Mao's
Bestiary

Mao's

EXPERIMENTAL FUTURES
TECHNOLOGICAL LIVES, SCIENTIFIC
ARTS, ANTHROPOLOGICAL VOICES
A series edited by Michael M. J. Fischer and Joseph Dumit

Bestiary

Medicinal Animals and
Modern China / *Liz P. Y. Chee*

DUKE UNIVERSITY PRESS DURHAM AND LONDON 2021

© 2021 Duke University Press
All rights reserved
Printed and bound by CPI Group (UK) Ltd, Croydon, CR0 4YY
Designed by Aimee C. Harrison
Typeset in Portrait Text by Westchester Publishing Services

Library of Congress Cataloging-in-Publication Data
Names: Chee, Liz P. Y., [date] author.
Title: Mao's bestiary : medicinal animals and modern China /
Liz P. Y. Chee.
Other titles: Experimental futures.
Description: Durham : Duke University Press, 2021. | Series: Experi-
mental futures | Includes bibliographical references and index.
Identifiers: LCCN 2020031117 (print)
LCCN 2020031118 (ebook)
ISBN 9781478011903 (hardcover)
ISBN 9781478014041 (paperback)
ISBN 9781478021353 (ebook)
Subjects: LCSH: Materia medica, Animal—China. | Pharmacognosy—
China. | Animals—Therapeutic use—China. | Traditional medicine.
Classification: LCC RS162 .C445 2021 (print) | LCC RS162 (ebook) |
DDC 615.3/60951—dc23
LC record available at https://lccn.loc.gov/2020031117
LC ebook record available at https://lccn.loc.gov/2020031118

To my "uncle" and cat

CONTENTS

ACKNOWLEDGMENTS

This book has been helped along by many people with diverse backgrounds and perspectives, including historians, anthropologists, doctors of Chinese medicine, museum directors, and animal welfare activists, not to mention librarians and archivists. I have room to cite only a few of them here.

My longtime mentor, Professor Gregory Clancey of the National University of Singapore, never ceased to believe in this project, and provided inspiration and support all the way through. The atmosphere he created at Tembusu College and in the STS Cluster of the Asia Research Institute (ARI), where I served my postdoctoral fellowship, could not have been better for a young academic. I also thank my many helpful colleagues at the college for their patience and aid. Professor Jonathan Rigg, the director of ARI, was equally supportive of a lengthy book project like mine in an age when short-term projects dominate university metrics. Professor Prasenjit Duara, who directed ARI when I was hired as a postdoc there, also deserves my thanks, as does the current director, Professor Tim Bunnell.

Professor Francesca Bray was generous enough to take me on as the first graduate student in the Edinburgh University–National University of Singapore Joint Doctoral Programme, and this book has profited from her guidance. I also thank the other academics in this pioneering program who contributed in various ways to my scholarly growth, including Professors Steve Sturdy and Jane Calvert of Edinburgh.

Mr. John Moffett, librarian at the Needham Research Institute in Cambridge, was an important guide when I was beginning my research, and Professor Christopher Cullen invited me back to speak at the institute when I had something to say. Professor Sean Lei of Academia Sinica in Taiwan likewise opened important doors and provided sound advice in the later phases of my research, as did Professor Angela Leung of the University of Hong Kong.

Ms. Jill Robinson of Animals Asia taught me a great deal about the bear farming phenomenon, and has inspired me at every turn.

This book would not have been possible without the assistance and hospitality given me by colleagues in China, particularly Professor Yu Xinzhong from Nankai University and Professor Zheng Hong and his staff from Guangzhou University of Chinese Medicine (GUCM). Professor Zheng, who now holds a position at Zhejiang Chinese Medical University, was exceptionally generous with me, in terms of both his time and inviting me into his network. Staff members of the GUCM Museum were also generous with their time and resources. I am also grateful to the following Chinese libraries and archives for allowing me access to their materials: the National Library of China (NLC) in Beijing, the Second Historical Archives of China in Nanjing, the Tianjin City Archive, and the Zhongshan Library in Guangzhou.

Professor Michael Fischer of MIT deserves my special thanks for being so encouraging of my project from an early date and for soliciting my manuscript as part of his book series at Duke. I also thank Mr. Ken Wissoker at Duke for providing sage advice as he shepherded the manuscript through the review process.

Professor Kim Dong-Won, who was a visiting professor at Tembusu College while I was finishing my research, kindly invited me to report my work before senior scholars at a D. Kim Foundation workshop, which helped sharpen many of the arguments in this book. Similarly, Professor Stephan Kloos of the Institute for Social Anthropology of the Austrian Academy of Sciences (ÖAW) introduced me to a number of ideas that proved important in framing my work.

Mr. Wang Wei was the perfect research assistant.

Going further back, to my undergraduate years, Professors Huang Jianli and Teow See Heng of the NUS History Department were important influences in introducing me to, respectively, Chinese and Japanese history. I also thank Professor Tan Tai Yong, now president of Yale-NUS, for welcoming me into the NUS History Department (from Japanese studies), thus initiating my turn toward China.

INTRODUCTION

This book is about the use of animals as drugs in the state medicine of modern China. Historians in recent years have produced a rich literature explaining Chinese medicine as a complicated, varied, and evolving set of theories, practices, and materials, rather than a clearly codified and unchanging tradition.[1] Much of this scholarship has been directed toward early Communist-period innovations that brought global recognition to Chinese medicine, such as new acupuncture therapies, the barefoot doctor program, and the isolation of the antimalarial drug artemisinin, to name but three. Medicinal animals, on the other hand, have largely escaped historical attention. This is despite many of them being products of this same period and having had an equally important, albeit largely negative, impact on the reputation of Chinese medicine as a domain of healing.

Animal-based drugs arguably fall into the category of "less orthodox therapies" that, as Bridie Andrews points out, were "explicitly rejected" as subjects by some influential Western historians of the 1970s and 1980s "in their efforts to upgrade Western perceptions of Chinese medical accomplishments."[2] This was despite the almost frenetic development and deployment of animal-based drugs in China during the same decades. The growing contemporary concern with wildlife conservation, animal ethics, and zoonotic diseases provides even more reason for those with similar instincts to find the subject uncomfortable. Yet as the field of science studies has taught us, the perception of illegitimacy, unorthodoxy, or controversy of a scientific (or medical) project is all the more reason to take a closer look.[3] Indeed, a focus on medicinal animals can contribute to a more complicated picture of how Chinese medicine has been shaped since its state-supported institutionalization in the 1950s, particularly its increased materialization in the form of new drugs and drug therapies. It also represents an opportunity for historical scholarship to inform current and ongoing ethical and political debates with wide policy ramifications.[4]

With the coming of globalization, demonstrating the efficacy and safety of Chinese medicine, particularly its drugs, has become a major preoccupation of institutions that support and promote it. This has generated an infrastructure of laboratories and test protocols, laws, and regulatory bodies that increasingly mimic or parallel those clustered around biomedicine.[5] The greater sanction this has given to Chinese medicine has not quelled all skeptics and has even generated debate within that domain on the legitimacy of using biomedical theories and benchmarks. But one has only to look at its expanding global constituency, its recognition by international health organizations such as WHO, and the recent award of a Nobel Prize to a researcher self-identified with the field to see that acceptance of Chinese medicine's efficacy, safety, and utility has been on an upward trajectory in the early twenty-first century.[6] Even the COVID-19 pandemic has become an opportunity for the Chinese state to increase its already-strong promotion of Chinese medicine in the domestic health-care system, and as an element of "soft-power" politics abroad.[7]

The "animal issue" in Chinese medicine, on the other hand, has become only more charged and controversial with time. If Chinese medicine retains an Achilles' heel in the present century, it is the widespread perception that it is contributing to a holocaust among wild creatures, reducing biodiversity, and in so doing supporting a global criminal enterprise the profits of which rival those of narcotics and arms trafficking.[8] Nor is the animal issue entirely divorced from that of efficacy, as medicines based on the parts and tissues of endangered species are regularly condemned in the global media, and by some Chinese physicians, as being as ineffective as they are unethical. The naming, poaching, and trafficking of so-called medicinal species has dramatically increased in the current century and spread to even more areas of the globe, leading to the perception, as an article in *Nature* framed it, that "traditional Asian medicine is on a collision course with wildlife conservation."[9]

The animal issue sows division not only between two growing global sociocultural movements (alternative/indigenous medicine and species conservation), but also among individuals, groups, and institutions within

Chinese medicine, both in and beyond China. At stake is their shared understanding of Chinese medicine's history, trajectory, boundaries, and ethics. Some Chinese medicine practitioners have declared animal drugs, particularly those from endangered species, to be outside the scope of their practice, particularly following the Chinese government's ban on the importation of tiger bones, rhino horns, and other parts of endangered species in 1993.[10] This policy was, as Volker Sheid points out, convergent with the government's increased efforts to promote Chinese medicine abroad as a global health practice.[11] More recently, however, with the intensified promotion of Chinese medicine across Asia and the world as part of China's Belt and Road Initiative, other powerful voices have reaffirmed medicinal animals as a fundamental ethnomedical resource. Some have even challenged critiques by conservationists as "Western," despite a growing movement for animal conservation in China, among the Chinese diaspora, and within the realm of Chinese medicine itself.[12] The announcement by China's State Council in 2018 that it would even lift its ban on the medical use of "farmed" tiger and rhino parts, and its subsequent rare about-face due to global and domestic protest, demonstrates that tensions over medicinal animals have only been intensifying as the sixth mass extinction continues apace.[13]

As this book goes to press, the COVID-19 pandemic is bringing this controversy over medicalizing wild animals to an even wider audience, and fundamentally changing the nature of the debate. Regardless of which species passed the virus to humans, or exactly how and where it was transmitted, the pandemic has broadened the animal issue in Chinese medicine beyond ethics and efficacy to include the specter of zoonotic disease. The response of the Chinese state to the increased profile and notoriety of faunal medicalization has so far been mixed. Pangolins, which were early identified as a possible intermediate host for the virus, and have heretofore been the most heavily trafficked of all medicinal animals, were officially removed (with caveats) from the Chinese pharmacopeia in 2020. Yet the state's heavy promotion of Chinese medicine as potentially alleviating COVID-19 symptoms has not excluded the lucrative bear bile industry, despite there being legitimate herbal substitutes for its product. How the pandemic will affect the medicalization of animals in the long term remains to be seen, but better understanding the history of this process will do much to clarify its relation to Chinese medicine more generally, and hence the possibilities of reform.[14]

In debates involving medicinal animals, all parties usually accept the chronological and discursive space of "thousands of years of use" in China, thus arraying history against positions based on ethics, efficacy, or even public health. By focusing attention on a more recent and clearly defined period—the 1950s through the 1980s—this book will add significant nuance to such arguments, lightening "the weight of the past" as an impediment to serious discussion about the present and future. The chapters that follow locate the increased deployment of animal-derived Chinese drugs in a largely unexplored place and time: drug discovery, innovation, and production in early Communist China. This realm of experiment-based activity was influenced as much by modern political policies, slogans, economic incentives, institutional priorities, and in some instances foreign sources of knowledge and practice, as by long-standing traditions of use by the Chinese people. Pharmacological policy in the early Communist period initially concentrated on plants, and fauna only gradually came to loom as large on the agendas of medical reformers, mainly from the time of the Great Leap Forward. Many of the animal-based medicinals or therapies of the early Communist era were new innovations, some were locally specific practices suddenly promoted on a national scale, and some represented new powers and efficacies suddenly bestowed on old and familiar substances.

The "experimental future" of animal-based therapies that emerged in the Mao period, this book argues, is the historical underpinning of Chinese medicine's present animal-based dilemma. The most commonly stated explanation for the rising consumption of animal drugs in the current century—that Chinese have become rich, so can "finally" afford what they have always craved—is in that sense ahistorical. A heightened degree of awareness, desire, and, above all, industrial production had to develop behind such drug-taking practices first, and here the history of the early Communist period is an overlooked watershed. A range of new animal parts and tissues in many varied forms became increasingly common in Chinese medicinal circulation from the late 1950s onward, thus habituating a large population to using more of it, more often, and for more reasons than ever before. The new enthusiasm for animal parts and tissues did not have its roots only in Chinese practice, moreover, but was influenced as well by external factors such as Soviet organotherapy and North Korean bear bile extraction technologies. Once the scope of this change and the mechanisms behind it is understood, the contemporary scourge of endangered species in Africa, Southeast Asia, and China appears not just as the continuation of a tradition. It is also the result of an evolving interest in and appetite for animal-based drugs, which increased in breadth and range from the early Communist period onward.

Faunal Medicalization

The phenomenon I call *faunal medicalization* was the process of fashioning and refashioning animal-based drugs for service to Chinese state medicine and, in the import/export realm, the larger Chinese economy. One has to be clear from the beginning, however, that animal-derived medicinal compounds have a long use in China, as they have in some (but not all) indigenous medicinal practices elsewhere in the world.[15] More than four hundred are listed or discussed in the sixteenth-century *Bencao Gangmu*, and both their numbers and the types of ailments they were meant to treat only grew and became more refined in subsequent pharmacopoeias.

When asked about the reasoning and utility behind the use of animal parts in materia medica, Chinese physicians among my informants often refer to slogans or sayings taken from classical literature, for example *yi du gong du* (using poison to attack poison), and *yi xing bu xing* (using shape to nourish shape). On the strength of the first slogan, animal venom such as that of snakes and scorpions would be advisable to use in treating fatal diseases. *Xing* in the second saying, basically referring to organs or parts, is often interpreted to mean that a particular animal organ or part can help nourish the same human organ, or one of similar appearance.[16] This also accounts for the medicinal attraction of the plant ginseng, which resembles the human body, and of walnuts, which resemble the brain.[17]

Animal parts are also referred to in classical sayings such as *xuerou you qing zhi pin* (products with passion in both blood and flesh) or *bu yi jingxue* (enriching and benefiting essence and blood), suggesting that they have more vitality or power than plants. Zu Shuxian believes that "animal medicine originated from the worship of animals," which would place them in a different ontological category than herbs.[18] Like much else in Chinese medicine, animal-based drugs have magical origins. Michel Strickmann reminds us that cow bezoar, to take one example, was once "the most highly prized of all medicines" in China because of its demon-dispelling qualities.[19] The medical doctor turned anthropologist Johann Frick found that magical attributes were still considered important to a drug's efficacy in the village in Tsinghai province, where he lived just prior to the Communist Revolution: "Magic and medicine are inseparably associated in the minds of the people, so that even when the medicines are 'good,' in themselves, greater confidence is often placed in the magic power than in the strictly medical effects. The people see superhuman forces at work in every sickness, so that when merely natural healing agents are pitted against them these latter must be endowed with higher than natural powers." Frick lists many animal-derived (and human-derived) substances that had such properties in his village, most of which involved not killing their hosts but harvesting renewable tissue (e.g., dung, urine, and the webs of spiders).[20] Animal-derived materials were more often accompanied by herbs in physicians' prescriptions as part of a complicated polyherbal recipe, but even then they often stood out as the most dynamic components.

According to He Shaoqi, the phrase *bu yi jingxue* was coined by the famous Tang physician Sun Simiao, known as the King of Medicine (*yaowang*).[21] Sun Simiao was also, however, "the first Chinese author to have devoted a separate section of a paradigmatic nature to questions of medical ethics," according to Paul Unschuld.[22] And the use of animals as medicine was among Sun's ethical concerns:

> Whoever destroys life in order to save life places life at an even greater distance. This is my good reason for the fact that I do not suggest the use of any living creature as medicament in the present collection of prescriptions. This does not concern the gadflies and the leeches. They have already perished when they reach the market, and it is therefore permissible to use them. As to the hen's eggs, we have to say the following: before their content has been hatched out, they can be used in very urgent cases. Otherwise, one should not burden oneself with this. To avoid their use is a sign of great wisdom, but this will never be attained.[23]

There is even a legend associated with Sun in which he heals a wild tiger by extracting a donkey's bone from its throat, and the animal remains with him out of gratitude, even carrying his medical bag.[24] Sun's example is often cited by those contemporary practitioners and users of Chinese medicine who advocate expunging animal parts from the Chinese pharmacopeia. Many other classical writers, however, included animal-based ingredients in what were otherwise plant-based recipes or prescriptions, along with minerals, and even parts of the human body, such as placenta.[25] The issue of efficacy aside, it was more likely scarcity and expense rather than ethics that kept animal parts subsidiary to herbs in the historical development of the Chinese pharmacy.

In the contemporary urban Chinese medical marketplace, however, animal-derived components are startlingly abundant, from whole lizards and ground beetles, on the lower end, to bear bile and cordyceps at the higher one, and rhino horn and tiger bone in illicit corners.[26] Although this cornucopia may appear traditional to both buyers and sellers, many of its elements are new not only in their availability and uses, but also as a lived set of practices and materials. With globalization, even species with no prior status as medicinal, or any prior relationship to China, have taken their place in this market. The spontaneous medicalization of jaguar parts by Chinese construction gangs working in South America, for example, has caused Vincent Nijman to describe Chinese engineering projects in forested countries, many driven by the Belt and Road Initiative, as "giant vacuum cleaners of wildlife," sucking any available exotic animal tissue into China's medical marketplace.[27] In a like manner, the recent medicalization of the gills of manta rays has been attributed to Chinese seafood salesmen, who, faced with a declining shark fishery, created a multimillion-dollar market for what was formerly a waste product.[28] China is of course not the only Asian society in which some people have bestowed new curative powers on both familiar and unfamiliar species, as attested by the well-publicized case of elite Vietnamese businessmen seeking African rhino horn as a hangover cure.[29]

Much of the modern discussion of Chinese medicinal animals focuses on tigers and rhinos, given their current endangerment, the huge profits involved in their trafficking, and their shared charisma as apex species. The most trafficked of all medicalized animals in the early twenty-first century, however, is likely the lowly pangolin, added to the Convention on International Trade in Endangered Species (CITES) list of critically endangered species in 2016, and removed from the state-managed Chinese pharmacopeia only in 2020 because of its possible association with COVID-19.[30] Rhinos, tigers, and pangolins share the attribute of wildness, often considered a central attraction for consumers of animal drugs. Yet neither wildness nor exotica can explain the perceived potency of the blood of chickens, which became one of the most important animal drugs during the Cultural Revolution, nor the fact that the majority of medicinal species, then and now, are actually farmed. Likewise, village donkeys are being skinned alive by poachers in Africa because of their perceived medicinal benefits in China, leaving their already-poor owners further impoverished.[31] If we are to understand the modern rise of animal-based drugs and therapies in a more holistic way, we must recognize that faunal medicalization is a process potentially inclusive of all species, yet one that has arisen in relation to specific political contexts, economic imperatives, and inventive strategies with heretofore opaque origins.

The range and voraciousness of faunal medicalization centered on China and its diaspora, according to one journalistic account, extends "far beyond anything that TCM authorities are able to discourage or contain."[32] Just who "TCM authorities" are, however, and to what degree they have discouraged, contained, or advanced such practices, is not easily resolved. The surfeit of animal parts in such places as Guangzhou's vast Qingping Market is some-times dismissed as in the sphere of "folk medicine" and therefore outside the purview or concern of Chinese medicine as an organized community of schol-ars, practitioners, and regulators. It is indeed true that contemporary Chinese medical colleges and hospitals do not account for much of this animal-based materia medica in their instruction or clinical practices. But the boundary between "folk" and "classical" medicine, especially when it comes to the use of animal tissue, is not a hard one, and was in fact willfully confounded in the Mao period. As we shall see, authorities in the form of state actors, Chinese physicians, Western-trained doctors, pharmacists, agricultural researchers, and others were very much involved in initiating the current wave of faunal medicalization, even if its goals, targets, and scale have now extended beyond what could have been imagined in the Mao and Deng eras.

Indeed, as the variety of animal parts in China's medical marketplaces has increased since the early Communist era, the numbers of animals cited in published, physician-authored sources as "medicinal" has likewise bur-geoned. If we can take the four hundred animals in the *Bencao Gangmu* as a historic baseline, they represent just a fraction of those medicalized in pub-lications of the Mao and Deng periods, and continuing into the present day. With the publication of the two-volume *Zhongguo yao yong dong wu zhi* (Chi-nese medicinal animals) in 1979 and 1983, the number of such species more than doubled, to 832, capping a period of intense animal-drug discovery and farming over the previous three decades.[33] In the 2013 revised and updated version of this compilation, the tally of medicinal animals has grown to 2,341 (inclusive of subspecies). Thus while faunal medicalization may have its roots in premodern practice, it is neither bound nor overly determined by it. Indeed, the authors of the most recent edition cite the "30-year research pro-gress of zoology and medicinal animals," which relied on "modern molecular biology and other emerging science[s] and technolog[ies]" as the reason for issuing a new edition.[34] Like medicinal herbs, whose variety has similarly increased in published compilations, animal tissue is the stuff of ongoing "research and development." In that sense its roots are as firmly planted in the laboratory as in the marketplace, farm, or legal or illegal trade network.

Innovation and Tradition

To their contemporary consumers, animal-based products hold the aura of tradition, and hence historicity. But under Mao, the allure of animal-based medicines was at least equally dependent on their being seen as "new drugs"—the product of science-based innovation. That association has never fully abated, even if it is no longer foregrounded in the way such drugs are marketed. In that sense, historical research on faunal medicalization can also shed new light on the phenomena of innovation and invention within Chinese medicine and science in the early Communist period, and the way that fragments of the historical and traditional were spliced into this process.

The long-standing view of the Mao period, and particularly the Cultural Revolution, as antiscience has undergone significant revision in the last decade. Miriam Gross, for example, has described "scientific consolidation" as central to regime dynamics under Mao, by which she means the mass cultivation of pragmatic technical skills intended to spark "an experimental and innovative mind-set" for party-directed projects.[35] Likewise, Sigrid Schmalzer's work on scientific farming in the same period shows how innovation in agriculture relied on a "patchwork of methodologies" that "cannot easily be characterized as 'modern' or 'traditional'" but were, in all instances, declared to be "science."[36] The thrust of these and other recent studies is that innovation under Mao was broadly encouraged and cultivated, even if it required tying particularistic concepts of science, tradition, and politics together in new and contested configurations.

The promotion of innovation in this period likewise extended to the creation of new drugs and therapies within the domain of Chinese medicine. This has been well-chronicled in the case of acupuncture therapies and herbology, but not for animal medicines.[37] Medicinal animal farming and the proliferation of novel animal-based "cures" are nonetheless among its prominent examples. This period saw the training of a new class of pharmacists and pharmacologists uniquely experienced with both Chinese and Western drugs and geared toward research. Physicians with Western medical training were also induced for the first time to experiment with new therapies involving indigenous materia medica, while communes were encouraged to farm a wide array of formerly wild animals for medicinal purposes, some for home consumption and others for export. Through this convergence of agents and agencies, fueled by political ideology and pragmatic need, the types and quantities of animal-based drugs in the Chinese pharmacopeia began a process of expansion and reformulation that has continued into the present day.

The medicinal farming and drug-making sector in the early Communist period celebrated its own modernity and inventiveness while simultaneously tapping in to classical, folk, and literary references in concocting new animal-based products; this imbued such drugs with complex and overlapping claims to efficacy. Alongside a drug's historicity might be the development of new delivery methods and protocols replicating those common to biomedicine. Chinese interest in Soviet medicine also sanctioned the spreading use of animal tissue, via mutual interest in "tissue therapy," while a shared ecosystem along the China-Soviet border encouraged such practices as medicinal deer farming on an industrial scale. The Maoist view that medical science and drug discovery should be projects inclusive of workers and peasants, with a strong emphasis on production, also contributed to the gathering up of new fauna as materia medica. At the same time, the ideological turn to folk medicine converted local animal-based cures into national practices with political sanction. By these and other means, a new matrix of mutually reinforcing associations—of science, socialist politics, low cost and efficiency, and, in some cases, even miraculous curative effects—were attached to an increasingly wide range of animal tissues, helping to propel their production or dissemination. This also extended to foreign trade, as Chinese-produced animal-based medicines became an attractive source of foreign currency in the capitalist Chinese diaspora, thus extending the charisma of these products beyond China's borders.

The long-standing characterization of faunal medicines as "products with passion" was also given new meaning through innovation. Traditionally used as an ingredient in polyherbal recipes, animal tissue was now increasingly a research material, and consumable substance, in its own right. Administered in "pure" form through injections or pills, some substances were promoted as able to cure diseases, such as cancer, that had tested biomedicine's limits. A premium was also put on quick action, in the manner of antibiotics, thus reversing the perception of Chinese medicinals as slow-working. The sense that Chinese medicine could offer "miracle cures" became pronounced in such Mao-period innovations as chicken blood therapy, and remains a propelling agent in faunal medicalization today, if not the clinical practice of Chinese medicine more generally.[38]

The values attached to faunal medicalization in the Mao period, however, were not always convergent with those driving the process today. Charging exorbitant prices for "authenticity" is characteristic of the present marketplace for animal-based medicines, and helps subsidize and expand the cross-border trade in endangered species, whereas substitution and economy were watchwords of many early Communist-period animal drug therapies. This may seem like an utter break with the past, but the medicinal animal farming that began in the early Communist period has arguably helped further the contemporary global assault on animals in the wild. The farming industry as developed under Mao not only habituated people to the use of faunal remedies through increased availability, but also demonstrated that almost any animal, or animal part, could be rendered into a medicinal product for urban consumers. Although this would have its ultimate effect on species outside China with Deng's reforms and the rise of a Chinese consumer class, it began to have similar effects on species within China much earlier. Species extinction combined with market forces have subsequently made increasingly rare animal parts "good investments," and their soaring prices have given rise to a gifting economy, in which the medicinal animal might never actually be used as medicine, but only as an offering(s) to higher-status individuals who appreciate it as a form of insurance: either a miracle cure in case of medical emergency or an appreciating asset to hedge against a financial one.[39]

Pharmaceuticalization

The forty-year period I have chosen for this study, from the start of Communist government to the end of the first decade of Deng's reforms, is an iconic one in Chinese history, full of dramatic political events and accompanying slogans. I agree with Mei Zhan that "dynamic forms of traditional Chinese medicine emerge through particular kinds of encounters and entanglements."[40] Medicine and politics in this period were deeply entangled, and the material and therapeutic forms that emerged from their encounter were particularly dynamic. I have tried to be sensitive to how each major political shift affected my topic, and in so doing demonstrate the primacy of political policy in giving rise to the wider production of, and knowledge creation around, animal-based drugs. Communist-era policies and resulting slogans about Chinese medicine are well-known, but have rarely been studied with reference to pharmaceuticals and drug-making.

Stephan Kloos has challenged us to "take seriously the process of pharmaceuticalization as a defining but understudied moment in the ongoing modernization of traditional Asian medicines."[41] Animals aside, pharmaceuticals and drug-making under Mao has heretofore not been well documented, and has indeed occupied a subsidiary role in histories or discussions of Chinese medicine as a modern institution.[42] This despite the fact that pharmacology in this period developed an outsized importance within the world of Chinese science and medical research. A team of American pharmacologists, chemists, and other experts touring China in 1974 under the auspices of the National Academy of Sciences found that, "relative to other biologic sciences, pharmacology occupies an exalted position in the People's Republic of China, where the emphasis given to pharmacology is greater than in many other countries. This distinction is, however, perhaps more the result of political action than of scientific achievement."[43] While a politically informed history of Chinese pharmaceuticals is beyond the scope of this book, it is necessary in the early chapters to account for the existence (and origins) of this large, varied, but little-understood industrial sector, in order to provide a baseline for the eventual emergence of animal-based drugs within and around it. As we shall see, animal-based substances were not of initial concern in the immediate postrevolution years and, even after becoming an important focus of research, were never exclusively the domain of state pharmacology and industrial production. But faunal medicalization under Mao clearly converged with the rising status of pharmacology, and thus provides a window into the growing materialization of Chinese medicine, which it has arguably come to exemplify. I therefore offer enough background in the history of pharmaceuticals in this period, in the early part of the book, to frame the emergence of animal-based substances as among its eventual products.

Chinese drug development in this period roughly followed what Laurent Pordie and Jean-Paul Gaudilliere describe as a "reformulation regime," in which "new traditional drugs" were crafted amid changed circumstances, which in this case were both political and economic.[44] Such drugs become the productive centerpieces of "Asian industrial medicines," the term Laurent Pordie and Anita Hardon prefer to "traditional Asian medicines" as better foregrounding their materialization and commodification.[45] More recently Stephan Kloos has deployed the term "Asian medical industries" to put even greater emphasis on the consolidation and size of this sector, which incorporates not just "industry" in its classical sense of manufacturing and marketing, but "the entire field of sociocultural, political, technological, scientific, and medical phenomena involved in the generation of surplus value (monetary and otherwise)."[46] Most analysis and discussion of reformulation regimes in Asian medical industries relate them to post–Cold War globalization. But Chinese drug development experienced some of the characteristics of an "industrial medicine" much earlier, first with so-called patent medicines in the Republican period, and later with the developments I chronicle under the early Communist regime. Terms like "market" and "consumer," however, seem somewhat misplaced when applied to China before the period of Deng's reforms, and are particularly inadequate for some of the drug-making practices I chronicle, which did not involve what could reasonably be called "consumable goods." The injection of chicken blood into one's buttocks or the drinking of goose blood directly from that animal's neck were not practices that even China's state-owned drug manufacturers could easily commodify. Yet these and other seemingly eccentric innovations were not unrelated to larger and more organized projects like the farming of deer antlers for home consumption and export, the later farming and sale of bear bile, or the trade in rhino horns and tiger bones, a connection that would be obscured if one were to concentrate exclusively on marketable or packaged drugs and their circulation.

Given this book's focus on innovation and invention, I naturally spend more time among makers than among distributors or consumers. This concentration on "making" also reflects the bias in my sources, and the whole tenor of this period in Chinese political history, during which invention, innovation, and production were emphasized almost regardless of demand or need. There was clearly demand for Chinese medicinal exports, however, and I hope that understanding the push factors in mainland China will propel future research that traces demand (pull factors) for Chinese medicinals in Hong Kong, Taiwan, Southeast Asia, and even Korea and Japan, where market forces were more controlling. Mei Zhan has valuably described how Chinese medicine has been remade "through trans-national frames."[47] Animal-based drugs were prominent exemplars of this process. I refer not just to the obvious presence of a consuming diaspora in East and Southeast Asia, but less obvious research and production links to the Russian Far East, Korea, and Japan. Likewise, this period saw the intensified importation of exotic (now endangered) species into China from Africa and Southeast Asia, a topic of such continuing importance that it deserves a study in its own right, and for which the present book can provide only a baseline.

Terms

I use the term "Chinese medicine" (*zhongyi*) rather than its more popular and political English translation, traditional Chinese medicine (TCM), throughout the text to refer to the broad set of practices, theories, rituals, materials, beliefs, technologies, and the like that were bundled under that name by the early Communist period. I am sensitive to the fact that some practitioners and consumers of Chinese medicine withhold that term from many animal drugs, calling them "folk medicine," or arguing more broadly that Chinese "drugs" and Chinese "medicine" are different realms that should not be confounded. Such positions are partly grounded in historical usages, some of which I discuss below. But they are also partly a reaction to contemporary critiques equating all Chinese medicine with animal drugs, which is hardly true or fair. Acupuncture, moxibustion, exercise therapies, and most herbal drugs and prescriptions have nothing to do with animals, and the variety of these materials and practices demonstrate Chinese medicine's diversity. But animal-based drugs are also, undeniably, within this domain. Arriving at, let alone policing, a definition of Chinese medicine is not my project, however. Most of the time I simply follow actors, authors, and informants in using this and other terms as they do, while sometimes pointing out contradictions or peculiarities in their deployments.

Most historians agree that the term "Chinese medicine" arose as a counterpoint to "Western medicine" as soon as the latter term began to be used in China.[48] The dyad is now so accepted, and has so informed the majority of scholarly and popular works on medicine in China, that it is not easily dispensed with. I have chosen to use the term "biomedicine" to refer to Western medicine, however, as it is not geographically directional. This will also cause less confusion when I introduce concepts from Soviet medicine, which has many of its own characteristics.

That said, almost all the Chinese medicines and medicinals I deal with in this period had hybrid elements and were influenced in some manner by their encounters with biomedicine, as well as their location within a twentieth-century socialist nation-state politically invested in their "survival," in one form or another. The slogans of the Communist regime through this whole period were insistent that Chinese and Western medicines mingle, combine, and learn from each other. In other words, for most of this period, the state had a strong bias against maintaining either system in pure form, were that even conceivable. Their relationship had grown complex as early as the Republican period, as Sean Lei points out, when the idiom "neither donkey nor horse" was used to disparage practices considered in between, which were nonetheless proliferating and would later be favored in the new Communist regime. Lei helpfully refers to this nascent process as "speciation"—the formation of a new type of modern medicine fundamentally different from what had come before.[49] Bridie Andrews uses the term "combination medicine" to make a similar point, and excavates the previously underrated Japanese influence on Chinese pharmacological research.[50] My own story supports our growing picture of Chinese medicine in this period as a self-consciously modernizing and highly experimental realm, and complicates it further by adding the influence of Soviet medicine, which included many therapies and research projects that never gained traction in "the West."

As with the term *zhongyi*, I use the term *yao* (drugs) in the widest sense to describe whatever actors believed to be medicinal substances. I reserve the term "pharmaceuticals," however, mainly for drugs that were more main-stream or mass-producible, within biomedicine or Chinese medicine. The heads of frogs and the blood of geese, for example, were promoted and used as drugs, but the term "pharmaceuticals" is too evocative of lab-based industrial production to really fit such materials. The term "materia medica" is perhaps most useful, and thus conventional, in covering the broadest range of substances, as is the term "medicinals."

The word "science" is more problematic in the Chinese context than is "medicine," given that it did not exist in the Chinese vocabulary prior to the encounter with the West, but thereafter became deeply and explicitly intertwined with the politics of nation-building.[51] The concept was even personified as "Mr. Science" (*Sai Xiansheng*) after World War I, and later made into a verb (to scientize, or *kexuehua*). The Communist Revolution further distanced the word "science" from the sense of "investigation of nature," because Marxism itself was now presented as the ultimate science. Thus nearly everything under the early Communist regime was open to "scientization," including Chinese medicine. As Lei points out, "scientize is a word used almost daily in modern Chinese, Japanese, and Korean; many native speakers would find it puzzling that Westerners can do without it."[52] It likewise occurs regularly in my source material, very often as a substitute for specificity. Suffice it to say that almost every actor or speaker in these pages would have felt comfortable defending his or her own ideas or policies as advancing the scientization project. This is important to note, given that many lingering products of their actions are now presented as exclusively belonging to the realm of "tradition."

As for "animal tissue," this is my term to describe everything from discrete pieces of animals, such as gecko tails or deer antlers, to extracts such as goose blood or bear bile, or whole animals such as beetles, centipedes, or toads, when used as medicinals. As discussed, animal tissue has always been present in Chinese medical traditions, and has never been fully segregated from herbs, minerals, or even human tissue as an available medical resource category. But it began to stand out more sharply in the modern period, when it came to be distinguished by aggressive promotion, heightened production, and exalted claims for efficacy, such as the ability to "cure 100 diseases," reverse aging, or melt cancerous tumors. Animal tissue of course took on an additional political meaning with the rising interest in species conservation and the ethical treatment of animals in the late twentieth century, neither of which was a concern during most of the period I chronicle except as it related to ensuring a viable population for sustainable production.

Sources and Methodology

Partly because of the range of materials, actors, and practices one needs to tap in order to describe faunal medicalization during this period, organizing this topic into a single story line with a small set of characters or institutions at its center is not possible. Indeed, the dispersed and fragmented nature of the evidentiary base is likely another reason that the subject of animal tissue in Chinese medicine has not previously attracted historians, despite its importance and topicality. There was no well-bounded group or institution responsible for, or consistently involved over time with, this gradual change in Chinese materia medica. Agency has been dispersed and, hence, elusive. And even then, one can't transparently rely on statistics or facts, given the exaggerations and distortions of Mao-era documents. The evidentiary base comes down to a series of descriptions, claims, admissions, reports, proposals, and statistics, mainly in the form of articles in professional journals and reports. With a few exceptions, such as chicken blood therapy and the bear bile industry, the material is also difficult to organize as case studies.

Animals are, in other words, not found as a ready-made and presorted category in one or more discrete archives. The faunal medicalization of the Mao period resembles what Kloos has described elsewhere as an emergent "assemblage" that "doubles as an ontological entity and analytic-methodological approach."[53] Animals emerge here and there, in this article or that, in parts of biographies, and reports on production. One thus has to piece together many textual scraps to see them emerge at all. But emerge they most certainly do, and more and more strongly with time.

My major (though not exclusive) sources for this book are a wealth of untapped pharmaceutical journals, published from the 1950s through the Cultural Revolution, most of which are collected in the library of Guangzhou University of Chinese Medicine (GUCM). Within the constellation of Chinese medical universities, GUCM is particularly well respected as the most important such university in southern China. The faculty there was kind enough to host me through years of doctoral research, offering themselves as instructors, informants, and, in some cases, close friends. Despite my research location in southern China, however, the sources that I have used are mostly national and, with some exceptions (e.g., deer and bear), make little editorial reference to specific regions (even if individual articles and papers were written from such localities) but rather attempt to create a national discourse around practice(s) of drug-making. Besides providing insights into official policies, these journals and related sources also provided a forum for the various groups and individuals constituting the loose Chinese drug-making community, from physicians and Western-trained doctors (who were also called *daifu*, an archaic term for physicians) to, more prominently, pharmacologists, pharmacists, medicinal farmers, and medical bureaucrats. Publications from this period sometimes give us glimpses of groups with particular interests, but at other times even the identity of specific authors is cryptic.

I have supplemented journal sources with books, yearbooks, published reports, pamphlets, and other types of texts produced by actors as disparate as elderly Chinese physicians, bear farmers, and ministry officials. Oral history has proven less useful as a tool, except in gaining the trust necessary to be referred to written sources by my informants. Most of the influences that led to the increasing use of animal parts after 1950 remain unclear to Chinese physicians themselves, because they occurred gradually, were spearheaded by other state or private actors, or have more recently become controversial and thus not so easily open to discussion. For example, everyone in the world of Chinese medicine knows that rhino horns and tiger parts are officially banned substances, but not all agree that they should be. Everyone is also aware of the ethical controversy around bear farming, and that the majority of Chinese are against it. There is also considerable embarrassment about chicken blood therapy, which is widely considered an isolated aberration of the Cultural Revolution. Indeed, any discussion of the Great Leap Forward and Cultural Revolution periods with foreigners is uncomfortable for some otherwise helpful Chinese. My key Chinese informants have greatly encouraged my research direction, however, and this book would not have been possible without them.

Outline of the Book

Chapters 1 and 2 provide a base for understanding the eventual rise of state interest in animal-based medicinals by tracing the birth of the state-owned Chinese drug-making sector in the early to mid-1950s. As there is no general English-language account of drug discovery and drug-making in early Communist China, these chapters fill that gap and create a foundation for the subsequent structure of the book. Together these two chapters cover the period up to 1958, or the threshold of the Great Leap Forward, when animal tissue begins to figure more prominently in Chinese medicine, and in my text.

Chapter 1 explains how a state-owned pharmaceutical industry was crafted through the creation of new factories, on the one hand, and the consolidation of older medicine shops, on the other. Bound up with these developments was the emergence of *yao* (drugs) as a more clearly articulated area or field within Chinese medicine, and one more in line ideologically with Marxism's emphasis on materiality. The phrase "Abandon *Yi*, Retain *Yao*" (*Fei Yi, Cun Yao*), although pre-dating the Revolution, animated actual programs into the 1950s, when Mao argued for the preservation of *yi* as well, but in "combination" with biomedicine. Thus native herbs common in Chinese medicine were used by state enterprises in this period to create imitations of previously imported biomedicines. Land surveys were also conducted in various parts of China in a search for hitherto untapped medicinal resources. A keyword of the era was *chuangxin* (to innovate), and the new class of Chinese pharmacists (*yaogongshi*) was encouraged to take up that task rather than rely on tradition. I argue that herbs were much more a source of enthusiasm within state medicine of this period than were animal-sourced drugs, excepting those associated with brand-name Chinese medicine companies, which continued to deal in substances like rhino horn and tiger-bone wine. The relative absence of "Chinese" animals in the early state pharmacy demonstrates that their subsequent "scientization" and inclusion in the state pharmacy signals a new creation rather than a simple continuity with existing practices.

Chapter 2 looks at the Soviet Union's crucial influence on Chinese drug-making policies and practices in this same period, particularly in relation to faunal medicalization. "To Learn from the Soviet Union" was a well-used phrase in the early to mid-1950s, and Chinese articles on this theme abounded. The Chinese goal of making drugs from local raw materials was convergent with the experience of the USSR, which had to build its own pharmaceutical industry using domestic resources after the October Revolution. The Russian influence also complicates the category Western medicine, as certain Soviet pharmacological interests, practices, and theories were relatively unique. Chinese drugs such as ginseng and deer antler, for example, were also native to Siberia, and some Soviet experts sent to China studied Chinese materia medica in order to create cross-border knowledge. Just as significantly, the Soviet innovation of "tissue therapy," virtually unknown in the West, became widely popular in China and directly encouraged animal-based therapies. Chinese medicine's historic use of animal drugs in raw form alienated it from Western biomedicine, but such practices overlapped with Soviet promotion of organotherapy, which provided modern and scientific sanction for the Chinese fascination with faunal drugs.

Chapter 3 chronicles the rise of animal farming in modern China, beyond the farming of deer. It concentrates on the Great Leap Forward, when the stepped-up effort to drive production in all sectors led to a policy of intense cultivation of plant- and (increasingly) animal-based medicinals. Based on Chinese pharmaceutical journals as well as English-language reports and official statistics found in Hong Kong archives, this chapter also traces the growing importance of the export-oriented sector to medicinal production. The list of farmed animals in this period grew to include tokay geckos, ground beetles, seahorses, and many other species. In so-called laboratory farms, crossbreeding experiments took place in an effort to increase and improve the quality of yields. Under the banner of production, the population was encouraged to find new uses for known animal medicinals at the same time they were taught, often for the first time, that certain animal-based substances had healing qualities. This expansion and institutionalization of medicinal animal farming and mass collection, based partly on the Sino-Soviet precedent of deer farming, brought animals of all kinds into the domain of state medicine.

Chapter 4 turns from an emphasis on production toward innovation, and extends discussion of the Great Leap Forward into the Cultural Revolution. Despite the increase in overall supply of both plant- and animal-based medicinals through systematic farming, most of the Chinese population did not have access to such products. The lack of medical care and supplies was likely one reason for the rush to discover, record, and legitimate folk-healing practices. Another was ideology. The turn to folk medicine resulted in an expanded repertoire of animal-based drugs and cures being incorporated into state medicine. The emphasis on innovation, however, also resulted in hybrid therapies promising miraculous cures using animal tissue, the most notable of which was chicken blood therapy, which I present as an important case study.

This chapter goes on to discuss animal-based drugs and therapies of the later Cultural Revolution, which went further down the path paved by chicken blood therapy. Claims of efficacy for these drugs reached well beyond treatment for "traditional" ailments, to include cancer and other conditions that biomedicines could not seem to cure, an attribute that has become standard in the marketing of many animal-based drugs today. At the same time, politics dictated that cheaper and more popular substitutes be found for luxury animal medicine like rhino horn, even as the cultivation of export animals like musk deer became more intense.

Chapter 5 traces faunal medicalization into the period of Deng's early rule and new policies related to market reforms. Medicinal animal production and use, having established a solid base under Mao, became even more popular as part of the official policy to enrich farmers, some of whom now became "entrepreneurs." Bear farming was the signature innovation of this period and was ultimately destined to create more controversy than even chicken blood therapy, though for entirely different reasons. Historical documents suggest that bear farming first took place in North Korea before entering China via the northeastern border. Captive bears were farmed essentially for their bile, the healing properties of which were supposedly sanctioned by Chinese classical texts. Arguments for the efficacy of bear bile, however (and the types of ailments it could treat), were expanded in the twentieth century after the isolation of its active ingredient by Japanese scientists.

Interludes at Golden Boten City and
Golden Bear Private Limited

No scholarly project emerges from a vacuum, so let me describe one of the several contexts that fostered mine. Like many Singaporeans of Chinese descent, I have taken Chinese drugs and consulted Chinese medicine doctors all my life, while simultaneously patronizing biomedical hospitals and clinics. And, like an increasing number of my countrymen, I have also been active in the cause of conserving wildlife and biodiversity in the Southeast Asian rain forest that constitutes our mutual home. For most Singaporeans of my age and younger, a Chinese medicine without animals of any kind is not only a preference, but a largely accomplished fact. Rhino and tiger parts have been largely eliminated across this city-state through undercover work by local NGOs in cooperation with a generally cooperative government, sensitive as it is to international opinion and respectful of international treaties like CITES. Even in Singapore, however, the elimination of endangered animals' tissues from the Chinese medicinal marketplace has not been complete. The horns of endangered saiga antelope continue to be sold here as I write, ironically because they have been promoted as a substitute for now-banned rhino horns and were stockpiled by medicine shop owners prior to the animal's CITES listing.[54] As for the surrounding Southeast Asian region, it continues to be "at the heart of the [global] wildlife trade," according to the organization TRAFFIC, with Singapore ironically acting as a major trans-shipment point because of the efficiency and status of its port.[55]

I first conceived this book during a working trip to a Chinese-owned bear farm in Laos in December 2009. Shortly after joining a Singapore-based animal welfare organization, I was sent to what was then called Golden Boten City, a cross-border gambling den located in the most northern part of Laos bordering China's Yunnan province. Boten was then part of a Chinese development plan to convert an approximately two-thousand-hectare Laotian land parcel into a casino and recreational resort. It was to be the next Macau, but one catering to regular Chinese people rather than high rollers. Sometime in 2009, my organization received a tip-off about a bear farm operation in the city that was possibly contributing to an epidemic, not only among captive bears, but also among other useful animals such as horses. Local authorities were worried that the disease would continue to jump the species barrier, in the manner of SARS or bird flu, and thus affect tourism. Our Australian veterinarian and Singaporean founder formed the first group to travel to Laos, intent on using the epidemic as an opportunity to save the remaining bears, and I followed a few weeks later.[56]

The journey to Boten City from Luang Prabang airport was a harrowing ride at breakneck speed through steep mountain roads, along which locals (some of whom had been evicted from Boten City) had built homes. Located right up against the Chinese border, Boten was so minimally connected to Laos that even the Laotian national currency was not accepted there, only Chinese yuan. Laotian police and border guards were present, but they seemed to defer to the Chinese who ran the city, and all were deeply connected to the casinos. We heard rumors of Chinese gamblers who could not pay their debts being murdered and their bodies dumped in the jungle.

Looking around the reception area of the hotel, I discovered a little booth at one corner selling "Chinese medicine" in red packaging, obviously meant to be purchased as gifts. I approached the Chinese lady sitting behind a glass display case full of boxes of bear bile products and asked to see one. The saleslady was no pharmacist. She had no answers to my questions about the medicinal uses of the products she was selling for very high prices. Like other products for sale in Boten, bear bile seemed to exist more within a gifting economy than a medicinal or curative one. On the other hand, the medicinal capital invested in bear bile was real and powerful, and, as I would learn in time, the product was intended to sell itself with little need of physicians, pharmacists, or other medical professionals to give it further sanction.

The following day, I was brought to the actual farm where the bear bile products I had seen the previous evening were made. It was nestled in a hill overlooking the city and next to a house belonging to the farm owner. Inside were two rows of cages supported on thin metal rods the height of a five-year-old child. Most of the cages were empty because so many bears had been killed by the epidemic, but two adults and one cub had survived. The adults were hardly recognizable as bears because they had rubbed most of their fur off against the bars of the cages and had grown very long toenails through disuse of their feet.

As for the cages, they were terribly small. There was an adjustable plate in one that, I later found out, was for pinning down the bear so that the farmer and his assistants could go underneath and "milk" her from a catheter permanently placed in her gallbladder, down which bile would drip. As I absorbed the scene around me, one adult bear reached his paw out to the farm owner, who in return extended his and touched the bear. I asked the owner what he thought their relationship was, and his reply was, "We are just like family." He was, however, sporting a huge scar on his face, evidence of being mauled by one his captive bears.

The team from Singapore was invited to drink hard liquor every night with the police chief and the head representative of the development company, as was Chinese custom, while negotiating the surrender of the bears and other wild-caught animals, such as the iguana hanging in cages at a nearby restaurant. The town was full of wild animals in cages, many endangered, and nearly all illegal to trade under Chinese law. Those not eaten were likely destined for the trade in exotic medicinals or as pets. My companions were mostly nondrinkers (as is typical of Singaporean Chinese), which put them at a disadvantage in negotiating. As their junior, I was assigned to do most of the drinking. Boten City was a resort for Chinese gamblers, but is also close to a rain forest, and the farm owner had taken advantage of that convergence to market exotic animal medicinals to Chinese tourists. The casino owners had now lost patience with the bear farmer, however, so were cooperating with us in closing him down and repatriating the remaining bears. Their plan, however, was to still have the bears make money, as exhibits in a "bear sanctuary" or glorified zoo, which they hoped would be funded and run by animal-loving Singaporeans.

There were no Chinese doctors in Golden Boten City, no Chinese pharmacies, and no obvious sites of intersection with institutions of Chinese medicine. But there were many, many animals and animal parts being sold as medicine by people who could offer little explicit advice on how such substances should be used. The animals themselves were not Chinese (i.e., not living in China prior to being caught) but Laotian. Moreover, Boten City was one of a number of such gambling/medicine sites that exist close against the border of China and its Southeast Asian neighbors. In all of them, exotic animals from the surrounding forests were being sold for high prices as medicine to Chinese gambler-tourists, who were perfectly healthy at the time of purchase. In Boten, ironically, even sick and diseased animals were being converted to "medicine" for the comparatively rich and healthy, in an atmosphere of risk, danger, and criminality.[57]

A few years later, having decided to pursue animal medicinals as a scholarly project in the Edinburgh University–National University of Singapore

(NUS) Joint PhD Program, I traveled to China and was hosted during my archival research and fieldwork at the Guangzhou University of Chinese Medicine (GUCM). In this capacity I had the opportunity to accompany a professor of Chinese medicine on a visit to Golden Bear Company Private Limited in Conghua, Guangzhou, China's third-largest bear farm and a family-run enterprise. On entering its gates, Golden Bear is an impressive sight, different in every way from the decrepit appearance of the farm in the Laotian jungle. The central building, five to six stories tall, is covered with shiny yellow-tinted tiles, evidently to match the name of the company. It was literally gleaming in the sun on the day I arrived. The attached premises span roughly two hundred *mu*, or thirty-three acres, and the visitor can't help but be struck by its picturesqueness. Its centerpiece is a large man-made waterfall. A family member revealed in the course of my visit that the company planned to tap in to Conghua's reputation as a hot-spring destination to eventually turn Golden Bear into a *yangsheng zhongxin*, or health cultivation center, for tourists.

Unlike in Golden Boten City, it would be easy for visitors to Golden Bear to imagine they were entering a paradise for animals. But in fact the tall building is a factory, processing bile collected from an attached farm containing some four hundred bears. An additional two hundred are kept in Chaozhou, where the family had established their first enterprise—a zoo. The founder's son described the zoo as displaying all kinds of "queer gourds and fruits" (*shenqi gua guo*), as well as a crocodile, an ostrich, Bama pigs, a camel, and just a couple of bears. A 2001 visit to the zoo by a professor of Chinese medicine had induced the family to expand its horizons. Noticing the bears, he introduced the owners to the concept of bear bile farming and its potential for profit.

The Golden Bear grounds still have something of a zoo flavor. In addition to bears, they include a deer farm where easily a hundred deer are kept for their antlers, also a highly valued medicinal, which the company produces on the side. A camel (from the original zoo) is kept in a separate enclosure among scores of Bama pigs and piglets. Two trams take tourists on tours of this menagerie.

We proceeded to one of two lackluster cement buildings, which was full of bear cubs. Bears below the age of three are not suitable to have their bile milked, according to our guide, and so are kept separate from the adults (whom we were not invited to see). As we walked through the narrow walkway, the bears—two or three to each enclosure—approached the metal fencing between us. We stopped at one enclosure and our guide reached out to shake the paw of what looked like an enthusiastic bear cub. On closer inspection, the paw was deformed. According to our guide, the cub was born wild and had had its paw caught in a trap laid by poachers. Forest rangers discovered the bear, who then delivered it to the company.

This time the scene of hand (paw) shaking between farm owner and bear did not surprise me, as it had at Golden Boten City. I realized that farm owners use this gesture to convince visitors that their bears are not suffering, but are cooperative partners in a profitable venture. By showing us a bear that was formerly wild, trapped, and then rescued, the company also sought to demonstrate its existence as a pseudo-sanctuary. This image was further boosted by an official certificate recognizing the company's role in conservation efforts. Our guide stressed, however, that two-thirds of their bears resulted from captive breeding, while those caught from the wild were all "rescued" bears.

The company's customers are not only mainland Chinese, but also Hong Kong, Taiwanese, and Japanese dealers. A Japanese pharmaceutical company had even offered to buy the farm. Bear bile is an essential ingredient in making Japan's household drug *Sokko kyuushingan* (*Suxiao Jiuxin Wan* in Chinese), or simply *kyuushingan*.[58] It is also the main ingredient for *Matsui yuujingan*, an Edo-period concoction linked to the Matsui family. In fact, Matsui Yuji, the CEO of what is now Matsui Pharmaceutical Company, was on record as stating that no other animal bile could effectively replace bear bile as a medicine.[59] Our Chinese guide likewise dismissed Ursofalk, a synthetic substitute created by German drug-maker Losan Pharma GmbH in 1979, as not having the properties of "the real thing."

My last stop was in a reception hall, where the family's patriarch was waiting to greet me and my colleague, who was a high-ranking Chinese physician. I noticed on the table in front of us two shot glasses held firmly by a plastic supporter, just like two *temaki* rolls. The glasses were filled with a thick, golden-colored liquid, and before I could ask what it was, our host told us to "finish it in one gulp," as we would a shot of liquor. My companion did as he was told, but I was revolted on the first sip. The taste of raw, untreated bear bile is indescribable. I politely excused myself and went to the display section, where I saw different grades of bear bile tea, pure bile liquid and powder, all with elaborate packaging. These products had the trade name Professor Bear or *Xiong Boshi*. There were also various wine concoctions such as "bear bile-lingzhi wine," "deer antler and blood wine," and "deer antler-deer penis wine."

Before we left, I was induced to drink up the last of the bear bile in my shot glass by being reminded that ten milliliters of the stuff—the glass contained fifty—was worth at the time 600 yuan (or over 80 US dollars). Our host spoke enthusiastically about its benefits, including its ability to cure cancer and reduce pain in critically ill patients, and recommended drinking it every day as a "natural antiseptic." Back in the hotel, I brushed my teeth twice and ate only desserts for dinner, but the taste of raw bear bile lasted in my mouth for hours.

Despite the different scales and situations of the two bear farms, their similarities were more pronounced than their differences. Both seemed to rely on their product to sell itself, producer and consumer having equal faith in the medicinal being potent and sanctioned by tradition. Unlike the farm in Laos, Golden Bear is a member of the China Association of Traditional Chinese Medicine (*Zhongguo Zhongyao Xiehui*), which is bear farming's strong lobbying arm. But in neither place is the presence of the Chinese physician, let alone the lab or the clinic, obviously apparent. In both places medicine is embedded within a menagerie, accompanied by visual and oral references to threatened forests, on the one hand, and zoos, wildlife sanctuaries, and tourism, on the other.

Bear farming may seem to illustrate the distance currently prevailing between the industrial production and use of animal-based drugs and more academic conceptions of Chinese medicine—that such drugs are indeed no more than a bad taste incidental to, and hence unreflective of, classical modes of health and healing. From one angle, the practice seems to embody what Elizabeth Hsu has described, in a slightly different context, as the rise of "an autonomous 'pharmacy' decoupled from the physician's clinical practice."[60] Yet state-institutionalized pharmacology in the early Communist period indeed paved the way to Golden Boten City and Golden Bear Private Limited, and, as we shall see, academic physicians and clinicians played a strong supporting role in this process, and still do today. Bear farms have their origins in Soviet-sponsored deer farms, the export of "luxury medicinals" like musk, and claims that injecting chicken blood into humans could cure a hundred diseases. They interweave references from ancient Chinese texts, Japanese laboratory reports, and North Korean experiments in veterinary surgery. They originate in the development of a drug-discovery and drug-making culture in the mid-twentieth century with strong political as well as economic imperatives—a culture that might have left medical animals behind as an artifact of a previous era, but instead chose to expand their exploitation. Animals in the twentieth century became the raw materials for a modern Chinese medicinal industry that presents an ecological, ethical, and public health challenge in the current generation. How and why that happened is the subject of the chapters that follow.

CHAPTER ONE

"Abandon Chinese Medicine, Retain Chinese Drugs"
Creating a State Pharmaceutical Sector

 Before focusing on animals, we first need to trace the larger institutional and policy changes reshaping pharmaceutics in the first decade of Communist rule. These changes related mainly to herbal medicine and only incidentally to animal tissue, which was initially undervalued and underdeveloped within the new regimes' plans for its pharmaceutical sector. The later medicalization of fauna in the form of medicinal farming and novel drug therapies nevertheless depended on this early turn to pharmacy as a prominent state interest, linked as it was to the concept of merging Chinese and "Western" medicines around the common theme of drug discovery. That "Chinese" animals (those commonly used in Chinese medicine) were initially outside the project of creating a new, science-based Chinese pharmacy indicates that they were initially viewed as a different and more problematic resource than herbs.

Although this chapter summarizes discussions that began before the Revolution, its primary focus is the period between 1950 (the first full year of the new regime) and 1957, the last year before the Great Leap Forward. The most significant policy event of this period was China's initial Five-Year Plan (1953–1957), which constituted the regime's first serious attempt to weed out private firms and construct a socialist economy—including a pharmaceutical sector—on the Soviet model. Among the developments this chapter chronicles are the perceived shortage of medicines of all kinds (Chinese and Western) following the Revolution; the government response of creating pharmaceutical factories (with embedded laboratories) to produce "new drugs" using "native resources," including herbs shared with Chinese medicine; the government's takeover and consolidation of private drug companies producing Chinese medicines, some of which already sold animal-based medicinals in overseas markets; the continued importance of these overseas Chinese medicine markets to the Chinese economy; and the simultaneous training of new categories of persons—pharmacists and drug factory workers—as well as the expansion in the numbers of pharmacologists, which was both a result and a lever of these changes.

It is important to note, however, that these developments were not simply economic imperatives or responses, but reflected political ideologies and programs that also shifted on a regular basis. Such political shifts were usually signaled by slogans or new idioms that, precisely because they were incomplete in meaning and intent, allowed for flexible interpretation by those repeating them. Even the concept of "drugs" (*yao*) was not simply descriptive or neutral at the beginning of this period, but was used to draw a contrast between materia medica, on the one hand, and the theory and practice of Chinese medicine, on the other, with important stakes for medical politics. This new focus on drugs and drug-making helped set the stage for the flurry of animal-tissue-based innovations we later encounter from the Great Leap Forward and onward.

Indeed, the rise of the pharmaceutical sector is as fundamental to understanding how Chinese medicine was institutionalized after the Revolution as is the better-known creation of a state-managed educational system for doctors of Chinese medicine that occurred simultaneously. The earliest state-supported Chinese medicine schools had been set up in the late 1940s, but many more were founded during the first Five-Year Plan, such as the present-day Guangzhou University of Chinese Medicine (established in 1956 under the name Guangzhou Chinese Medical College), which was the base for my fieldwork.[1] In this college, as in others, trends that began in the 1950s eventually resulted, in 1972, in the establishment of two curricular streams, embodied in separate departments, to teach *yi* (medicine) and *yao* (drugs).[2] This marked a break from past tradition, wherein less distinction was made between the actual knowledge of physicians and drug-makers pertaining to medicinals, even if those roles were embodied in different individuals.[3] Well before these reforms in higher education, however, a new class of pharmacists and drug factory workers was created from what were formerly medicine shop workers (*yaogongshi*). This was part of the larger attempt to institutionalize Chinese medicine according to Chinese understandings of how biomedicine was organized in the West. This new professional group and its practices allowed for new enactments of Chinese medicine as a more material (i.e., drug-focused) system and less a body of theory, heritage, and skill embodied in the physician.

These and other reforms had their root in slogans like "Abandon *Yi* (Chinese medicine), Retain *Yao* (Chinese drugs)" (*Fei Yi, Cun Yao*), which pre-dated the Revolution but were influential into the early years of the new regime. Mao's more-famous statement made at the end of this period (1958), that Chinese medicine constitutes a "great treasure house," is not entirely inconsistent with this earlier slogan, as both invited a new materialization of Chinese medicine through pharmaceutical research, a program that grew only more powerful through the rest of the century. In fact, Mao's exact statement was that "Chinese medicine and drugs" (*zhongyiyao*) were a treasure house, though the word "drugs" is invariably edited out of contemporary English translations.

The activities around drug discovery and drug-making take us beyond the clinic and hospital, which are the usual settings for the study of institutionalized Chinese medicine, and into the factory and factory-based laboratory, as well as the research laboratories of universities and agricultural stations. In subsequent chapters they will take us into villages engaged in the mass collection of insects and gizzards, "farms" where deer were shorn of their antlers and bears tapped for their bile, and even into city streets where people lined up with live chickens under their arms, waiting to be injected with the animals' blood. Drugs also involve us in the import and export of medicinal raw materials, which continued in 1950s China despite the country's increasing geopolitical isolation.

Drugs (*Yao*) versus Medicine (*Yi*)

The concept of Chinese drugs being separable from Chinese medicine, and thus constituting a different realm of value and action, was initially bound up with the project of making biomedicine the state medicine of China. As Sean Lei has chronicled, this policy and its theoretical underpinnings originated in the Republican period and was particularly associated with the Japanese-trained physician and medical reformer Yu Yan. Yu and other Western physicians (Chinese nationals trained in biomedicine) attempted to use the new Ministry of Health to abolish Chinese medicine and entrench the practice of biomedicine, but with the concession that some Chinese drugs likely had efficacies that should be subjected to discovery by modern pharmacology, beginning with the isolation of their active ingredients. The name given this project was Scientific Research on Nationally Produced Drugs (SRNPD) (Guochan Yaowu Kexue Yanjiu), which Lei explains was also a way to split the constituency for Chinese medicine by enlisting drug manufacturers at the expense of physicians. It was the faction around Yu who were associated with the slogan "Abandon *Yi*, Retain *Yao*" (*Fei Yi, Cun Yao*).[4]

This program caused a backlash among Chinese doctors, who organized themselves into a National Medicine Movement in 1929, which henceforth was as politically active as their Western-trained opponents. As Lei further explains, Chinese drugs became a boundary object between these two camps, even as reformist elements among Chinese physicians eventually embraced the idea that their materia medica might be "proven" to have medical value by surviving trials in Western laboratories.[5]

The study of *yao* "in its own right" had its origin in Japanese pharmacology, with which Yu was intimately familiar. As Benjamin Elman and Bridie Andrews have each pointed out, Chinese reformers during this period were not influenced directly by Western sources as much as by Japanese ones.[6] Ding Fubao, a scholar and practitioner of both Chinese and Western medicines, was among the earliest members of the Chinese medical community to travel to Japan, where he learned that Japanese pharmacologists were using chemical analysis to search for active ingredients in Chinese herbs in order to reformulate them into drugs acceptable to biomedical practice. This inspired Yu, who also studied in Japan, to set up his own pharmaceutical factory in China to reformulate *zhongyao* into Western-style drugs.[7]

Emphasizing the *yi/yao* divide thus initially served to help salvage *yao* as a material resource for the advancement of biomedicine in China, yet at the same time salvaging "things Chinese" as a resource for biomedicine generally. Republican-period reformers like Yu equated Western medicine or biomedicine with "social medicine" and as belonging to the larger movement for "social revolution." Western medicine had by that time diverged into a number of specialized subfields—including pharmacological research—which only reinforced its perceived usefulness in political and social reform. It was seen as effective in addressing specific social issues such as infectious diseases (preventive medicine), genetic defects (eugenics), crime (forensics and psychology), and social welfare (medical insurance), which Chinese medicine seemingly had no answers for. As such, Western medicine was considered an answer to the "all-round crisis" that China was facing.[8]

Western medicine was also considered "social" in the sense that it was seen as serviceable to the Chinese population writ large, as opposed to the intimate one-on-one relationship of the Chinese physician and his patient.

In Republican China, the relatively new germ theory was coming to be understood as a basis for disease. Yu Yan, in defending Western medicine, was also advocating for public health as a new state-directed realm. Chinese medicine by contrast seemed narrowly focused on the individual body rather than the national one. Yu coined the term "individual medicine" as the new and derogatory term for Chinese medicine, further reinforcing the idea of Western medicine as closer to socialism (a formula that the Communist regime later rejected). Yu also wove his narrative around a new/old dichotomy, with the two medicines representing different eras of human development. He suggested Chinese doctors registering themselves under "old medicine" should "undergo re-training in the basics of public health, while those above the age of fifty would be exempt from such classes but forbidden from treating known infectious diseases and also certifying death."[9]

Yu and others of his generation went to the extent of likening Chinese medicine to witchcraft.[10] In that sense, isolating out the corpus of Chinese drugs for chemical investigation was perceived as an act of demystification. Lei has described this as a "re-networking process," by which drugs that were deeply networked into Chinese medical practice would be re-networked into biomedicine through the medium of chemical analysis, clinical trials, and publication in scientific journals. Such practices were considered essential to validating a drug's effectiveness in the eyes of the international medical research community. Once the individual herb or other ingredient was in the lab, it could theoretically be reformulated into even more powerful or at least different medicines. The researcher would now understand it in a new and more precise way, and could presumably become the instructor to the physician, much as Western pharmacologists regularly provided Western doctors with new drug products along with instructions on their use.[11]

In the early years of the Communist regime, such ideas still held currency among medical policy-makers, most of whom were Western- or Japanese-trained doctors. At the same time, however, the sympathy of Mao and other party leaders toward Chinese medicine strengthened the ability of Chinese doctors to push back. In 1950, Wang Bin, who was then health minister for the northeast region, wrote an essay in the journal *Dongbei Weisheng* (literally, northeast hygiene), detailing plans to phase out Chinese medicine, much along the lines of Yu's earlier proposals. The essay became influential throughout China, especially after being reprinted as a booklet under the title *The Road Ahead for the Medical Worker*. At that time, Wang's plans to replace Chinese medicine with Western medicine were praised by many as "the practical example of exercising Marxism but especially dialectical materialism" in health care. Five years later, however, in the midst of high-level political struggles, members of an increasingly organized and self-confident Chinese medicine community rediscovered Wang's statements and contrasted them with Mao's advice, made as early as 1944, to give equal weight to Chinese medicine and, if possible, "combine Chinese and Western medicines."[12] That same year (1955), Wang was forced out of office, along with Deputy Health Minister He Cheng, who was accused of harboring similar sentiments.[13]

Although portrayed as an enemy of Chinese medicine in its entirety, Wang and those who shared his beliefs actually intended, like Yu and others before him, to salvage Chinese drugs. Wrote Wang, "Chinese physicians are not qualified doctors. They are effective only in terms of providing solace and comfort to farmers. . . . On the other hand, we should accept Chinese drugs (*zhongyao*), conduct scientific analysis, and then incorporate them into the next pharmacopoeia. This is the only way to secure and further our national essence."[14] These similarities with the policies of the Republican-era medical elite allowed Wang's critics to argue that he was opposed to a Marxist science, which was increasingly characterized as experiential learning by the masses. As one critic put it, "There is science in Chinese medicine although it may not be the language of modern science. Yet again, how does one even define science?"[15] This last question never received a clear answer during the early Communist period, the terms "science," "scientific," and especially "scientization" being present in the writings of advocates on both sides of nearly every policy.

In 1959, by which time Chinese medicine was safely institutionalized and above political censure in the PRC, Western-trained doctor Chen Xianyu described the thought process of he and his reformist colleagues in early Communist days as follows:

> Before taking lessons on Chinese medicine, I was of the opinion that Chinese medical terminologies such as *qi, yin, yang,* external, internal, cold, and hot were all too abstract. They were to me the products of human imagination with no proofs in science. I did not bother to find out the actual meanings of those terms. On the other hand, I had seen and heard of healings from ailments using Chinese drugs and realized their effectiveness. I can therefore understand why Chinese medicine and Chinese drugs were gradually seen as two separate entities, thus befitting the earlier slogan "Abandon *Yi*, Retain *Yao*."[16]

Being material substances, drugs were more easily constructed as "real" than traditional ideas about them, which could be assigned to superstition. Scientific research into their efficacy, it was hoped, would make them even more real, by creating new formulations and maybe identifying and proving new efficacies based on biomedical protocols. In fact, no field was seemingly more amenable to achieving Mao's policy of unification than pharmacology, given that Chinese materia medica was a research object that Chinese doctors trained in both Western and Chinese medicines could appreciate the significance of, despite their different theoretical and clinical practices.

The efficacy of Chinese herbs was still openly questioned in China in the early 1950s, however, especially given the increasing availability of "miracle drugs" like penicillin. Those advocating "Retain *yao*" thus represented a middle ground between traditionalists and those who would ignore Chinese materia medica altogether. Denigrating names for Chinese medicinals abounded in this period, such as "naughty powder" or "lying pills." Medicinals whose given names seemed to exaggerate their healing power were evoked to question the relevance of the whole corpus.[17] There were also accounts of Chinese physicians burning their entire book collections or denying their profession soon after the Communist victory. Even though Wang Bin and his like-minded colleagues were eventually expelled from their positions, and Chinese medicine was once again reinstated as an officially sanctioned practice by the mid-1950s, the suggestion that Chinese drugs could be studied, analyzed, and even reworked with scant reference to Chinese medical theory continued to be influential, particularly among those who would create a new pharmaceutical sector.

It must be noted, however, that the enthusiasm of Western-trained doctors for isolating active ingredients in Chinese drugs in this early period did not extend to drugs based on animal parts and tissue. The reasons are not hard to discern. Western caricatures of Chinese medicine as odd, backward, or even dangerous had often led with descriptions of animal-based drugs being used in raw form. As Linda Barnes and others have pointed out, raw animal parts had once been common in European materia medica as well. But their gradual elimination with the rise of "modern medicine" in the eighteenth and especially nineteenth centuries made them into one of the principal markers between what was, by the twentieth century, considered scientific as opposed to primitive in medical practice.[18] Western medicine had hardly severed its relationship with zoology, as we shall see, but cultivating the border with botany seemed the safer and more reasonable approach to those who would re-network Chinese medicine into biomedicine in the early to mid-twentieth century.

Yet Western discomfort with Chinese animal-based drugs (and Chinese understanding of that perspective) does not fully explain why animal-based drugs were not as subject to early lab analysis as herbs. As one contemporary Chinese scientific journal article points out, "Animal drugs are complex mixtures containing hundreds or even thousands of different chemicals, proteins, or other [substances]. Thus to identify the active ingredients of these animal materials in molecular detail through experimental methods is still intractable."[19] Pharmacological analysis of protein-based tissue was all the more intractable in mid-twentieth-century China. For both these reasons, the search for active ingredients in plants was pursued with far more energy and resources in Chinese labs than was animal-based materia medica. The most notable "breakthrough" regarding a Chinese-sourced animal drug by the 1950s—the isolation of what came to be called ursodeoxycholic acid (UDCA) from bear bile ("urso" referring to bears)—was almost entirely a Japanese research project, although initially pursued using bears imported from China. Even then, UDCA was not subjected to clinical trials until the 1970s, by which time it had already been commercially synthesized from chickens and pigs.[20] This lack of what would then have been considered "fundamental" research on the chemistry of animal-based materia medica extended through nearly the whole period we are considering. Yet it did not slow the production and use of such medicinals when more attention turned to fauna during the Great Leap Forward and afterward. This demonstrates that the search for active ingredients came to be considered only one of many paths to "scientization" of medicinals in this period, and not one favored for animal-based drugs.

"Scientize Chinese Medicine, Sinicize Western Medicine"

Despite continuities from the Republican period, the previous equation of "science" with Western-derived bioscience was no longer unreflexively accepted by the early Communist regime. The Maoist emphasis on "combination" and "unification" of the two medical traditions meant that, from early in the new regime, there was a sense that Chinese scientific paths might (indeed should) diverge from Western ones, especially regarding the role of the scientist as expert (which we deal with at length in subsequent chapters). As Sigrid Schmalzer and others have pointed out, the term *xiyihua* (westernize) was no longer politically correct, yet the verb *kexuehua* (scientize) was now even more charismatic than it had been under the Republic, and was applied as a referent to almost all areas of life.[21]

The new slogan that came to guide such medical policy in the early 1950s was *Zhongyi Kexuehua, Xiyi Zhongguohua* (scientize Chinese medicine, sinicize Western medicine). This was a more conservative rephrasing of Mao's earlier message to "combine Chinese and Western medicines." Rather than be forced into combination, both medicines were to evolve in order to eventually meet at the same understanding.[22] It would not be the last reformulation of this elusive goal, however, which remained in one form or another as the political principle guiding medical policy throughout (and beyond) the period of Mao's rule.

But how to activate such slogans in practice? When the Chinese doctor Xu Yecheng encountered difficulty grafting Chinese clinical practice onto Western medical understandings, he wrote to the journal *Xin Zhong Yiyao* in 1950 asking for clarification. The editors responded:

> Do not confuse "scientize" with "westernize." We are basically harnessing the weapons of science to transform Chinese medicine into an evidence-based practice. There were earlier attempts to merge Chinese and Western medicines into one understanding, starting with Tang Rongchuan from the Qing dynasty. Unfortunately, all efforts were in vain. It is impossible to explain Chinese medicine using the principles of Western medicine since they are totally different. For instance, there is no Western equivalent for the twelve meridians . . . and any attempt to find one is futile. It is, however, possible to understand Chinese medicine using Western science. To do so, we have to rely on scientists or the scientific knowledge gained from pursuing advanced studies.[23]

It was likely unclear in the mind of the writer, not to mention the reader, what such phrases as "harnessing the weapons of science" meant in practice. But in requiring that Chinese medicine become "evidence-based," this writer and others reaffirmed the belief that laboratory- or clinic-based proofs would eventually validate Chinese medicine to skeptics, rather than transform it along the lines of Western biomedicine.

For many observers, the easiest path to fulfilling this ideological imperative to "Scientize Chinese Medicine, Sinicize Western Medicine" was to analyze Chinese materia medica using Western chemistry, hoping to find active ingredients and thus convincing proof of the effects of such substances in curing ailments. In other words, continuing the Republican-period SRNPD project, but now for the glory and benefit of Chinese medicine rather than as part of a strategy of replacing it. By the 1950s, China could cite two Republican-period projects as having already accomplished that goal. The first was the creation of the anti-asthma drug ephedrine from the Chinese herb *mahuang* in the 1920s by a research group in Peking. The second was laboratory research that led to recognition by Western-trained scientists in the 1940s of the antimalarial properties of the Chinese herb *changshan* (a plant of the hydrangea family). The seeming success of these two projects suggested that a systematic investigation of all Chinese medicinal substances, which had never been attempted in the Republican period, would yield many more such "breakthroughs."[24] Indeed, another success was to come in the early 1970s with the creation by Chinese researchers of the antimalarial drug artemisinin from the traditionally used medicinal plant *Artemisia annua*.

But there were objections to this project from the standpoint of Chinese physicians. One was that Chinese herbs were traditionally combined by Chinese doctors into recipes and not prescribed individually. Thus, studying *zhongyao* for active ingredients, as one writer in 1955 put it, meant "a focus on individual herbs rather than collections [i.e., recipes involving multiple herbs] which constitute the underlying principle of Chinese clinical practice." Finding the active ingredients of specific Chinese herbs would add to the corpus of biomedicine but provide no evidentiary reinforcement for the prescriptive knowledge of Chinese physicians. Here was recognition, and fear, of the "re-networking" process as Lei has described it.[25]

This issue of whether to research the properties of individual herbs or concentrate on physicians' multi-herb recipes tended from the beginning to divide Chinese pharmacological researchers from Chinese medicine doctors, and to some extent still does to this day. A closely related point of difference was whether a given medicinal had only one "active ingredient," or several, some of which might only be activated in combination with other substances. This issue was raised as early as 1950 in a new journal published in Shanghai under the title *Xinhua Yiyao* (New Chinese medicine and drugs; later renamed *Xin Zhong Yiyao*), whose mission statement was "A scientized Chinese *Yi* as the New *Yi*, A scientized Chinese *Yao* as the New *Yao*."[26] A paper in the second issue was co-authored by Yu Yan, whom we encountered in the Republican period as an opponent of Chinese medicine and an advocate of subjecting single Chinese herbs to chemical investigation based on the Japanese research model. Under the new regime, however, he had become more critical of such "foreign" research schemes. The paper gave credit to Japanese and European researchers for having been the first to analyze the chemical makeup of Chinese herbs and extract their main active ingredients. But their attempts at understanding the pharmacology of Chinese herbs had failed, the authors went on to claim, because they had tried to isolate only one active ingredient in each herb. "The majority of Chinese drugs are plants. . . . Each plant has more than one active ingredient, some even exceeding ten. Whilst active, the ingredients do not perform the same function. Some are either to help enhance or suppress another ingredient, while others play no role at all. An ingredient that has been singled out using scientific means could turn out to be neutral. It cannot therefore represent the herb in its entirety." Previous drug discovery programs had also set false limits on the useful range of each herb, they argued, *mahuang* being cited as an example. Until Chinese pharmacologist Chen Kehui alerted Japanese researchers to its anti-asthmatic property, the authors wrote, the latter had tested only its ability to improve eyesight. The existing pattern of searching for only one active ingredient, they concluded, thus ended up delimiting the curative power of the herb to a few specific complaints. The authors of this article conceded the importance of analyzing Chinese drugs in a laboratory setting in order to demonstrate their efficacy to the world. They also sought to use lab research to ensure that artificial substitutes could be concocted should domestic supplies of raw ingredients run out. Yet whether from patriotism or from a genuine concern with research directions (or both), they were arguing that the task of chemically analyzing and testing Chinese herbs be done in China, and with more understanding of the way materia medica was actually used by Chinese doctors.[27]

Casting doubt on, or even rejecting, the project of searching for active ingredients in Chinese medicinals was a stance that, in the future, would often be invoked by those advocating the modern use of animal drugs. As has been indicated, animal tissue was extremely chemically complex even when isolated, and all the more so when used as one ingredient in polyherbal recipes. It was also in many cases far less uniform than material from plants. Thus arguments initially crafted by more conservative physicians or researchers to complicate the search for single active ingredients in plant-based materia medica became even more compelling when applied to animal parts. The efficacy of such materials, it was claimed, could not be absolutely proven in the laboratory given their complexity, but their mass production or use must not be held up by this circumstance, given (to use the common phrase) "their long history of use by the Chinese people."

Consolidating a Pharmaceutical Sector

The new concentration on drug research and discovery, partly ideological and partly pragmatic, was accompanied in the early to mid-1950s by a new concentration on drug production, which was activated most clearly by the first Five-Year Plan. "Production" emerged beside "scientize" as an important key word of this period, and had a controlling effect on which scientific projects were now pursued. Projects that did not have a productive component (and even links to actual factories) were no longer in favor, as what in the West was called "pure science" was now increasingly considered "bourgeois."

When the Communists came to power, China was actually in the midst of a severe shortage of Chinese medicinals. The tumultuous war years—both the civil war and the Japanese invasion—had severely interrupted production and trade, and there were many accounts of hard-hit medicine shops engaging in dishonest trading of inferior goods or, worse, complete imitations. Exports from China to the overseas Chinese market also took a beating as a result. To worsen the situation further, private medicine shops and pharmacies reportedly engaged in secret stockpiling to inflate prices. Authorities in the 1950s described them as "yellow cows," a Chinese term for black marketers.[28]

Stockpiling was decried as counter-socialist in 1954, and citing this problem, the government released plans in January of that year to co-opt all private enterprises in the pharmaceutical sector. The aim, officially, was to "stabilize production in order to meet public needs."[29] The co-optation of factories also allowed, however, for the implementation of new national policies relating to drug discovery and distribution under the Five-Year Plan. By the late 1950s, a network of *yiyao* companies (state-owned Chinese drug companies) and "herb collection stations" had been established throughout China to solicit, collect, and deliver raw materials to factory-based pharmaceutical laboratories. Some of these production facilities were created from scratch, while others were crafted by consolidating existing private firms.

Because of these reforms, many cultivated Chinese herbs became raw materials for processes of drug discovery in factory-based labs.[30] Herbs from the Chinese countryside began to be used experimentally in an attempt to produce biomedical drugs or their imitations.[31] In 1953, the Chinese Communist Party had published its first official pharmacopoeia, which listed mostly biomedical as opposed to Chinese drugs.[32] From this point onward, a principal concern of Chinese pharmacology would be to reproduce those medicinals in the official pharmacopoeia using locally available resources, following a similar policy implemented in the Soviet Union. The Chinese motto in the early years of Communist rule was to follow the Soviet example, including its ambitious drug-making program (a matter dealt with in detail in chapter 2). Politics notwithstanding, the government also wanted to reduce spending on medicinal imports that would otherwise drain national coffers.

State-sponsored efforts in this area began even before the first Five-Year Plan. In the southwest region, for instance, pharmaceutical factories were set up in the provinces of Guizhou, Yunnan, and Sichuan to directly access supplies of local herbs. China did not have a well-developed road system in the early 1950s, and the only solution was to build regional factories. Drugs produced by these factories were either imitations of Western drugs or new formulations—collectively known as "new drugs"—both of which were mainly for consumption within the region. Sourcing for local raw materials also helped prevent overreliance on strategic or nationally traded ingredients. For example, Daxin Pharmaceutical Factory in the same southwest region produced glucose from a local herb instead of from sugarcane and alcohol, the standard sources used in the West.[33]

These "new drugs" were generally formulated for domestic consumption. Low cost of production, affordable pricing, and portability were among the criteria set for their production. A wide variety of such "new drugs" appeared in 1954, reportedly in the thousands, though sources from this period regularly inflate the progress of China's pharmaceutical sector since the Revolution. Nearly all begin with stock phrases such as, "In the last four years, drug production in China has achieved an impressive state of development." That was the actual title of an article published in the newspaper *Renmin Ribao* in 1954, which opened with these words: "China's pharmaceutical industry continues to gain strength. Before Liberation, most drugs for local use had to be imported. Under the current leadership of both the Central Health Ministry and Ministry of Light Industry, however, the pharmaceutical sector has undergone a significant change. Among the hundreds of pieces of medical equipment and drugs that state-owned enterprises produce, individual ingredients alone amount to seventy kinds. The production of 'new' drugs increased by thirty more varieties in 1953. Important drugs like penicillin and sulfa guanidine can now be locally produced."[34] Penicillin was one of the first pharmaceutical "breakthroughs" of the early Communist period, when a drug factory in Shanghai managed to replicate an Austrian process for producing the drug.[35]

By the mid-1950s, many journal reports like this one were claiming scientific breakthroughs in drug discovery. While some lauded scientists for successfully following and replicating foreign processes, such as the one that had resulted in Chinese penicillin, others argued that drug discovery should begin with the examination of Chinese materia medica. In 1954, pharmacologist Jiang Daqu pointed out that except for minerals, a subgroup of Chinese medicines, the pharmacological properties of Chinese plant- and animal-based ingredients were greatly under-researched. While recognizing that "previous generations of physicians have used Chinese drugs successfully without knowing their exact chemical makeup," Jiang argued that this was no longer possible in the new China. He did, however, encourage the use of classical texts to inform pharmacologists, and gave the antimalarial drug *changshan* as an example of effective modern drug discovery, which he claimed was based on two ancient works, *Zhouhou Fang* and *Waitai Miyao*. The example of *changshan* as a Chinese medicinal herb whose active ingredients had been isolated and proven effective against malaria was cited nearly as often as penicillin in celebratory accounts of Chinese pharmacology. These neatly provided two complementary paths of drug discovery, one in which China replicated a foreign process and the other in which Chinese materia medica (and Chinese laboratories) were the points of origin.[36] Thus did the very term "new drug" blur the boundary between Western-derived and Chinese-derived ingredient, process, and product.

One difficulty in subjecting Chinese materia medica to any form of laboratory investigation, it was early realized, was standardizing the names of herbs. The "same" herbs collected from different localities might not be the same at all, and result in nonreplicable results. Research scientists pointed out the confusion arising from one herb having multiple common names, or one common name applied to multiple herbs. This eventually became a research problem in its own right and led to the publication of more codified versions of Chinese materia medica.[37] While this same issue of classification and nomenclature should have by right also applied to medicinal animals—for example to differences between sub-species of tiger or rhino—it was almost never raised in this period, and rarely in later ones when medicinal animal farming began in earnest. This had partly to do with the far greater commonality of herbs used as medicinals, and hence the stronger established connection between Chinese medicine and botany, as opposed to zoology. Zoological links would be forged later, and mainly as a result of medicinal animal farming. Yet even then, ignoring rather than highlighting differences between animal sub-species would remain normative, and prove convenient for those eager to link them to references and recipes in classical texts.

These and other difficulties in creating "new drugs" from Chinese materia medica led to increasing collaborations in this period between branch offices of the Chinese Pharmacology Association, hospitals and research institutions, and even some Chinese medicine doctors. The project also tapped in to the existing knowledge of workers who handled Chinese herbs. In Tianjin, for instance, these workers were enlisted to provide information on plant names under earlier classification systems. Field trips were then made for hospital personnel to learn the process of herb farming from cultivation to harvest. Specimens were subjected to chemical analysis in labs, but longtime employees, especially *yaogong* workers, were often consulted regarding herb authentication. As such, a typical research committee might be made up of laboratory researchers (biologists, chemists, and pharmacologists), Chinese doctors, and sometimes-skilled workers. Each research committee focused on herbs grown in its region, which ranged from a handful to tens of varieties.[38]

From Drug-Makers (*Yaogongshi*) to Pharmacists (*Tiaojishi*)

The roles of *yishi* (doctor) and *yaogongshi* (drug-maker) were well differentiated even prior to the Revolution, a situation that Fang Xiaoping tells us had prevailed "for thousands of years."[39] *Gong* connotes labor and signals the technical nature of the job of the *yaogongshi* compared to that of the *yishi,* who was expected to understand and apply theories. Yet again, both were expected to be knowledgeable about materia medica. Medicine shops might dispense drugs according to a physician's prescription, or might sell them without one. A Mao-period physician named Yan Cangshan also described how some physicians used to "carry medicine bags on their backs"—in other words, dispense drugs directly.[40]

The new emphasis on pharmacology, however, and the creation of a more integrated medical system, required the creation of a new breed of pharmacist or pharmacological worker. Their distinction from doctors would remain, but they would now seek greater status using the title *tiaojishi* (pharmacist). Another phrase to describe them that began to appear in post-revolutionary literature was *jishu renyuan* (technician). The latter designation was then considered prestigious because it fit the description of "being scientific" (*kexue de*). Medicine shops and pharmaceutical factories were still linked in people's minds to capitalism, even though they had come under state management, and after the Revolution it was no longer respectable to engage in commerce.[41]

As we have seen, in postrevolutionary China the word "scientize" (*kexuehua*) was highly charismatic, and ubiquitous. At the same time, however, Western scientific terminology often required reform in the Chinese context to make what was historically an elite and esoteric practice seem more socialist. Clause 95 of the new "People's Constitution," for example, declared that the Chinese population was free to engage in creative literary, artistic, or scientific "labor." Writing soon after the constitution was promulgated (1954), pharmacology professor Xue Yu followed many contemporaries by introducing himself as "a worker in scientific research" rather than a "scientist"—a term considered individualist, if not elitist, now that "scientific labor" had become the province of the people.[42]

An avid contributor of articles to Chinese pharmacological journals throughout the Mao period, Xue was typical in claiming that under Kuomintang rule there was neither government funding nor infrastructure to promote pharmacology, a situation he claimed that Mao had reversed: "After Liberation, the National Pharmaceutical Research Institute [Guoli Yaowu Yanjiu Jigou] was set up. Each pharmaceutical factory now has its own research department to study foreign drugs. . . . Scientific research creates the material foundation for a socialist society. It is not only the basis for China's current industrialization program, but also a means to better the life, both materially and culturally, of its people."[43] As Xue makes clear, pharmaceutical research was intended to contribute directly to China's industrialization. He emphasizes the location of pharmacological research in the research departments of factories, which conformed to the Chinese policy of emphasizing the close marriage of research and production. Xue's statement also makes clear that Chinese pharmacology would prioritize the study and replication of foreign drugs. This did not rule out, however, the search for substitutes using Chinese materia medica. In fact, raw Chinese medicinals would come to be considered crucial to the project of replication.

The creation of factory labs was accompanied by educational programs to produce a cadre of pharmacists, pharmacologists, and drug-producing technicians. A two-page editorial in the front pages of a newly established pharmacology journal of 1954 noted that while training schools had been set up throughout China (presumably in factories), education was not yet standardized, a reform the author urged. He pointed to the existence of what he described as malpractice in factory labs, and quoted a 1953 report by the Central Health Department claiming evidence of fake or unqualified drugs in the market. Only centrally directed education along the Soviet model, he argued, would raise standards.[44]

This was not, however, the direction that training would take. Factory-based education for pharmacological workers (including those conducting research) would remain the norm, with only a small elite of pharmacologists trained in institutes. This conformed to official policy under Mao to produce a nation of "science workers." Not only were factory schools set up, but books written by Chinese authors on Western pharmacology began to appear (though often to poor reviews by Chinese commentators), to educate and inspire this new class of worker-researcher.[45] Traditionally, Chinese medicine shop workers had been trained under apprenticeship, but night-school classes began to be established as early as 1950 to supersede this system. Drug factory workers were eventually required to attend classes six nights a week, except Sunday, each class lasting two hours. The skills needed to work in a Chinese or a Western-style drug factory or dispensary were also eventually standardized, so that the two became almost interchangeable.[46] Thus while the distinction between the "Chinese" or "Western" doctor lingered in post-revolutionary China, despite slogans calling for convergence, merger was more easily and quickly achieved among those who handled drugs, from factory workers to pharmacologists.

The drugs that students learned about in these classes were mainly biomedical ones—those listed in the official pharmacopoeia of 1953, with occasional reference to local drugs such as *changshan* and *yadanzi*. Students were required to know both the Chinese and Latin names for each drug and its characteristics, including its pharmacological action, recommended dosage, and, finally, the different ways of administering it. In pharmaceutics, students learned "the responsibilities of working in a pharmacy such as the mixing of drugs." Missing in this first iteration of a pharmacy curriculum was basic science and, especially, theory.[47]

The motto for ambitious *tiaojishi* was *zhuanyan* (research). This was seen as the key to elevating pharmacists above, or at least on par, with physicians. Journals of the period often presented pharmacists in this light—as workers in a pioneer industry who needed to create and not just apply knowledge of the kind held by doctors. The successful Chinese production of crystallized penicillin was a commonly cited example from the realm of industrial lab research. Although Chinese researchers had learned from Western journals that potassium acetate was the main ingredient for making crystallized penicillin, they were not aware of the steps in this process and had to learn them through reverse engineering. The implication was that pharmacist-workers would have to come up with their own technical solutions, given that foreign journals often failed to explain processes in detail.

Pharmacy journals of this period began to feature articles written by workers who, lacking full knowledge of a procedure, had taken the initiative to innovate (*chuangxin*). One article was by a pharmacist named Zhang Zhongde who, with his work group, had been given the task to "seal an ampoule," a glass container for liquid substances. He was perturbed that no one in the team had even seen an ampoule before, not to mention the action of closing one up. They turned to existing literature but found only vague information like "experience is required to seal an ampoule." Zhang described his experiments as follows: "I chose twenty unsealed ampoules that had longer necks and poured distilled water into them. I placed each neck over the flame of a burner. . . . After experimenting for two hours, I finally found the technique for sealing them. I was elated! Now, I will introduce my findings."

Most workers, concluded Zhang, could make up for the lack of theoretical knowledge by being practical and having an innovative spirt. To Zhang, it was wrong to think that formal schools were the only place where one acquired knowledge. One could learn equally well in the workplace, and then share the experience with others. Such a "practical" experimental culture was aided, of course, by the burgeoning journal culture that allowed techniques to be reported and shared with a national audience, thus helping create a research instinct among young members of the nascent profession.[48]

Despite this, articles and letters in pharmaceutical journals of this period are still full of angst and uncertainty about the status and skills of pharmacists in comparison with physicians, as well as uncertainty as to where to draw the line between them. That some trainees considered themselves subordinate to doctors angered more ambitious practitioners. Cai Yumin, a teacher from Shandong Medical College, remarked that most of the practicum reports he read by pharmacy students were of poor quality, which he attributed to poor morale. According to Cai, recent graduates did not appear content with their lot, and many chose not to stay in the pharmaceutical sector because of its low prestige. This to Cai was un-Communist behavior. He also criticized the passivity of some pharmacists who thought that "filling a prescription is basically to take from the shelves what the doctor has written. It doesn't matter if the patient consumes more or less of what has been prescribed." Cai wrote that although the role of a pharmacist was indeed "to prepare drugs in strict accordance with the doctor's prescription and the rules listed in the official pharmacopoeia," it was not a dead-end job. He likened both pharmacists and doctors to screws and bolts, meaning they were equally seminal to the nation-building effort.[49]

The suggestion was that pharmacists and pharmacy workers now had access to a knowledge realm separate from that of physicians, and that the advancement of that realm required innovation on their part. It was no longer just "decanting," which is the way drug handling before the Revolution was now lampooned. This message had to be constantly reinforced in the journals, and was often presented as coming from the voice of youth, sometimes in rebellion against their teachers.

In June 1955, the Chinese Pharmacology Association published a letter by a young pharmacy student or trainee named Wu Ming in its journal *Yaoxue Tongbao* with the title "Overqualified or Too High an Expectation." Wu presented himself as an ambitious person who was unhappy with the low expectations and knowledge level of his instructor, whom he called only "the pharmacist." His letter portrays himself and his workmates or classmates (the setting of his instruction is unclear) as constantly pushing for more inspiring training to awaken their creativity:

Comrade Xiao Zhang [another student] had one day said this to the pharmacist: "During class, you merely recited from the textbook. You never mentioned anything beyond the textbook. We do not feel you have taught us much." Comrade Xiao Deng (a second student) gave the following feedback: "We received a prescription to combine glycerin and *qingmeisu* (penicillin) the day before. We asked the pharmacist about the need to observe any combination taboo. His answer was to follow what everyone else was doing. This is the pharmacist's attitude to problem solving." In yet another incident, a patient had experienced discomfort after using an eye drop solution. We suggested improving the recipe, but the pharmacist disagreed and said it was unnecessary. How appropriate is the pharmacist's approach to healthcare?[50]

Wu's letter was not unusual in expressing frustration that he was not being sufficiently challenged. But it was also controversial, eliciting a number of follow-up letters suggesting that he curb his ambition.[51]

Although none of these letters "from the field" were particularly reassuring as to the opportunities in Chinese pharmacy in the early 1950s, their tenor demonstrates the hopes and tensions of a new professional group looking for a secure niche in the formative state medical realm. This realm was bifurcated between "Chinese" and "Western" doctors, whereas their own loyalty and developing expertise was to drugs and drug discovery, and not to either specific tradition. The more ambitious among them would work to develop drug discovery and drug-making into a knowledge realm that, although never divorced from that of physicians, would take on a life of its own through "innovation." Their material of interest initially was herbs, but by the dawn of the Great Leap Forward, would expand with similar enthusiasm in the direction of animal tissue.

Animal-Derived Substances in
Early Communist State Medicine

So far, we have made scant mention of animal-derived substances because they appear so infrequently in texts of the early 1950s, in contrast to later periods. This omission indicates that, with a few significant exceptions, they were initially not as prominent in the concerns or consciousness of those setting drug-related policies or dealing with drug production. Many varieties of animal parts and tissues were certainly then in use by Chinese doctors, and as folk medicine, as they had been for centuries. Yet most Chinese "medicinal animals" were, unlike herbs, not yet a concern of state pharmacology.

Only a handful of animal-derived substances (twenty-seven in total) were listed in the official Chinese pharmacopoeia of 1954, almost all of them associated with Western biomedicine. Lanolin and lard were prominent, along with fish liver oil, beeswax, and bovine vaccine. Except for beeswax, animal parts and tissues from the classical Chinese materia medica were not included until ten years later, in the second edition, which indicates that Chinese animal tissue was not initially targeted as a subject for drug discovery. Most of the foreign-origin animal-based substances listed in 1953 were compounds made from the fat of sheep, pigs, and cows, animals common in Western as well as Chinese farmyards.[52]

Certain of the animal fats listed in the 1954 Chinese pharmacopeia were not even being used in China at the time of publication. The minutes of a pharmaceutical meeting held in 1956 presented them as new knowledge; even the Soviets, the Chinese source claimed, had not been familiar with the medical use of many animal fats until 1946, when they were finally added to the eighth edition of the Soviet pharmacopoeia. It is likely that the Chinese choices closely followed Soviet precedent. Two kinds of lanolin, for example, were recorded, with the comment that the Soviet Union used mostly the former.[53]

When Chinese research on animal-based drugs did occur in this early period, it generally followed the work of Western or Soviet biomedical labs, with no explicit reference to Chinese medicine. In 1954, for example, a report appeared in the Chinese pharmaceutical journal *Yaoxue Tongbao* describing an experiment to extract histidine monohydrochloride from the blood of cows. Author Wang Shizhong wrote that he had followed the methods of American organic chemist Henry Gilman.[54] The Chinese "breakthrough" of creating artificial insulin in the same decade of course followed earlier research on the extraction of insulin from dogs and then cows, based on work by Canadian researchers in the 1920s. As historian of medicine Walter Sneader points out, "By the middle of the 20th century, the majority of drug prototypes were no longer gleaned from the plant kingdom. The animal organism had now become the single greatest provider of drug prototypes. It has retained that role, rivaled only by prototypes obtained from fungi and microbes."[55] Bovine insulin represents a prime example, though by the 1950s it was the human organism that was increasingly yielding prototypes. In other words, a certain number of animal-derived drugs were used in American and European biomedicine that Chinese labs were also keen to either replicate or synthesize, as were labs around the world, and with no reference to Chinese tradition.

Most of the animal parts and tissues that were used in Chinese laboratories (and later factories) for drug-making purposes during this period were simply by-products of the agricultural sector, where they were either "leftovers or considered useless."[56] In this way they paralleled the close relationship that had been established in the West as early as the 1920s between the drug research lab and the slaughterhouse. An article on retrieving deoxycholic and cholic acids from animal bile thus began, "Bile of animals is a by-product of the animal slaughter industry. When left untreated, they are sometimes given to farms to be used as fertilizers or simply gotten rid of. Under the new directives to expand production by leaps and bounds, to increase product varieties, and to find and explore new resources, the use of animal bile is therefore part of the official agenda. This is because the bile of animals such as cows, sheep, pigs, and rabbits contain rich amounts of bilirubin and other essential acids."[57] This article was written during the Great Leap Forward, by which time large-scale farming of specifically Chinese "medicinal animals" was beginning to take place all over China (as we explore further in subsequent chapters). But some research in the 1950s on the medicinal use of animal parts and tissues overlapped with similar experiments in North America and Europe with agricultural animals common to both cultures, even if the bile of livestock (cows, pigs, and sheep) did became an essential ingredient for making drugs important in Chinese medicine, such as artificial bezoar.[58]

One cannot discount early twentieth-century biomedical breakthroughs involving animal tissue as a contextual factor in the later Chinese enthusiasm for "scientizing" the medicinal animals of the Chinese pharmacopeia. On the other hand, there were significant contrasts between the ways Chinese and Western (and even Soviet) research construed the nature of animal-based drugs. Only in the Chinese case was it important that a drug's identification with a specific animal not disappear—that it not be reduced to the molecular level, as was the case with Western animal-derived drugs like insulin and heparin. And, as we have seen, not much Chinese effort was put into identifying active ingredients for most animal drugs, in contrast to research being done in the same period in China on plant-based medicinals. This foregrounds the continuing importance of the symbolic and, in many instances, the ethno-historic as an attribute of Chinese animal medicines, and why they were generally avoided in this early period.

"Chinese" Medicinal Animals Enter State Medicine

Chinese animal-based drugs may have initially been outside the focus of the pharmaceutical industry, but they soon entered the official pharmacy through a different route: the state's takeover and consolidation of private Chinese medicine shops. In the early 1950s, medicine shops in China were mostly small-scale operations hiring not more than ten workers to process or convert raw ingredients into saleable forms of drugs. Most were family-owned businesses, and their workshops were located just behind the stores that sold the drugs. By 1954, there were reportedly 10.4 million of these private Chinese medicine shops throughout China, many of them undoubtedly selling locally sourced animal medicines as well as herbs. That year the government began merging individual shops into larger operations of a few to a hundred, however, in order to reinforce state management, but also to facilitate large-scale processing. For instance, the 580 Chinese medicine shops located in Beijing were regrouped into just seven pharmaceutical factories.[59]

A few of the Chinese medicine shops had grown into relatively large businesses by the Republican period and had developed national and even overseas reputations selling mainly high-end proprietary medicines, most plant-based but some including animal parts and tissues. A famous example was Beijing's Tongrentang, which had supplied drugs to the imperial household prior to 1912.[60] Another was Darentang, whose founder had had connections with Tongrentang but established headquarters in Tianjin. Each medicine shop worked to differentiate itself from the rest by touting special formulas or processing techniques. Guangzhou-based Chenliji, for example, was famous for not only inventing a beeswax pill coating but also developing a process to preserve tangerine peels for as long as a century (or so it claimed). These shops were not spared in the process of regrouping, but the government sometimes preserved their brand names and even product lines. For example, one of seven Beijing factories was organized around Tongrentang and kept its famous name, though under the new system the former owners were relegated to the status of employees.[61] Chenliji was merged in 1956 with shops making drug ingredients such as wax to become Guangzhou Chenliji Joint Pharmaceutical Factory.[62]

As mentioned above, the only animal tissue in the 1954 pharmacopeia with a clear history of use in Chinese medicine was beeswax, considered effective as an actual medicine in Chinese practice besides its use as an excipient. Traditionally, beeswax had been used externally for cuts and ingested as a way to stop bleeding, kill germs, and promote tissue growth; it was also a major export item. Even though the interwar years had greatly affected beeswax production, it was still substantial compared to other faunal materials. Beekeeping, which began in the late 1920s, mainly in and around Beijing and Tianjin, was in that sense the earliest instance of organized "medicinal animal farming" in China. Tianjin-based Darentang, famous for its honey products, had set up the earliest bee farm, though most others were smaller scale, operated by individual families from private homes.[63] Honey was also considered a medicinal in China, used overall to protect against especially toxic ingredients that would otherwise "cause harm to the spleen and stomach." It was also used as a complement to drugs for treating chronic diseases, since it was believed honey could help prolong the drugs' effects in the human body.[64]

Such shops had also long sold medicines that incorporated rare animal parts like tiger bone (in the form of tiger-bone wine) and deer antler, and they continued to do so under the new regime. In the autumn of 1955, two staff members of the Beijing Third Municipal Hospital visited Tongrentang Pharmaceutical Factory and described seeing "antelope and rhino horns being sliced, while deer antler are cut into thin pieces." The Revolution had not stopped the importation of exotic animal parts, nor presumably their transshipment abroad.[65] Besides meeting local and national needs, the "traditional" pharmaceutical sector was seen as a potential source of overseas revenue, especially in marketing Chinese medicine to the Chinese diaspora. This meant preserving, within the new pharmaceutical system, some existing Chinese medicine shops that had developed famous drug brands. Their products were not to be marketed as "new drugs" but as "Chinese medicine" for mostly overseas consumers. Thus, through the takeover of such firms, the Chinese government first entered the business of producing "traditional" animal-based medicines, even if these were still a comparatively minor (but profitable) part of such companies' product lines.

The reorganization of the larger "traditional" Chinese medicine shops put a premium on expansion, the greater use of technology, and heightened production.[66] In 1955, for example, the newspaper *Da Gong Bao* (or *Ta Kung Pao*) published an article titled "Old Tongrentang Grows Younger," describing how the firm had been totally reorganized under state direction. For more than two hundred years, the report stated, a series of single overseers had been in charge of everything, including the company's accounts and all stages of production. Under state management, however, the government created five key positions, four manufacturing workshops, and a separate sales department. The restructured Tongrentang extended sales of its drugs

1.1 Advertisement from the 1950s from a Chinese medicinal company based in Hong Kong, featuring ginseng and deer antler (collectively known as *shenrong*) from mainland China. *Shenrong* became the generic name for all rare, expensive medicinals. COURTESY OF THE GUCM MUSEUM.

beyond physicians, its traditional customer base, to co-op stores, *yiyao* companies, and hospitals. It also began the process of mechanization by acquiring from Tianjin two machines to convert herbs into pill form, two mixers, one pulverizer, and a slicer. The report ended by quoting manager Le Song Sheng—originally direct heir to the owner before the government takeover—as saying the new figure reflected "an unprecedented phenomenon in Tongrentang's history."[67]

As for Tongrentang's product line, it initially remained unchanged despite expansion and reorganization. As one report described it, "Tongrentang produces more than five hundred kinds of ready-made drugs, and they come in the form of *wan, san, gao, and dan*. These drugs garner seventy percent of total sales, followed by 'tiger bone wine' which makes up twenty percent. It is effective for curing *fenghan* (wind-cold). The remaining ten percent goes to ginseng, deer antler, and herbs that are already processed. Tongrentang produces the most number of ready-made drugs and they are famous throughout China. This is because only the finest ingredients are used, thus securing public trust." This description shows that Tongrentang relied for at least a quarter of its business at the time on "high-end" animal products and herbs like ginseng. These were together referred to as *shenrong*, which combines the last characters for ginseng and deer antler, but generically described all expensive medicinals. As we will see, *shenrong* production did not stop but actually increased under the Communists.[68]

The government invested such careful attention into this branch of the pharmaceutical industry because during the 1950s, *zhongyao* remained one of China's important sources of foreign revenue. An article of 1950 focusing on southwest China noted, "Herb cultivation is a common farming activity there in order to service the demand of its Southeast Asian neighbors."[69] Xiao Ge from the Ministry of Agriculture wrote in more concrete terms:

> Chinese medicinals are popular among local as well as overseas Chinese. Products such as ginseng, deer antler, *danggui*, and wolfberries have high economic value. These and 200 other varieties are major export items. The revenue gained from last year's [1954] exports of Chinese medicinals can be exchanged for 7 million tons of steel or 1500 tractors, and 14 million tons of fertilizers. For every ton of *baishu* exported, for example, we can purchase 45 tons of steel or 30 tons of fertilizers, and six tractors. . . . As such, Chinese medicinals provide our country the financial means to build an industrial nation.[70]

Although the statistics can't be trusted, the quotation makes clear that high-end or "luxury" medicinals, which included animal products such as deer antler, were considered important sources of revenue, and thus would remain in production under Communism, but mainly to be sold to overseas Chinese in capitalist countries.

Conclusion

The Republican-period project of separating Chinese medicine from Chinese drugs continued into the early Communist period, but with a different set of emphases. Rather than attempting to re-network Chinese herbs into Western medicine, the two realms of Chinese and Western medicine were to "learn from one another," and medicinals were to constitute an important boundary object constructing this shared space. That space was to be occupied not just by Chinese and Western physicians with their clinics and hospitals, however, but also by a newly consolidated pharmaceutical sector, which incorporated even "traditional" medicine shops into a factory- and lab-based system. This consolidation provided an opportunity to train a new set of people—drug factory technicians, pharmacists, and pharmacologists— who were encouraged to see domestic materia medica (at this stage, mostly herbs) as the raw material for science-based innovation.

Animal-based Chinese drugs, despite being widely used, were initially not emphasized in this new drug-making culture. Research and production in this period focused on either "Western" or Chinese plant-based medicines, continuing the Republican-period project (and enthusiasm for) discovering the "active ingredients" in Chinese herbs through lab research. The initial absence or sidelining of Chinese medicinal animals in this research program was likely because of the far greater difficulty of conducting lab work on animal tissue, not to mention the opprobrium attached to Chinese medicine in the West because of its very use of raw parts from wild animals. Although Western biomedical pharmacology also developed a significant number of animal-based drugs in the twentieth century, they were highly processed, in forms such as insulin and heparin, and hence alienated from the creatures whose tissue was sacrificed—tissue drawn, in most instances, from agricultural slaughterhouses.

Chinese "medical animals," such as tigers, rhinos, and deer, were in the early 1950s still mostly caught in the wild, and used in forms that clearly preserved, if not highlighted, their origins and identities. Their continued identification as specific animals and parts of animals was important to both those who prepared them and those who used them as drugs. In that sense they were not easily re-networked into biomedicine, even had their efficacy been sanctioned using biomedical research protocols. The Japanese project that yielded ursodeoxycholic acid from bears is in that sense the exception that proves the rule for this period. Chinese medicinal animals did not enter the Chinese state-directed pharmaceutical sector in this period through the laboratory, but the product lines of medicine shops like Tongrentang that served a mostly luxury market, both domestically and for export. The consolidation and technological upgrading of these firms, however, would have future consequences for their animal-based products.

Given the circumstances described in this chapter, it was not inevitable that medicinal animals would constitute a significant part of the state pharmacy under the new regime. As we shall see in chapters 2 and 3, however, during the course of the 1950s a number of factors would combine to reverse this initial disinterest in animal tissue by drug researchers and producers, and medical animals would emerge more strongly, and in greater variety, as state assets.

CHAPTER TWO

"To Learn
from the Soviet Union"
Russian Influence on
Chinese Pharmaceuticals

 Historians of Republican China have documented in detail its borrowing of biomedical knowledge from Europe and North America, and the important influence of Japan on both "Chinese" and "Western" medicine.[1] Starting in the early 1950s under the new regime, however, there was a decisive turn toward the Soviet Union. The relationship with the Soviets brought with it a number of factors that were either absent from or underplayed in China's previous encounters with foreign sources of medicinal knowledge or learning. First, and important for our purposes, was a shared interest by the Soviets and Chinese in indigenous herbology and the medicinal use of animals, which were closely linked. In forms such as "tissue therapy," this Soviet interest would eventually give new sanction to faunal medicalization in Chinese medicine, in contrast to the denigration that Chinese use of raw animal tissue had encountered in the West. A second factor in this relationship was a shared geography and ecosystem, which saw plants and animals native to the Russo-Chinese borderlands used as medicines in both places. A third was a common need in the political economies of the two countries to use local resources to formulate replacements for drugs that were no longer being imported from the West. This led to intensive searches for substitutes and a renewed strong interest in local flora and fauna as a strategic resource.

In these and other ways, the Soviet model played a major role in shaping China's drug-making and drug-discovery culture from the middle of the 1950s. Plant-based drugs loomed largest in both pharmacies, but Russian pharmaceutical innovation extended almost seamlessly to fauna-based drugs. A full history of this relationship has yet to be written in any language (and would require a close look at Russian as well as Chinese sources), but much can be learned through a critical reading of Chinese writings and translations alone, which form the bulk of the evidence for this chapter.

The Soviet influence is important because, in analyzing the policy of "combining" Chinese medicine and biomedicine, we can too easily suppose that the latter category is synonymous with American and (Western) European medicine. During this period, however, biomedicine was filtered through a specifically Soviet lens and, in some instances, touched on a specifically Russian interest in its own indigenous or folk medicine, which continues to this day. The Soviet emphasis on self-sufficiency, and on conducting laboratory research into locally derived ingredients to replicate or replace foreign drugs, converged with and helped sanction China's bioprospecting of its own flora and fauna, particularly those used in Chinese medicine. Chinese attempts to make modern medicines from "traditional" materia medica were at the least reinforced if not directly influenced by Soviet attempts to do the same.

At the same time that Soviet learning was being heralded across all knowledge realms, however, the imperfections and shortcomings of scientific and technological "transfer," combined with the Maoist proclivity for grassroots innovation, meant that the very act of learning from the USSR triggered widespread experimentation. Workers in the drug-making sector were encouraged to experiment (*shiyan*) and innovate (*chuangxin*) in order to complete Soviet-sourced projects that were often only half understood. Soviet models were also naturally selected and edited to fit Chinese realities, as is the case with almost any act of "borrowing" across cultures.

An overlapping natural geography was a crucial factor in this relationship. China and Siberia shared medicinal plant and animal species, something that was not true of China and other Western countries. Moreover, shared materia medica like ginseng and deer antler, because of their rarity and high price, were considered worthy of significant investments of resources in both countries and became the objects of joint research. Because of Tsarist-period expansion into the "Far East," interest in the materia medica of Chinese medicine had begun early in Russia, and there was already a significant Russian-language literature on that subject on which Soviet experts working in China could build. Shared material, together with a shared desire to produce modern drugs from indigenous sources, gave Chinese and Soviet experts a strong basis for collaboration during their decade of cooperation in the 1950s.

The Soviets through Chinese Eyes

In the early 1950s, Chinese workers in the pharmaceutical sector were told, "The Soviet Union of today is our tomorrow. Learning from the Soviet Union is the direction that all Chinese should take, and this is also the official policy."[2] During the first decade of Mao's rule, China referred to not just the USSR but all members of the Eastern Bloc as "brother countries," sources of direct assistance as well as role models. In health care, or *baojian*, as in other sectors, efforts were thus made to study Soviet priorities, organization, and philosophy in detail, and Chinese book publishers and medical journals translated and introduced massive amounts of existing Russian medical literature. From 1955 onward, the pharmaceutical journal *Yaoxue Tongbao* included a reference section dedicated solely to Russian works, nearly all of it uncritically received. The works of Russian physiologist Ivan Petrovich Pavlov were particularly influential, and a nationwide campaign was organized in 1953 to popularize Pavlov's thoughts.[3]

Reading Chinese pharmaceutical journals of the early to mid-1950s, it can often seem that one is in the USSR rather than the PRC, given the ubiquity of references to the Soviet Union and the many whole articles translated straight from Russian sources. Of course many writers of the period felt themselves to be part of one socialist world, so the cultural, historical, and even practical borders simply did not impress them as they do us today. It is important not to ignore this material as being irrelevant to China, however, because many writers were looking not just for models, commonalities, and convergences, but also for differences. In other words, the Chinese image of Soviet pharmaceuticals was edited to fit Chinese circumstances and situations, but also help propel change in specific directions.[4]

The given history of Soviet pharmaceuticals as presented in Chinese publications can be summarized roughly as follows (my account amalgamates a number of Chinese journal articles, one of which was a translation from a Russian source). As soon as the October Revolution ended in 1917, the Bolsheviks had set about creating a domestic pharmaceutical industry nearly from scratch, much as the Chinese claimed to be doing after 1949. The former Russian Empire had relied mainly on ready-made drugs imported from Germany and France, while local "drugs" were mainly raw herbs, considered inferior to foreign imports. The final pharmacopoeia produced by the imperial government before its downfall reflected this trend by listing mostly foreign medicinals and only a handful from local sources. Clearly herbal and even animal drugs were used by the population, but there was yet no organized effort to consolidate them.[5] When World War I broke out, Germany had cut off drug supplies to the Russian Empire, and the resulting shortage contributed to the spread of diseases such as typhoid fever, dysentery, and cholera. As such, one of the major initiatives by the Bolsheviks after the revolution was to produce modern pharmaceuticals from local herbs, which were also known as "folk medicinals," since they were previously used only by the informal medical sector.[6] One can already see in this narrative a privileging of the indigenous and a push for self-sufficiency that would directly influence subsequent Chinese efforts.

Following World War I and the Russian Civil War, the Soviet Union began conducting an extensive study of native medicinal resources, mostly plants, a project that was made much of in Chinese journals. According to Tang Guang, who wrote an article in 1954 describing Soviet progress in pharmaceutical research, the aim was "a centralized planning system which guaranteed a steady supply of raw ingredients." In 1925, the Soviet National Planning Committee had announced that research on locally derived ingredients would be conducted on an expansive scale. The project involved experts from various fields such as agriculturists, botanists, chemists, pharmacologists, and doctors. For the next thirty years, researchers conducted land surveys—eighty of them, according to Tang—and consolidated their findings in hundreds of publications, mainly handbooks with information about useful and potentially useful plant species in different regions of the USSR, including their scientific names and purported medicinal properties. Pictures of plants in the form of hanging charts were also produced. These surveys would become a model for those later conducted in China. Although Tang generally praised this and related Soviet projects, he claimed that the medicinal uses the Soviets had discovered in some plant species shared with China were already well-understood in Chinese medicine.[7]

Supplementing the surveys, laboratory research was also mounted to discover and isolate active ingredients in a range of medicinal herbs. Soviet scientists managed to formulate new drugs from plant-derived glycosides, for example, and the claim was made in Chinese sources that one-third of the discoveries of alkaloids in plant species made worldwide could be attributed to Soviet researchers. These and other claims of breakthroughs caused Tang to enthuse in 1954 that the Soviet Union was "number one in the world in pharmaceutical research." This ranking is disputed by historians of Russian pharmacology like Mary Conroy, however, who writes that Soviet pharmaceutical research in this period still fell well behind that of America, Japan, and even Eastern Europe.[8] Still, the Soviet aim was not to win Nobel Prizes but to reduce imports by replicating foreign drugs using local substitute materials, or synthesizing them, a policy that would be pursued even more diligently during World War II. By 1954, wrote Tang, the Soviet Union was also able to cultivate many ingredients formerly sourced from abroad, such as cinchona, squill (sea onion), and other important medicinal herbs, and domestic drug production generally was meeting 40 percent of local health-care needs, with imports from the Eastern Bloc making up most of the rest.[9] These reported achievements, and especially the reliance on research into native substitutes for formerly imported drugs, would greatly inspire Chinese planners.

The Soviet system of drug distribution was also presented as a model in Chinese publications. A 1955 translation of a Russian article in a Chinese newspaper claimed that, prior to the revolution, there were few pharmacies in Russia, and the medicines they sold were unaffordable expect to an urban elite. After the revolution, however, the new government set up a network of pharmacies throughout the federation, with locations in "cities, workers' quarters, the countryside, and even remote villages." It was reported that Ukraine alone had more than 5,500 pharmacies and herb supply stations combined. As impressive as this might have been to the Russians, it also demonstrated that they had started well behind China at the start of its own revolution, given the greater ubiquity of Chinese medicine shops.[10]

Despite the general desire to learn from the Soviet example, Chinese policies, emphases, and organization diverged in some respects from Soviet models. The philosophy and structure of higher education is one example. Officially, and on the highest level, Chinese pharmaceutical (and medical) education was directly modeled on the Soviet system.[11] But unlike in the Soviet Union, Mao wanted "the masses" and not just a group of professionally trained pharmacists/pharmacologists to share in scientific and technological innovation. *Shijian* (experimentation) was in many quarters valued over classroom learning, and credential-building was questioned if not devalued.[12] In China's pharmaceutical sector, factory and farm venues would become as important for research and innovation as the institute or the academy. In terms of propaganda, they would loom even larger, as "pure" research results were de-emphasized in favor of those that could be linked to production.

The Soviet Pharmacopoeia and
Its Influence on Chinese Pharmacology

Soviet and Chinese organization of their pharmaceutical sectors thus differed in some respects, but there was great convergence in their goals and methods. The emphasis on locating and studying indigenous resources in order to find substitutes for foreign drugs was a major shared element. In this sense, the existence of a wealth of indigenous flora and fauna in both countries was viewed as a huge opportunity from the standpoints of both research and production.

The first Soviet pharmacopoeia was published in 1925, but was commonly referred to as the "seventh edition" the nomenclature suggesting continuity with publications under the old regime. It was distinguished from previous editions, however, by emphasizing locally sourced over foreign medicinal ingredients. The goal of the Soviet Union, as one Russian scientist wrote, was "to eliminate dependence on foreign imported drugs especially those made from plants."[13] The sixth edition, published in 1910, had listed 124 plant-based drugs, over half of which were imported. By the seventh edition, however, local ingredients accounted for 70 percent of the 104 drugs derived from plants. By the time the eighth edition was published in 1946, only twelve foreign plants were still mentioned. Even then, the Soviets continued to source for locally produced replacements. With a few notable exceptions, such as cinchona, it was also Soviet policy to search for indigenous substitutes for nonnative or foreign plants rather than attempting to cultivate them locally. For instance, the Soviets stopped the cultivation of the Canada yellow-root once an alternative native source of berberine was found.[14]

Chinese promoters of the Russian model, such as Tang Guang, considered the 1946 or eighth edition of the Soviet pharmacopoeia their primary reference book.[15] Tang and others made much of the Soviet policy of indigenous substitution, emphasizing that, in the Chinese case, the substitutes would be found in Chinese materia medica. Citing Russian publications from as early as 1866, Tang complimented the Soviets not only for progressive localization of drug sources, but also for weeding out foreign herbs, some of which he claimed had little or no medicinal value. Examples he cited were anise, nutmeg, orange peel, and South American condurango. The eighth edition also showed a new awareness, he went on, that only specific parts of the plants had medicinal value. For instance, only the leaf and flower of *junyingcao* (lily of the valley) was now considered medicinal in the USSR, whereas previously every part was sanctioned for use. He cited microanalytical techniques as among the new methods contributing to a more detailed authentication of herbal effects. He concluded,

> Our country is undergoing major economic reconstruction. We have huge responsibilities ahead of us. The current healthcare program has driven the demand for medical supplies. As such, there is an urgent need to revise our collection of Chinese drugs. There are two objectives to fulfill. First, retain and expand research on the scientific aspect of Chinese drugs. Second, discover new uses for both plant and animal-based medicinals, and produce better quality breed types. Between the two objectives, we should put more attention on the latter, which is the formulation of new drugs. The Soviet model is our best example.[16]

Here he explicitly and casually links the Soviet model of drug development with the long-standing Chinese project of testing the materia medica of Chinese medicine in order to formulate "new drugs." This Republican-period project thus becomes reformulated as a Communist one, and linked to the Soviet model of socialist self-sufficiency.

Herb-based medicine was to be a source of real convergence between Soviet and Chinese medical establishments, and helped pave the way for cooperation in animal medicines as well, given their common designation as "folk medicines" on both sides of the border. The convergence also allowed for more equality in the exchange of information and practice than did the creation of synthetics under biomedical protocols, where the Soviets were clearly ahead. The center of this research in the USSR was the All-Russian Research Institute of Medicinal and Aromatic Plants, located on the periphery of Moscow. Its primary responsibilities included identifying the active ingredients of native herbs considered medicinal and applying them to actual clinical practice, a program that the Chinese could fully embrace.[17] For instance, Chinese articles of the period described how the Soviets discovered they could use varieties of *Rehmannia* (or *dihuang* in Chinese) to imitate drugs like digalen and digifolin—used mainly for treating heart-related diseases—and a local variety of *Adonis* to replicate adonigen.[18] In situations where herbs like cloves and camphorwood were unavailable, scientists searched for indigenous alternatives before attempting to create synthetic versions. All this led Ye Sanduo, a pharmacologist who helped compile the 1953 Chinese pharmacopoeia and early textbooks on pharmacognosy, to enthuse that Soviet chemistry had virtually become alchemy, demonstrating that "all things from the natural world can be made to have similar uses through scientific research."[19]

This Soviet strategy of substitution encouraged Chinese pharmacists to attempt their own substitutes of locally available resources for those listed in the official (national) Chinese pharmacopeia. For example, some pharmacists used *yuanzhi* (*Polygala tenuifolia*) or *guazijin* instead of senega (a different species of *Polygala*) as written in a doctor's prescription, thus making up their own minds as to the most appropriate drug based on available local resources.[20] Ye wrote approvingly of this, and encouraged "using only local ingredients to make drugs in the pharmacopoeia following the Soviet example." On the other hand, substitution could also give rise to mismatches. Ye noticed that there were "some new pharmaceutical factories using Chinese *gansong* to replace *Valeriana officinalis*, which is incorrect since they contain entirely different ingredients." In the countryside the problem was an over-reliance on herbs specific to that region. For example, there were cases of deaths from *Chloranthus* poisoning in Zhejiang province because the plant grew there in abundance. This oversupply encouraged overuse, leading in turn to overdosing.[21]

As in China, some Russian phytotherapists (then still a relatively new description for advocates of herbal medicine) even criticized the project of re-networking herbs from folk medicine to biomedicine through targeting single active ingredients. They instead encouraged the use of plants in their whole form, called for a closer examination of traditional methods of healing, and used the term "folk medicine" positively in their writings. For example, a 1952 Soviet drug handbook was quoted in a Chinese source as advising that "phytotherapy drawn from the experiences of folk medicine is the most effective."[22] This position had its opponents, however. In 1955, V. P. Kalashnikov expressed his disapproval of phytotherapy in the Soviet journal *Pharmacology and Toxicology*, an article that was translated and republished in Chinese. He argued that most components of a plant were dregs that could and should be removed by modern technology. He also frowned on the Russian phytotherapy movement's focus on herbal tea as a medication, calling this therapy "a form of magic." If folk remedies had not been replaced by medicinals based on scientific research, Kalashnikov argued, "Russians would still be eating mold or drinking the urine of pregnant women instead of penicillin and steroids."[23]

This Soviet controversy had obvious resonance for China. Thus when the same Russian journal published, in the following year, a critical response to Kalashnikov by a Soviet scientist identified as Y. P. Kefalov [*sic*], both papers were translated together by the Chinese journal *Zhongyao Tongbao*. The Chinese editor also included a short comment, however, indicating his support for the views of phytotherapist Kefalov. Kefalov argued that most Russian scientists did not actually ignore the holistic properties of plants, even when attempting to identify their active ingredients. He pointed out that Russian scientists were still unable to pinpoint the active ingredients for a majority of plant-based drugs, yet to discontinue their use in clinical practice would be to ignore their efficacy. Kefalov gave instances in which Soviet doctors prescribed raw opium or the leaf of foxglove (known as *yangdihuang* in China and from which drugs like digalen and digifolin—and today digitalis—were made). "We may already know the chemical composition of bread," he wrote, "but we do not eat pills made from bread extracts." The parallel here with arguments made in favor of Chinese medicine was clear. While not denigrating the search for active ingredients, Kefalov commended scientists who, even if they did not belong to the phytotherapy movement, had investigated folk medical knowledge of a drug before conducting laboratory work on it, concluding that "it is only when research is conducted in this order" that it can be effective.[24]

This debate shows that the use of folk or traditional medicinals on both sides of the border resulted in similar disputes, with Russian phytotherapists deploying many of the same arguments made by more conservative Chinese physicians. The position that specific materials or combinations of materials in the form of recipes had properties too complicated to be reduced to single active ingredients would be repeatedly articulated in China in the coming years, and having Soviet sanction for this was clearly useful. Moreover, the Soviet phytotherapists' advocacy of medicinals taken in raw form would resonate beyond herbalism in the Chinese context, also informing approaches to the use of animal-based drugs, where the search for active ingredients was de-emphasized.

Russian Interest in Chinese Medicinals

Not only was there convergence between Chinese and Russian theories and policies on the use of indigenous medicinals, but certain plants and animals existed on both sides of their common border and were of shared interest to the two drug-making cultures. Russian interest in such medicines had historical roots in the Qing period, paralleling the nineteenth-century Russian colonization of Siberia and incursion into Manchuria. A survey of Chinese herbs by physician and sinologist A. A. Tatarinov, published in 1856, was praised in a Chinese source of 1954 as "an extensive and detailed work on the wealth of Chinese herbal resources combining the arduous task of determining their active ingredients through scientific means."[25] Even more celebrated in China was Emil Bretschneider, a Baltic German in the service of the Russian Empire, who, between 1882 and 1895, produced three volumes on plant species in China. Titled *Botanicon Sinicum*, all three volumes were written in English, and so received a global readership. These seminal works remained influential into the twentieth century, by which time scholars from Britain, America, and Japan had taken an increased interest in Chinese herbology.[26]

Chinese commentators in the 1950s (and after) criticized most early foreign works on Chinese medicine as non-scholarly, claiming that they tended to approach the subject as nonscientific, and inferior to Western medicine. Bretschneider, by contrast, was praised for having had a genuine belief in the efficacy of Chinese medicinals. He was a doctor attached to the Russian legation in Beijing when he read *Bencao Gangmu*, the most comprehensive Chinese compilation on materia medica. Between 1866 and 1895, he devoted himself to reformulating understandings of Chinese herbs based not on laboratory research, but on learning the properties of plants and picking up authentication techniques by visiting medicine shops and drug-production sites. He also read widely in both Chinese and foreign sources.[27]

A 1955 article by Zhu Sheng put Bretschneider's scholarship above all other foreign works, including that of Hong Kong physician Bernard E. Read, who was considered the chief British scholar of Chinese medicine. The latter, according to Zhu, "underestimated the ability of Chinese herbs to treat more diseases than the few that he had listed." Following the Russian commentator Vyazemsky, Zhu gave credit to Bretschneider for conducting the first "unbiased" study of Chinese medicinals. "Most Western doctors in the past had overly focused on the abstruse nature of *zhongyi*," wrote Zhu, "until Bretschneider, who was passionate about learning how we employ medicinals."[28] The elevation of Bretschneider was clearly influenced by politics as much as by the content of his work. But it is significant in representing Chinese attempts to highlight and create depth around the shared Chinese-Russian interest in indigenous herbology.

Despite Bretschneider's passion for Chinese learning, flora and fauna shared by China and Russia had different histories of use and, thus, different ways of being understood. At least in the 1950s, Russian uses and understandings were consumed by Chinese more often than the other way around. One of the primary examples of a shared medicinal object—a "Chinese" plant serving as the raw material for Soviet lab investigation—was *Schisandra chinensis* (Chinese magnolia in English, or five-flavor fruit in Chinese, *wŭ wèi zi*), which was native to both Siberia and northern China. The plant became a candidate for research during World War II based on reports it improved the stamina and even night vision of indigenous Siberian hunters, allowing them "to follow a sable all day without food." The People's Commissars Council decreed in 1943 that *limonnik* (the plant's Russian name) be studied as a "tonic substance" for Soviet soldiers and defense workers, thus initiating, according to one Russian historical account, "a new era of the intensive study of medicinal plants." Soviet findings that the herb had an invigorating effect on the central nervous system, first published in 1945, spurred a research program that produced about twenty-five articles on the plant in 1959 alone. As a result, *limonnik*, already a fundamental herb in Chinese medicine, also became an official medicine in the Soviet Union in the early 1960s, and encouraged further lab research on herbs, much as *changshan* had done in China itself in the same period.[29]

Soviet scientists became interested in a variety of plant-based Chinese medicinals, but it was ginseng that elicited the most attention as a medicinal crop.[30] The Soviet Union began cultivating the plant in earnest in the 1950s, while also participating in shared agricultural experiments in China.[31] The Russian scientist A. P. Kiriyanov spent a total of three years and two months in China beginning in April 1955, advising the Chinese Academy of Medical Sciences on the study and cultivation of medicinal plants, but particularly ginseng.[32] Kiriyanov also encouraged his Chinese hosts to study their own folk medicine, which he called an "invaluable resource for our research work."[33] On the other hand, the focus of his research was improving and innovating the way ginseng was grown, and expanding its range, which meant overturning much of the "folk knowledge" surrounding its cultivation.

The first large-scale *shenchang* (ginseng farm) in China had been established only in 1946, and its location changed after each harvest, due to the belief that a piece of land should be used to grow the crop only once. Other beliefs that were passed through generations in the form of popular verses included, "King of all grasses, a delicate plant that will rot at the sight of feces"; "It is the work of man to cultivate ginseng, but that of heaven to harvest them"; and "Ginseng will rot if not die under sunlight." So delicate was ginseng that it became widely described as *jiaosheng guanyang*, a Chinese phrase that meant to be spoilt and pampered. It was the tradition therefore to leave the plants alone throughout their cultivation period.[34]

Kiriyanov argued that these practices were unsuitable, given state policy to increase production of high-end medicinals, and worked with members of the Chinese Academy of Medical Sciences on joint research to foster cultivation on permanent plots within agricultural communes.[35] The Russian scientist claimed that farmers had initially been discouraged by the Communist state from growing ginseng because it was a luxury item, and its cultivation would thus foster capitalist thoughts. Also acting against the crop was that ginseng required a long cultivation period, between four to six years, and was therefore difficult to account for in a society obsessed with yearly output quotas. These impediments were removed in 1954, however, as the government pushed to increase drug supplies, and Kiriyanov's research demonstrated how to cultivate the crop on what was previously considered unsuitable land. Between 1955 and 1957, land for the cultivation of ginseng in Jilin province alone increased from 44,700 square meters to 359,200, and the number of ginseng farms from three to five.[36]

Organotherapy and the Turn to Animal Tissue

A shared interest in herbology and plant- and animal-based folk remedies and the push for creating "new drugs" from indigenous raw materials were important links forged between Soviet medicine and Chinese medicine in this period. Yet another was Pavlovian science. The research and theoretical work of the Nobel Prize–winning physiologist Ivan Pavlov was influential in China even before the Revolution, and became dogma in the years following.[37] Pavlov's contributions to neuropathology included the idea that the central nervous system was fundamental in regulating bodily functions ("nervism," in Russian parlance), a concept that had appeal in China to those who equated the acupuncture meridians with the nervous system. Pavlovian science, broadly defined, would be the overarching framework within which much Chinese medical research in this period would be contained, including work in pharmacology. Its major influence on animal-based medicinals, however, would occur in an area only tangentially related to the research of Pavlov himself, and with a less solid evidentiary basis: organotherapy.

Organotherapy was both a movement and a set of practices that had at its core the idea that certain human health deficiencies could be treated using "secretions" from animal tissue administered through injection. "Internal secretions" from glands had been a new object of medical research in the late nineteenth century, out of which grew hormone therapy (United States), organotherapy (France), and, eventually, endocrinology, the last of which would sweep the others before it to become an established field of medical research. The enthusiasm started around 1890, when the respected French medical researcher Charles-Édouard Brown-Séquard self-injected an extract from guinea pig testicles and reported that he felt "rejuvenated," and with no side effects, a result that most contemporary commentators attribute to the placebo effect. According to the historian Nicolai Krementsov, "physicians around the world enthusiastically began to apply extracts of various animal tissues as a cure for a variety of diseases," a search that lasted for at least four decades in the West and even longer in Russia.[38] In 1914, American physician Henry R. Harrower called organotherapy "one of the greatest achievements of modern medicine." By that time, however, endocrinologists were expressing skepticism over claims by organotherapists that injecting animal tissue directly into human bodies had any health benefit, and were cautioning about the dangers. By the late 1920s and early 1930s, they had succeeded in branding organotherapy a pseudoscience in America and Europe.[39]

Organotherapy had a longer run in the Soviet Union, however, where, uniquely, it had begun in veterinary science. Krementsov has described how veterinarian Iakov Tobolkin and medical professor Vasilii Shervinskii created extracts from animals like goats and monkeys. Though they began their research in earnest prior to the revolution, they were able to sustain state patronage into the Communist period, when the government even established a primate breeding station in order to secure monkey glands for human transplantation. In the Soviet Union, the modern discipline of endocrinology was more a partner if not a product of organotherapy, rather than a competitor or antagonist.[40]

The charisma of organotherapy in the socialist world was boosted in the 1930s by the invention of a specific form of organotherapy called "tissue therapy" by the ophthalmologist Vladimir P. Filatov. Tissue therapy, or sometimes histotherapy (known in Chinese as *zuzhi liaofa*), was the transplantation of tissues derived from humans (including placentas and corpses), animals, or plants (strictly speaking, the leaves of aloe vera) underneath the human skin. The idea was to graft the living tissue of plant or animal directly onto the affected area. Filatov had invented it to treat patients with corneal diseases, but soon claimed its effectiveness for organs and parts of the body other than the eyes. He called the concept "biogenic stimulation," and it was promoted, by his Filatov Institute, as effective for many chronic diseases.[41] Filatov's political connections were such that tissue therapy spread widely in the Soviet Union, and its success was approaching orthodoxy by the time of the Chinese Revolution.[42]

Tissue therapy was being discussed in China as early as 1946, and by the time of the Revolution the treatment had been experimented with in various parts of the country, but especially the regions bordering the Soviet Union.[43] In March 1951, the Chinese Ministry of Health released a notice promoting the use of tissue therapy nationwide, including a list of medical conditions (about nineteen) that it believed reacted positively to the method but suggesting that it might be effective for even more. At the same time it cautioned against overreliance on tissue therapy, citing incidences of fatalities, which suggests that the practice was widespread enough to generate such reports.[44] On October 12 that same year, the health ministry released the "Five Interim Provisions on Tissue Therapy," in which a number of diseases were recategorized based on their responses to the therapy as a curative tool.[45] Many Chinese translations of Russian writings on tissue therapy appeared around the same time, and experiments were conducted in China to apply it to even more conditions, like stomach and intestinal ulcers, as well as asthma.[46]

As historian Xi Gao has pointed out, tissue therapy was "the first Soviet medical therapy officially promoted by the Chinese government," and the health ministry accordingly directed that it be taught and discussed by all hospitals, medical associations, medical journals, and the like. By early 1952, more than fifty thousand patients had been treated with tissue therapy in one form or another, with the ministry declaring positive outcomes in the majority of instances.[47] As we shall see in chapter 4, this enthusiasm was to contribute to one of the most dramatic and controversial medical innovations of the Great Leap Forward and later: chicken blood therapy.

Organotherapy (and tissue therapy) had a particular appeal in China given the sanction they seemed to provide for the long use of animal and even human tissues in Chinese medicine. Links between them had actually been made in the early twentieth century, but mainly by Western opponents of both practices. In a section titled "Charlatanism and Animal Therapy," Harrower wrote in 1914 that organotherapy was unfairly equated with quackery in the West, because, for example, "many Chinese 'physicians,' whose ideas we scorn, still use such animal preparations as powdered deer's horn, hoof of a white horse, thigli [sic] of a grey horse, eyes of a tiger, etc." For Western promoters of organotherapy such as Harrower, in other words, distancing it from Chinese medicine was important. In the political environment of the 1950s, however, Russian promoters were unashamed to compare it to Chinese practice, and Chinese were quick to embrace it for the same reason.[48]

Some Russian sources were even willing to give China priority in the development of organotherapy. Such was the case in a 1954 article by the Russian E. S. Vyazemsky, introducing classical medical works such as *Shennong Bencao* and *Bencao Gangmu* to a Russian audience, which appeared in translation in the journal *Yaoxue Tongbao*.[49] Singling out *Bencao Gangmu* as "the most comprehensive," Vyazemsky recommended that all the medicinals recorded in it be analyzed in a laboratory setting and their active ingredients identified and tested, including animal-based ones. Even in the absence of laboratory-based proof, however, Vyazemsky was ready to accept the efficacy of Chinese materia medica based on experience. He wrote, "Chinese physicians had very early discovered the use of sheep liver to cure night blindness, and pig's stomach for anemia and chronic gastric problems. The Chinese have every right to say they were the first to invent organo-therapy (*Zangqi Zhiliao Xue*) and hormone therapy (*He'ermeng Zhiliao Xue*)." He also mentioned deer antler, whose "ability to strengthen the human body has been proven."[50]

The "proofs" of the medicinal effects of deer antler, with which Vyazemsky would have been familiar, were actually the product of Russian lab research. The Sino-Russian push to expand ginseng cultivation was paralleled by a similar initiative, in the same region, to expand medicinal deer farming. Just as ginseng and deer antler were intimately linked in the marketing of Chinese medicine as *shenrong* (a common name for both products), so they were linked by their mutual study and cultivation in Siberia. As with ginseng, it is unclear whether the Russians had independently arrived at the medicinal use of deer antlers or had borrowed that idea from Chinese medicine, one Russian source admitting, "they [deer antlers] were first used successfully in Chinese medicine."[51] Clearly, however, Russian scientific research on deer antler, which began as early as the mid-1930s, was considered by the Chinese to be in advance of their own. Moreover, the first large-scale Chinese deer farms (discussed in chapter 3) appeared only in the late 1940s as part of Soviet-assisted development in the border region.[52]

The key Russian figure in medicinal research on deer was the pharmacologist S. M. Pavlenko, who claimed to have found high levels of male hormones in deer antler, and "preserv[ed] all the good hormones into a single extract" that he called "pantocrin." Pavlenko's claims for pantocrin included successful treatment of male sexual disorders, which conformed to one of its many therapeutic uses in Chinese medicine. Enhancing male virility was likewise a long-standing goal of European hormonal research, and in particular of organotherapy. The real innovation of pantocrin, however, which would be repeated in many subsequent Chinese research projects involving animal tissue, was turning deer antler velvet into a concentrated substance, which could be taken either as an injection or in pill form. Thus did pantocrin become a pioneering product of the Moscow Organo-Therapeutic Drug Factory, beginning in 1942, along with the drug campolon (derived from animal livers).[53]

Pantocrin was sometimes incorrectly described as the "active ingredient" in deer antler, but it was actually just an extract rather than a single molecule. Nonetheless, mass-produced and one step removed from its natural source, pantocrin was likely the first internationally vended modern pharmaceutical to be based on Chinese medicine, despite its Russian invention. Russian pantocrin would also find a market on the Chinese side of the border.

Pantocrin began to be produced in China itself in 1954, using Pavlenko's technique, at the state-owned Harbin Chemical and Pharmaceutical Factory. A Chinese text recounting the development of pantocrin described the USSR's adoption of deer antler as "a creative way of providing healthcare for its people," and by the 1950s the drug was indeed being prescribed not just for sexual dysfunction, but also for "general disability." Its proponents claimed that pantocrin could induce sleep, increase appetite, reduce fatigue, and promote kidney function. A Chinese article praising this development actually denigrated traditional Chinese deer antler recipes in comparison, which it described as a "mishmash of ingredients," including inefficacious ones, in comparison to the purity of the Russian product.[54]

Despite the "purity" of pantocrin, Chinese research on complex recipes containing deer antler continued in the same period, likely encouraged by Soviet recognition of its medicinal value. One "breakthrough" reported around the same time involved the formulation of a "deer antler syrup" by Taiyuan Gangtie Hospital in Shanxi province. Besides deer antler, the recipe used herbs like ginseng, wolfberry, *danggui*, and *dihuang*. The hospital explained that it had referred to both Chinese and Russian formulas in concocting the new recipe, suggesting that even in the case of multi-herbal drugs containing animal tissue, Soviet experience was considered an important touchstone.[55]

Even beyond organotherapy and its variations, the Soviets were more comfortable than their Western counterparts in experimenting with the medicinal use of animal tissue of many types. Some of this can be attributed, as with herbs, to wartime exigencies, and some to general fascination with folk medicines. Conroy reports "strange remedies" in Soviet press reports around 1940 involving "the venom of vipers, and the effect of extracts of flatworm on the intestines" and that, during World War II, "a great deal of faith was placed in [medicinal] items derived from animal substances," of which pantocrin was only one. By 1944, the Soviets were producing as many as forty "endocrine products" from animal tissue. The extent to which some of this research was inspired by folk medicine, writes Conroy, "pushed Soviet mainstream medicine into a different trajectory from American medicine."[56]

This same trajectory, on the other hand, brought Soviet medicine into closer convergence with that of China, a legacy that would outlast even the expulsion of Soviet experts during the Great Leap Forward.

Conclusion

I have argued in this chapter that the category "Western medicine" is too general to account for the particular relationship that Chinese medicine cultivated in the 1950s with its Soviet counterpart, which would have long-lasting effects in the pharmaceutical realm. As the herbalist Igor Zevin has pointed out, "the study of herbalism and folk healing became a type of state-run industry in the Soviet Union," which helps account for the status Russian medicinal preparations still hold, alongside Chinese ones, in the global marketplace for "alternative" drugs.[57] Pantocrin, for example, is still widely vended through the internet as I write, perhaps in greater quantities, and certainly in more places, than in the period we are examining in this book. The Russian and Chinese "indigenous" medicines are usually considered to have had separate if parallel histories, but this chapter has shown that they were linked in space and time.

An important overlapping element in the Chinese and Soviet (Russian) experiences of drug discovery was the will toward self-sufficiency that, along with the states' recognition of their comparative poverty and large rural populations, suggested they fall back on available resources, including "folk medicinals." The two countries also shared common medicinal species in their borderlands following Russian expansion into the "Far East" during the Qing period, a history that was productively recalled in the 1950s by those Chinese and Russians intent on forging stronger relations between their two state medicines.

The lack of distinction the Soviets made between floral and faunal medical resources was also quite different from the attitude of Western medicine toward Chinese practices, and would provide a shared frame for research and production by the mid-1950s. Soviet organotherapy and tissue therapy helped provide a scientific sanction for preexisting Chinese practices, particularly regarding animal-based drugs, as would Russian comfortability with zootherapies more generally. Though outside the acceptable bounds of biomedicine as it had evolved in Western Europe and America, these and related Soviet therapies would have a lingering influence in the socialist world, and particularly China. Even the greater Soviet interest in herbology, and particularly the medicinal plants of Siberia that were shared with China, helped in creating animal-based drugs as a shared resource. Research-led cultivation of deer and ginseng went hand in hand in Siberia, just as they did in the marketing of the two materials in Chinese medicine. As we will see in subsequent chapters, some of these influences would inspire efforts to "scientize" the use of animal tissue in Chinese medicine long after China had broken its political ties with the USSR during the Great Leap Forward.

CHAPTER THREE

The Great Leap Forward and the Rise of Medicinal Animal Farming

 Soviet models, initiatives, and theories gave new and scientific sanction to faunal medicalization in China, but it was only during the so-called Great Leap Forward that animal-based drugs became a commonly discussed topic in Chinese pharmaceutical publications. The ideologically driven increase in production quotas during these years affected all sectors, including drug production, which in turn focused more attention on animal tissue as an underutilized medicinal resource. There was also even greater emphasis in this period on producing medicinals for needed foreign exchange, and certain animal-based drugs commanded high prices when marketed to overseas Chinese. Taken together, these trends favored the development of medicinal animal farming on a much larger scale, and affecting more species, than had been the case under the first Five-Year Plan. While herbal medicine continued to be the main focus and concern in drug-making, this period would see a "great leap" in the attention paid to animal tissue of all sorts in journals, handbooks, and other published sources. Although most of this attention related to medicinal farming, the organized collection of animal tissue, from insects to the stomach linings of chickens, also flourished from this period onward.

The Great Leap Forward has been well discussed by historians as an infamous attempt at rapid industrialization that eventually collapsed as a result of unrealistic goals and aspirations.[1] The project was launched in 1958 under the slogan "Overtake Britain in 15 Years," inspired by the USSR's own stated goal of overtaking American industrial production in the same time frame. Besides pushing forward the production of steel—remembered as the policy's major focus, and failure—China also aimed to surpass Britain in other less-discussed areas, including drug-making. Britain was a formidable target in this instance, as it was then the world's largest exporter of drugs, including to its colony Hong Kong. Chinese authorities from various ministries (but primarily Health and Chemical Industry) began to hold regular meetings on drug production, conducted in a manner befitting the slogan "Let a hundred flowers bloom, let a hundred schools of thought contend."[2] As a key strategic driver of the post-revolutionary economy, China's newly created pharmaceutical industry became even more export-oriented with the Great Leap Forward. Ready-made drugs notwithstanding, China gave equal or more attention to raw medicinals as export items. Bioprospecting land surveys were conducted on the Soviet model in order to "peel and unveil new terrains," from which to tap hitherto unknown sources for drugs.[3] Animals as well as plants were swept up in this nationwide project.

Animal Medicinals, Foreign Trade, and the Second Five-Year Plan

In 1956, the Central Committee issued the so-called 1956–1967 Agricultural Development Policy Outline, which included as a goal increasing the production of Chinese medicinals. By 1957, the Ministry of Health had come to handle all affairs related to drugs, including those products with export value (which had previously been managed by the Ministry of Foreign Trade).[4] It was hoped that such restructuring would allow better coordination between material production and actual health-care needs. Still, the ability to meet overseas demand for medicinals (raw ingredients and pharmaceuticals) had become a priority, since, to quote health ministry official Meng Qian, in charge of drug administration, "The revenue obtained from such exports helps build and underpin our country's economy." The primary consumer audience were Chinese living overseas, who had long relied on medical substances from China and for whom pipelines were retained through Guangzhou and Tianjin long after the Revolution had begun to choke off other types of trade with the capitalist world.

In late 1958, Meng raised concern over supply falling behind an overwhelming demand, foreign as well as domestic, for Chinese medicinals. As he wrote in the journal *Zhongyao Tongbao,*

The current rate of drug production, though faster than before, still cannot meet the needs of the people whose standard of living has greatly improved. This is especially the case for plant-based medicinals that require long cultivation periods, and prized animal parts and tissues. At the moment, the supply of Coptis root (*huanglian*) meets only 17 percent of total demand, while ginseng, deer antler and musk meet 27 percent, 33 percent, and 19 percent respectively. Also due to supply shortage, imports are still being carried out for about 60 different types of drugs. Some examples are betel nut, frankincense, and rhino horns of both the African and non-African species. Under correct leadership of the Communist Party, Chinese medicine and drugs are enjoying a growing international reputation. In the last few years, foreign visits to China for the purpose of studying our medical tradition are on the rise. Our drugs are also well sought after. In the first half of 1958 alone, Beijing Tongrentang received thousands of letters from 24 countries to sign purchase agreements. This is proof that Chinese medicine and medicinals will flourish beyond this country.[5]

Until this time, authorities had not put as much stress on production quotas as on the need for reorganization and the establishment of systems and institutions. There had even been an official instruction to "prevent a flowering of the land expanse";[6] in other words, attempts to expand cultivable land had sometimes been discouraged. The beginning of the second Five-Year Plan in 1958 changed this policy. Emboldened by the overall success of its first phase of industrialization, the government became increasingly ambitious and set ever-higher targets for everything. The general rule was to produce the most in the shortest possible time, and this included medicinal ingredients.[7]

The fact that Chinese medicine had also been rehabilitated and institutionalized at the levels of universities, hospitals, and clinics also meant that demand for Chinese drugs by state institutions was now at a high point. Previously informal means of collecting, processing, and distributing were to be increasingly regularized, incentivized, and controlled. In the end, this meant creating "national" infrastructures over what until then had often been highly local practices.

Meng argued that another long-term solution, in addition to increasing the number of "herb collection stations" and locating them even in remote places, was to dispel the notion of "regional medicinals" (*didao yaocai*), in order to create the mind-set of national medicines. The real meaning of the term *didao yaocai*, Meng argued, "is nothing more than the impression that a particular site is conducive to the cultivation of a particular drug," a principle did not fit well with existing plans to become self-sufficient in the supply of medicinals. At the time only three hundred of the 2,600 known Chinese herbs were being circulated nationwide, or outside the specific areas they had been associated with historically. To discredit the concept of *didao yao-cai*, the government assigned it to the realm of superstition, invoking the official slogan, "Down with Superstitions" (*Dapo Mixin*).[8]

Given its long-term goal to achieve self-sufficiency in domestic drug production, the government also intensified the process of import substitution. It had even managed to export some of these "replacement" products, including pharmaceuticals like penicillin and sulfa drugs. Although major Western powers like the United States and, to a certain degree, Britain had instituted trade barriers, China maintained active trade relations with its socialist allies, and many other capitalist countries had been eager to make specific agreements. Britain even partially lifted its trade embargo on China under pressure from merchants in Hong Kong and elsewhere. One source reported that "over one thousand foreign ships called at Chinese ports in 1956."[9]

As Meng's article made clear, exports of traditional Chinese medicinals were not to be neglected, despite domestic shortages. Guangzhou retained its historic place even after the Revolution as the major port and coordinating center for the overseas trade in medicinals and much else. The Chinese Export Commodities Fair, also known as the Canton Trade Fair, was held there twice a year beginning in 1956, in order to showcase Chinese goods to overseas buyers, particularly those in Hong Kong.[10] One Chinese historian writes, "After the establishment of New China (i.e., Communist China), all Chinese medicinals from the Western and Southern provinces were exported via the port of Guangzhou." The city also retained its role as one of the major centers for the import of raw materials (including animals) used in the manufacture of Chinese drugs.[11] The second major port for this trade was Tianjin, which mainly gathered medicinals from the northern provinces like Hebei. In this manner China was able to maintain its traditional overseas customer base for "luxury medicinals," as well as its ability to import certain exotic raw materials used in their processing.

Exports of such medicinals were indeed on the rise from 1950 onward, if we can believe historical statistics published in 1990 by the Ministry of Foreign Economic Relations and Trade. Under the category "Chinese Medicinals," it claimed exports more than doubled from US$5,390,000 in 1950 to US$12,720,000 in 1957, with only slight dips in 1954 and 1956. The same upward trend held for the subsequent years. The average annual export value for medicinals even during the Great Leap Forward—1958 to 1961—

3.1 Opening of the first Chinese Export Commodities Fair (*Zhongguo Chukou Shangpin Zhanlanhui*), on November 19, 1956, in the Sino-Soviet Friendship Building in Guangzhou. *RENMIN RIBAO*, NOVEMBER 20, 1956.

was US$13,260,000. Surprisingly, it was during the Cultural Revolution that exports of medicinals are recorded to have peaked, their value rising to US$28,820,000 in 1966, and further climbing to US$34,400,000 in 1968.[12] Accounting for unreliability in the reporting of specific figures, this and other sources agree that exports of Chinese medicinals in the early Communist period did not stop or slow down but increased relative to the Republican period. The increased organization of the sector and increased demands put on domestic production, as well as the revenue that could be had from a loyal overseas Chinese consumer base, doubtless all contributed.

Publications from provincial bureaus handling foreign trade often categorized their exports, and it is in these sources that we see medicinal animals emerging prominently as trade items. In a thousand-odd-page volume covering the period from 1953 to 1963, for example, Hebei Province Foreign Trade Bureau provided a breakdown of specific medicinals and the countries they were traded to.[13] Musk, cow bezoar, deer antler, and deer by-products (tail, penis, and sinew) were among the animal parts and tissues being shipped overseas from Tianjin port. Deer by-products accounted for the largest single category, followed by deer antlers. The rarest medicinal commodity was cow bezoar (the indigestible objects trapped in the animal's gastrointestinal system),

Table 3.1 **Export figures of medicinal animal products from Hebei province during two five-year plans**

NAME OF MEDICINAL	UNIT	FIRST FIVE-YEAR PLAN (1953–1957)	SECOND FIVE-YEAR PLAN (1958–1962)
Deer by-products (ossified antler, tail, penis, and sinew)	kilogram	16,106	39,946
Deer antler (*lurong* or deer velvet)	liang	48,319 (approx. 1827 kg)	29,531 (approx. 1117 kg)
Musk	liang	19,909 (approx. 753 kg)	6,470 (approx. 245 kg)
Bear paws	kilogram	27	0
Tiger bone	kilogram	0	12
Bezoar	liang	16 (approx. 0.6 kg)	0
Yaojiu (medicinal wine)	American dollar	70,274	150,806

Source: Hebei Sheng Duiwai Maoyi Ju, Hebeisheng Tianjin Kouan Duiwai Maoyi Tongji Ziliao 1953-1963 Nian (Chukou Bufen) Di Er Ce (1965).
Note: Author's conversion from *liang* to kilogram.

of which Hebei province exported sixteen *liang* during this period, all to Vietnam.[14] There is no mention of bear bile, but twenty-seven kilograms of bear paws were sent overseas in 1957. Statistics also showed that Hebei produced twelve kilograms of raw tiger bone for export in 1958. There is, however, a separate figure for *yaojiu* (medicinal wine), which likely also included tiger parts (see table 3.1). Among the socialist countries, the greatest demand for animal-based medicinals came from Vietnam, followed by North Korea.

Targeting British Pharmaceuticals

In March 1958, in the spirit of the Great Leap Forward, the Ministry of Chemical Industry set its goal of matching or even surpassing Britain in drug production. It established the ambitious target of four hundred "new drugs," and declared it would produce 95 percent of them by the second year of the Five-Year Plan. These drugs were intended largely as replacements for standard biomedicines using Chinese ingredients. The directive, however, caused an explosion of innovation in the making of "new" medicinals that were neither clearly "Chinese" nor "Western," and did not replace existing drugs so much as attempt to create new niche markets. The propensity of innovators to reach beyond herbs and into relatively unused or entirely novel animal tissues was one unintended consequence of this directive. For its new slogan, the ministry selected the Chinese proverb *Kuai Ma Jia Bian* (whip the horse to speed it up) to evoke a sense of urgency.[15]

The close attention Chinese sources began paying to British drug-making in this period in some sense mimicked the attention paid to Soviet pharmaceuticals slightly earlier. In 1958, Britain was the top exporting country for pharmaceuticals worldwide. Exports to its colonies (including Hong Kong) and its commonwealth made up one-third to three-quarters of the value of its total production, according to Chinese sources that monitored that trade. American drug exports, according to the same sources, accounted for only 13 percent of its domestic production.[16] Moreover, most of the medicinal products shipped from Britain were ready-made drugs, whereas the United States, West Germany, and Japan focused on exporting individual chemical compounds.[17]

The Ministry of Health launched its own campaign against Britain by holding an exhibition in 1958 to showcase the medical achievements of various research institutes. Opening on July 1, to mark the founding of the National People's Congress, the exhibition was dedicated to furthering China's goal of "becom[ing] a world-class nation within the next three to five years." One banner announced the ministry's aim to "bring medicine and drugs to every possible place," and four full rooms were filled with drug samples, which the ministry claimed represented a production "somewhere in the thousands."[18] In relation to the exhibition, the Central Drug Testing Center announced it was compiling a *Handbook on Chinese Medicinals* (*Zhongyaocai Shouce*), which would indeed be published in September 1959, almost three years ahead of schedule. This was among the first work to enshrine *zhongyao* as an important resource for drug-making in Communist China.[19]

Given this environment, it was now the duty of medical institutions to become even more productive by either setting high benchmarks or benchmarking themselves against other institutions. Open competition now reigned as a way to increase productivity and overall performance.[20] Animal-based medicines were prominent in such schemes, perhaps because the quantities produced in comparison to herbs had heretofore been modest, and it was believed that more attention to research could dramatically increase yields. For example, in April 1958, Beijing Tongrentang declared on the front page of the journal *Zhongyao Tongbao* that two of its factories would combine efforts to overtake Beijing Pharmaceutical Factory in both research and worker training. Tongrentang's research aimed to improve the overall quality of honey and determine the exact amount needed for the production of traditional medicines. It would also sponsor scientific studies to replace the use of African rhino horns with those of the Asian species, which were called *guangjiao* in Chinese. The word *guang* came from Guangzhou, since all Asian rhino horns entered China via this city. They also intended to contribute to research and production of artificial bezoar, given shortages in the natural product. Regarding labor, Tongrentang gave itself the target of producing two hundred skilled workers by 1961.[21]

Rhino horn (*guangjiao*) was given a particularly large production quota, and authorities went to great lengths to fulfill it. Regular imports could not suffice, so another strategy was to collect cups made from rhino horn from around the country, some quite ancient, and then grind them down for reuse as medicine. Tianjin Medicinal Company actually conducted a series of tests on such cups in its research lab before declaring them to be acceptable for medicinal use (by what criteria one can only speculate).[22] "Inferior" grades of horn were also sanctioned for medical use for the first time. In August 1956, the central agency in charge of medicinal companies issued a notice to its branch offices allowing the use of worm-infected horn.[23] The notice read,

> Due to an increase in demand for *guangjiao*, but faced with the difficulty in sourcing for them, our company recently imported a batch of infected *guangjiao* via Tianjin. Prior studies conducted on early samples showed that it was safe to use the non-infected areas. A report presented at the Chinese medicine conference held recently in Beijing writes: "This has happened in history before, but it is important to remove the infected area before using the rest of the horn." As such, it is based on this decision that infected *guangjiao* were imported to meet market needs and satisfy medical needs.[24]

In April 1957, Tianjin authorities estimated that the city required at least 1,800 *liang* (about 90 kilograms) of rhino horns for the rest of the year, but that its repository held only two hundred. Guangzhou authorities agreed to supply three hundred *liang*, but Tianjin still lacked one thousand *liang* even after confiscating rhino cups from its residents. Artificial replacements for rhino would henceforth be pursued, continuing into the Cultural Revolution (see chapter 5), but the setting of new quotas based on perceptions of "shortages" also meant increasing importation from foreign suppliers.[25]

Such documents suggest that at least some of the seeds for the global scourge of rhinos in the late twentieth century were planted with the production demands of the Great Leap Forward. Indian and later Chinese merchants in Zanzibar had been coordinating with African poachers to ship rhino horns to China at least since the 1920s.[26] When the first statistical reports on the global trade in rhino horn were compiled in the late 1970s, however, mainland Chinese traders were found to be sourcing the material through Hong Kong middlemen, as well as importing directly from East Africa and, later, from middlemen in Yemen. Although the Chinese in Southeast Asia were major consumers as well, along with the Taiwanese, Japanese, and Koreans, China was the second-largest importer of African rhino horn by the 1970s, after Yemen (which also re-exported a portion of its supply to China). Medicine shops in Southeast Asia tended to stock whole rhino horns, from which small quantities of powder were prepared for individual customers, while Chinese firms imported mostly shavings to be used in tonics.[27] Over the long term, this trade would help seal the fate of species like the northern (African) white rhinoceros.[28]

The most important short-term result of this push to develop drugs of every sort, however, and in ever greater quantities, was to turn to species that had not previously been exploited commercially. The medicinal use of sharks began in this period, for example, not for their fins (which had long been used in soup) and not so much for Chinese medicine, but as the basis of a Chinese effort to replicate a Western medicinal: cod liver oil. Cod liver oil had long been a staple of European and North American medical practice for use in curing "deficiency diseases," given its richness in vitamin A. During World War II, however, when the cod fisheries of northern Europe were disrupted, the United States and Latin American countries turned to shark fishing, and shark liver oil temporarily became a global commodity. Cod liver oil regained its place of prominence after the war, and shark liver oil essentially disappeared from marketplaces, at least in the West. In China, however, far from the Atlantic cod fisheries but with sharks along its coastline, the wartime experience had suggested new possibilities.[29]

Shark liver oil was a rare example of a new animal drug being introduced into the modern Chinese pharmacopeia as a substitute for an existing Western animal-based product. Sharks had never been prominent ingredients in

Chinese medicine. Their fins, however, were a gourmet item in Chinese cuisine, and the existing high culinary status of sharks in China, and Asia more generally, likely aided the reception of shark-based fish liver oil among that continent's consumers. By contrast, the necessary use of sharks to make fish liver oil in the wartime West, where cod were food and sharks were not, often had to be masked from consumers and was abandoned as soon as cod liver oil again became available.[30]

Thus in January 1958 the Xiamen Fish Liver Oil Factory announced that it would surpass the leading English brand, Scott's, in both quality and quantity of creamy white fish liver oil over the next two years, but using the livers of shark rather than codfish. The development of its product, called Xingsha, was narrated in a publication of the period as the typical story of a worker with little or no formal education making outstanding contributions to production through innovation:

> Yang Pi from the Xiamen Fish Liver Oil Factory is an exceptional member of the Communist Youth League. He left home at the early age of ten to become an apprentice, and in 1953 joined the fish liver oil factory. Yang has always been passionate about work, hardworking, and obeyed deployment orders. He therefore has a wealth of experience in many aspects of production such as packaging, washing of bottles, and manufacturing. In 1954, Yang was transferred to the Number Two Plant to assist in the production of creamy white fish liver oil. Within six months, he figured out how the operation worked. Yang and his team also focused on repairing mechanical parts to ensure smooth operation of the factory. Since 1957, Xiamen Fish Liver Oil Factory experienced an unprecedented high utilization rate of its machines.[31]

The account goes on to describe how Yang reduced the main emulsifying and stabilizing ingredient, tragacanth, by one-third, succeeded after more than thirty tries in thinning the consistency, eradicated signs of uneven fermentation and the appearance of black residues on bottlenecks, and created a smoother color effect. In April that same year, it was announced that Xingsha had met its goal of overtaking Britain's Scott's brand one year and nine months ahead of schedule. The announcement claimed that "the new recipe not only replaced Scott's as the top consumer choice in the international market, thus bringing glory to China, it also helped the country save as much as three million yuan." It concludes, "Yang's unremitting efforts to enhance the factory's performance continued even after Xingsha declared victory over Scott's. He enlisted the entire workforce in his section and in

August the factory recorded seventeen thousand kilograms of creamy white fish liver oil in production. This was by far the largest monthly yield and exceeded even the national target. Yang also improved the quality so that even overseas consumers were impressed. This year alone Xingsha saw a twenty-fold increase in exports."[32] *Fang weixing* (satellite launching) was a common expression of the Great Leap Forward to describe this sort of effort, invented following the successful launch of Sputnik by the Soviets in 1957. In the Chinese pharmaceutical context, the expression referred to a factory having exceeded its production target by achieving some breakthrough in research. For instance, one title that appeared in the journal *Yaoxue Tongbao* reads, "Huabei Pharmaceutical Factory Launches Satellite in a Big Way." The factory was reported to have successfully improved the quality of two drugs, benzylpenicillin potassium and streptomycin sulfate, and was for the first time managing to export both overseas.[33]

Posters began to appear illustrating such developments at a speed similar to the Sputnik launch. An exhibition held in Hebei province showcased successful cultivation of nonnative medicinals. One even showed *dihuang* being launched like a satellite into the air, a celebration of the province's success in cultivating this herb. A separate article proudly announced that Anguo, one of Hebei's counties, had produced more than a million *jin* worth of *dihuang*. A sample was later presented to then Vice Chairman Liu Shaoqi during his visit to Hebei. The piece of land that created this miracle was thereafter known as "the satellite land plot."[34]

The Rise of Animal Farming

Until the Great Leap Forward, farming animals for medicinal purposes was not common in China, except for deer. Even then, industrial-scale deer farming, as we have seen in chapter 2, was a very recent development inspired by similar farms on the Soviet side of the border. Other medicinal animals (and for a long period, even deer) were usually caught in the wild. Not only did deer farms expand after 1958, but so also did the variety of animals newly subject to medicinal farming, and (as crucially) the numbers of medicinal uses some animal tissue was described as having. The logic of production itself suggested that more and more parts of each farmed animal be used as medicine, particularly large and expensive-to-raise animals like deer. This was due as much to an ideology of efficiency and cost considerations as to claims of medical efficacy, which were often based on stray references or selective readings of classic texts. Few if any accounts problematized the ability to match species mentioned in early medical sources with those chosen for farming, though this issue had long been discussed in relation to herbs.

Although many articles describing the establishment of farms ritually point to "shortages," new markets for such products were obviously being created at the point of production, based on quotas. This was driven partly by the push to increase exports of materials for consumption by an ever-more-prosperous Chinese diaspora, but also by the particular logic of the Great Leap Forward, in which production of all sorts was stressed, with consumption playing a secondary role.

Translated into practice, this economic imperative begat the movement for "home cultivation," out of which much medicinal animal farming in this period likely arose. On April 7, 1958, Premier Zhou Enlai gave a speech that laid out concrete plans to tap the country's native medicinals. While encouraging their full and active utilization, he also warned against their exhaustion. Zhou was particularly concerned about "those medicinal plants with comparatively high economic value or having diverse uses." One solution, argued Zhou, was to begin "home cultivation" of medicinals in every commune. This was in line with the policy, previously discussed, of making cultivation national by resisting the "superstition" that particular products were tied to regional homes. He also encouraged artificial breeding of wild plants to make them suitable for farm production. Throughout his speech, Zhou stressed the importance of relying on the efforts of the people—*qunzhong*—and the government's willingness to "pay a reasonable price as incentive."[35]

This concept was soon extended to animals through modifying the slogan to read *Jia Yang Yia Zhong* (home rearing, home cultivation). Not only did the Chinese government increase the number of medicinal processing factories in this period, it also converted much more land to herb plantations and medicinal animal farms. In fact, medicinal animal farming was introduced in an official manual as "a new department."[36] Besides sika deer, animals such as musk deer, seahorses, beetles, and scorpions were all recorded as newly subject to farming by 1960. In Hebei province, a movement encouraged the farming of birds, insects, fish, and many types of mammals, though some of these were doubtless consumed as food as well as medicine. The farming of snakes—specifically, of the long-nosed pit viper or *baihuashe*—also began during this period.[37] Various minorities were also cited as experimenting with the farming of lesser-known species. For instance, the *baizu* (members of the Yunnan *bai* group) built a facility to farm river deer, while the *tongzhu* of Guangxi province attempted to rear tokay geckos. It was already recognized by this period that animals such as the Mongolian wild horse, tigers in the northeast region, pandas, and even the sika deer were in danger of extinction. Farming was thus sometimes presented as furthering "conservation," although their effects on the targeted wildlife generally had the opposite effect, stimulating the market for even wild examples of the same species. This was particularly true for "farms" that could not sustain self-breeding populations and had to rely on hunters to replenish their stock.[38]

Although there were seemingly no limits to the types of animals that could be farmed for medicine, deer remained the most commonly discussed. We have already seen that Russian efforts had encouraged Chinese deer farming in the northeast, including lab research that led to the creation of the mass-produced drug pantocrin. The industry's expansion was sustained at least in part by attractive remuneration from overseas sales. An article in 1955 explaining the state of deer farming in the northeast (or Dongbei) region relates, "Besides catering to domestic needs, most of the deer produce are exported out of China to earn the capital required to build the country."[39]

Claims for the medicinal properties of deer had first been made during the Qin dynasty, but the supply of deer antler in medicinal shops long depended on the skill of hunters. Hunting was still the primary recourse throughout the Republican period. Young male deer were stalked during the summer season when their antlers were considered the most potent. On spotting a family of deer, groups of hunters would chase after the lot to scare them, intending to stimulate their adrenaline so that blood would rush upward and accumulate in the antlers. Deer tended to fracture or otherwise damage their antlers while thrashing in their death throes, so after shooting them, hunters would rush to the wounded deer and immediately hack off its head with the antlers intact. They then took turns vigorously swinging their prize antlers to ensure that blood did not congeal but spread evenly throughout the rack.[40]

A limited number of Chinese medicinal deer farms did exist in the Republican period, belonging to famous and wealthy medicinal firms such as Tongrentang and Darentang. These operations were not large-scale compared to those that came later, however: a Singapore-based magazine reported in 1930, for example, that the farm of Beijing-based Tongjitang held only about seventy deer,[41] which was consistent with the status of deer antler as a luxury product. These Chinese farms were much smaller than Russian deer farms located across the Siberian border during the same period. One Republican-period document of 1928 recorded that the largest farm in Vladivostok held some nine thousand animals.[42]

It is likely that the proliferation of Soviet deer farms along the border in the early twentieth century grew up mainly to serve the Chinese market.

Until the late 1950s, Vladivostok was a large exporter of deer antler to China, given that Chinese domestic supply remained low and unstable, depending as it did on the luck and skill of hunters, most of whom were of minority races. As we saw in chapter 2, it was Russian scientists who provided the "scientific proof" for the medicinal use of deer antler, based on organotherapy. The method of processing antler for Chinese medicine remained elusive to Russian farmers, however, who found it more profitable instead to simply export antlers in raw form to China.[43] Because of their geophysical proximity, Russian antlers were indistinguishable from ones harvested in northern China, where it was believed by Chinese consumers that the best quality antlers originated. Even Beijing-based Tongrentang resorted to sending its farmed antlers to Shenyang to be artificially colored to look like northern antlers, prior to marketing and selling them as the real thing.[44]

As the Chinese government merged private pharmaceutical firms into larger, state-owned enterprises, Chinese deer farms began to grow in both size and number.[45] Antlers derived from young deer in which the trabecular bone had not yet formed were particularly regarded as *guizhong yaopin* (a valuable drug). Captive deer were thus kept alive for at least five years, during which multiple antlers could be harvested with no harm to the animal, while older deer, in their sixth or seventh year, were killed by the so-called slashing method, whereby "the antlers including the skull was removed by a quick stroke of the knife." Although concentrating on antlers, farmers also began to collect and "medicalize" many other deer body parts such as sinew, penis, and blood, all of which were now processed and sold as medicine, as demonstrated by the previously quoted export figures.[46]

The numbers of types of ailments that deer parts were promoted as treating also expanded with the increased production pressures. By the mid-1950s, *lurong*, or the antlers of young deer, were promoted not only for specific disorders, like impotence, but as a general health booster. Previously taken orally, deer antler in the form of pantocrin (discussed in chapter 2), was also reformulated for injection purposes,[47] resulting in "modernizing" the drug and elevating it as a medicinal in its own right, rather than as one ingredient in polyherbal recipes. But Chinese reformulations of deer antler did not stop at pantocrin. In the Harbin Pharmaceutical Factory, injectable pantocrin was made mainly from the antlers of younger deer. The antlers of older deer, named *lujiao*, were usually cooked into a paste (*lujiaojiao*) and used as a blood-stopping agent. Like the antlers, other parts of the deer, such as the sinew, blood, and even the fetus, were promoted for their ability to invigorate health on the whole, as well as for an expanding series of specific ailments.[48]

Few reliable statistics are available on the growth of deer farming, but from the later 1950s onward, articles on this and other types of animal farming proliferated in pharmaceutical and Chinese medical journals, indicating increasing energy and resources were being directed to this sector. Many articles took the form of local experiences and tips regarding innovation. Farms that had won awards based on the highest yield in a particular year would also share their experiences as a way to encourage others. For example, the Dongfeng Deer Farm in Jilin province was named the best deer farm in China in 1956 and, in March the following year, was invited to display a sample of its antlers at the National Agricultural Exhibition. The key to its success, Dongfeng claimed, was adopting new and more efficient methods of antler harvesting. Instead of restraining the deer, which was the existing method, Dongfeng learned from another farm that it could harvest antlers more quickly by hanging deer upside down (a method reminiscent of the pig-slaughtering technology of the "dis-assembly line" in nineteenth-century America). It also followed the practice of another deer farm in cutting antlers individually instead of in pairs. Dongfeng claimed it had increased its yield by 13 percent through these and other new practices. Dongfeng was considered the largest state-owned deer farm in Jilin province at the time the report was written, housing over a thousand deer. Even then, construction had started on a competing farm intended to house 2,500 deer by 1960.[49] Dongfeng continued to exceed quotas well into the Great Leap Forward.[50]

It is noteworthy that Jilin province would later emerge, in the 1980s, as the birthplace of Chinese bear farming. Like deer farming before it, this industry likely had origins across the border, this time in North Korea (this connection is discussed in chapter 5).

Few articles on animal farming in this period discuss the toll it was taking on wild animal populations. One exception is a story-like essay by Mu Ziguang, published in 1960, which begins,

> Deep in the forests of Changbaishan, Daxiaoxinganling, and Wandashanmai of Heilongjiang there lives a thriving red deer population. Every part of the deer's body is a treasure. Its meat can be turned into food and skin into leather. Its antlers, tail, penis, tendons, blood, and even fetus are precious medicinal resources but especially the antler, which is considered one of "Dongbei's Three Treasures." A pair of antlers from a dead deer fetches one thousand yuan. On the other hand, one can harvest up to ten pairs of antlers from a farmed deer and earn one million yuan in revenue. Every commune in my province has incorporated deer farming into its

sideline production plan. Until recently, the hunting and killing of deer for their antlers was the only method employed, and had caused three thousand or so deer to be killed each year. Even though deer farming has proven to be a promising enterprise, there is not much experience in capturing them alive. Most deer perish during the process. Out of the four hundred and twenty-three deer caught in this province last year, only one hundred and thirty-two survived (to be farmed).[51]

Despite the transition to large-scale animal farming during the Mao period, the continued reliance on hunting in order to source deer for farms indicated that a self-breeding population could not be maintained. Hunting wild deer was thus only encouraged by the existence of farms, and by the increased profit generated by expanding markets, a pattern that would later be seen to affect almost every species that became "medicinal." A 1960 manual published by the National Hunting Committee, for example, singled out deer as the most valuable game, since so many of its parts and tissues were now marketable as medicine. The animals were no longer to be killed in the field, however, but captured for breeding: "Deer antler, deer fetus, deer penis, and deer blood are all *guizhong* medicinals that not only guarantee the health of our people, but also help advance the medicine of this country."[52]

Trials were carried out in the same period on farming wild animals that had never before been farmed or had not been widely marketed for medicinal value. Published tracts encouraging the farming of these species often began by describing their "long history" of use and the ailments they would cure. One example was the farming of seahorses, which first took place in August 1958 in Shantou, Guangdong, under the direction of the local Water Resources Bureau. The bureau published a handbook the following year that covered everything from seahorse biology to ideal farming methods. It began,

> Seahorse is a sea product with very high economic value. It has long been used in this country and according to historical records and folk tradition has the ability to nourish [*bu*] the kidney and strengthen the heart, to give but two examples. It is particularly effective in treating diseases relating to the nervous system. Demand, both domestic and overseas, has always exceeded supply, but artificial farming [*rengong yangzhi*] of seahorse was never carried out. Neither did the rest of the world. In this Great Leap Forward Movement, effort will be made to institute seahorse farming since it has not only an economic significance but a larger political one.[53]

Here was an example of a preexisting local medicinal product (generally the bycatch of fishermen who were targeting other species) intended by its bureaucratic promoters to go "national" through farming, if not international (the reference to a political significance likely related to its value as an export). The bureau also asked for public advice. It had introduced seahorse farming as "a new project . . . [which] is imperfect due to lack of experience," so asked readers to write in with solutions. One major problem the bureau encountered was the lack of prawn feed: "We obtain most of our prawn feed from nature, and its supply is unpredictable. There were times when we totally ran out of prawn feed. It is therefore imperative that we conduct large-scale farming of prawns." The bureau also suggested changing the seahorse's natural habitat by replacing seawater with fresh water (or water of lower density). The reason, it claimed, was that "this will make seahorse farming easier . . . by being able to expand farm size and improve on current techniques."[54] A separate booklet on animal farming, however, cautioned against keeping seahorses in fresh water, as it would shorten their lives.[55]

Trial farming of insects and small reptiles also became popular in the same period. In fact, insects were identified in journals of the period as being in the greatest "shortage" of any animal type with claimed medicinal value. The infamous campaign to eliminate the four pests in the late 1950s—rats, flies, mosquitoes, and sparrows—was given as a reason for the dwindling population of even medicinal insects. People were apparently killing anything that moved and removing habitat for even "useful" insects.

Thus was the first farm started to cultivate ground beetles in August 1957. An article written the following year by one of its principals, Xi Tongsheng, described the project:

> The ground beetle has the ability to unblock meridians. It is also effective as a painkiller and can be used to treat all kinds of wounds and injuries. The best quality ground beetles are found in Guangdong and Jiangsu provinces. . . . Ground beetle thrives in damp places like most village kitchens and base of walls, loose soil and amongst grass-heaps. Its reproductive season is the period between the *duanwu* and mid-autumn festivals. In recent years, however, the effort to remove the four pests and raise the overall standard of hygiene has resulted in fewer breeding grounds for the ground beetle. Kitchens, floors, and even grass-heaps have become cleaner. The year-on-year decrease in their population has created a crisis for the pharmaceutical industry. Since 1957, we have carried out trial farming of ground beetles.[56]

This article makes clear that there was a preexisting market for ground beetles, although it does not tell us whether it was regional or national, primarily domestic or for export. At the level of ground beetle and seahorse, however, we are dealing with animal tissue far cheaper in price than deer antler, let alone imported substances like tiger bone or rhino horn. Despite the lack of information on distribution, it is likely that the mania for medicinal animal farming in this period was creating or expanding consumption, rather than being consumer-driven. The impetus for the experimental beetle, seahorse, and other such farms discussed in journals and yearbooks also seems to have resided within ministries and bureaus, with local authorities responding by creating novel farming systems on their own initiative, although the "Home Rearing, Home Cultivation" movement was presented as a popular or grassroots one.

Because of the new or enhanced status of such creatures as farmed medicinals, much new and even basic information on their habits and behaviors was observed and recorded in the pharmaceutical journals of this period, giving them more a zoological than medical flavor. For instance, Xi and his team claimed to have discovered for the first time that ground beetles hibernate in the winter. In February, six months after keeping them in an enclosed space, the ground beetles appeared almost lifeless, but sprang to life after Xi took them out and placed them under the sun. Three months later, in May, Xi sifted the ground beetles and discovered tiny, baby beetles passing through the sieve. This was evidence of successful breeding of the insect, which, according to Xi, required only loose soil and the husks of various seeds.[57]

Central health authorities also went about collecting the farming experiences of different localities and compiling them into booklets to be disseminated across China. In Shandong, provincial health officers were dispatched to scorpion farms to document methods and create handbooks. The information collected extended from the design of ideal breeding facilities to ways of attracting the flies that scorpions fed on. In Shandong, a so-called integrated farming system was introduced, whereby livestock, medicinal animals, and various herbs and vegetables were kept and cultivated together, thus conflating the boundary between food and medicine. Most such booklets concentrated on the farming of only one animal species or a plant type, however, reflecting the specialized nature of most Chinese medicinal farm operations.[58]

It is possible that the tradition of beekeeping may have contributed, along with deer farming, to the medicinal farming of insects and other animals in this period. Few articles describe transitions of embodied knowledge or techniques from one field of endeavor to another. But beekeeping was a medicinal farming practice even more widespread than deer farming in this period, with both "local" and supply-chain connections to urban pharmaceutical firms. As briefly discussed in chapter 1, beeswax and even honey were considered medicines in China, rather than food products. Traditionally, honey was used not only for medicinal reasons but also as a coagulating agent in the making of drugs in pill form, which meant the substance was a basic raw material in factory production.[59]

The spate of experimental farming activities carried out on insects and reptiles, though often presented as addressing "critical shortages," can also be seen as a kind of bureaucratic and pharmacological entrepreneurship, reflecting the revolutionary spirit of the Great Leap Forward. Authorities had raised the banner of daring innovation. The chanting of slogans like "Dare to Think, Dare to Do" (*Ganxiang, Ganzuo*) was meant to instill a mood of creativity. This atmosphere was well captured in a report by a Guangxi-based trial farm, which started a breeding program for the tokay gecko in May 1958. The report began with the claim that "previously no one had attempted nor thought it possible to farm tokay geckos, but following the injunction to liberate one's thoughts . . . we conducted many experiments . . . resulting in successful breeding."[60] Popular belief in the medical efficacy of the tails of tokay geckos was based, like many other examples of the use of animal tissue, on like-cures-like associations. The Guangxi report claims,

> The healing powers of the tokay gecko lie in its tail, which has strong growth ability. A tailless tokay gecko grows back its tail usually within ten days. It therefore has great potential as a regenerative medicine. It was found that patients suffering from tuberculosis show signs of healing after ingesting a tail or two. Our farm had experimented with different ways to remove the tail from a live tokay gecko. The steps are first to wipe the blades of scissors with alcoholic antiseptic, and after cutting the tail, apply the powder of the fungus lasiosphaera onto the gecko's wound.[61]

The trial farm also recommended baking the tail before using it as medicine. As with the ground beetle, the authors carefully noted and reported new knowledge of gecko behavior as a result of close observation of captive animals. To determine their eating habits, for instance, the farm fed geckos a variety of insects and found that they ate only wasps and locusts, and then only live ones. Like the ground beetle, the tokay gecko would also enter hibernation during the winter.[62]

In the contemporary (twenty-first-century) Chinese urban marketplace, whole geckos are commonly sold as medicinals. Documents like this one from the 1950s, however, clearly show that geckos were originally farmed only for their tails, and thus as a renewable resource. This illustrates a principle also seen with deer. Once a medicinal animal was farmed, there was pressure or incentive to justify the use of all of its parts, regardless of previous traditions that had often been quite selective as to which part should actually be taken as medicine, and for what purpose. The casual (and undocumented) reference to gecko tail as a cure for tuberculosis also illustrates the easy drift from modest to more dramatic curative claims in articles announcing new animal farming initiatives, which were in line with the generally hyperbolic language of the Great Leap Forward.

To supplement farming, the masses and especially schoolchildren were encouraged to catch and bring medicinal insects (and occasionally reptiles) to collection stations in communes. Such activities were particularly organized during school holidays. Children in the primary level were encouraged to catch only nontoxic insects such as cicada, ground beetle, and dung beetle, whose colloquial name was "the big general. Toxic "insects" such as scorpions and centipedes were left to secondary-school children.[63] Shandong and Inner Mongolia were among the earliest provinces to employ schoolchildren in the effort to collect and amass different types of insects for medical purposes.[64] Even into the 1970s, when farming of animals and insects had become well established, the government continued to depend on regular people collecting them as a by-employment. Posters with pictures of whole insects or specific parts of animals were put up to inform and educate the public about their medicinal value, which suggests that such knowledge was not already widespread, or that knowledge or practices from particular localities or traditions was being "nationalized" through poster campaigns.

Besides farming and collecting medicinal animals from the wild, Chinese authorities also educated people that certain by-products of livestock had medicinal value, and encouraged their collection at the point of slaughter. One example was *jineijin*, or the inner membrane of chicken gizzards, which was advertised to the masses as effective in treating ailments like indigestion, nausea, and diarrhea. Chicken gizzard was being recommended and used by elite physicians such as Zhang Xichun into the Republican period.[65] But an article in the journal *Yaoxue Tongbao*, in April 1958, explained that the Chinese people had looked down on *jineijin* as being "too insignificant and not worthy of the time and effort required to store and accumulate them in amounts substantial enough to sell." A *jineijin* weighed less than one *liang*. To educate and incentivize people to collect them, a so-called herb specialty company was formed to carry out publicity on *jineijin*, and collection boxes

3.2 & 3.3 Posters from the period of the Cultural Revolution meant to educate the public about the medicinal properties of plants and animal tissues and encourage their collection. One poster reads, "Chinese Medicine Is a Glorious Treasure Trove. We Have to Work Hard to Raise It Up." The other reads, "For the Revolution, Collect Medicines." The targeted animals include turtles, tortoises, chickens, brown beetles, squid, centipedes, and horses (for bezoar). COURTESY OF THE GUCM MUSEUM.

accounting for one yuan worth of *jineijin* (which were bought back by the company at one cent per *jin*) were distributed to communes as an incentive for people to collect gizzard linings in sufficient quantity.[66] Once a system was in place to collect and distribute it, *jineijin* was a particularly cheap and readily available medicine compared to deer antler and even seahorse, which may have been one reason it was so widely promoted.[67]

Musk: Communist Production of a Luxury Medicinal

While more and more common animals like insects and chickens were increasingly promoted as medicine in the Great Leap Forward, new high-end animal-based medicines were also cultivated in earnest, even if such products were entirely beyond the ability of ordinary Chinese to consume.

Musk, the product of a special species of small deer, was at the very top of China's export list because of its high value. Musk deer thrived in the provinces of Sichuan, Xikang, and Yunnan, and even in Tibet. Prior to the development of farming, hunters would kill the deer and simply cut off its pouch, from which skin, fats, and excess fur were removed before leaving it to dry on its own or in an oven. Although small-scale farming existed in the northeast region of China as early as the 1930s, during the 1950s the farming of musk deer in China expanded in tandem with animal farming generally, to include the Gansu region and Inner Mongolia.[68] The first farm had been set up in Sichuan province only during the Great Leap Forward.[69] Still, the largest amount of musk continued to be produced in Xikang province, while Tibet was considered to produce musk of the best quality.[70]

The musk deer was not an easy species to manage in captivity. Only the males produced musk, on a seasonal basis, and the amount that could be collected per head each cycle was insubstantial.[71] Furthermore, reproduction in a captive musk deer herd was slow, since the females conceived just once a year. Frequent attempts to farm these animals had not only ended in failure but also caused the musk deer population "to face near extinction," in the words of an insider, because replenishment was accomplished mainly through hunting. Even more than other deer species, musk deer did not easily adapt to life in captivity, so the mortality rate was even higher than for "regular" deer farms. Those that survived were also seen as producing musk inferior to that of wild deer because of the change in environment. It was claimed that millions of musk deer were killed each year through mistakes, inexperience, and the inherent incompatibility of "farming" such wild animals. The Beijing Medicinal Company alone killed as many as 5,640 musk deer a year in the mid-1950s to produce 2,400 *liang* of musk, which was still not enough to satisfy demand.[72]

During this same decade, however, China supplanted India and Russia to become the world's largest musk producer. Gao Minggong wrote in 1955 that China produced around 3,000 *jin* of musk each year for export, with only a small amount trickling in to domestic consumption. In the 1930s, China had exported its musk largely to European countries, with France as its largest market, and perfume rather than medicine its intended use.[73] After the Revolution, however, musk exports to East and Southeast Asian countries, included Japan, Hong Kong, and Vietnam, began to increase at the expense of the Western market. This suggests a shift away from its original use—as a perfume—to its use as medicine.[74]

As musk's identity as a medicine began to reassert itself at the point of production, it became possible to imagine more elements of the animal also serving a medicinal purpose. This expansion in the number of parts of the musk deer that could be marketed helped make up for previously low productivity and high mortality. One example was the secretion *sexiangzi*, another name for which was *sexiang neiyi* (musk's inner wear), which is basically the musk pouch itself. Before the early Communist era, this substance was never sold in private medicine shops, although it was considered to have medicinal value in some literature. The reason for its lack of popularity was that *sexiangzi* could not easily be converted into powder or some other easily digestible form. As we have seen, however, those working on animal farms, like workers in pharmaceutical factories, were encouraged in this period to innovate new uses for the animal parts and tissues they handled. Thus it was that a worker by the name of Ni Minggao discovered a way to process the substance into a powder. In 1956, the Beijing Medicinal Company No. 1 Wholesale Unit published an article detailing every step in Ni's inventive process, from the first successful experiment to the product's eventual official approval and marketing.[75]

Ni's narrative follows a typical pattern in worker-as-innovator accounts of the period: the intelligent or clever worker, having had their creativity long suppressed under capitalism/feudalism, now came forward with production solutions given the new spirit of grassroots innovation. Ni had been working with musk deer since 1931, and came under the mentorship of a Sichuan-based musk expert named Zhang Danian. As a buyer, Zhang had learned much from musk hunters, with whom he had direct dealings. He later passed on this knowledge to Ni, including the manner by which *sexiangzi* was formed. Based on that understanding, Ni began experimenting with ways to convert the substance into powder form. He finally found a method by first removing the white outer layer and then air- or oven-drying the core before crushing it into powder. The end product was, accordingly, "not too different from musk itself in terms of color, smell, and form."[76]

Another common characteristic in articles about worker-innovators was how their initial uncertainty grew into a determination to take their discoveries through to the stage of actual production. Ni had wanted to announce his innovation during the early 1950s, according to the article, but felt inadequate until he had worked out a system for large-scale production. It was not until the third quarter of 1955, according to the article, that he approached the company with his technique. By then, demand—both international and domestic—was far exceeding the supply of musk, and China was searching for alternatives to producing more of the pure product. For nine months the wholesale unit of Beijing Medicinal Company conducted both lab tests and human trials and found *sexiangzi* to be as medically efficacious as musk (by what measure the article does not say). Attempts to reproduce the product in the form of *wan* or pills, both at company premises and the Beijing Tongrentang Medicine Shop, were also successful, and the use of *sexiangzi* greatly expanded the market for musk-related products.[77]

This account of innovating a new animal medicinal does not mention "tradition," medical efficacy, or any testing regime used to determine the product's effects. The emphasis, as in many other accounts, is on innovation leading to increased production, thanks to humble workers with vision who in this instance also consulted peasants in the form of hunters. The production worker or technician thus takes on the role of pharmacist in conceiving and creating a new medicine, whose status as medicine is assumed because of its proximity (in the body of the animal) to other tissues sanctioned by longer or more common use. Thus does the logic of production expand the range of consumption.

The Science of Animal Farming and the Search for Substitutes

The story of *sexiangzi* illustrates quite clearly the push, not confined to deer, to create new products from new parts of medicinal animals, and particularly to reproduce them in modern forms, such as injections, powders, or pills. To do this, some farms had to turn themselves into experiment stations, where the task was not just to increase yield and production, but also literally to create new medicinals from the raw material of increasingly available animal bodies.

The most traditional way of increasing yields was of course to "improve" animals through breeding, which was widely practiced in medicinal animal farming. By 1960, there were many reports in Chinese journals of farm-based labs' successful breeding of plants and animals, often producing new strains. In the case of seahorse farming, the Shantou Water Resources Bureau (Guangdong) listed as one of its goals the crossbreeding of seahorses caught in the open sea with those from its local basin. The reason, it wrote, was that "all living beings have both good and bad traits. . . . Through the re-selection process, we hope to create a new breed of seahorse which is the result of combining the best of the two existing species."[78] As part of the program to equip Chinese physicians with "Western" scientific knowledge in this period, the Guangdong Health Bureau began to give lectures on animal biology, which included a presentation of Darwin as an animal breeder:

> Darwin once carried out research on livestock such as chickens, pigeons, and cows. He also did the same for crops like wheat and cabbage. Darwin found out there were many varieties of the same species. For example, he studied all the varieties of domesticated pigeons—some 150 of them—and chickens. Where do they originate? In Darwin's formulation, all living beings react and adjust to the changing environment. New traits acquired were not all desired, and thus began a process of selecting only the best qualities with the aim of passing them on to the next generation, and so on and so forth.[79]

The presentation went on to discuss that, in a particular setting, certain characteristics were deemed more important than others, and this changed the criteria for selection. For instance, some places focused on producing only fast-running horses, while another used horses as labor. When applying this concept to the production of animals for medicine, the rule was to favor traits that related to healing human diseases. How a breeder or researcher was to determine this for a medicinal animal was left unclear, however.[80] Nor was there any reference in this text to classical or folk sources on which the medicinal properties of seahorses must originally have been based. The category "seahorse" was assumed to be unproblematic across time and geography, and even capable of being bred in new forms to cure (perhaps) additional disease categories. The sense in this and some other passages is that premodern Chinese medicine had simply launched the animal species into the realm of healing, but that its full possibilities as a healing agent would be developed only through lab-based innovation.

Experiments in breeding aside, the most common reason that medicinal animals were the targets of lab-based research in this period lay in the hope of developing synthetics or substitutes, particularly when the animal in question was foreign, or in short supply, or both. Cow bezoar fell into this category, as a necessary ingredient in more than thirty existing drug formulas—such as Niuhuang Qingxin Wan (cow bezoar heart cleansing pill) and Huoluo Dan (meridian activating pill)—but dependent on supplies from India and North America.[81] Chinese research on artificial bezoar began in May 1955, and within four months it was reported that pharmaceutical workers at a Tianjin-based company had produced their first successful batch, using bile from livestock.[82] Local authorities then ordered not only the large slaughterhouses but also smaller-scale ones, and kitchens of the people's communes, to surrender (for a token sum) all animal guts to the Tianjin factory.[83] Collection points were also set up at *yiyao* or clinical stations throughout Hebei province to ensure no animal guts went to waste.[84] It was estimated that places like Shanghai, Qingdao, Bengbu, Zhengzhou, Wuhan, Changshang, Sichuan, and Ha'erbin together sent close to 11,500 kilograms of a specific ingredient—bile calcium—to Tianjin in 1957, and about 14,000 kilograms in 1958.[85] As cow bile became less and less available, further research was done on substituting the bile of pigs.[86] Tianjin subsequently became a center for research on artificial substitutes for many animal-based drugs. Success was also reported there in the making of artificial tiger-bone paste (*rengong hugujiao*).[87]

As with many "modern" animal-based Chinese medicines, the artificial bezoar project had been preceded and informed by foreign research. Chinese reports on this project cite the names of foreign scientists (mostly Japanese) who had conducted studies to synthesize bezoar as early as the 1930s.[88] Some of this work was conducted in prewar Manchuria, then a major center of Japanese scientific research.[89]

Species substitution was as much a subject of Chinese research as attempting to develop synthetic versions of animal tissue. It was first suggested in this period, for example, that antelope horn might substitute for rhino horn, based on the Chinese medical reasoning that both substances "perform the same function of bringing down heat in both the liver and lung channels."[90] Others recommended replacing both rhino and antelope horns with those of domestic water buffalo. An article of 1958 reported,

> In doing away with the superstitious belief in *guizhong* medicinals to treat warm diseases to the point of high fever or even coma, many regions are trying to use water buffalo horns to replace rhino and antelope horns. The Number Two People's Hospital in Foshan Special Region conducted

a study whereby 35 patients were given water buffalo horns and 28 took rhino and antelope horns. The first group experienced a reduced death rate of 8.57 percent, according to the report. The hospital concluded that water buffalo horns were more effective than rhino and antelope horns. The study thus contributed to the official spirit of More, Fast, Good, and Thriftiness [*Duo Kuai Hao Sheng*].[91]

This particular research program continued into the late 1970s and is discussed further in chapter 4.

Conclusion

We have seen in this chapter that the new emphasis on production in the Great Leap Forward, and in some cases just preceding it, had a transformative effect on Chinese medicinals in general and animal-based drugs in particular. Steep quotas for Chinese medicinals stimulated drug discovery and innovation of every kind as China sought to become not only self-sufficient, but to also "overtake" Britain in drug output. In the export realm, this involved such projects as increasing the size of deer farms, based on the Soviet example, and developing a fish oil industry based on sharks. On the domestic side, the emphasis on "Home Rearing, Home Cultivation" extended medicinal animal farming to many more species besides deer, such as insects, small reptiles, and seahorses. Innovation took the form of making existing processing more efficient and medicalizing more parts of animals, sometimes accompanied by new forms of delivery. Musk deer, for example, had their pouches rendered into a powder, and deer antler became an injectable substance. There was also a search for substitutes for rare and expensive animal medicinals, such as rhino horn and bezoar, as well as the first efforts toward synthesizing. Suggestions were even made to "improve" medicinal animals through breeding, which indicates that historical descriptions of an animal's medical efficacy were considered simply a starting point in their medicalization, with innovation being the order of the day.

Faunal medicalization at this juncture was only rarely focused on issues of efficacy, given that the "thousand-year experience of the Chinese people" was considered a solid base from which innovation involving medicinal animals could proceed. The focus was rather on production and the expansion of use within a command economy. The spirit of the time was to transform, test, supplement, reformulate, and mass-produce rather than to overly dwell on the lineage of a particular substance. This was, after all, part of a "great leap forward," not a return to the past. And as we have seen, the new realm of pharmacy was competitive with the old one of medicine. Animal medicines, having been an underutilized resource in comparison with herbs (although many of those were also considered underutilized) were particularly ripe for exploitation, and all the more so if such drugs could bring in foreign currency.

Yet economic factors were not the sole controlling agents in Chinese drug development—even animal-drug development—as we shall see in chapter 4.

CHAPTER FOUR

The Quest for Innovation
Folk Remedies and Animal Therapies

 As we have seen, incentives for innovation in drug-making were present from the beginning of the Communist period, though in the early 1950s they were driven largely by the perceived need to emulate the Soviet example. The Great Leap Forward and the simultaneous deterioration in Sino-Soviet relations—resulting in the sudden withdrawal of more than 1,400 Soviet experts from China in 1960—reversed the previous emphasis on "learning from the Soviet Union," however, or indeed from any foreign source. The new discourse was all about domestically sourced or "grassroots" innovation. This took a variety of forms, from attempts to revive previously ignored techniques and practices (culled from both classical references and folk sources) to the invention of hybrid therapies, some of the most important of which would involve the use of animal tissue. The influence of Soviet theories and practices based on organotherapy would linger, however, and continue to provide what was perceived as scientific justification for novel treatments.

The parallel developments in medicinal animal farming, discussed in chapter 3, both facilitated and, in some instances, reflected these trends. In other cases, however, "innovation" in animal-based drugs stood entirely apart from farming, the export trade, or even the normative state-directed production of pharmaceuticals. Indeed, the use of raw chicken blood (and many similar substances we shall trace in this chapter) as a "drug" pushes us beyond the concept of "pharmaceuticals" as it has been discussed so far, and even beyond the codified Chinese medicine institutionalized by the state in the mid- to late 1950s.

With the increased emphasis on innovation, perhaps spurred as well by the availability of novel animal-based therapies, the previous characterization of Chinese medicine as preventive now seemed overly conservative. Confidence increased from this period onward in the curative power of Chinese drugs, especially in the form of new and dramatic therapies that might work where biomedicine had failed. Indeed, the phenomenon of Chinese medicinals hailed as "miracle cures" for diseases such as cancer, well chronicled in the present day, was also present in Mao-period animal-based therapies.[1] Faunal medicines were promoted as potentially exceeding the powers of biomedicines and as matching their quickness of action, qualities not previously associated with the polyherbal recipes on which clinical practice had been largely centered.

Grassroots Innovation

The idea of mass innovation, "grassroots innovation," or the "mass line" (*qunzhong luxian*), to use Mao's formulation, has been well-studied in reference to such projects as "scientific farming,"[2] the campaign against snail fever,[3] and the tracking of portents to predict earthquakes and extreme weather by observing unusual animal behavior.[4] In the case of drugs, we have already seen that pharmacology, industrial drug production, and medicinal animal farming were also considered sites for worker initiative, research, and, ultimately, innovation. It was in the realm of "folk medicine," however, that the campaign for "grassroots innovation" would most fundamentally affect drug development.

With the launch of the Great Leap Forward in early 1958, Chinese authorities began to emphasize the need to draw knowledge and experience from the masses, while at the same time inculcating skepticism of both foreign and "expert" opinion. Yan Yi, deputy head of the Beijing Municipal Public Health Bureau, wrote, in 1958, "Workers and farmers have settled the problems that so-called experts were incapable of solving in the past. . . . There used to be the superstitious belief that all things foreign were good. We used to consult only foreign literature, and looked down on local inventions to the extent that we even stopped creating. Things have changed, however. The younger generation now knows that they should stop thinking capitalist thoughts and be bold to create. . . . They are determined to become red and expert." The phrase "Red and Expert" (*You Hong You Zhuan*) and the slogan "Dare to Create" (*Dadan Chuangzao*)—both of which were coined early in the Great Leap Forward—became new levers in the mission of technological innovation (*jishu gexin*). These expressions were applied across all fields, not just the medical sector, and were directed in part against the idea of a professionalized science. Yan, for instance, was of the opinion that "science" had no clear definition, but was simply "a set of reasons founded on trial and error and then reformulated as theory." He thus believed that anybody, not just professional scientists, could invent scientific principles, as long as the inventors had "tenacity and courage."[5] This was very much in line with the practical emphasis in Chinese pharmacology, as discussed in an earlier chapter, and the positioning of drug-making as a counterpoint to medical theory and practice.[6]

Mao emphasized grassroots innovation repeatedly in his speeches of this period; one of his stated reasons for launching the People's Movement (*Qunzhong Yundong*) was to dispel the "superstition" that nonprofessionals were unqualified to invent or discover. The expression "Dare to Speak, Dare to Think, Dare to Do" (*Ganshuo, Ganxiang, Ganzuo*) was coined to motivate the masses toward innovation. To quote historian Cui Luchun, "The mass population was enlivened with enthusiasm, and there were daily reports of new ideas being formed." Such activity grew in intensity after a full propaganda campaign was launched in May 1958.[7] Resulting new innovations were to be considered gifts to the government for its upcoming "birthday," 1959 marking the tenth anniversary of the Revolution. In a September 1958 report on various health-related achievements, sixty-four-year-old Health Minister Fu Lianzhang cited two lines from a poem: "The ink isn't yet dry on the last research breakthrough, and already a new record is established." The minister was not yet fully in line with the new emphasis on the masses, however, as his report made much of work by the Chinese Academy of Sciences, where "107 of 972 successful projects have even surpassed international standards."[8]

Across many sectors, besides medicine, old technologies and local techniques were simultaneously being revived in the form of *tufa* or "local methods." In fact, the expression *tu zhuanjia*, or "indigenous expert," was coined to describe amateurs with expert knowledge in a particular area or field. In 1958 the so-called Caifeng movement was launched to collect from the population "ancestral recipes, time-tested formulas, and popular *danfang*" (single-herb prescriptions). Mao had originally launched the movement to solicit folk songs and proverbs, but later expanded it to include folk remedies. Under this official banner, the Chinese people were to volunteer knowhow of all sorts, and journal articles on *tufa* proliferated from this time in Chinese pharmaceutical and medical journals.[9] Many substances and techniques were explicitly considered substitutes for modern technology, which was seen to be lacking, and the phrase *tuyang jiehe* (combining indigenous and foreign methods) was coined to encourage the use of indigenous (i.e., low-tech) methods to produce even Western drugs or chemical ingredients for drug-making. This of course paralleled the more infamous injunction to use "backyard furnaces" to produce high-grade steel.

In the effort to break away from institutional knowledge, doctors began to be sent to the countryside to learn from "the people" as well as serve them. City doctors were regularly sent down to the countryside in small numbers through 1965, when Mao would publicly criticize the health ministry for putting most of its attention on cities, preparatory to launching the barefoot doctor program. At that time he described the ministry as *chengshi laoye* (old city master, a derogatory term for the urban elite) and emphasized the need to "focus all healthcare work in the countryside."[10] Well before this injunction, however, many doctors and health-care workers had been sent to the countryside, with the mission to "find new ways in old methods, and Sinicize all ways Western" (*gu wei jin yong, yang wei zhong yong*).

But returning to the Great Leap Forward, the most immediate and ultimately sustained response to the new directives in the pharmaceutical field was to search out previously unknown or obscure healing practices, which were now resurrected as new knowledge or medical innovations. In 1959, the Department for Research on Chinese Drugs of the Chinese Medicine Research Institute wrote a report summarizing its achievements since the start of Communist rule. It included a section on folk prescriptions, which the department described as "the people's experiences with finding medical cures in concrete form." Two categories of folk prescriptions, *danfang* (single-herb prescriptions) and *mifang* (secret recipes), were introduced:

> Historically speaking, folk prescriptions were comparatively simpler. Their ingredients were not only cheap and easy to find, but also functional. *Danfang* were generally known through word-of-mouth. The symptoms which they targeted, their required dosages and contraindications, if any, were usually not found in written form. And due to past restrictions imposed by authorities and special requirements for certain *danfang*, some of them were even kept secret. In those instances, they became known as *mifang* and knowledge of them was only in the hands of a few people who were either related by blood, or teacher and student. Some of these prescriptions thus became lost over time. Zhang Zhongjing, famous Han-period physician, also wrote in his *Shanghan Lun* encouraging the mass acquisition of lay medical experiences.[11]

This work of seeking out and compiling folk prescriptions had started even before the Great Leap Forward, but beginning around 1959, such collections began to be published on a large scale. This particular compendium included 450 *danfang* and *mifang*, collectively called *yanfang* in the title. *Yan* came from the Chinese word for "experience." The reason for publishing them, the department wrote, was to encourage physicians "to first apply those methods to clinical practice in various medical institutions . . . and then find out the symptoms that they target."[12] Thus while their efficacy as medicine was largely accepted, matching their powers of healing to specific symptoms or modern disease categories was presented as research that could still engage China's clinicians. In practice, however, many journal articles in which clinicians described their use of such medicines focused more on safety or side effects than on efficacy. Efficacy had been mostly proven to the satisfaction of the writers (or editors) by "the people's experience."

This project of legitimizing local folk-healing practices had actually started in the provinces, and the seemingly sudden publishing effort of the Great Leap Forward period likely drew to some extent on previous provincial efforts. In November 1956, for instance, the Yunnan Health Bureau had conducted a meeting of doctors from various ethnic groups to gather and consolidate their prescriptions into a two-volume treatise. They recorded a total of 1,794 *yanfang*, which were recategorized to conform to Western medical specialties such as pediatrics and internal and external medicines. Besides medicine for human use, agricultural bureaus at the provincial level, such as Shanxi province, had also compiled folk prescriptions that applied to animals.[13]

That more doctors were now going into the countryside could only have aided the discovery project, though urban sources of information were not neglected. One example was the book *Applying Chinese Drugs to Clinical Practice*, the work of a class of students and their teachers from Guangzhou Chinese Medical College, published in April 1960. The preface began,

> This book is a response to the call by the Central Committee to "combine education and productive labor." In the winter of 1958, the students of Class 568 put together this book mainly from experience gained in the course of their practicum. There is a pressing need for reference materials on drug use in the Huanan region. Most of the wild medicinals in this region remain unrecorded and it is therefore important to gather and consolidate them. . . . In compiling this book we also referred to classical materia medica, and recent magazine articles introducing the latest healing abilities of certain *zhongyao*. Also we interviewed famous Guangzhou

physicians on their experiences. We even visited medicine shops and interviewed folk physicians.[14]

The book included many examples of the use of animal tissue in folk medicine. In this and other ways, hitherto unrecorded regional "wild medicinals" joined the available corpus of nationally recognized materia medica.

According to one source, by the end of 1959 more than 200,000 recipes and prescriptions had been collected nationwide, and the Hebei Province Health Bureau had published half of them under the title *100,000 Golden Prescriptions*.[15] Correspondingly, journals began carrying many reports of patients cured by these folk remedies. By the mid-1960s, lists of such remedies commonly appeared in pharmaceutical journals, though cautious editors sometimes advised care in their ingestion. One editor made the qualification that "while most of these ingredients have been applied to clinical practice, it is still best to take precautionary measures when using them." Some recipes were quite benign, such as using ginger, table salt, and the white-colored stem of spring onion to cure the common cold. Author Kang Zhengjia claimed he had tested that recipe on 107 patients, and most of them were cured within one or two days. There were also folk prescriptions using whole insects or animal parts, such as ground beetle for backache and pig's testicle and liver to cure asthma and vitiligo, respectively.[16]

It is important to point out that the enthusiasm for compiling national or provincial compendiums of folk medicinals was mainly an urban phenomenon, and had little effect on the existing medical regimes of rural people except to reinforce the sense, of state actors, that folk medicine was appropriate for them. Chinese versions of Western drugs were not yet produced in enough quantity to meet the needs of villages. Historian Fang Xiaoping sees this gap as gradually closing, from the mid-1950s, but notes that, through the 1960s, the "pharmaceutical sales network only reached the commune level," meaning commune hospitals and union clinics.[17]

While folk medicine was being promoted on all levels, a parallel effort was ongoing in this period to bring *all* Chinese medicine into the mainstream of Chinese pharmacology. A milestone in this regard was the publication by the Chinese government in 1963 of the second edition of the official Communist-period pharmacopoeia. Although published after the Great Leap Forward, the compilation was clearly a product of that period. The 1963 edition differed from that of 1953 in including an additional volume dedicated exclusively to Chinese medicinals, listing 446 types of such drugs, including 51 derived from animals. There were also 197 prescriptions for the making of *chengyao* (Chinese patent drugs) in various forms, some of which included animal tissue. Besides conducting even more land surveys to locate previously untapped drugs, the authors claimed to have consulted old medicine shop workers whose ability to distinguish differences among medicinals was much valued.[18] National and regional drug-testing centers accordingly took on the responsibility of finding and recording the words of elderly workers, with different centers targeting different drugs and drug types. The Tianjin Drug Testing Center, for example, concentrated on six *guizhong* (expensive) drugs: ginseng, deer antler, musk, tiger bone, antelope horn, and rhino horn. The testing center in Qingdao documented fivefold that number, but mostly herbs.[19]

The colorful language that old medicine shop workers used to describe drugs, but especially animal parts, was sometimes recorded in the new pharmacopoeia. For instance, the seahorse was described as an animal "with a head like that of a horse, and body like that of a snake but replete with lines just like an ark shell." In describing the rhino horn, however, geographical images were evoked. The side of the horn curving inward was known as the "heavenly ditch," while the larger base was likened to a mound. The uneven surface of the base was also noted, and compared with "toddlers' teeth about to emerge."[20] This represented an expansion from the language of the laboratory to include that of the medicine shop, but the transition was still incomplete. Nanjing-based medicine shop worker Zou Jianbai, for example, taught that one needed to activate all five senses when authenticating a drug specimen, a skill that could not be captured and described in print.[21]

Thus by the end of the Great Leap Forward, at least in the world of pharmacology, the lingering separation between Chinese medicine as a set of literate and elite understandings, on the one hand, and as a set of folk remedies or prescriptions, on the other, had begun to be breached. Chinese physicians might maintain distinctions, but all materia medica was now to be grist for the drug-discovery and drug-making mill. In fact, the move toward folk medicine, while partly ideological and economic, was also a natural extension of Chinese pharmacology's self-appointed mission to survey, collect, analyze, and, where possible, reformulate all available Chinese natural resources, be they vegetable, mineral, or animal.

The Case of Chicken Blood Therapy

The trends we have traced so far—namely the emphasis on innovating at the boundary between Chinese and Soviet medicine, the growing interest in folk medicine, the new emphasis on "cures," and the increased medical charisma of animal tissue because of its links to both folk medicine and Soviet-inspired organotherapy—all come together in the phenomenon of chicken blood therapy. For a treatment that stirred so much excitement in the late 1960s, it remains surprisingly under-commented-on in Western scholarship, likely because of its perceived eccentricity.[22] Although it is difficult to ascribe the emergence of this practice to a purely medical need, real or imagined, it well reflects the intimate links we have been tracing between medicine and politics, and how state interest in faunal medicine emerged at their juncture.

Chicken blood therapy describes the direct injection of chicken blood (from live chickens) into human bodies. Crafted in the early 1950s, the therapy emerged publicly during the Great Leap Forward, was suppressed, but then revived, reaching the height of its popularity during the Cultural Revolution. Its inventor described it as "meet[ing] the official standards of simplicity, convenience, and affordability," echoing Mao's injunctions to extend health care to the masses.[23] Although chicken blood therapy was originally intended for rural patients, it was mainly an urban phenomenon in practice, first taking off in Shanghai. It migrated to villages only after it had been suppressed in the cities, around 1970, when it showed up in training manuals for barefoot doctors.[24]

Chicken blood therapy has been likened in some retrospective Chinese accounts to witchcraft, because patients became hyperactive upon receiving it.[25] In fact, the Chinese expression *dajixue* (injecting chicken blood) has now entered colloquial vocabulary to describe a person in a state of overexcitement as the result of an external stimulant. It was probably not its novelty but its runaway popularity and, eventually, the politics around its promotion that caused scientists, health authorities, and a number of doctors to single it out for censure, then and now. Besides chicken blood, however, many types of animal tissue, from bear bile to musk and deer antler, were experimented with in the same period for use as injectable substances. Earthworm, fish liver oil, and pig bile would also become injectables in the 1960s. Many of these therapies were, moreover, promoted by reputable Chinese physicians and published in medical and pharmacological journals.[26]

The medicinal use of chickens (and geese) was not fully outside of Chinese medical tradition, but neither was it common. The twentieth-century medicalization of chicken blood can best be described as a fusion of references in early Chinese texts, with the Western technology of injection (and limited use of clinical trials), and the early obsession with Soviet tissue therapy. Its links to Soviet medical theory and the use of injection made it "scientific" in the eyes of its proponents, while the use of fowls gave it a vague link with "folk medicine" as interpreted by urban-dwellers. Ultimately, however, its identity as a new innovation, its forceful promotion, and its political location in the turmoil of the Cultural Revolution gave it a status unique among the many animal-based therapies of this period.

The inventor and lead promoter of chicken blood therapy was Yu Changshi, born into a landlord family in Nanling, Anwei province, in 1903, who had received a university education in Western medicine. Despite his upper-class lineage, Yu was drawn to socialist politics and briefly jailed by the government in 1931. Upon release, he was sent to work in Nanfeng county, Jiangxi province, where, according to his own account, he recalled chicken blood being mentioned in classical descriptions of materia medica, though only for external use, particularly as an eye drop.[27] He began experiments on chickens by sticking thermometers up their rectums to measure their average body temperatures, which he calculated as 43 degrees Celsius (109.4 degrees Fahrenheit). The unusually high temperature of chickens suggested to Yu that their ability to "fight germs and toxicity [du] must be exceptionally high."[28] This combination of modern veterinary research and reference to scraps of classical text induced Yu to develop the idea of injecting chicken blood into humans. That idea came to him in 1952, the year Mao launched the Five-Anti Movement (Wu Fan Yundong) to remove all forms of capitalism.

Yu also acknowledged, however, the direct influence of the Soviet concept of tissue therapy. "Tissue therapy was very popular then [the early 1950s]" wrote Yu, "and I began to think about using chicken blood."[29] To recall, this therapy was the brainchild of V. P. Filatov, based on earlier research in organotherapy, whereby the injection of substances made from human tissues like skin, liver, brain, placenta, bile, or lung fluid into another human could supposedly cure or fortify the same tissue from disease. Alternatively, raw tissue was to be inserted directly underneath the patient's skin. That chicken blood (according to Yu) had some tradition of being used in China as an eye drop likely also helped suggest the connection to Filatov's therapy, which was centered on eye repair.

Although Yu never referenced what the Soviets called "blood science," it is also notable that Russian scientists had previously forged links between socialism and the rejuvenation of bodies through blood transfusion. This theory, which had no equivalent in Western biomedicine, was advanced by the prominent Bolshevik Alexander Bogdanov, who founded a state institute to study and promote the rejuvenating effects of transfused blood in the 1920s. According to Krementsov, who chronicles this phenomenon in detail,

Bogdanov's ideas were related to a larger "rejuvenation craze" that swept the Soviet Union in that decade, making rejuvenation "a fixture of Russian popular culture" and "arguably the hottest topic in experimental medicine and biology." Bogdanov concentrated on human-to-human and not animal-to-human tissue exchange. But he argued that blood was the most vital human tissue, and that its transfusion should supplant the earlier obsession, spurred by organotherapy, with "vital secretions" of the glandular kind.[30]

There is also evidence that the Chinese experimented with cross-species blood transfusion during the Korean War, which may also have contributed to Yu's comfortability with the practice. In a 1976 instruction manual on blood transfusion written for barefoot doctors, in question-and-answer format, one question asks whether pig's blood serum can be injected into the human body. The answer, a qualified yes, relates that research on pig's blood had been conducted "during war-time," when human blood was scarce. According to the manual, that research had shown that animal blood in raw form was incompatible with that of humans, but could be injected into the human body after proper treatment. Even then, the barefoot doctor could administer treated pig's blood serum only to those patients with no history of allergy or hemorrhage, and in quantities of no more than six hundred milliliters a day.[31] This section was likely added precisely because of the intervening popularity of chicken blood therapy, which had dispensed with the manual's cautions.[32]

As is common in the history of clinical innovations, Yu's first patient was himself. In 1953, he injected 1.55 cubic centimeters of blood from a six-month-old male chicken into his shoulder muscle. He claimed not to have felt or noticed any side effects, but rather recalled being in very good spirits and having a good appetite a day or so after the injection, as well as sleeping better. By the fourth day, he observed what he called "a miracle." For ten or more years, Yu wrote, he had suffered from blisters, peeling on his feet, and an itching scalp. Suddenly he recovered from all those conditions, and his family even noticed a new glow to his skin.[33] By coincidence or design, Yu's report of his initial self-injection closely mirrored the moment in late nineteenth-century France when Charles-Édouard Brown-Séquard, the founder of organotherapy, had injected himself with an extract from pig's testicles and reported similar feelings of rejuvenation.

Encouraged by his experiments with self-injection, Yu began also injecting his fifteen-year-old daughter, who suffered from frequent stomachaches. He claimed that she recovered from that condition after only one treatment. Yu then started experimenting on his patients. He specifically mentioned peasants who had severe leg infections from working long hours in wet paddy fields, for example: "One peasant had cellulitis on his thigh, and came down with high fever for three to four days. Pus was beginning to form. Due to the lack of penicillin, I decided to inject the peasant with chicken blood. Both fever and pain stopped that very night. The peasant also slept better. He was completely recovered after the second injection." The "lack of penicillin" is noteworthy, because so much of the Chinese drug-discovery program in this period involved finding cheaper native substitutes for expensive Western medicines, including biomedicine produced in China. Yu's use of chicken blood was fully convergent with this goal. He soon expanded the therapy in his own practice as a substitute for even those biomedical drugs meant to treat severe diseases.[34]

Yu's research was temporarily interrupted, however, when he was transferred to Shanghai to work as director of the Yong'an nursing home. By his own account Yu became busy, having to attend to one hundred sick beds, and thus he abandoned further research on chicken blood until 1959, when he became inspired by the slogans and speeches promoting innovation that accompanied the Great Leap Forward.[35]

Yu relaunched his therapy in a dramatic way, appearing among workers of Shanghai Yong'an cotton mill at eight o'clock in the morning on May 26, 1959, and publicly injecting himself with chicken blood as a demonstration of its efficacy and safety. More than forty workers from the cotton mill reportedly went to Yu for chicken blood injections that afternoon. Even before this public demonstration, Yu had already given chicken blood injections to a number of workers, discreetly, and recorded more so-called miracles: chronic coughs stopping just five minutes after an injection, those suffering from insomnia due to breathlessness sleeping well that same night, and stomach problems clearing. Yu later claimed that he saw more than three hundred patients in the next couple of months, giving most of them one to two injections, but some five or more. According to Yu, those with the most injections made the most dramatic progress. Another Chinese source claimed that Yu reported his results in a letter to the Shanghai Municipal Health Bureau.[36] A follow-up investigation by health authorities showed that he actually saw only 203 patients, but this was still a large enough figure to create significant word-of-mouth publicity in Shanghai.[37]

By his own account, Yu had been apprehensive prior to his public demonstration and the resulting mass injections. He wrote, "In order to be effective, a doctor has to personally test the drug. I was worried that patients would have adverse reactions to chicken blood, and so I took the first shot."

Yu continued to inject himself daily with chicken blood and felt all right, drawing the conclusion that his therapy "promotes general well-being." In fact, he had by this time given chicken blood therapy another name: *qiangzhuang liaofa* (health-boosting therapy). He went on to list more than a hundred conditions—from low sex drive to leukemia—that the therapy had cured, buttressing his claims with personal testimonies like the following: "Many people gave the feedback that they developed a higher sex drive soon after the injection and that, at night, their *yang* element rose on its own. 'High libido after chicken blood injection' was the comment given by a female doctor at an enlarged conference of the Chicken Blood Small Research Team. Recovery was seen in those suffering from *yangkui* [impotency] and *yijing* [spermatorrhea]. Women who were barren or had missed their period also found cure in chicken blood therapy."[38] It was most likely hospital staff who made up the "small research team" reportedly founded by Yu. He had postings in a number of Shanghai institutions during the early 1960s, including Shuguang, Number Six, and Longhua hospitals, and claimed that, over a five-year period, chicken blood was used by himself and others between forty thousand to fifty thousand times, and "all proved effective after one shot" (*yizhen jian xiao*). Yu even quoted the director of the then Shanghai Public Hospital as saying, "Chicken blood is even more effective than the elixir mentioned in novels for treating gastritis, stomach cancer, and neurosis." The head of the eye department at Shuguang hospital, who also used chicken blood on his patients, commented, "We have achieved a 72.7 percent cure rate for conditions that elude even foreign specialists. We have surpassed international standards through the use of chicken blood."[39] This was the reason, according to Yu, that the health ministry had not popularized chicken blood therapy—its remarkable effectiveness made it a Chinese state secret.[40]

Some Chinese secondary sources weave a different story, however. According to them it was the government, and not Yu, that set up the initial research team, out of concern for its unorthodoxy. In April 1960, officials of the Health Bureau for Shanghai Jing'an district interviewed Yu's patients—all 203 of them—and found one-third had suffered from various side effects, though the rest reported improved health. The health bureau decided that more studies were needed to ascertain the therapy's efficacy and safety. In October the same year, a research team comprising representatives of the bureau and the district's labor union, and also Yu himself, carried out more closely monitored clinical trials at a laboratory set up at the Sanitary and Epidemic Prevention Station (*weisheng fangyi zhan*) in Jing'an. Earlier, the team had found serum reactions in the animals used for testing chicken blood, though they were mild compared with their reactions to similar substances, such as horse blood. Between October 1960 and December 1962, according to one account, the research team conducted experiments on more than 1,300 human subjects. Seventeen participants eventually withdrew. The report produced at the end highlighted the severity of side effects, which accordingly incurred the wrath of Yu. He then accused "experts" in the team of being conservative and having falsified the report.[41]

The report did demonstrate some positive results, however. On the whole, patients showed short-term healing from problems like excessive menstruation and gastric ulcer. Many reportedly gained in appetite and slept better. Yet again, the negative side effects were considered so drastic that even though these cases made up only 16 percent of total trials, they quickly overshadowed the positives.[42] These were patients who had received more than four chicken blood injections and who, by the fifth or sixth day, developed hot flashes, diarrhea, nettle rash, and fear of cold. Six patients fell into a coma, but were given "emergency revival" so that no deaths occurred during the experimentation. The official interest in chicken blood was great enough, however, that discussions began about mitigating its worst effects, which were thought to relate to the direct cross-species transfusion of untreated blood. Thus did the Jing'an District Health Bureau and Shanghai Biochemical Factory collaborate to treat and reproduce chicken blood in powder form according to the same procedures for making dried, powdered placenta. They then tested chicken blood powder on fifteen thousand people and found no side effects.[43]

Yu strongly refuted the claim regarding side effects, however, and in addition to that, accused authorities of defying official guidelines by making the therapy more expensive through processing it into powder. According to Yu, sixty *yuan* was needed to produce one hundred grams of chicken blood powder, which was costly at that time.[44] Eventually, Yu left the team and set up his own practice specializing in raw chicken blood injection. Representatives from the Shanghai Municipal Health Bureau approached him several times to close his practice but failed. Probed by its Beijing headquarters, the Shanghai Municipal Health Bureau in June 1965 convened a meeting of experts to discuss the safety of administering chicken blood injections. Everyone in the meeting agreed that injecting chicken blood into humans could cause severe allergic reactions (due to a non-compatible protein kinase), and on July 23, 1965, the Central Health Ministry banned chicken blood therapy nationwide.

Chicken Blood Therapy and the Cultural Revolution

Chicken blood therapy might have been remembered as a footnote to the Great Leap Forward had it not been for Yu's zeal in continuing to promote it into the period of the early Cultural Revolution, when it was given a second birth. In October 1965, Yu wrote to prominent political figure Kang Sheng (one of the architects of the Cultural Revolution) and eventually gained his ear. A year later, in August 1966, Yu defiantly produced and distributed a handbook titled *Chicken Blood Therapy*, promoting his banned direct-injection method. Four months later, in December 1966, the health ministry suddenly lifted the earlier ban.[45] The ministry's reversal was likely spurred by more than one source of pressure. Yu's therapy became an issue of medical politics just at the time the Cultural Revolution was beginning, and soon became caught up in that movement. Mao's severe criticism of the health ministry as elitist had come at nearly the very moment that the therapy was banned, thus making it emblematic of economical grassroots innovations that official medicine had rejected. Yu naturally took full advantage of the political turn, making his chicken blood therapy the very expression of "red medicine."

The Red Guards and "revolutionary teams" also played a significant role in reviving Yu's innovation. As one account from the period relates, "After the launch of the Cultural Revolution, Red Guards from both the capital Beijing and Shanghai set up an investigation team. They traveled throughout the country and confirmed that for eight years the Chinese people were deprived of the use of Chicken Blood Therapy. Upon their return to Beijing, the investigation team received official support and on 28 December 1966 the 'old city master' that is the Health Ministry, removed the ban on Chicken Blood Therapy."[46] In the same document, no less a figure than Prime Minister Zhou Enlai was quoted as saying, vehemently, that "the Central Health Ministry has defied Mao Zedong's thoughts in the way it handled Chicken Blood Therapy!" The Red Guards and revolutionary teams held both the Ministry of Health and Shanghai Municipal Health Bureau responsible, and castigated them in the fashion typical of the Cultural Revolution, using words like *zaofan* (literally, to make revolt). When the health ministry finally issued a statement to reinstate chicken blood therapy at the end of 1966, a Red Guard unit enthused that "this revolt was well-made, correctly made, and excellently made."[47]

Yu's handbook was reprinted in 1967 by the so-called Qinghai Province Eight-One-Eight Post and Telecommunications Revolutionary Team.[48] In

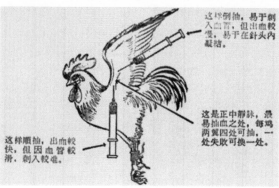

4.1 & 4.2 The cover of the booklet *Chicken Blood Therapy* (*Jixue Liaofu*) and one of its illustrations, showing Yu's recommended method of blood extraction, using a needle inserted underneath the chicken's wing. QINGHAI SHENG BA YI BA YOUDIAN ZAO-FAN TUAN BIANYIN, *JIXUE LIAOFA* (1967).

July that year even the Ministry of Health, fearing more attacks, created its own Red Heart Revolutionary Team, one of the main tasks of which became gathering Red Guards from Beijing and Shanghai and sending them in groups of fifteen to spread the news about chicken blood therapy throughout China. More specifically, they were told to highlight its contribution to the national slogan, "Prepare for War, Prepare for Famine, and Serve the People" (*Bei Zhan Bei Huang Wei Renmin*).[49] As China became increasingly estranged from the outside world, the revival of chicken blood therapy came to be seen as part of a "political war" against not only the bureaucracy, but also China's enemies abroad. The expansion of the Five-Anti Movement to include not just capitalism but "everything from cows, to ghosts, to snakes and all kinds of gods" basically gave the Red Guards free rein over what or whom to denounce.[50]

In the case of medicine, the broad target of the campaign was elite expertise.

In November 1966, Shanghai Chinese Medical College issued a declaration in the name of the Red Guards, which interpreted Mao's formulation of the mass line (*qunzhong luxian*) as encouraging people to "educate" and "liberate" themselves through innovation. The Red Guards defined the phrase "achieving (or surpassing) international standards" as any innovation that "has been proven through practice [*shijian*], and caters to the needs of the world's population." They coined the term "classless medical professionals" to reinforce Mao's idea that even the uneducated public could invent cures. The Ministry of Health was accused of practicing "political tutelage" (*xunzheng*), a phrase associated with the Kuomintang.[51]

A subsequent letter to the public, titled "In Defense of New Matter in Medical Research," zeroed in on chicken blood therapy as the ideal of red medicine. According to its authors, by dismissing chicken blood therapy as "not science," the health ministry had promoted a Western understanding of "experts" and "scholars" that excluded the wisdom of the general population. The authors questioned the meaning of science-based medicine and provided their own definition as "anything that removes pain, cures diseases, and proves effective." The writers related how, prior to the Health Ministry's ban, "the people would each carry a chicken and wait in line for the doctor, or they would inject themselves with chicken blood [but] some cities encountered a shortage of chickens and injection tools," which was the fault of the ministry. The letter also expressed indignation over the treatment of Yu by health officials, who were accused of confiscating his research materials and letters, and denying his right of speech.[52]

The radicals claimed that there were neither major side effects nor occurrences of death from the use of chicken blood. This they based on their own experiments, which they conducted separately from those of the health ministry. In fact, another round of tests conducted by the ministry, from March 1966, was described as "attempts to plot against Chicken Blood Therapy." These experiments were considered by the radicals as "nonscientific," since they were conducted in elite medical institutions (Beijing and Shanghai hospitals) and not in clinical settings. A year later, the Eight-One-Eight Post and Telecommunications Revolutionary Team of Qinghai Province wrote about its own experiments: "First, we conducted preliminary investigations by interviewing *daifu* and patients who had used Chicken Blood Therapy. . . . On 4 August 1967, we launched our battle by injecting chicken blood into sixty or so people. The results were significant and totally matched the research findings of Yu. . . . On 29 of August, we set up our own clinic to administer Chicken Blood Therapy (limited only to Post and Telecommunications staff and their family members)."[53] It was clear from their writings that the radicals were using chicken blood therapy as a lever in their fight against the health bureaucracy in general. In fact, the letter to the public declared the writers were speaking for all the "new matters" that were invented by nonexperts, and not just chicken blood therapy. That Yu was himself a Western-trained physician was never mentioned.

There were also more pragmatic reasons behind the revival of chicken blood therapy. Red Guards had considered large-scale medicinal farming to be a form of capitalist activity, and the production of herbal medicines thus fell sharply during the Cultural Revolution.[54] The resulting shortage in regular pharmaceuticals may partly explain why chicken blood injection became much sought after. There were stories of long queues at hospitals (with patients bringing their own chickens), and the conviction among some that chicken blood could forestall death. A story set in Kaifeng, Henan province went,

It was the early 1970s. There began somewhere in China a new treatment called injecting chicken blood which created much fervor. This was bad news for the chickens, however. Only young roosters were used. Blood was drawn from under their wings and straightaway injected into the human buttock. Chicken blood if cooled would lose all healing abilities. Or so it was believed. Both my parents were doctors, and nobody I knew had taken chicken blood injection except my father's friend who was also a doctor in a district hospital. His doctor friend would visit us every day and rave about new happenings at his workplace, especially chicken blood injection. My father's friend was heading the outpatient department when this treatment reached Kaifeng. He charged ten cents for each jab and had a nurse do the job. The hospital would earn ten to twenty *yuan* each day from this. For half a year, the doctor friend injected chicken blood into his own father after he got a stroke. When his father eventually died from a second stroke, the friend lamented that due to financial difficulties he had not given his father more chicken blood injections.[55]

Chicken blood therapy eventually traveled as far south as Guangzhou. As in most places, the craze there lasted about ten months between 1967 and 1968. According to author Wu Zhijing, who lived through this period, morale in the city was then low because of the excesses of the Cultural Revolution, and there was chaos day and night. Food, medicine, and housing were scarce, and there was little or no work. Civilians were given a meager sum of between twenty to thirty *yuan* at the end of each month. The arrival in Guangzhou of chicken blood therapy, according to Wu, temporarily transformed the overall mood of frustration and fear. On hearing that a certain hospital team was offering the injections, many immediately put their faith in the new treatment, and soon the usual long queues began to form outside hospitals and *weisheng* stations. Patients brought their own chickens, and those who left written accounts of this episode recalled scenes of filth developing around health-care premises caused by chicken feathers and feces.[56]

As chicken blood therapy became widespread, alternate accounts of its origins began to appear, some of them apocryphal. Sang Ye, who lived through the Cultural Revolution, retrospectively recorded this version in a 1992 essay:

> During the civil war, a former Kuomintang medical officer was captured by the CCP police and given the death penalty. In exchange for his life, the officer offered up a "secret recipe" for longevity that was chicken blood injection. Apparently, Kuomintang leader Chiang Kai-shek had kept himself alive by injecting chicken blood. On hearing this, the chief of a hinterland province ordered his nurse to administer the injection and soon news of it spread. There were plans to revive China using this medical practice, but were dropped because of the vastness of the project (China was simply too big) not to mention its connection ultimately to Chang and his Kuomintang party. Nevertheless, it was the upper echelon of Chinese society that had invented Chicken Blood Therapy and by 1965, had popularized the saying "Injecting Chicken Blood to Cure a Hundred Illnesses" (*Da Jixue Zhi Baibing*).[57]

4.3 A retrospective illustration showing people during the Cultural Revolution lined up in front of a clinic with chickens under their arms, waiting to be injected with raw chicken blood. FROM JING FANG, *WO SHI LIU LING HOU 1969–1978* (BEIJING: NEW STAR PRESS, 2010).

Sang Ye's narrative continues into the Cultural Revolution, when the same chief of the hinterland province had fallen from grace. During an interrogation session by the Red Guards, the chief confessed that he had taken chicken blood injections to prolong life, but remained elusive when asked why he did not share this with the people. The former chief's reticence on the treatment was interpreted by the Red Guards as capitalist behavior, and he was publicly shamed.[58]

Although chicken blood was advertised as curing up to a hundred diseases, most people likely took it as a source of nourishment (*busheng* or *yangsheng*). Patients reportedly felt stronger and had redder cheeks after the injection. A later medical article explains, "These physical manifestations were only reactions from the human immune system. During the Mao period, people did not have much medical knowledge to discern the difference, not to mention during the Cultural Revolution, when bizarre discoveries like chicken blood injection were actually welcomed."[59] Mao Xianglin, who had injected chicken blood into more than two hundred people, recalled, "There were certainly side effects, but there was nothing we could do since medical care and facilities were lacking. One basically threw oneself to any medical option available."[60] And when the Ministry of Health announced in 1967 that chicken blood therapy was the latest cutting-edge invention in medical research, the treatment attracted the attention of even more people, though some intellectuals secretly called it a "strange hormone."[61]

Dissent was not restricted to experts. Some regular Chinese also had doubts about the treatment. Su Zhiwu wrote,

I was in junior high school and so old enough to remember what actually happened. My father worked as a factory accountant and was educated. He made the sharp comment that since blood types must be matched before a transfusion could take place, shouldn't chicken blood be subject to the same test? Although my mother was only a housewife, she was wise enough to stay out of the craze. She joked about not needing asses and horses since even rabbits were strong enough to pull carriages after being injected with chicken blood. Still, my mother constantly warned my brother and me against publicly sharing those comments as they could potentially get the family into trouble. One afternoon while having lunch, my brother suddenly remembered seeing in the newspaper our second commander-in-chief looking absolutely emaciated and said he should really go for chicken blood injection. My mother turned to look at my brother wide-eyed, and then beat the living daylights out of him.[62]

According to some sources, only young roosters were to be used. The best chickens were considered to be those weighing more than two kilograms, white, with nice feathers and voice, which were rare to find during the Cultural Revolution. Foreign breeds (especially Italian) were preferred.[63] There was also a rule about not drawing blood from the same chicken more than once.[64] As such, it was common to find households in cities including Beijing keeping three to four chickens solely for injection. Up to one hundred milliliters of blood was drawn each time but used over a number of patients. The recommended number of injections was two a week.[65] The needle used to draw the blood from the chickens was usually replaced by a new one when injecting it into humans, though some recalled seeing the same needle being used for both procedures.[66]

Yu claimed, erroneously, that all chickens belonged to the blood type O and so were safe for transfusion.[67] Although he strongly recommended the blood of young roosters, especially those that were just learning to crow, since "they contain the most male hormones," Yu also allowed the use of female chickens in non-gynecological settings. He advised the number of injections be three a week, and on alternate days, and identified the shoulder muscle, and not the buttocks, as the best point of injection. Yu also suggested mixing chicken blood with other drugs such as liver extract, Novocain, and vitamins B12 and B1. He even gave specific instructions (with illustrations) on how to draw blood from the chicken: "Under the wing of a normal chicken is a long, visible vein. It is the same as the median antebrachial vein of a human. Blood can be drawn from both sides. First, remove all feathers on one end of the vein. Second, apply iodine tincture and then alcohol to kill all germs. Lastly, use needle no. 7 or 8 to draw the blood. I recommend shortening the needle (by a quarter) to prevent blood clots. Blood drawn in the morning is of the best quality."[68]

By the early 1960s, the technique of injection had become common in China, promoted by such popular books as *An Introduction to Painless Injection*. Published in 1957 by a nurse named Liang Jielian, the book sought to overcome the acute pain felt by both young and adult patients when punctured by needles, to the extent that "some collapsed out of fear even before the injection took place." Thus had the author began a study of the possible causes of pain and clot formations from taking injections, but (she claimed) had only made serious breakthroughs following the Revolution. Wrote Liang,

> After 1943, I was burdened by tedious housework. The old society [that is, under Kuomintang rule] did not provide measures to lighten the load

of working mothers. I had no choice but to leave my nursing job for as long as eight years. In 1949, under the enlightened leadership of the Communist Party, China was not only liberated but also institutions like the nursery were set up in increasing numbers and speed. In 1950, the nursery managed by the Department of Heavy Industries accepted my two children. A few years later, they entered the affiliated primary school with boarding facility. I was freed from domestic duties, and could devote more time to research.[69]

At the time she wrote, Liang was working at the Ping'an Hospital in Beijing, and had been dispatched to work at the treatment room. Through direct clinical study, she devised a number of methods to help reduce pain experienced during injection with the idea of increasing its acceptance. Thus even painless injection was presented as a "new innovation" by a humble medical worker, one that not only accompanied chicken blood therapy but likely contributed to its widespread use.[70]

Injection had become so common in China by the mid-1960s that notices began to appear advising against its overuse as a drug delivery method. In 1965, the regulatory department of a provincial health bureau wrote, "In recent years, sixty percent of drugs administered have been in the form of injection. While some of these were necessary, most were because the patients demanded it. Unknown to even doctors, injection can lead to detrimental results."[71] The department went on to list a number of side effects, such as a sudden rise in temperature leading to muscle dysfunction. The writer also mentioned witnessing many cases of severe allergic reactions to injection when doing his rounds in the hospital, and highlighted the danger of injection directly into the vein.[72] Yu, on the other hand, had argued that chicken blood therapy was most effective when injected in just that manner. The effect, to quote him, "is even better" than the more usual use of the buttocks or shoulder.[73]

Yu's chicken blood therapy depended on a large network of actors and circumstances for its proliferation. Even after Yu left the research team organized by the Shanghai Jing'an district, he did not work alone but had the support of a core group of doctors who continued to administer chicken blood despite the official ban.[74] The Red Guards and higher communist officials were clearly actors in the therapy's propagation, as were health workers who, lacking medical supplies, made "red medicine" out of chickens and needles. Chinese "folk," however, in the form of peasants or urban workers, were not involved in the invention or promotion of the therapy, except as patients, which made its actual connection with the masses highly tenable.

When news of deaths from chicken blood injection began to surface and be reported in 1968, the therapy came to an abrupt end in the larger Chinese cities, though its practice continued for some time in towns like Kaifeng in Henan province and Xishuangbanna in Yunnan province. Despite overall skepticism, the fact that health authorities conducted extensive studies on chicken blood therapy showed they were willing to consider it as a medical option. This is in line with the broader sociopolitical context of the time, when all resources were potentially medicine, and innovation of all sorts was encouraged. By the middle of the Cultural Revolution, however, chicken blood therapy had proven itself to be a craze that, likely because of its political associations, could not sustain itself as politics changed. It did, however, open the door to many similar therapies that, while equally unusual, were not so wrapped in revolutionary fervor (some of which we examine below). Chicken blood injections have occasionally resurfaced into the current century, but in contrast to the 1960s, the therapy's later promoters or adherents have been almost universally dismissed as tricksters or charlatans, though "miracle cures" remain a steadfast tradition in Chinese medicine and continue to periodically induce novel therapies.[75]

Beyond Chicken Blood Therapy:
Toads, Geese, Ducks, and Lizards

Chicken blood therapy is remembered in China today as an eccentricity of the Cultural Revolution, one that was eventually stopped through the exercise of reason. But there was actually a proliferation of similar new therapies based on animal tissue during this period, some invented even into the mid-1970s, years after chicken blood therapy had been banned. Many were the projects of well-educated physicians, like Yu, operating before a national audience (i.e., writing books and publishing in journals) and claiming folk practices as their initial inspiration. And, as in the case in chicken blood therapy, many of these cures were presented as unusually powerful alternatives to biomedicine, whose shortcomings in curing fatal diseases like cancer were increasingly stressed.

One example was the rise in the popularity of toad therapy during the mid-1970s. Because Mao's health was declining due to old age, medical research began focusing on folk cures to alleviate the effects of aging and, in the process, discovered folk recipes involving toads.[76] Thereafter toad research proliferated. In 1976, for instance, the physician Ge Hanshu contributed an article on the subject to the journal *Xin Zhongyi*. He began by assigning the animal characteristics based on Siqi Wuwei (four natures, five tastes), a standard formula in the use of traditional materia medica. Ge described toad tissue as poisonous, acrid to the taste, and having an overall cooling effect. He also listed a number of its traditionally understood healing abilities, the most important of which was its antiseptic nature. He lastly gave examples of both historic and recent prescriptions using whole toads or toad secretions as ingredients.[77]

The bulk of Ge's article, however, described his own clinic-based experiments, most of which involved using raw parts of the toad, especially their heads. In treating patients with abscesses on their fingers and toes, Ge cut off the heads of live toads and inserted them like finger-puppets on the infected digits. He recommended between one to three applications on alternate days, with a fresh toad used for each. Ge scrupulously provided case studies with the surnames of the patients/subjects followed by their gender, age, and both the commune and production brigade to which they belonged. For example, he described thirty-four-year-old Duan, a male worker from the Yitao brigade of Yitao Commune, as having suffered a cut toe while working in the fields. Duan left the wound untreated and it became severely infected. Ge tried all kinds of other treatments without success. Duan recovered, according to the account, only after covering his injured toe with the heads of toads in three separate applications.[78]

Ge went beyond folk tradition, however, in claiming that toad-based recipes could treat even more serious diseases, such as asthma. His instructions for curing that condition included dropping twenty white peppers into the mouth of a live frog or toad, wrapping it in mud, and baking it in a furnace. The toad was removed from the furnace once the mud turned red, and then crushed into powder. Ge suggested one toad as a weekly dosage, with the resulting powder taken twice daily. He named his invention "toad pepper powder" (chanyu hujiao san). Like the responsible researcher he claimed to be, Ge was careful to observe and note side effects. In cases of overdose, patients became nauseous and some vomited. There were also instances in his experience wherein the mouth or the entire body of the patient became numb. As a solution, Ge proposed either drinking green bean soup or reducing the dosage. Only in the worst-case scenarios had he stopped the medication altogether.[79]

Even after chicken blood therapy had been officially discredited in the late 1960s, therapies involving goose and duck blood surfaced in the early 1970s as alleged cures for dysphagia (i.e., difficulty swallowing) and gastric cancer. Again, this became a research program among reputable physicians, whose reports purported to follow normative research conventions. In this instance, however, the initial origin point for the project was not only folk medicine, but also the supporting "discovery" of neglected references in classical texts. Zhang Mengnong of Hubei Chinese Medical College contributed a number of articles on this topic between 1973 and 1976, providing detailed summaries of his clinic-based experiments. Zhang also wrote extensively on the historical folk use of goose and duck blood, especially in the treatment of the condition called *yege*, the symptoms of which he claimed were similar to those of dysphagia, in that patients had difficulty swallowing or digesting their food. *Yege* was considered incurable by ancient physicians since its cause remained unknown. Wrote Zhang, "Our ancestors were limited in their means to pinpoint the etiology of *yege*. While some argued that it was the result of a malignant tumor that prevented certain organs from working properly, many believed that the main causes were blood stasis and *qi* stagnation." It was not until the Cultural Revolution, Zhang claimed, that *yege* was found to be synonymous with the Western disease categories of esophageal and gastric cancer. Zhang credited this finding to the "correct path taken by medical personnel to combine Chinese and Western medicines."[80] In this and other instances, the popular slogan *Zhongxiyi Jiehe* (combine Chinese and Western medicines) was interpreted as innovating Chinese medicine to cure disease categories recognized by both medical traditions.

Zhang humbly described himself as an eighty-one-year-old physician suffering from coronary heart disease who "does not possess broad knowledge." But sources told him that duck and goose blood had been used as early as the Ming period, when physician Li Shizhen sanctioned their medicinal qualities, and even recommended the use of duck and goose feathers. Clearer evidence of its use was a 1695 compilation of twelve volumes of writings by Zhang Luyu, titled *Zhang's Medical Annals* (*Zhangshi Yitong*). The contemporary Zhang described these as *yanfang*, that is, prescriptions based on clinical experience alone. One described a patient, by the surname Wang, who vomited every time he ate. Wang consulted many physicians, but none knew the cause of his illness. He took such medicinals as cow and horse bezoar, tiger's stomach, and cat placenta, without effect, until an advice came to "drink the hot blood of a live goose." Wang followed the advice and was supposedly cured.[81]

Besides medical books, Zhang also provided a list of Qing-period novels that exhorted the efficacy of duck and goose blood. Two examples were *Gusheng* and *Xiangzu Biji*, both written in the early eighteenth century.[82] One story in *Gusheng* was about a monk who died and had his body burnt to ashes, leaving behind only bones. A duck was later killed and, upon contact with its blood, the monk's bones immediately dissolved. Zhang clarified that such stories were not to be accepted without question, but were to serve as a basis for contemporary research into substances historically recognized as having special powers.

Zhang next described his own experiments, which he claimed had extended over three decades and had resulted in scores of dysphagia patients being cured with goose blood.[83] Zhang aimed not only to prove earlier claims, but also to test the healing ability of goose blood on diseases without effective biomedical cures. For instance, Zhang reinterpreted the Chinese term *du* (poison) to also mean cancer. He wrote, "The blood of white goose and duck can be used to counteract all kinds of poison. Whether one sees it or not, anything that comes into contact with the human body and brings suffering (or even death) is poison. Today, some consider a tumor as a form of contagious poison. To quote our ancestors, the hot blood of geese and ducks can 'counteract the effects of raw gold and silver, *danshi*, arsenic . . . and even revive the dead.' As such, I believe that their ability to remove poison [*jie du*] far surpass all other medicinals."[84] Zhang attempted to add additional weight to such claims through reference to animal physiology, particularly lessons allegedly proven through dissection. He claimed to have discovered snail shells (in powdered form) mixed with duck and goose droppings in farmyards, leading him to conclude that both geese and ducks could swallow and digest whole snail shells. Given such unusually strong powers of digestion, Zhang was led to the conclusion that both animals "must also possess a special substance to fight cancer," by which he meant to dissolve tumors. His friend Xu Shoucheng thus performed an experiment by inserting a copper coin into the crop of a duck. The following day, Xu killed and dissected the duck and found the coin half-dissolved. Zhang also cited a similar study conducted by the tumor research center at Zhengzhou City Third Hospital, in which a duck was stuffed with glass marbles. Researchers killed and opened up its body the next day to find that half the amount had been digested. The next stage in Zhang's reasoning was that the blood of ducks (and geese) had properties similar to those of its strong digestive juices. Thus he concluded that ingesting the animal's blood might cure not only dysphagia, but also all kinds of cancer, by breaking down or "digesting" tumors.[85]

Zhang was not alone in conducting serious research on goose blood. A 1974 article in the journal *Qunzhong Yixue* (Medicine of the masses),[86] for instance, also argued for its exceptional healing properties based on research done on the animal's physiology. This work was a joint project of the pathology department of the Shanghai Navy Hospital and the immunity research (and teaching) team at Zhejiang University School of Medicine. The report began by characterizing geese as a species that developed mature bodily functions at an unusually early age, had unusually high levels of immunoglobulin in its blood, and had a higher percentage of white blood cells than other birds. Encouraged by these and other characteristics, the researchers claimed to have conducted actual clinical trials using goose blood in both human and animal subjects, which ended with the conclusion, echoing Zhang, that the substance was effective in the treatment of cancer. The Zhejiang team even posited the possibility of an "anti-cancer gene" in goose blood that could be absorbed into the human body through digestion.[87]

The journal in which this article appeared, *Qunzhong Yixue*, was first published in 1974 and mainly featured reports on the discovery and testing of practices from folk medicine. The editor quoted Mao as saying, "We need collective effort to create a newspaper, not just by a selective few." A contributor by the name of Wang Zhongliang even put together a song based on various new/old healing methods that the journal had documented. Titled "The Herb Song" (*Caoyao Ge*), the first stanza began by advocating the use of "all new matters" as part of Mao's plans for the Cultural Revolution.[88]

Chicken blood therapy had attempted to capture some of the charisma of biomedicine by using injection as its delivery method. But with toad, goose blood, duck blood, and other such therapies of the late Cultural Revolution, recommended methods of administration often veered toward the primitive in a search for greater authenticity.[89] According to Zhang, no attempt should be made to combine goose blood with other drugs, as that might alter the overall effect. Patients were advised to drink the blood raw and untreated. Zhang gave detailed instructions for choosing and killing the animals that would have made even the advocates of chicken blood therapy take pause:

> Geese and ducks of any sex and age can be used. Their feathers must, however, be completely white. Once the animal is caught, cut off its neck. The patient must immediately suck its hot blood from the neck till not a drop is left. Most patients, except those with serious conditions, experienced no adverse reaction from this method. Alternatively, pluck all feathers off the animal's tail, burn them into fine ashes, mix in rice soup, and drink up. A third method is to remove its gullet including the crop and gizzard (retain the yellow inner skin). Wash and mince thoroughly. Add an egg, water, and little salt, and steam until cooked. Eat this once every day three to seven times.

Zhang acknowledged that all these methods, especially the first, were "very unscientific, and require improvements to be made." He mentioned that some hospital units were experimenting with making goose blood syrup and tablets, and had achieved a "sixty-five percent success rate." Goose blood syrup was the more effective of the two, he claimed, but had a shorter shelf life. He was suspicious, however, that some effective ingredients were lost during the manufacturing process, and therefore recommended sticking to the old method of simply drinking fresh goose blood until more research was done. In a bow to chicken blood therapy, he did suggest goose blood might be made into an injectable substance in order to "increase its efficacy and expand disease targets." And he advised putting more research efforts on ducks rather than geese since the former were cheaper and available in greater quantity, although classical texts, he admitted, did not make much of duck blood.[90]

In the cases of goose- and toad-related therapies, we see a greater transition toward the primitive and raw as guarantors of authenticity. Chicken blood therapy had been presented not so much as "tradition" as innovation, and its references to Soviet tissue therapy and biomedicine (through the delivery system of injection) gave it some of the charisma of modernity. On the other hand, and perhaps because of the controversy surrounding chicken blood therapy, the promoters of subsequent therapies were even more careful to describe sources, present case studies, and, in the case of the Shanghai-Zhejiang team, even conduct what they claimed were clinical trials. Instead of "curing 100 diseases," these therapies were now aimed more toward specific ailments, but important and serious ones, like asthma and cancer. In making claims regarding disease categories that had been defined by Western and not Chinese medicine, they were (in their eyes) rediscovering new and powerful substances, neglected in the West, which would have curative effects as dramatic as those of antibiotics. In that sense, the project of "combining" Chinese and biomedicine still animated these projects in the eyes of their proponents, even as the turn toward folk prescriptions introduced ever more exotic elements into their protocols.

Unlike chicken blood therapy, the use of goose blood seems to have escaped official comment. It may have been its lesser promotion, or that experimental animal therapies had become so normative toward the end of the Cultural Revolution that all such practices were increasingly allowed.[91] Chicken blood even resurfaced in this period in other contexts, such as using blood from chicken combs to treat light burns. Ke Zexun, a member of the so-called Bravery Brigade at a Sichuan commune and most likely a barefoot doctor, claimed in 1976 to have cured more than seventy patients using this method during the previous decade.[92] Unlike Zhang, who documented his research in great detail, Ke relied only on a few references to successful treatments to support his claimed innovation. He gave the example of a six-year-old, surnamed Li, whose face was severely burned by a stove during winter. Zhang applied the blood from a chicken's comb to Li's face once a day. By the fifth day, he claimed, a scab was formed, and by the ninth day Li completely recovered.[93]

Ke reasoned that chicken blood was effective against germs since it hardened quickly upon contact with the human skin. Like some of the goose blood researchers, he also theorized the presence of a "gene" that could kill all kinds of germs, thus encouraging growth of new tissues. To prepare and use the ingredient, Ke gave the following steps: "First, use alcohol to disinfect the chicken comb (regardless of male or female chickens). Pierce and let the blood drip onto the burnt area until it covers approximately 0.5 cm of the surrounding skin. It is not necessary to bandage the wound or wipe off blood from the previous application before dripping a new layer. Do this once a day and always check for pus or any kind of secretions. If any of such substances are found, add salt in lukewarm water and wash the wound. After that, drip another layer of chicken comb blood."[94] References to genes, as well as to curing cancer, were increasingly common in discussions of animal medicines in this period. Along with their novelty, and perhaps the lingering tradition of Soviet-style tissue therapy, this made animal drugs now seem a research frontier more compelling than herbology.

No animals were too insignificant to be tested for the possibility of providing cures for cancer and other serious diseases. A *weisheng yuan* (hygiene institute) at a commune in Guangdong province claimed to have experimented with folk treatments for cancer since June 1974 using insects. It gave the example of a patient with the surname Cheng, who suffered from ascending colon cancer. For the first thirty-five days, he was prescribed honeycomb (two *liang*), the corpses of baby silkworms (two *liang*), seaweed (two *qian*), orange peel (five *qian*), *huanglian* (five *qian*), and lizards (one *liang*). All the ingredients were mashed into powder form. Cheng reported that his overall condition improved, but he did not continue with the same prescription because of a lack of ingredients. For the next twenty days, he was prescribed plant-based medicinals, but developed a splitting headache. According to the institute, Cheng had eaten cuttlefish porridge, which did not go well with the medicine. The earlier silkworm-and-lizard-based recipe was reverted to, but this time augmented by thirty centipedes. Cheng's headache disappeared and he regained his appetite. At the end of 1974, Cheng went for an X-ray and showed negative for cancer or other complications.[95]

This report and others like it focused on individual cases seen by a particular hospital, clinic, or individual physician rather than presenting statistical evidence based on formal clinical trials. Claims were sometimes made in articles that larger trials had been carried out, as we saw in the case of the Shanghai-Zhejiang team (and which we later encounter with water buffalo horn). Although this would seem to reflect respect for the clinical trial as a step in establishing efficacy, the purpose in most instances, as with chicken blood therapy, seems to have been to test safety rather than to prove or disprove a drug's usefulness. The tone of the reports never includes skepticism as to whether a substance "works," as its effectiveness had seemingly been proven by its long history of use, or rediscovered references from earlier times. The questions guiding the research with patients mainly involve dosages and combinations, as well as potential side effects, and sometimes whether a substance would cure a more expanded or serious set of ailments than the one for which it was targeted. The evidence produced thus usually augments an argument rather than disproving it.

Research on animal-based therapies grounded in classical or folk medicine was nonetheless considered so promising by the mid-1970s that even some Western-trained doctors enthusiastically experimented with substances they would not have touched twenty years earlier. One such Western-trained physician, Ye Haichang, wrote an article reporting his experience with using lizards, a therapy he claimed to have traced to Ming-period physician Li Shizhen and some less-famous healers. According to Ye, lizards were effective historically as a calming agent and painkiller,[96] but he also used them to treat scrofula (tuberculosis of the lymphatic glands, especially at the neck) and enlargement of lymph nodes. These were of course foreign disease categories, which would have been familiar to Ye given his Western medical background.[97] But Ye needed to develop his own preparation methods in the absence of detailed historical guidance. He thus experimented with baking and mashing the lizards into a powder, or simply eating them raw. In another instance, Ye advised this elaborate preparation: "First, make a hole into an egg. Then, shove a live lizard into it and quickly seal the hole with rough paper. Wrap the egg in mud and put it over fire until burnt. Crush into powder and ingest with water."[98]

Most of Ye's prescriptions incorporated other animals and insects besides lizards. One in particular included centipedes, whole insects, and *jiangcan* (dead silkworm larvae) as ingredients to be cooked and consumed together.

Another was strictly for external use and required fourteen lizards, with tails intact, and more than twenty spiders. They were baked, crushed into powder, and then mixed in vegetable oil to form a paste. As in many accounts of this period, these therapies were also defended as being more appropriate for the masses than expensive biomedicines. Ye reminded readers at the end that lizards were "easily available, cheap, and have practical value."[99]

Ye cited only classical texts to demonstrate a Chinese tradition of using lizards, rather than attempting to legitimize them through reference to folk medicine, which departs from other accounts I've reported from this period. Other sources interested in lizards did reference folk medicinals, however, adding "evidence" to buttress the use of an animal that had only begun to be farmed during The Great Leap Forward. Articles from that period promoting tokay gecko farming had provided no evidence to buttress claims of their medicinal importance. The sudden popularity of lizards from the 1950s onward, however, may have been linked to the research of Zheng Yihua, who in 1954 had described lizards as yielding *zuzhiye* (tissue fluid) another reference to Soviet-inspired tissue therapy. Zheng had written, "Since June last year, we made an injectable substance out of lizards and began treating patients with chronic diseases. Within six months, we manufactured 20,000 milliliters of lizard extract and found it particularly effective for intestinal and stomach problems (including indigestion and lack of appetite), and also neurosis."[100] Zhang's and Ye's projects were related in material and purpose (though not in the disease categories each were targeting), but Ye did not reference the earlier research, if he even knew about it. By this time all explicit references to Soviet influence had been erased from research lineages, leaving only classical and folk traditions as acceptable touchstones.

Seeking Replacements for "Luxury" Animal Medicinals

Given the turn to folk medicinals, it is hardly surprising that during the Cultural Revolution, medical prescriptions using "luxury medicinals" (*guizhong yaocai*) were declared counterrevolutionary. Two staff members of a hospital affiliated with the Beijing Zhongyi Research Institute even suggested throwing away old textbooks and formulating new ones based on folk medicine alone, because of a previous overemphasis on expensive materials. They wrote,

> Many *gufang* [old prescriptions] and recipes in old textbooks use luxury medicinals like musk, bear bile, pearl, *shidan* [stone bile] and *yuxie* [jade fragments]. Such gold, silver, jade, and stone-derived ingredients are not

only expensive but also difficult to find. They are not serviceable to the labor force that is the Chinese people. On the other hand, the cheaper, more convenient and well-tested practices of the rural region are way underutilized. These also include Chinese herbs and acupuncture. Those old textbooks are divorced from what is practical, divorced from the needs of the workers, farmers, and soldiers, and also divorced from the fundamental direction to serve the medical needs of the people.[101]

The authors claimed that Mao's earlier advice to "thoroughly reform all textbooks, and simplify some of them" was left unheeded until the Cultural Revolution, when every effort was made to disassociate China from its previous intellectual history.[102] "Criticize Lin Biao, Criticize Confucius" (*Pilin Pikong*) was a landmark phrase of this period to encourage a disregard for what was regarded as elite knowledge. Ancient sages were openly castigated, and deposed political figures such as Lin Biao were accused of reviving useless elite practices. The Beijing authors were clearly in league with this way of thinking, writing, "The culture that underpins socialist democracy is a scientific one. . . . All feudalistic as well as superstitious thoughts should be removed."[103] Folk knowledge was now "scientific," while the accumulated canonical knowledge of classical Chinese medicine was feudal and superstitious.

As we shall see, however, such pronouncements did little to affect the farming of high-value medicinal animals, which actually increased during the Cultural Revolution, because it continued to contribute needed cash through foreign trade. They did, however, encourage an even greater effort to find cheap synthetic or naturally occurring substitutes for high-end drugs so as to make such medicines more available to the masses. A main target in this regard was rhino horn.

Despite efforts made in the 1950s (discussed in chapter 3), the matter of replacing rhino horn with cheaper substitutes had still not been resolved by the 1970s, when published research on rhino versus water buffalo horn again became common. A 1977 article gave a justification:

Rhino horns are the horns of rhinoceros' found in Southeast Asia and Africa. They are rare animals and their horns are regarded as luxury medicinals. Rhino horns have the ability to clear heat, counteract the effects of poison, cool blood, and stop bleeding. They are particularly effective for high fever and viral meningitis. Not only are rhino horns imported from overseas, they are also very expensive and difficult to source. In 1957, 129 kilograms of rhino horns were imported into the country at a cost of 1,430

American dollars per kilogram. This was the highest amount imported so far. By 1974, the cost increased to 2,156 American dollars per kilogram. Such imports cannot satisfy domestic medical needs.[104]

Since 1970, the article continued, research units in Beijing and Tianjin hospitals had been studying water buffalo horns, which it claimed had been proven by folk medicine to reduce fever. Researchers tested their use in prescriptions that originally called for rhino horn, and concluded, as did the studies of the 1950s, that the two did not differ much in their effect. In one experiment, researchers changed the famous prescription *angong niuhuang san* to include buffalo instead of rhino horns, and administered the new combination to 518 patients with viral meningitis. The researchers claimed a cure rate of 82.4 percent. The original (rhino horn) prescription had been given to three hundred patients, and 82 percent found it effective, according to the study. The same comparative study was also applied to *zixue san*—a prescription using rhino horn (as one ingredient) to cure high fever—with similar results. Further research led to the claim that water buffalo horns were also effective for a host of other conditions, such as infection and inflammation. Such clinical trials were supposedly supported by technical analysis of the components of both materials with the help of modern equipment.[105]

Here was a rare instance in which an animal-based drug was reportedly the subject of an extensive clinical trial involving a number of hospitals and research institutes, and whose results were reported in the form of statistics. The long use and high status of rhino horn within Chinese medicine might explain the enthusiasm for finding newer and cheaper substitutes.[106] This in turn animated a number of competing research teams, and their disagreements may have also pushed the argument in the direction of well-documented clinical trials, as had eventually happened with chicken blood therapy. One team, for example, disagreed that rhino and water buffalo horn were similarly powerful and recommended increasing the dosage when using the latter. Zhejiang Huzhou Pharmaceutical Factory believed the horns of the two animals possessed similar abilities, such as clearing heat, but advised using buffalo horn only for adaptive diseases.[107] Zhang Haoliang from Jiangsu New Medical College cited a claim by Tianjin Pediatric Hospital that neither material was effective on its own and had to be mixed with other ingredients. Zhang's institute also conducted studies on the horns and hooves of other common animals and found them to be equally suitable replacements. Some examples were hooves of cow, sheep, and even pigs.[108] The institute replaced rhino horns with pig's hooves in the prescription *xijiao dihuang tang* (rhino horns-rehmannia soup) and clinical observations claimed positive results in the treatment of purpura. Other institutes recommended substituting the horns of oxen, artificial bezoar, and the shell of the hawksbill turtle.[109]

There was even research aimed at replacing rhino horn with *shancaoyao*, or wild herbs. A 1973 article by a Chinese medical hospital presented a recipe of *shancaoyao* that might substitute for both antelope and rhino horn: "Both antelope and rhino horns are effective in the treatment of encephalitis, but are highly expensive and not easily available. To lessen the burden of the masses, and consolidate the new cooperative medical system, we recommend the following substitutes for the two animal parts." The hospital combined a number of herbs that each matched a specific curative principle claimed for the animal tissue. For instance, it claimed that the function of antelope horns were "to flush liver heat, clear lung heat, and put out wind."[110] The herbs that purportedly fulfilled each of the three healing properties were *gougancai*, loofah, and cat's claw. Rhino horns, the article continued, "flush heat and counteract the effects of poison, cool blood, and clear the heart, but can be substituted with centella, spreading hedyotis, mondo grass (only its juice extract), and fresh danzhuye."[111] There were also calls to substitute *angong niuhuang wan*, a well-known prescription using bezoar, with a less expensive one involving an entirely herbal recipe.[112]

Such research on substituting common and cheaper animal tissue or even herbs for the parts of expensive and rare species was increasingly common in this period, and not just for imported animals like rhinos. Other examples cited in the literature included substituting antelope horn with goat horn, donkey hide with pig hide, and musk with the secretions of civet cats. Some researchers even decided that dog bone could replace tiger bone. A team from Shandong province succeeded in making wine from dog bone that, like tiger-bone wine, was used to treat rheumatoid arthritis.[113]

Based on these research results, the ministries of health and commerce both began to officially promote the use of water buffalo horns in 1977.[114] This represented not just "substitution," as rhino horn was rarely prescribed, given its rarity, but in some sense the popularization of what had previously been a therapy for the elite. Although rhino horn research was intended to lessen Chinese dependence on imported animal parts and find cheap substitutes, it likely had two unintended effects that linger into the present century, to the great detriment of rhinos. The first is that all this research seemed to strengthen the theory that rhino horn (and, by extension, its substitutes) was a highly effective medicine. The second is that such substitutes likely induced a more widespread consumption of, and demand for, animal horn of all types among a stratum of the population that had not regularly used it. This would have devastating consequences for world rhino populations when, in a later period, the Chinese people became middle-class consumers able to afford the authentic product.

The Intensification and Expansion of Medicinal Animal Farming and Collection

Although the atmosphere of the Cultural Revolution led to criticism of luxury medicinals, it did not greatly affect existing Chinese (domestic) cultivation of such drugs for an overseas market. In fact, production of some high-end animal medicinals actually increased in this period. The categories of animals farmed and systematically collected for medicinal purposes also continued to expand, particularly at the lower end, where greater varieties of insects and sea creatures with supposedly medicinal properties were now brought to market.

State-owned medicine companies continued in this period to carry out an organized search for animal- (and insect-) based drugs. In the journal *Zhong Caoyao Tongxun*, articles often mentioned the need to supply a national market. An article on "whole insects" (*quanchong*) related, "Whole insects, a commonly used Chinese medicinal, are currently lacking in supply. They are scattered throughout the country and highly seasonal. The medicine company of Yi county, Hebei province organized the masses to go deep into the villages to catch and harvest them. In just three months, the company acquired more than 5,000 *jin* of whole insects. This figure amounts to more than 50,000 *yuan* worth of investment for agricultural production. This is double the expected number of whole insects gathered this year, and 12.5 times the total collection for last year."[115] To facilitate such growth, the company not only increased the number of "collection stations" (*shougou zhan*), but also provided training on the hunting and processing of insects. Members of communes (especially barefoot doctors and students) were sent into the mountains, where insects thrived. At the same time, they kept a lookout for other medicinal herbs such as red ginseng and *chaihu*. The article concluded that such activities not only "provided the finances to fight drought, but also helped support the cooperative medical system."[116] This indicates how closely such efforts to collect animal tissue had been woven into commune life by the late Cultural Revolution.

Beetle farming, which began during the Great Leap Forward, had become particularly well developed and widespread by the Cultural Revolution. The Golden Bridge brigade from the Maji commune in Jiangsu province wrote that it began keeping ground beetles in the late 1960s, starting with only one small breeding pond. By 1974 they had 106 such ponds. The reason for raising so many ground beetles was to satisfy what was now a national market. The brigade wrote, "Besides satisfying demand within our own unit, we use some to exchange with our brother units for the things that we lack. We then hand the rest over to the country as a medicinal resource," presumably to be marketed in cities, or regions where beetle cultivation was not as common.[117]

At the other end of the spectrum, farming continued of what were clearly luxury animals such as deer and musk deer, despite the rhetoric about their elite nature. Even here, however, there were attempts to reform practices based on supposedly more authentic folk or classical ones. An article published late in the Cultural Revolution, for example, suggested reforms in the way deer antlers were processed based on such a reading. The contemporary method was to boil them in hot water (referred to as "frying" in practice) after they were removed either by sawing or hacking. It described that process:

> Once sawed (or hacked), the deer antler is attached to a hanger. It is then "fried" in boiling water, its sawed end facing upwards. After 2–3 minutes, the antler is removed and lightly cooled. The same process is repeated many times until all the blood is drained out. The skin that comes out at the end of the antler is secured with a nail and hanged to dry. According to old medicine shop workers, the three reasons for boiling deer antlers are: (1) to prevent rotting by draining out all blood; (2) to clean the deer antler and remove oil crust and fishy smell; (3) to give it a nice color and shiny coating.[118]

The writer argued, however, that none of the above steps were sanctioned by tradition. For example, Ming physician Li Shizhen instructed only to "harvest in the summer and dry in the shade," and "once broken, keep dry."[119] The handbook of the Beijing Medicinal Company, published the year before, was also cited as advising that blood be kept in the antler, as it could "nourish the qi."[120] In boiling, not only the blood but all water-soluble ingredients ended up in the water. According to the author, some farms in Jilin province, following this new advice, had begun separately retaining the blood or converting the water for medicinal use. Another in Sichuan province followed the new (but historically sanctioned) advice by simply airing and not boiling the deer antler. Such antlers were now called "blood antlers" (*xuerong*). The writer believed that their quality was better and encouraged more research into traditional preparation methods to further improve their processing.[121]

As for musk deer, experiments continued into the Cultural Revolution to better understand the animals' biology, with the aim of increasing quality and yield. In Shanxi province, a so-called experimental farm documented that the front muscle of the musk pouch basically controlled the secretion. Other experiments reported during this period included determining the prime season for musk secretion, learning the best way to artificially harvest the material, and proving the efficacy of musk for conditions like hair loss.[122] Unlike in the case of deer antler, there were no references in any of this research to conforming with classic or folk methods of harvesting or use, perhaps because the product of these animals was already so valuable.

Interest also increased in this period in the medicinal use of marine animals and their by-products. A 1972 article related, "The 1970s heralds an age of exploration into the uncharted realm of the marine world. . . . Members of both the marine and medical professions place great importance on retrieving medicinals from the sea."[123] One example was pearl, which was promoted as a medicine "to clear heat and benefit the yin, calm the heart and soothe the nerves, clarify one's sight and counteract the effects of poison."[124] It was, to quote an article, "also an important export item," presumably for nonmedicinal uses.[125] From the late 1960s onward, various provinces began conducting artificial cultivation of river oysters as a result. For instance, the so-called Five-Seven Cadre School, belonging to the revolutionary committee of Yiyang region in Hunan province, carried out crossbreeding of two species of oysters in order to improve pearl quality.[126]

Pearl had been mentioned in classical medical texts, but the medicinal properties of many marine animals were considered new discoveries. In the *Bencao Gangmu Shiyi* of 1765, only about seventy of the more than two thousand medicinals recorded were marine-based. The glut of sea animals that are sold in twenty-first-century medicinal marketplaces like the Qingping Market in Guangzhou likely have their source in folk recipes retrieved during the early Communist era, and are the result of farming or directed catches of marine species that date from the same period.[127] The drug department of the Shandong Marine Research Institute wrote, "Under the enlightened leadership of the party and Chairman Mao . . . the mass movement to explore and discover the treasure trove that is our *yi* and *yao* soon picked up pace. Local publications of *tufang* [indigenous prescriptions], *yanfang* [experience-based prescriptions], and reports on pharmaceutical research proliferated like bamboos sprouting after a heavy spring rain." Shandong Marine Research Institute (formerly the Marine Research Institute of the

4.4 & 4.5 Examples of dried marine animals (seahorses and starfish) sold at the Qingping Zhongyaocai Specialty Market in Guangzhou. PHOTOS BY AUTHOR.

Chinese Academy of Sciences) had, since 1969, been conducting interviews in fishing villages from six provinces and collected more than one hundred healing recipes using marine resources.[128]

This process of collecting marine medicinal medicines was likely aided by a new group of barefoot doctors who appeared by the early 1970s, called "fishermen doctors" (*yumin yisheng*). In 1970, Guangdong Zhongyi Institute accepted its first batch of students from nearby fishing villages such as Wanshan Island in neighboring Zhuhai. Upon graduation in 1973, the students returned to their homes to perform medical duties, though presumably they were also involved in surveying local marine resources that could be medicalized.[129]

By the end of the Cultural Revolution, therefore, many more animals (land- and sea-based) and insects were being harvested and sold as medicinals. In 1977, a year after Mao's death, a comprehensive treatise on Chinese medicinals published in Shanghai (*Zhongyau Da Cidian*, or *The Encyclopedic Dictionary of Chinese Pharmacology*) recorded 5,767, out of which 740 were animal parts and tissues. This far exceeded the number of animal-based drugs recorded in the Ming-period materia medica, *Bencao Gangmu*.[130] The numbers of animals designated "medicinal" increased even further with the publication of the two-volume *Chinese Medicinal Animals* in 1979 and 1983, a trend that has continued into the present century. Jin Yilang, a member of the *Zongyua Da Cidian* research team noted this new emphasis in writing, "especially since the Cultural Revolution, when the mass-oriented Chinese Medicinal Movement was launched, every place focused on uncovering and studying not just plant but also animal-based drugs. It was in the process of preventing and treating diseases at the mass level . . . that a batch of animal drugs were discovered." One example he gave was cow bile, which, according to Jin, "was found to be an effective anti-inflammatory agent only in the last couple years." He attributed its discovery to barefoot doctors, one of whose tasks was to source for medicinal resources in industrial and agricultural by-products, in addition to surveying folk practices.[131]

Conclusion

We have seen that the turn to folk medicinals during and after the Great Leap Forward greatly expanded the official Chinese pharmacopeia and, not incidentally, the process of faunal medicalization, by collecting references to many more animal-based cures. At the same time, the emphasis on innovation reveals that this process was not simply one of discovery. Such materials and therapies were subject to further research and "scientization," primarily through clinical application but also, in some instances, laboratory testing, creating new delivery methods, or discovering new efficacies that mapped onto modern disease categories.

Chicken blood therapy was emblematic of this period because it managed to combine so many references: classical Chinese texts, the charisma of Soviet tissue therapy, the aura of lab research, the political dictate of economy, the association of chickens with rural areas, and injection as a modern system of drug delivery. It was eventually wielded as a political weapon in the Cultural Revolution, only to be banished as the winds of politics shifted. But other therapies related to the blood of fowls, the heads of toads, the eggs of lizards, and the like continued to be seriously experimented with until the time of Mao's death, indicating that chicken blood therapy was no isolated eccentricity, but part of a growing movement to find cheaper alternatives to biomedicine, and potential "miracle cures" in previously neglected animal tissue. Behind this was a greater sense of competition between Chinese medicine and biomedicine (at least from the perspective of some Chinese innovators) to cure serious diseases like cancer, which had seemingly revealed the limits of the latter. Animals were increasingly seen as a new/old resource from which stunningly innovative and effective cures might be coaxed. Yet at the same time, mundane animals were likely becoming nearly as normative as herbs (in visibility if not in number) in the production and supply chain of Chinese materia medica, as well as the research programs of would-be medical innovators.

The intensification of animal farming in this period, with the export trade and the domestic attraction of medicinal by-employments, also continued to be major factors sustaining the project of medicalizing fauna. Pronouncements against luxury medicinals as bourgeois did little to slow musk deer farming, while the intensive research on rhino horn substitutes for the masses only focused more attention on animal horn as a medicine. The growing charisma of faunal medicalization within modern Chinese drug development, set by the Great Leap Forward and continued through the Cultural Revolution, would result in the commodification of additional species under Deng's subsequent reforms, as we shall see in chapter 5.

CHAPTER FIVE

"Economic Animals"
Deng's Reforms and
the Rise of Bear Farming

 In the vast literature on Deng Xiaoping's reform policies, little has been written about their effect on Chinese pharmaceuticals, although this sector was destined to become almost emblematic of the new liberalization. The revival in 1978 of the Four Modernizations—first proposed in 1963 by then premier Zhou Enlai—and the new emphasis on export-led growth, resulted in an expanded global market for Chinese drugs, with animal-based drugs having a prominent place. By this time, the exploitation of animal tissue for all manner of drug-making was well established, and had long been a staple of the overseas trade. But, as we have seen, during the Cultural Revolution animal-based research had taken a turn toward folk medicine and idiosyncratic cures, of which chicken blood therapy was emblematic though hardly unique. Under Deng, the production of animal-based medicines would be discursively and practically relocated in the realm of the economy, signaled by the use of the term "economic animals" (*jingji dongwu*) to include even more species with supposed medicinal value.

Industrial-scale bear bile farming was as emblematic of this period as chicken blood and other folk therapies had been for the Cultural Revolution. The farming of bears and other new animals in this period of course had roots in the successful state farming of deer, which had been a growth sector since the 1950s. It can also be seen as part of a reemphasis on production following the confusion of the Cultural Revolution, although state-directed quotas were now replaced by incentives for entrepreneurship. The discussion in this chapter examines these larger trends in animal exploitation, but focuses on bear farming as its major case.

———————

With China's increased engagement with the outside world, animal-based drugs were celebrated more consciously in this period as products of Chinese tradition and, simultaneously, as one of China's contributions to cutting-edge global research in pharmacology. In 1979, Zhang Tianmin, from the pharmaceutical department of Shandong Medical College, described animal drugs as *zangqi zhiji* (organo-pharmaceutics) needful of serious research and development. The active ingredients of most such drugs were still unknown, he pointed out, mainly because of their highly complex molecular structures. Furthermore, he continued, "their combinations are sometimes necessary in order to exercise efficacy," echoing what we have seen was a long-standing suspicion of Chinese medical doctors toward the reductionism of biomedical laboratory research. He still maintained faith, however, that modern science would be able to "separate and purify" these substances, converting them into *zangqi shenghua yaowu* (organo-biochemical drugs) for more general use. Zhang was well informed on the use of animal tissue in Western pharmaceutical research, but thought China held certain advantages:

> We have a long history of using internal organs to prevent diseases, and this is an important component in our medicinal legacy. Ancient doctors already had experience in using animal organs to cure various diseases. Cow bezoar, bile, placenta, and chicken gizzard—all these were commonly used medicines. In fact, Li Shizhen's *Bencao Gangmu* recorded a substantial number of animal-based substances that could be called organo-pharmaceutics. Their main functions were to supplement, regulate, bring to control, replace or even correct the human metabolic system. Such drugs have low toxicity and few negative side effects, and are easily absorbed by the human body. They are highly effective as a form of intrathecal therapy, which means to deliver drugs to a targeted body part. The medical use of animal organs is considered a new development in the international medical scene, and an important resource for prevention as well as cure.[1]

There were, Zhang believed, some four hundred "organo-biochemical drugs" being developed in China and worldwide at the time he wrote. Prior to the Revolution, he claimed, China produced "none, or at most 4 to 5 of them." But since then, he calculated, 160 had been developed in China alone. Still, Zhang believed Chinese pharmacological research on animals was behind related efforts in countries like Japan and the United States— that China was, in other words, now in global organo-pharmaceutical competition.[2]

Bureaucratic reforms helped reinforce this greater emphasis on animal-based medicinals as potential drivers of the economy. Such emphasis had always been present with high-end export products like musk and ginseng, but now became more general, to include potentially all animal medicines. One result was the reduction, by the early to mid-1980s, in the governance role of the Ministry of Health, with the regulation of some Chinese medicinals being parceled to bureaucracies less concerned with the health system. Raw medicinals were reclassified as "crude drugs" (*yuanliao yaocai*, but more commonly known as *zhongyaocai*) and regulated by the agricultural ministry. The forestry ministry was also given decision-making power over wild medicinal animals, excepting marine life, and would essentially manage China's forests as extraction sites. Only Chinese patent drugs (*zhong chengyao*) and Western drugs remained under the full regulatory control of the health ministry. This categorization scheme not only differentiated types of drugs by sector, but also affected the way they were managed and, ultimately, marketed and consumed. This in turn opened the door to an even greater exploitation of animal parts and tissues as medicinals, given the increased profits to be made in their commercial farming. The term "economic animals" (*jingji dongwu*) was coined during this period, particularly to describe wild (or formerly wild) animals, in order to more explicitly recognize their commercial value.

With agriculture identified as one of the four keys to China's economic growth, the official position on "crude drugs" (both plant- and animal-based) from this period onward was that their production needed to expand and further differentiate. In this political context, animal farming, the growth of which had plateaued during the Cultural Revolution, was further expanded to include even more species, and their use in a wider variety of products. This push was accompanied by rhetoric reminiscent of the Great Leap Forward, including the slogan, "Home Rearing, Home Cultivation." Mao and Deng both stressed the importance of exporting drugs, but Deng's policies allowed private profit, and animal medicinals seemed to represent a growth area. This expansion in the marketing of Chinese medicine to include even more animal-based substances did indeed bring great profits, but would eventually (in the very late twentieth and early twenty-first centuries) help bring Chinese medicine into disrepute internationally as a scourge of animals, endangered and otherwise.

Controversy particularly swirled around "farmed" bear bile, perhaps the signature animal-based drug of the Deng period. For this reason I examine bear farming in this chapter in some detail. Although bear bile was given medicinal sanction in classical texts, its mass production through farming and accompanying mass-marketing was wholly a product of the 1980s and later. It was never easily available in premodern times, when bears had to be hunted to obtain their gallbladders. Then, too, foreign (Japanese) rather than Chinese researchers had been instrumental in finding the active ingredient in bear bile (ursodeoxycholic acid or UDCA), which helped support its modern claim to efficacy, and the expansion of its medical use well beyond the advice, knowledge, or opinion of the ancients. Likewise, farming techniques borrowed from North Korea formed the basis for the Chinese practice. Despite these modern and even foreign influences, the term *chuantong zhongyao* (traditional Chinese medicine) would be extensively and casually used as a marketing tool by pharmaceutical companies to give bear bile and other modern farmed animal products needed authenticity, both within China and for a newly expanded diasporic market.

By the end of the Deng period, there were increasingly few limits on which animals and their parts could be promoted as medicinal, and for what curative purposes. In his projection of the future for animal drugs, college student Chi Cheng wrote in 1989, "As long as there are animals, one can find a medicinal use for every part and tissue." This was echoed by the popular phrase, used in conjunction with many "economic animals" in the 1980s: "The entire body of X is a treasure," with "X" being almost any species.[3] A list drawn up by Chi of animal parts and tissues with curative value included leopard's bone and the feces of wolves.[4] Although marketing claims now rested more and more on "tradition," and classical or folk references could almost always be found for this or that substance, such claims were increasingly outside the authority or control of any recognized Chinese medical professionals. This was in contrast to even toad, chicken, and goose blood therapy during the Cultural Revolution, whose promoters had all been physicians.

To understand these developments, however, we first have to examine the further expansion of animal farming and farm-based experimentation under the Deng regime.

Medicinals as Agricultural Resources

Exhortations to produce drugs in the early Communist period were normally made in the language of national and bodily need (e.g., shortage), of
patriotism, and sometimes even of military necessity. A late example of this
long-familiar rhetoric was an essay published in the inaugural issue of a 1983
yearbook, which begins by paraphrasing a previous article by Yao Bang titled
"Shanghai Faces Serious Shortage of Over One Hundred Herbs":

> Comrade Yao Bang has always been concerned about the development of
> Chinese Medicine, and has on many occasions given important instruc-
> tions to solve related problems. In response, the National Headquarters
> for the Management of Healthcare has begun work to spread [Comrade
> Yao Bang's message], learn, and implement ways of reform. The National
> Headquarters has also invited pharmaceutical companies from the three
> cities of Beijing, Tianjin, and Shanghai to help with listing herbs that
> have low stockpiles, and with sorting out the reasons for the shortage. A
> conference was also held in which the head of the National Medical De-
> partment and managers of pharmaceutical companies agreed with Com-
> rade Yao Bang's advice that work on solving low herbal supplies should be
> carried out at the leadership level.[5]

This was the language of central planning: ensuring supply and preventing
shortages, and mindful of the hospital and clinic dispensary as the primary
sites of consumption.

Under Deng's reforms, however, with their new emphasis on commercialization, some medicinals started to take on more the identity of "agricultural produce," and agriculture bureaucracies began to create policies that
affected the production, status, and use of drugs. In this way Chinese medicines began to develop markets less clearly anchored to clinics, hospitals,
medical schools, theories, practices, and the like, becoming, more and more,
commodities for simple production and sale in what was now a national and
soon international marketplace. At the same time, bureaucratic control and
regulation of such substances fragmented. This would have major ramifications for animal-related products, some of which could command much
higher prices than herbs.

An early sign of this drift were guidelines issued in July 1981 for the pricing
of agricultural products (*nongfu chanpin*), which now included "thirty-four
expensive *zhongyaocai* [Chinese medicinals]." The list included musk, bezoar,
deer antler, tiger bone, leopard bone, bear bile, "whole insects" (*quanchong*),

toad venom (*chansu*), donkey-hide gelatin (*ejiao*), rhino horns from both Asian and African species (*xijiao* and *guangjiao*), and antelope horn.[6] These guidelines accompanied a new push to increase production in line with quotas for agricultural products generally. The state department for the administration of pharmaceuticals even revived the Great Leap Forward slogan *Jia Yang Jia Zhong* (home rearing, home cultivation) to encourage mass farming of those listed medicines with a domestic origin.[7] At the same time there was a turn to the language of resource protection, perhaps in anticipation of a higher degree of exploitation, but more likely as part of an argument for "conserving" wild plants and animals by farming them. Under the provisions of a 1984 drug law, for example, the government expressed the need "to protect wild medicinal resources, and so encourage cultivation."[8] Two new slogans reflecting the official position on plant and animal-based medicinals were "Harvest, Protect, Cultivate" and "Protect, Rear, Hunt."[9]

As "wild" medicinals became subject to agricultural policies, this further blurred the line between wild animals and livestock. In Jilin province, for example, one of the main goals for the seventh Five-Year Plan (1986–1990) was to build an export-oriented economy using animal parts and tissues. In a report on developing agriculture in the province, the northeast tiger, bear, white fox, and golden money leopard were among the wild animals singled out for the potentially high economic value of their parts. The plan was to extend beyond deer antlers (known as one of the "Northeast's Three Treasures"), which were producing 1,000–1,600 *jin* worth of exports yearly, to include even more types of farmed animal tissue, most notably bear bile.[10]

Jilin province was so associated with medicinal animal farming in Chinese journals of this period that the discussion that follows concentrates on its enterprises, understanding that they were destined for a national and international medicinal marketplace. The province may have not been unique in seeking to exploit its wild animals, but it had certain characteristics of physical and even political geography that made it a particularly important center for such projects. Among these were its existing experience with deer farming, its comparative closeness to Beijing and the ports of northern China, and its border with North Korea.

Outsourcing Farm Laboratories

As in the Great Leap Forward, animal farms in this period (the early 1980s) again began to be described as scientific laboratories. The phrase *tianjian shiyan shi* (laboratory in the field) was coined to emphasize the importance of farm-based research to production. Liu Dezu, who held a managerial position at Jilin Agricultural University, quoted the government as saying, "The countryside is currently undergoing professionalization [*zhuanyehua*], commercialization [*shangpinhua*], and lastly, modernization [*xiandaihua*]." Liu interpreted this to mean the beginning of a closer relationship between farms and academic research centers such as Jilin Agricultural University. He wrote, "It is therefore important to set up experimental-farm stations [*shiyanchang zhan*] affiliated to the university in order to promote teaching, research and practical exhibition all in one location." Liu summarized this argument in three characters, which translate to "Three Combines" (*San Jiehe*), meaning university-based research would contribute more directly to China's economy.[11]

Experimental-farm stations run by universities had existed as early as 1961, during the Great Leap Forward. They operated separately from state-owned farms, even though research was being carried out in both establishments to improve plant and animal breeds. Such college-affiliated farms were then known as experimental stations (*shiyan zhan*) and managed by either animal husbandry and veterinary science departments or departments of agricultural studies. They were discontinued during the Cultural Revolution, however, when many schools, including Jilin Agricultural University, had been ordered to relocate, and higher education had generally been disrupted.[12] Not until 1978 were college-owned farms reinstated, but with the new focus of making research a commercially profitable venture. According to Liu, such farms were now receiving little or no government funding, so "it is therefore imperative that all research projects be directly beneficial to the farms." Some farms fell into disuse because they could not turn a profit or had made a substantial loss while trying. At the same time, Liu warned against the self-serving ways of faculty members who used farms to promote private research projects, which suggests that such practices were becoming widespread.[13]

Jilin Agricultural University solved its own financial problem by contracting or outsourcing its experimental farms to third parties. This idea was borrowed from the so-called household contract responsibility system, which was introduced in the early 1980s as a way to increase agricultural productivity in the countryside. The new system proved effective, Liu claimed, in allowing experimental-farm stations (which still belonged to the college) to make a profit for the first time in fourteen years. Moreover, he went on, "individual workers are getting rich."[14] Liu likely meant "contractors" when using the word *zhigong* (worker).[15]

Among the medicinal animals of interest to Jilin Agricultural University's farm stations, deer were the most important. At the time Liu wrote, the college owned four hundred sika deer in addition to regular livestock such as pigs and chickens.[16] Experiments on deer were conducted mainly with the goal of increasing antler growth. One particular experiment lasted three years (1981–1983) at the Huadian County Number One Deer Farm (Huadianxian Diyi Luchang), and tested whether exposing young male deer to light could induce early shedding of spike antlers, thus promoting even more antler growth. The abstract stated,

> The authors used the *Cervus nippon* Temminck (sika deer) in their experiments. A total of 82 trials were conducted in three years, and the results showed that deer with increased exposure to light shed their spike antlers 31–39 days earlier. The first set of antlers produced under such conditions was 5–13 percent more than the normal yield, while subsequent sets were even higher (about three times). As such, the average production value for each deer increased by 50–80 yuan. Authors also found that less time was needed for post-mating recovery in their deer samples. Even older and weak deer exhibited strength after being exposed to light.[17]

The overall goal, therefore, was to make formerly wild animals (in this instance, deer) less conditioned to their natural environment and more like bred livestock in industrial farms, where controlled (indoor) environments could contribute to increasing yields.

Increasingly, too, animal-based research in this period was carried out in dialogue with Western (e.g., American and Japanese) laboratories, given the increasing Chinese accessibility to foreign scientific journals. It was an American researcher, for instance, who had first proposed the idea of stimulating growth of deer antlers through artificial means. The Chinese report cited the works of zoologist Richard J. Goss, who had carried out his experiments (between the 1960s and 1970s) not on farms but in an urban laboratory, transporting deer and a host of other animals to "the fifth floor of Brown's [University] new Biomedical Center." Indeed, Goss was more concerned with pure zoological research, his Chinese counterparts applying his findings to practical or economic purposes. They learned from Goss that young male deer produced more testosterone when exposed to light. This caused the skin around the antler burr to peel off, thus allowing the deer to shed its antlers. Applying this principle in a farm setting, the aim was to send a sensory signal to the deer's cerebral ganglion, from which the hormone was released. Through their own experiments, Chinese researchers confirmed that deer under increased exposure to light produced more antlers, and fuller sets. Some deer also developed faster than usual. Between 1981 and 1983, the period during which the experiments were conducted, the hours of light exposure were raised from approximately 770 in the first year to more than 1,700 in the last, meaning that deer were essentially kept in lighted barns at night in the manner of cows or horses.[18]

Jilin Agricultural University was not alone in conducting such sophisticated experiments on deer. The Northeast Forestry University received an award in 1989 for its research on the red deer species. Its reported breakthrough was in creating the condition for red deer to shed their antlers more frequently.[19]

Another species subjected to laboratory experimentation was musk deer, which had been considered particularly difficult to farm since the Great Leap Forward. Liang Fengxi from the Economic Animals Research Institute wrote a paper based on observational studies conducted on wild Siberian musk deer between 1977 and 1983. According to Liang, the purpose of the study was to better understand their biology in order to convert them, like the sika deer in Jilin, into a domestic farm animal (*jia yang*). The introduction read,

> The Siberian musk deer is one of those animal-based medicinals unique to China. Musk—the secretion from the pouch of the male deer—is a famous *guizhong yaocai* [expensive medicinal]. Siberian musk deer of the Northeast region thrive in the Greater and Lesser Khingan Ranges, and also the Changbai Mountain. . . . Since ancient times, the Siberian musk deer have been hunted and killed as described in the saying "kill the chicken to retrieve its eggs." No deer was spared during the process, and if not their musk, the female and their young were killed for their meat. Hunting also took place during the reproduction season, when even pregnant deer were killed. Coupled with large-scale deforestation and attacks from predators, their habitat has reduced drastically. As such, wild resources have been greatly impacted. To convert the wild Siberian musk deer into house breed, we must first study their biology, and then start taming them so that they become suitable as domestic livestock.[20]

Not just the Siberian musk deer, but other formerly free-range medicinal species became more closely housed and subject to yield-related experiments under their new status as "economic animals." At the same time, more wild animals also became designated as medicinal. For example, one farm affiliated with the Jilin Agricultural University captured a raccoon dog in 1983 and killed it to study its anatomy with a view toward breeding it for medicine. This species had never been systematically exploited for any economic or medicinal purposes. Pure zoological studies were rare in scientific journals of this period compared with those that set out to exploit wild animals as resources, though the latter category incidentally produced much information on anatomy and behavior.[21]

The Rise of Bear Farming

While Deng's reforms stimulated more scientific research into existing practices like deer farming, in order to increase their productivity, it also opened the door to potentially profitable new enterprises using new types of animals, such as bear farming. Jilin province in the 1980s was the origin point of Chinese industrial-scale bear farming, an enterprise fully consistent with the trends discussed above, but without the historic precedence of deer farming. Jilin is located on the border with North Korea, and there is evidence that bear farming had its origins in that country and migrated across the Yalu River to Jilin in this period. A retrospective report on bear research published in 1988 made reference to experiments conducted in the Liberation Army Hospital no. 226 in Yanbian in 1984, which mimicked or borrowed North Korean techniques. Other details about the North Korean connection remain murky, however, and will likely remain so given the impossibility of conducting research on that side of the border. Even Chinese researchers had limited access to early reports on experimental bear farming such as the one described above.[22] The geographical proximity of this research to the North Korean border, however, and the prominence of Korean-Chinese actors in the early enterprises on the Chinese side, remains strongly suggestive of such connections.

In 1993, the most extensive handbook on bear bile farming up to that time, *Bears and Bear Bile*, was published in China by four editors with the surnames Jin or Kim, indicating their ethnic Korean origin.[23] The book is one of our best sources for tracing the origins of the Chinese industry, which the authors had been instrumental in creating by the time it was written. The book not only celebrates their achievements, but also looks forward to expanding bear farming even further into new profitable areas convergent with national priorities: "According to recent studies, the bear species is the only animal that does not contract osteoporosis. It is therefore the ideal animal to carry out research on orthopedic diseases. Not only that, its hibernating pattern is very unusual. The fact that female bears give birth and breastfeed during winter make for an interesting research project. As such, cultivating bears for research purpose is meaningful not only for the medical field, but also the emerging fields of bionics and aerospace research."[24]

The earliest commercial research on bears was carried out in Yanbian, which is located in the easternmost part of Jilin province and just across the border from North Korea. Jin Jichun, one of the book's authors, claimed to have been the first to experiment with bear farming, and to have set up the first pharmaceutical factory in 1986 to produce bear bile powder. Jichun was credited with creating China Baitoushan Industry Co., Ltd., which was the result of the merger of a company (most likely Jichun's) specializing in bear bile production with another specializing in ginseng products.[25] Ginseng, as we have seen, was already a high-end medicinal with an established overseas market, the cultivation of which had been improved with Russian help. Baitoushan would later expand into other ventures such as the hotel and service industries. But bear farming remained essential to its profitability, and in fact a large-scale farming facility to house a thousand bears was under construction at the time the book was written.[26]

The book's language is reminiscent of the Great Leap Forward rhetoric of self-taught innovation, but now overlaid with the new language of entrepreneurship, which is evident in its description of Jichun's foray into bear bile production:

> Entrepreneur Jin Jichun, founder (currently general manager) of China Baitoushan Industry Co., Ltd., was not only hardworking but also an avid learner and a risk taker. In a business trip that he made in 1984, Jichun found out about the medical value of bear bile. Having lived in Changbaishan, he was deeply aware of the changes in the ecosystem especially the dwindling bear population. Jichun reckoned that human effort was required to ensure a ready supply of bear bile. He then decided to embark on the business of bear farming, even though Jichun knew there were many obstacles to overcome. . . . For the sake of raising bears, Jichun taught himself animal biology, veterinary science, and pharmaceutics. He also read books on Japanese and Korean styles of business management. When in doubt, Jichun asked for advice and in the end acquired professional knowledge. He went to many places to get funding and almost collapsed as a result.[27]

Jichun, like most entrepreneurs of his time, received assistance, if not in the form of direct funding, from the government. The difference between "entrepreneur" and "farmer" blurred during the 1980s, when the new government under Deng promoted agriculture as an industry. The term *zhi fu* (to bring wealth) became the key word of the era, despite the use of the phrase "socialist-based farming enterprise" (*shehui zhuyi nongye qiye*). In the mid-1980s, the government launched the so-called China Spark Program (Zhongguo Xinghuo Jihua) and clearly stated its goal of promoting agricultural development using modern technology.[28] The word *xinghuo* or "spark" was derived from an old Chinese saying popularized by Mao, "A single spark can start a prairie fire."[29] To quote an official website, it was hoped that "the spark of science and technology will extend over the vast rural areas of China."[30]

The two slogans Jichun gave as his "secrets to success" were "three dependables" (*San Kao*) and "three catches" (*San Zhua*). The "three dependables" were to depend on the government's strategies and policies, on science and technology, and, lastly, on what was called "a scientific style of management" (*kexue guanli*). Under the first dependable, Jichun's plan to set up a bear farm received support from all levels of government (from the Ministry of Forestry to the government of Yanji City where China Baitoushan Industry Co., Ltd., was later headquartered). That Jichun's business goals "are in line with the basic trajectory [*jiben luxian*] of the Communist party and the idea of a township enterprise [*xiangzhen qiye*]" was listed as the reason he gained official support. As for the second dependable, Jichun had worked closely with Yanbian Medical Institute, Yanbian Agricultural Institute, and Jilin University to develop the technology of bear farming. In 1986, for instance, China Baitoushan Industry Co., Ltd., and Yanbian Medical Institute signed a contract, under which Professors Jin Yuquan (one of the four authors of *Bears and Bear Bile*) and Li Chengri conducted research. In 1987, the project came under the provincial Spark Program and the education committee's list of "important research programs." To achieve the third dependable, Jichun spent more than two million yuan on business management books each time he traveled, the study of which allowed him to weigh and combine various management styles.[31]

San Zhua (the three catches) were to catch the right employees and collaborators (*zhua rencai*); to catch available funding opportunities (*zhua zijin*); and, lastly, to catch efficiency (*zhua xiaoyi*). Jichun's company hired five professors from various disciplinary backgrounds to collaborate, and "through a number of adjustments, fifty-eight percent of technicians and management staff achieved a higher level of education." As for the second catch, besides self-funding, Jichun procured loans from a bank and searched for foreign investors. He also strove to increase demand by improving the quality of his product, which is what he meant by efficiency. He set up a quality-control laboratory, and Professor Jin Yuquan, one of the coauthors for *Bears and Bear Bile*, worked to identify and neutralize germs in freshly extracted bile. In May 1991, Jichun became the "role model for the Youth Spark Program at the rural level."[32]

The book by the four Jins is mainly a celebration of their own entrepreneurship (albeit with the strong and necessary backing of state authorities), but the technologies they used to succeed in farming bears were the result of research by Chinese academics working at experimental farm stations. In 1987, Yanbian Agricultural College published an article by three researchers, who again shared the same surname of Jin. They each came from different bureaus, including the Yanji City People's Park, suggesting a widespread local network was being established around this new industry. Their experiment was conducted on one male black bear and one female brown bear, and describes the origin of techniques that have since become standard in Chinese bear farming.[33]

The Yanbian experiment was conducted in four stages, likely based on the Liberation Army Hospital experiments of 1984, which, as we have seen, had links to North Korean practice. The first was the so-called adaptation stage (*shiying jieduan*), wherein two bears were kept in one single cage for eight days prior to the surgery. The report explained, "Bears are vicious animals with a hot temperament. Caging the bears [together] is so that they adjust to the new environment." This likely meant to reduce their natural defenses through exhaustion and stress. Second was the "anesthesia stage." The bears were shot with an anesthetic gun filled with ketamine. When they were confirmed unconscious, ropes were tied around their bodies to drag and secure them to the sides of the cage. More ketamine and tranquilizer were administered to ensure the bears were in a deep coma before transporting them to the operating table. This brought researchers to the third stage: cutting open the bears to locate their gallbladders. A pair of pliers was used to hold the organ while a researcher took samples of bile using a syringe. After that, a tube was inserted into the gallbladder and secured with thread made from animal gut. The wound was then stitched up with the tube protruding from the animal's body, like a tap. The exposed end of the tube was then attached to an empty container especially made for bile collection. Before being put back into the cage, the bears were each made to wear a "metal coat" (*tiejiayi*).[34] In this way the living bear was essentially made into a vat with an attached spigot. The Chinese government would much later ban this technique and order all bear farms to switch to the "free dripping method," arguing it was a less painful way of extracting bile. Still, small-scale, illegal bear farms continue to use the original method to this day because they consider it more cost-effective.

The fourth and last stage of the experiment was to collect and process the bile. Bile was collected once every twenty-four hours, and baked for four to five days in a thermostatic oven at a temperature of 40 degrees Celsius. According to the lab report, the bile collected using this method contained essential acids besides ursodeoxycholic acid, which Japanese scientists had earlier identified as the main active ingredient. In pointing this out, Chinese researchers may have been agreeing with the Chinese medical principle that it was a combination of substances, not a single active ingredient, that gave drugs their power.[35]

The researchers also included a short description of the bears' condition: "Other than a slight drop in body weight, there were no signs of abnormal behavior during the experiment. Even after the tubes were removed, there were no side effects. Both bears have regained their weight and can be used for tourist viewing." There was mention that antiseptic agents were applied to the wound daily to prevent infection. When the experiment ended on the tenth day, researchers performed a last surgery to seal the wound up. The conclusion was that bile extracted using this method was safe and effective. This was preferred to hunting, which researchers regarded as "a barbaric method of gathering medicinals." They further claimed that the lab samples "fully conform to requirements in the state pharmacopoeia"—diagrams showing normal levels of acid content in captive bears were presented—and encouraged further research to "improve and perfect the technique of extracting bile from live bears."

Laboratory standards of this type were rarely replicated in private practice, however. In actual bear farms, manned by nonscientists, the bears' wounds would usually be left exposed and unattended, while cages were often so small that bears rubbed their fur off against the bars simply by moving.[36]

Initially, bear farming and bear bile was discussed almost exclusively in agricultural journals, underlining the strongly economic motivation for the practice. Only with the 1991 edition of the *China Pharmaceutical Yearbook* (the inaugural edition covered the years 1988–1989) did bear bile began to be mentioned in pharmacological publications, and from the 1992 edition onward, reports began to proliferate on the use of (and research on) this particular substance for medicinal purposes. The commercial availability of the product, in other words, created the conditions for new research on its medical efficacy, rather than the other way round. Most official statements such as the ones presented in the *Pharmaceutical Yearbook* are essentially reports based on research done on bears and other animals in captivity, with many of these coming from the bile factories of Jilin province.[37]

Bear bile farming, like farming of other "economic animals," also generated spin-off opportunities for publishable research in zoological journals. Captive bears that died were given to universities to be dissected and studied. In 1988, Yanbian Agricultural College received two dead bear cubs from a farm. Researchers used them to conduct close studies of bear anatomy, such as a detailed investigation of bears' tongues.[38] Chinese zoologists were thus upbeat about future bear research, which researcher Bi Pengfei attributed to the opportunities presented by farms.[39] Into the 1990s, almost all Chinese scientific studies on bears were government-funded projects connected to the farming enterprise. Observational studies commissioned by the Jilin provincial government, for example, showed that black bears produced most bile during the months of July through September, and the least in January through March. Male bears were found to produce more bile than female bears. Research was also carried out on how to best put bears under anesthesia, and to determine their daily nutritional intake and metabolic rates.[40]

In the cases of both bear bile and deer products, substances presented as "traditional Chinese medicine" were thus sustained and transformed by a modern industrial process backed by government-funded laboratory research. Both products also had a transnational character. Deer farming was a practice originating in the border regions of China and the Soviet Union, with elements of cross-border exchange. Likewise, bear farming and bile collection was a technology crafted in the borderlands of China and North Korea, and additionally influenced by lab work conducted in Japan.[41]

There is much discussion in Chinese sources of North Korean medicine in general being ancillary to or otherwise closely linked to that of China. The 1986 edition of the *China Pharmaceutical Yearbook* placed North Korean medicine within the category of *minzuyao* (indigenous) medicine, but one that had taken root in Chinese soil because of immigration: "From the mid-nineteenth century onwards, the North Koreans crossed the river to escape a widespread disaster and finally settled down in the area close to the Jilin border. It was here that [their] traditional indigenous medicine developed and flourished." According to Zhang Wenxuan, Chinese medical precepts were seminal in the formulation of the so-called four constitutions theory on which Korean medicine was based.[42] In these and other ways, Korean medicine was constructed, at least in China, as very much convergent with Chinese practices.

On the other hand, North Korean medicine was arguably influenced by modern Japanese practices to a much larger extent than by medicine in China. *Dongyi* (Eastern medicine), the Chinese term for North Korean medicine, had its own history of materia medica, while new medicinals were incorporated into Korean practice following Japanese scientific findings regarding their active ingredients. Other differences between Chinese and Korean medicine stemmed from divergent horticultural classifications. The authors of one report, comparing the use of fifteen plant-based medicinals in Yanbian with the 1985 state pharmacopoeia, found that different species or parts of a plant were used despite the similarity in names, because of the Korean influence on border medicine.[43] In other words, Yanbian prefecture (and Jilin province) was in many senses a "middle zone" between Chinese and Korean indigenous medicines, and bear farming was probably only one of many local manifestations of exchange. It was, however, unique in its impact on Chinese pharmaceuticals.

Expanding Claims for the Medical Efficacy of Bear Bile

As discussed above, the farming of bears in China pre-dated the research interest in bear bile on the part of the Chinese doctors and medical researchers. There was, however, a history of foreign interest in the medical uses of bears that Chinese researchers built on as soon as the commercial product began to proliferate and look for a market. That market was ultimately much larger than just people suffering from diseases of the eye, who had formed the principal patient base for bear bile in the pre-Communist period.

The use of bear gallbladder as a medicine was first recorded during the Tang period, when it was called *xiongdan*.[44] More specifically, it was believed to cure a handful of diseases like fever, jaundice, and dysentery. In the Ming-period *Bencao Gangmu*, however, author Li Shizhen gave bear gallbladder a fuller list of curative properties such as the ability to "reduce heat, clear the heart, sooth the liver and improve vision by removing unwanted tissue growth in the eye."[45] Later classical works—mostly of the Ming and Qing dynasties—would narrow the efficacy to being a clarifying agent for the eye, and recommend external rather than internal application. The bile was to be made into cream or powder form to be applied directly to the affected area.

It was a Japanese scientist (M. Shoda) who, in 1927, was responsible for isolating bear bile's active ingredient—ursodeoxycholic acid, or UDCA—and, in so doing, expanding its efficacies beyond those mentioned in Chinese texts, claiming it was also effective in treating coughs, lowering blood pressure, suppressing muscle spasms, and even useful as an antibacterial agent.[46] None of these curative properties had been recognized in earlier works on Chinese medicine, but would become quickly incorporated into bear bile's modern profile. A Japanese pharmaceutical company (Tokyo Tanabe) synthesized the product in the late 1950s (from cattle and pig bile, not bears), and marketed the highly purified compound as Urso. The success of this synthetic product, whose spectrum of clinical use in Japan and elsewhere then grew with time, certainly contributed to the charisma of the "original" material, raw bear bile. The isolation and synthesizing of its active agent thus made bear bile one of the few "organo-pharmaceuticals" in the pantheon of Chinese animal drugs that had the seeming sanction of foreign laboratory research and widespread clinical use outside China.[47]

Even before this development, however, Japanese patent medicine companies had displayed an attraction to bear bile similar to Chinese companies' attraction to tiger bone. The Japanese patent drug Rokushingan (*liushen wan* in Chinese, or, pill with six ingredients of magical power) included bear bile, as did other medicines advertised in the Japanese marketplace in the late 1950s. Whole bear gallbladders were also sold in Japan as medicine, as in China. In any case, by the time the Chinese began to develop bear bile farms in the 1980s, the existing Asian market for that product extended beyond China and its diaspora. In 1988, when the Indian government banned all export of bear products in an effort to conserve its bear population, Japanese researchers began visiting Chinese bear farms and brought back samples in order to compare the difference, if any, between the bile quality of farmed and wild bears.[48] Until the CITES convention was tightened to include bears in 1992, Japan imported "vast" amounts of bear gall and related bear products from China, a development that could only have confirmed the economic logic of developing bear farming as a new Chinese industry.[49]

Bear bile would eventually be marketed in China as curing everything from liver ailments, including hepatitis, to the common flu, hence becoming the most elaborate example of faunal medicalization in the modern Chinese pharmacy. To increase domestic sales, Chinese companies even went to the extent of marketing it as a tonic suitable for daily consumption, an aphrodisiac, or a "hangover cure for well-to-do businessmen who engage in nightly carousing," a claim that would much later be applied to rhino horn in Vietnam.[50] In other words it became a "health supplement," capable of not just curing disease but sustaining a healthy lifestyle. This new category of health supplement was helpful in expanding the market for animal-derived substances like bear bile once the strictly medical market had been saturated (a subject discussed in more detail below).

Although the efficacy of bear bile was buttressed by foreign medical research and interest, the active ingredients of many other Chinese medicines remained vague, and their effectiveness unproven by clinical trials. Laboratory research on their chemical makeup, however, became ever more precise, and their constituents were now often mentioned (and listed on the labels) of Chinese drugs as a way to signal that they had been tested and understood scientifically. For example, bilirubin is the chemical name for a substance found in the bile of many animal species.[51] In the 1950s, there was much discussion in Chinese medicine journals of the uses of "biles" from specific animals, but "bilirubin" was hardly mentioned.[52] By 1990, however, such chemical names were more commonly cited in discussions of Chinese drugs, giving them the imprimatur of the laboratory. The growing specificity with which the ingredients of animal-derived drugs were discussed was due not only to the growing importance and sophistication of research, but also to the need to suit Western marketing formats (and regulations) by listing chemical components.[53]

The Emergence of "Health Supplements" (*Baojianpin*)

Farmed animal medicinals were expensive to produce and market, especially as many were relatively new and considered more luxuries than necessities. It was therefore natural that medicinal animal farms would look to expand their markets beyond substances that required the prescription or advice of a physician, or that need be consumed only by sick or generally unhealthy people. Their solution was to exploit a new category of product called "health supplements"—substances in between medicine and food. Like some earlier Chinese patent medicines, modern health supplements could be sold as preventive rather than strictly curative. They could also be considered a modern version of an older Chinese category called "food cures" (basically foods that were considered health-giving or health-restoring). Food cures were not often mentioned in early Communist-period literature, but the term was repopularized in the 1980s in publications related to the government's hygiene movement, and then often discussed in relation to animal-based products.

"Food cure" (*shiliao*) is an ancient category, though one not unique to China.[54] Galen, for example, studied and wrote extensively on the medicinal effects of food.[55] The historian Ute Engelhardt has pointed out that a Tang tradition of producing *materia dietetica*, compilations of foodstuffs, grew out of (and in turn influenced) materia medica, although the categories "food" and "drug" maintained a distinction in that period as in the modern one. One dividing line was the perception of greater potency attached to the category "drug," and hence the need for safety and, ultimately, state regulation.[56] The promoters of animal-based drugs through most of the period we've been dealing with were very clear about the identity of those substances as drugs and were often concerned with issues of safety, but were just as often invested in their product being perceived as potent. Some producers of farmed animal products in the 1980s, however, began walking back from claims that their products were always drugs. The revived discussion of food cures, together with the translation of foreign terms like "health supplement," helped open the space for this loosening of categories.

Food cures were a common theme in the magazine series titled *Zhongguo Weisheng Huakan* (China health pictorial), published by the government in the 1980s to educate the public about hygiene (*weisheng*). The magazine's view of hygiene was very broad, including everything from the "scientific way" to arrange one's kitchen utensils to healthy eating habits to the proper use of food cures. For instance, articles warned against swallowing fish bile to cure various diseases, which was a common practice in the countryside, or eating eggs that were rejected by farms. Some articles were in the form of answers to public queries, mostly written by medical experts. Others informed about or revived the use of certain unusual ingredients.[57]

Although intended for a popular audience, the journal tried to strike a "scientific" rather than a folkish tone. This was particularly apparent in articles involving the medicinal qualities of animals. One example was titled "The Peculiar Food Cure—Ants":

> Tremendous progress has been made in research on ants as a food cure in the last 6–7 years. Joint efforts have been made among experts to improve "Xuan Ju Tonic Wine," a *yanfang* [experience-based prescription] that uses the *Podomyrma* ant species from Guangxi province. This project has spearheaded research on uses of ants as a food cure. Currently 30 kinds of ant-based products have been launched. A technological development center has been set up in Pinggu, Beijing to develop a series of tonic wines using ants. Some examples are the "China Jingang Wine" and "Mountain-Ant Bone Strengthening Fluid (*ye*)." Drugs to counter rheumatoid arthritis will also be launched.[58]

It was also the style of the magazine to draw on foreign evidence to buttress its claims. The same article went on to report that "countries like America, the Soviet Union, and Philippines are eating chocolate-coated ant sandwiches, drinking wine soaked in ants, and even selling them in cans," mistaking the sale of minor novelty items for significant food trends. This way of writing about ants was little different from what we have encountered previously, except that the word "food" was now being used, and articles promoting their consumption were being placed beside articles about kitchens.[59]

The introduction by Chinese pharmaceutical companies in the 1980s of the Western term "health supplement" could be taken as an attempt to give a contemporary and scientific flavor to food cure, another way of stopping just short of identifying certain substances as drugs.[60] The Chinese term for health supplements is *baojianpin* (literally, products that protect one's health). In the West, most health supplements were obviously not food and were normally associated with pills, such as vitamins. The boundaries could sometimes blur, however. For example, in *Life and Health* (*Shenghuo Yu Jiankang*), a monthly Hong Kong lifestyle magazine of the 1980s, advertisements introduced chicken soup as a form of health supplement. In the United States and United Kingdom, chicken soup was clearly marketed and consumed as food, but believed by some to have the property of curing common colds.

In 1987, the Ministry of Health recognized the new category of health supplement and issued a law indicating the kinds of Chinese medicine that could fall within it. Accordingly, health supplements made from *zhongyao* or Chinese medicinals "should be nourishing, nutritious and effective as a protector of health. They should not cause harm when used long-term." There was also the stipulation that such products "are not derived from endangered plants and animal species, nor also foreign imports."[61]

Still, "health supplements" remained ambiguous from a regulatory standpoint, as substances marketed this way still had to be classed for regulation as either a food (*baojian shipin*) or a drug (*baojian yaopin*), but not both. In 1995, an article by Zhong Jianguang sought to clarify the difference. According to him, products registered under *shizihao* (literally, a number in the food category) meant that their main components were essential to human health. Zhong gave the example of proteins and amino acids. Such products should not include traditional medicinals as ingredients, according to the official Food Hygiene Law, and advertisements for them were not allowed to claim medical efficacy. Substances with a *yaojianzihao* (a number in the drug category) could, by the same logic, not be advertised as nutritious food.[62]

Despite Zhong's attempt to achieve clarity, the category health supplement remained powerfully ambiguous, to the consternation of regulators but the profit of drug companies. Or, to put it another way, the ability it presented to cross the food-drug boundary, and provide both nutrition and health in one package, made it an ideal marketing category for the new, more open economy of the Deng period. The category was particularly important for animal-based substances, which were now being industrially pro-duced and mass-marketed. Formerly rare, or sparingly used in comparison with herbs, their existing market as medicines was therefore limited, even as their production was more expensive. But as ingredients within health supplements, they could increase the value of such products, while finding a much wider and more regular market (i.e., healthy consumers rather than sick people). Bear bile, as one prominent example, could be marketed as a pure medicine, but it could also be made into an ingredient of wine, tea, or even toothpaste, which could then be marketed as maintaining one's health.

Sensing abuse, the Chinese government warned in the late 1990s that it might scrap the *baojianpin* category altogether, though it ultimately decided to merely tighten it by removing the *baojian yaopin* (health supplement–drug) subcategory.[63] Thus in September 2001 the Ministry of Health forbade sales of bear bile as a "health product," emphasizing its status as a controlled drug.[64] Still, *baojian yaopin* never disappeared as a trade term; the China Health Care Association was still using it as late as 2011, and a paper published in 2016 provided a market update on the category.[65] Investigations by the Chinese media into the bear bile products firm Guizhentang revealed that, despite the 2001 ruling, the company had still not registered most of its products as drugs, thus allowing them to be sold over the counter and without the need of prescription. This included bile tea, one of Guizhentang's bestselling products, and one that had no "traditional" sanction.[66]

Some of these new products were also made from "protected" animals. On October 1987, the Chinese State Council issued a guideline for the use of "wild medicinals," in which medicinal animals were listed according to their level of endangerment. In the first, most-endangered, category were only four species: tiger, leopard, sika deer, and the saiga antelope. Two clauses in the guideline relating to this group were contradictory, however, in that while one clause forbade their hunting, another allowed the sale of their products, although not overseas. Even then, Chinese pharmaceutical companies were selling and advertising such products to Hong Kong–based customers after the issuance of the 1987 guideline. Not until after China signed the Convention on International Trade in Endangered Species of Wild Fauna and Flora (CITES) did it announce, on May 29, 1993, an official ban on all sales of rhino horns and tiger-bone products. Hong Kong followed suit two years later with a similar law.[67] This of course opened the door to a huge and still-flourishing black market in what were now illegal animal products, for which, by the early 1980s, a strong demand had already been created.

Conclusion

The period of Deng's reforms saw another significant expansion of faunal medicalization as targeted species now became "economic animals" as well, in line with the expansion of both domestic and overseas markets. This expansion built on the earlier Mao-period trade in luxury animal products, such as deer antler and musk, but the new market-driven medicalization potentially extended to nearly all animals, and nearly all their parts. Surveys of folk medicinals in the Mao period had greatly expanded the corpus of animal-based drugs, and with market reforms these species now became subject to larger-scale and more efficient exploitation.

As the signature medicinal animal of the Great Leap Forward period had been the deer, and that of the Cultural Revolution had been the chicken, the animal most emblematic of Deng-period pharmaceuticalization was the bear. As in these previous instances, bear bile farming would depend as much on contemporary (and foreign) innovation as on ancient recipes. Whereas Soviet research had partially inspired both deer farming and chicken blood therapy, Japanese laboratory research and North Korean technology were both essential for bear bile farming to take root in China and be raised to the level of industrial-scale pharmaceutical production. Laboratory-based research increasingly loomed large in faunal drug research in this period, even as innovation disappeared from the rhetoric of marketing in favor of "tradition."

Indeed, animals (especially rare and endangered ones) would be increasingly identified with the domain of Chinese medicine from the Deng period onward, even though plant-based medicinals continued to make up the majority of the Chinese physician's corpus. As we have seen, the increased presence and profile of medicinal animals was the result of deliberate state engineering having its origins in the Mao period. But the creation in the 1980s of the category "health supplement" not only expanded the usages for already farmed animals, but also provided pharmaceutical companies with a category under which even more animal tissue could be marketed for commercial purposes. And although China put regulations of such products on the books, their spotty enforcement was a concession to both the ambiguity of such products and pressure from producers and distributors to expand existing markets.

CONCLUSION

The rise of an animal-intensive drug-discovery and drug-making culture in the early Communist period is an aspect of Chinese medicine that is under-accounted-for in most histories and ethnographies of that domain, despite its contemporary relevance. Part of the reason for this absence, in addition to the more political ones we have already recounted, is the heterogeneity of its origins. The post-Revolution drug sector was not solely the creation of Chinese physicians, who are the normative subjects of scholarly attention in this field. Nor was it simply a continuation of the old Chinese drug business, but was a new set of interests, practices, and materials that would contribute to making the Chinese pharmaceutical sector a "different animal" than it had been in the Republican period. Faunal medicine was also a realm of invention and innovation, even when its actors claimed to be following classical texts and folk remedies, a process by which increasing numbers, amounts, and types of animal parts and tissues were brought into the modern Chinese pharmacy cabinet from many different sources.

It was not absolutely inevitable that animals would, along with plants, join the modern Chinese state pharmacy, any more than it is inevitable that they remain there. Although animal parts and tissues had always been present in Chinese materia medica, availability had naturally restricted their use. Chinese materia medica in everyday clinical practice comprised mostly herbs, and any animal components were, with few exceptions, collected from the wild. It took positive action to select animals, subject them to detailed research, mass-produce and mass-distribute their parts and tissue, and per-form the many other functions necessary to re-render such a vast array of creatures in the form of modern drugs. But as this study has demonstrated, drugs derived from animal tissue eventually emerged as central to the larger process of pharmaceuticalization, or making Chinese medicine what Pordie and Hardon have called an "Asian industrial medicine."[1]

The process I have described as faunal medicalization was not simply the old medicine in a new form. Once the farming and collection of animals for medical purposes began to become state policy, new types of animals (and new parts of animals) became part of an ever-expanding list. This expansion set the stage for increased experimentation with all sorts of faunal tissue, by farms, companies, universities, and individual physician-researchers, culminating in short-lived blood-related animal therapies of the Cultural Revolution, on the one hand, and stable industries producing large quantities of farmed animal parts, on the other. These were, however, two manifestations of the same phe-nomenon, which has continued ferociously into the present day.

Through this process, animal tissue whose use was sanctioned by classi-cal texts or folk usage took on new curative properties or was recommended for use against diseases and conditions unknown to classical writers. From asthma to cancer, diseases that continued to bedevil Western biomedicine through this period seemed more and more to invite the seeming power if not mystery of animal-based cures. Their delivery systems also "modern-ized," to include injections, eye drops, new types of pills and powders, incor-poration into foodstuffs, and so on. These developments were particularly significant in giving Chinese medicine the character of a drug-based practice rich with animal tissue, an identity, if not a stigma, it continues to carry today. This was in turn emblematic of a more general pharmaceuticaliza-tion of Chinese medicine, which began as early as the Republican period but adapted new forms in the Mao and Deng eras.

Including folk remedies in the drug-discovery process was part of a logic of production that considered every material a potential resource, but one that was also driven by political ideology. Therapies involving such materials as chicken blood, goose blood, and toad heads were clearly more than the re-discovery of local or forgotten practices. Communist slogans about mining the experience of the people, on the one hand, and innovating all aspects of life, on the other, created unprecedented marriages between local folk medi-cine cultures and nationalizing drug-discovery ones.

I have also demonstrated the large role Chinese export policy had in push-ing the farmed production of a range of animal parts. Chinese medicinals were a significant source of foreign exchange income for the regime from the 1950s onward, given the increasing wealth of the Chinese diaspora in the same period, and the continuing willingness to buy animal-derived products from the mainland. That such "luxury" medicinals remained a production priority even through the Cultural Revolution helps account for their expansion into other areas, such as bear bile farming, in the post-Mao period. To separate the luxurious and expensive from the mundane and cheap, however, would be to lose sight of the increased production in farms and research labs of animal parts across a whole range of prices and delivery methods, and for a large range of ailments and customers. I have argued that habituating Chinese people to this new availability and charisma of animal tissue should be seen as a general legacy of this period, one that transcends the history of use of any one animal-based material or product.

The twenty-first-century association of Chinese medicine with the consumption of endangered animal species and the exploitation of bears for the use of their bile must therefore be contextualized within the rise from the 1950s onward of a growing "animal-consciousness" or faunal medicalization within Chinese pharmacology, which was closely bound up with the rise of drug development and production as a national project. The notorious global trade in the parts of tigers, rhinos, and other species, which reached its first peak in the 1970s, was a pan-Asian phenomenon that involved and yet transcended the PRC, and thus demands a deeper and broader historical treatment than can be provided here. But when a more "open" China had become wealthy enough to scour the world for more exotic animal-based materials in the period following the one I've chronicled, their use had been conditioned by the increased familiarity since the 1950s with insects, lizards, oyster shell, toad powder, chicken blood, and a hundred other examples of animal tissues that had entered state medicine in one form or another during the Great Leap Forward and Cultural Revolution. The massive marketing and consumption of "traditional" Chinese drugs as a result of Deng's reforms, in other words, has its roots in Mao-period innovation.

Besides economics, politics, and bureaucratic priorities, the influence of Soviet medicine on Chinese pharmacology was particularly important in the period before and into the Great Leap Forward. Previous accounts of Chinese pharmacology under Communism have rightly discussed it as a hybrid combination of indigenous and biomedical practices and theories, but it was a biomedicine mainly cycled through a specifically Soviet experience. This included a shared Soviet-Chinese need for import and substitution of Western drugs using indigenous materials, plant- and animal-based. It also included research and production related to shared natural resources along their common border, such as deer and ginseng. Moreover, Pavlovian science and the strong Soviet interest in organotherapy and tissue therapy, as well as a Russian tradition of scholarship around Chinese medicine, provided additional points of contact between animal-based therapies in the two socialist states. The cross-border connections with North Korea (and Japan) are equally important, and deserve more research.

As early as the 1980s, however, the history of drug discovery and innovation in the early Communist period began to be downplayed or erased from memory, at least in terms of how products were presented to consumers. The huge mass of animal-derived products became simply the stuff of "tradition."[2] This was particularly true as the Chinese economy began to develop in a capitalist direction, and the need to write advertising copy grew. As a 1980s Tongrentang advertisement for tiger-bone wine read,

> Chinese medicinal wine has a long tradition and is famous both within and outside China. It is only the tiger bone wine, however, that strengthens tendons and bones, and at the same time reduces pain and rheumatism. Its origin can be traced back some two thousand years. Until the Ming dynasty, there existed different variations of tiger bone wine recipes. Tongrentang's tiger bone wine was founded on years of experience of its predecessors, and is exceptionally effective as a healing agent. Towards the end of the Qing dynasty, it became the imperial recipe for the court's exclusive use but still produced by Tongrentang. The product has a long history of 150 years and continues to enjoy good reputation. In 1924, it received an award at an international convention and recently, was conferred the national prize for top quality.[3]

Although this history is largely true, at least as regards tiger-bone wine, the early Communist period of Tongrentang's existence is notably absent, as it is from nearly all literature produced by contemporary Chinese drug manufacturers. This erasure of innovation or artifice produced a very different frame for these drugs than they had had in the Mao period, when contemporary human intervention, heroic, creative, and scientific, was more often stressed.

Animal Medicinals after Deng as Opportunity and Threat

As Chinese medicine has globalized in the period since Deng, medicalized fauna has continued to play a central, if increasingly problematic, role. As discussed in the introduction, the rise of environmental conservation and the new category "endangered species" has in a sense created a clash of two values. One is the value that modern societies, including those in Asia, increasingly attach to certain wild animal species, particularly large mammals like tigers and bears, but arguably any species that comes into consciousness as threatened with extinction. The other is the value these same species continue to have in the marketplace, and not just as regular drugs, but in many cases "miracle cures" and even investments, given their increasing rarity. This clash is too easily exploited, however, as one between "Western" love for animals, in the abstract, and "Chinese" understanding of (and need for) such animal medicines as life-saving cures. In reality, many middle-class Chinese, both on the mainland and in the diaspora, and within Chinese medicine itself, have been on the front lines in the battle to save endangered species from poaching and consumption and to reduce or eliminate their presence in Chinese materia medica, a movement that parallels Chinese efforts to end the practice of eating shark fin soup.[4]

This new ethical dimension in debates over Chinese medicine is best illustrated by the reaction in China and its diaspora to the growth of large bear-farming companies with Deng-period roots. The phenomenon is worth chronicling in some detail, since, unlike the more famous plight of tigers and rhinos, most of the affected animals live in China or its immediate borderlands, and most of the parties to the debate have therefore been of Chinese ethnicity, and living in Asia. It also brings us full circle to the story I tell in the introduction of visits to two bear farms—experiences that inspired this study.

By the 1990s, an estimated four hundred bear farms in China contained tens of thousands of animals.[5] In February 2012, however, Guizhentang Pharmaceutical became the first bear-farming company to offer its stock publicly, which set off a firestorm of protest against the industry on Chinese websites. Originally orchestrated by anti-bear-farming activists, the incident ultimately involved hundreds of anonymous social media posters who sympathized with the bears and against the company. The public outcry was so strong that Guizhentang abandoned its attempt at a public offering in 2013, and again a few years later, although the company, and the bear bile industry, continues to survive and remain profitable to this day.

Some voices in the Guizhentang debate used the opportunity to question the efficacy of Chinese drugs more generally, while others claimed to speak in the name of Chinese medicine from various positions of authority. The strongest of these latter voices came from the China Association of Traditional Chinese Medicine (*Zhongguo Zhongyao Xiehui*), a trade group representing bear farms that was not shy in animating history and science in its favor. Some influential Chinese physicians also defended bear farming as a natural development in the scientization (if not industrialization) of their practice. Dr. Xin Yan of Guang'anmen Hospital in Beijing, for example, said, "[The drug] heparin is extracted from the small intestines of pigs and ox's lungs, and is used to treat pulmonary thrombosis, and its manufacturer is listed on the stock market. . . . It's against nature to milk a cow every day, but we have to develop the dairy industry."[6] Guang'anmen Hospital is one of the leading Chinese medicine training centers in China.

Xin's statement sought to conflate wild animals with livestock (and ignored major differences in extraction techniques), but a more common argument, held by some Chinese medical practitioners, was that farming was necessary because there was no substance to replace bear bile. This ignored, however, the large investment in searching for (and finding) synthetic substitutes for this and other rare animal tissue that I have previously chronicled in the early Communist period. As early as 1954, Japanese scientists claimed to have found an alternative in the bile of chickens,[7] and in 1984, a drug research institute in Liaoning province had produced a synthetic version of bear bile that, according to one authoritative source, "proved equally efficacious as a cholagogue, an anti-inflammatory agent, and a host of other functions."[8] Professor Jiang Qi, at what is now Shenyang Pharmaceutical University, had been committed to developing a synthetic replacement for bear bile since the early Deng period. By the early 1990s, other Chinese researchers found what they judged to be additional substitutes in the bile of rabbits and pigs.[9]

Thus, even before the Guizhentang controversy, some Chinese physicians had switched to using the bile of non-endangered animals or even herbal substitutes. But the use of substitutes in Chinese medicine has resurfaced as an issue in the twenty-first century, as conservative voices within Chinese medicine argue that substitutes or synthetics delimit the full healing abilities listed in classical materia medica. Such physicians do not accept that isolating and synthesizing an active ingredient like ursodeoxycholic acid will be as effective as using raw bile, because they do not accept the premise of a single ingredient being responsible for the material's curative powers. And even if they accept the substitution, they might not agree with the concept of targeting a specific ailment. The raw product, to their minds, cures in a different way, or along different and more complex paths. This helps explain why Professor Jiang's synthetic substitute for bile is looked on with skepticism by conservatives in the Chinese medicine community, despite his having conducted numerous clinical trials with positive results. Professor Li Lianda of the Chinese Academy of Engineering (Zhongguo Gongcheng Yuan) commented, "Bear bile contains scores of active ingredients and not just ursodeoxycholic acid. Used as a whole, bear bile is a powerful drug. . . . Professor Jiang has only proven his product to be effective for minor illnesses like eye cataract, piles and high-blood pressure, when in actual fact bear bile is highly potent in curing the more difficult ones [*yinan zazheng*] like coronary heart disease, influenza, and even SARS. It is probably for this reason that Chinese Food and Drug Administration has not yet approved [Jiang's] drug."[10] In proposing bear bile as a virtual cure-all, and preferring the raw material to laboratory-produced substitutes, the claims in this statement resemble those made for many of the earlier animal-based therapies we have chronicled, such as chicken and goose blood. And as in these earlier instances, such claims strongly part company with classical texts, relocating their products in the very modern arena of innovation, and among disease categories the ancients had never encountered. On the other hand, in rejecting the idea of an active ingredient, clinical trials, and the search for synthetic substitutes, Li's defense of bear bile is equally a rejection of the Mao-period project of combining Chinese and Western medicine.

In addition to arguments over efficacy, and the availability of substitutes, ethical concerns regarding animals' lives and their suffering have emerged as a new issue in Chinese medicine, one that more than any other has inflamed resistance to bear farming. At the height of the 2012 controversy, the chairman of the China Association of Traditional Chinese Medicine, Fang Shuting, was quoted as saying in a press conference, "Bile collection is as simple as opening a tap. It is natural, painless, and when done, the bears go out to play on their own. I don't feel anything strange, and in fact, the entire process looks comfortable." This led to a scientific controversy over the levels of pain experienced by bears. When Fang's statements were ridiculed in a series of cartoons,[11] he countered by presenting seemingly independent laboratory reports purporting to show that farmed bears showed no indicators of pain while being tapped. Further investigation by a reporter for an online news agency, however, revealed that the pharmaceutical industry had paid for the research that formed the basis for Fang's statements, discrediting it in the eyes of critics.[12]

That scientific research was employed to quantify yet dismiss the pain of bears stirred even more response from the Chinese academic community. Three faculty members from the College of Biological Sciences and Biotechnology at Beijing Forestry University wrote to the international journal *Nature* in protest, citing "a wave of condemnation across the country" against Guizhentang's claims and its attempts to expand by offering public stock. The authors called for an end to bear farming, condemning as unreasonable the preference of wealthy consumers for natural bear bile when synthetic substitutes were available. They additionally pointed to the product's role in the gifting and bribing economies, its status as a luxury being ultimately more important than the purchasers' need or desire to use it as medicine. They even cited sympathetic voices among delegates to the National People's Congress, who had stated that such an industry was intolerable in a modern civilized society.[13]

Allowing bear farming to become an emblem of Chinese medicine thus threatened to weaken the reputation of that domain at a moment when high-level Chinese state actors were forcefully promoting it abroad. In 2007, Vice Minister of Science and Technology Liu Yanhua had described Chinese medicine as "having the greatest potential for original innovations among all other academic disciplines in the country," by which he meant converting Mao's "treasure house" of materia medica into biomedical drugs with a global market. That same year, Vice Premier Wu Yi outlined a three-year program to promote Chinese medicine as a "world intangible cultural heritage," with more funding, patent protections, and citations in regular medical textbooks. Even before the Guizhentang controversy, this refortifying of Chinese medicine by the state had elicited a counterreaction on a scale not seen since the early 1950s, as philosopher of science Zhong Gongyao of South Central University collected more than ten thousand signatures on a petition to remove Chinese medicine's special status from the Chinese constitution. Zhong referred to Chinese medicine as "a lie that has been fabricated with no scientific proof," while also citing its threat to biodiversity. Zhong was reprimanded by the National People's Congress Health Committee, but his arguments lingered and found a fresh audience with Guizhentang's attempted stock listing five years later.[14]

Zhong was hostile to Chinese medicine regardless of the animal issue, but the controversy over bear farming illustrated how the resurgent use of animal parts and tissues (at least from mammals) threatened to fracture Chinese medicine itself as a community of physicians, patients, drug suppliers, and healthy consumers as it clashed with modern sensibilities over animal welfare and conservation. One example of the issue's effect was the industry's felt need for rebranding. A visit to Guizhentang's bear farm in Quanzhou city by reporter Wang Yu at the height of the controversy found no public display of words like "bear bile" or "farm" on the company's signboards. In fact, Wang claimed, Guizhentang security guards used the term *shengtaiyuan* (ecological park) to describe the facility. This was also the company's official line for making its shares public, to create "A Land of a Thousand Bears" covering 3,000 mu or approximately 495 acres.[15] Golden Bear Ltd., which we encountered in the introduction and was part of the same trade group as Guizhentang, undoubtedly crafted its public image as a wildlife preserve as a result of the same conditions. Guizhentang simultaneously rebranded itself as high-tech, now registering under the name Fujian Guizhentang Biological Development Co. Ltd. As the Chinese government set its sights on building a biopharmaceutical hub in the south, with high-profile projects like the Guangzhou International Biological Island, the company likely hoped to lend itself legitimacy by resonating more closely with official policy.[16] This same strategy was used by Jin Jichun, China's first bear farm owner, to ensure success of his business venture in the 1980s. One company executive was even quoted as saying, "Going against us is as good as going against the state."[17]

Like the better-known controversies over the use of tiger and rhino parts, opposition to bear farming has also had international reach, particularly in the Chinese diaspora. The most prominent voice opposing the practice has probably been the Animals Asia Foundation, an animal welfare organization based in Hong Kong that has enlisted sympathetic Chinese physicians in its Healing without Harm campaign.[18] NGOs like Animals Asia and WildAid also turned to the voices of Chinese celebrity activists (e.g., Jackie Chan, Yoa Ming, Sun Li, Li Bingbing, Jay Chou, Lang Lang, Angelababy, and others) to answer those defenders of bear farming who claimed the authority of history and culture. Thus has the animal issue greatly expanded the numbers and types of voices and actors, domestically and internationally, with a claimed stake in the future shaping of Chinese medicine.

Singapore, a city-state with an ethnic Chinese majority population, not otherwise known for citizen activism, has also developed an unusually strong animal welfare movement in the last two decades, well keyed in to controversies in China. As early as 2001, ethnic Chinese students at the National University of Singapore (NUS), where I work, were publicly displaying a full-sized mechanical bear in a small cage in an effort to raise awareness of the cruelty of bear farming among their peers. In 2010, at the founding of NUS' residential Tembusu College, students voted to name their five "houses" after endangered Asian animal species, and have subsequently institutionalized awareness-raising projects that sometimes include faunal medicalization.[19] Since 2006, the local Animal Concerns Research and Education Society (ACRES) and the Singapore TCM Organizations Committee (STOC) have cooperated on an endangered species-friendly TCM labeling campaign with the goal of an animal-free Chinese medicine.[20] Similar groups exist in Hong Kong and Taiwan, which further belies the notion that Chinese Asia is blind to animal welfare and biodiversity issues.[21]

Despite rising ethical concern around faunal medicalization inside and outside China, the practice remains immensely profitable, and thus politically influential. The Chinese State Council's brief lifting in 2018 of the decade-old ban on the medicinal use of tiger and rhino parts drew renewed attention to what are essentially domestic tiger farms, modeled on bear farms and operated in the guise of "tiger parks" for tourists. Their owners, together with the developers of similar rhino parks in China and South Africa, wish to extend the medicinal farming culture, which began with deer and other animals, and has proven so profitable with bears, to even non-Chinese apex species. Their influence and that of more conservative Chinese physicians is seen to be behind the Chinese government's aborted attempt to loosen restrictions on the medical use of both animals, despite their critically endangered nature. As with bear farmers, the owners of such parks claim a conservation mantle, converting an endangered species into a renewable resource. In doing so they have made animal medicines even more emblematic of Chinese medicine at a moment when the Chinese government has again increased its global promotion in conjunction with the Belt and Road Initiative.[22]

The effect of the COVID-19 pandemic on faunal medicalization is only beginning to be felt as this book goes to press. But the emergence of pangolins as probable intermediate hosts of the virus has laid bare the irony of trafficking disease-bearing wild animals to support human health. The removal of the highly endangered pangolins from the official Chinese pharmacopeia a few months into the crisis was applauded by the Chinese and global conservation communities, and was a particular victory for the China Biodiversity Conservation and Green Development Foundation (CBCGDF), an NGO that had long advocated for that reform.[23] In temporarily banning the wildlife trade, however, the Chinese government left a large loophole for medicinal animals. Even pangolin scales remained legal for use in patent medicines, and hospitals were allowed to draw on "existing stockpiles," which are notoriously difficult to police.[24] The inclusion of an injection containing bear bile powder on a government-issued list of remedies to fight the virus was also indicative of the continuing power of that industry, and its ability to promote its product as all-purpose in the manner of chicken blood therapy, even for zoonotic diseases.[25] Concern was also expressed by environmental groups that newly banned wildlife farms would use the Chinese medicine exemption to medicalize animals that they had previously raised as food. An advisory from the National Forestry and Grassland Administration seemed to suggest that strategy, with the snake farming industry in Guangxi province being among the first to respond.[26]

As these issues play out in the linked arenas of animal ethics, conservation policy, public health, and Chinese medicine itself, the history of faunal medicalization is too rarely invoked, except to repeat the ahistorical mantra of thousands of years of use. Recognizing Chinese medicine as a rich, varied, but ultimately dynamic domain, driven by political considerations and business interests as well as tradition, and with a modern as well as ancient history, can better inform debate by recognizing the possibilities of choice and change. The future shaping of Chinese medicine will involve not just elite actors, however, but the scores of consumers who increasingly participate in discussions of these matters and choose to buy or boycott animal-based medicines. Whether they will reinvent the pharmacology of Chinese medicine as a practice less reliant on animals, endangered or otherwise, thereby reversing the pattern we have traced from the 1950s, remains a vital question.

NOTES

Introduction

1. The historical and ethnographic literature on Chinese medicine in twentieth-century China is vast and growing. Among the works that have most closely informed my own account, given their overlap in period and/or theme, are (in no particular order) Sean Hsiang-lin Lei, *Neither Donkey nor Horse: Medicine in the Struggle over China's Modernity* (Chicago: University of Chicago Press, 2014); Kim Taylor, *Chinese Medicine in Early Communist China, 1945-63: A Medicine of Revolution* (London: Routledge, 2005); Carla Nappi, *The Monkey and the Inkpot* (Cambridge, MA: Harvard University Press, 2009); Mei Zhan, *Otherworldly: Making Chinese Medicine through Transnational Frames* (Durham, NC: Duke University Press, 2009); Paul Unschuld, *Medicine in China: A History of Pharmaceutics* (Berkeley: University of California Press, 1986); Bridie J. Andrews, *The Making of Modern Chinese Medicine, 1850-1960* (Honolulu: University of Hawai'i Press, 2015); Volker Scheid, *Chinese Medicine in Contemporary China: Plurality and Synthesis* (Durham, NC: Duke University Press, 2002); Elizabeth Hsu, ed., *Innovation in Chinese Medicine* (Cambridge: Cambridge University Press, 2001); Sherman Cochran, *Chinese Medicine Men: Consumer Culture in China and Southeast Asia* (Cambridge, MA: Harvard University Press, 2006); Judith Farquhar, *Knowing Practice: The Clinical Encounter of Chinese Medicine* (Boulder, CO: Westview Press, 1996); Miriam Gross, *Farewell to the God of Plague: Chairman Mao's Campaign to Deworm China* (Berkeley: University of California Press, 2014); Xiaoping Fang, *Barefoot Doctors and Western Medicine in China* (Rochester, NY: University of Rochester Press, 2012); and Martin Saxer, *Manufacturing Tibetan Medicine: The Creation of an Industry and the Moral Economy of Tibetanness* (New York: Berghahn Books, 2013).

2. Bridie J. Andrews, "China: Medicine," in *Reader's Guide to the History of Science*, ed. Arne Hessenbruch (New York: Routledge, 2000), 136. The two historians cited as working to "upgrade Western perceptions" are Joseph Needham and Nathan Sivin. Andrews contrasts their scholarship with that of Paul Unschuld and Donald Harper, who are equally fascinated by the unorthodox.

3. As Bruno Latour puts it, "We have to be as undecided as the various actors we follow as to what technoscience is made of; every time an inside/outside divide is built, we should study the two sides simultaneously." Latour, *Science in Action: How to Follow Scientists and Engineers through Society* (Cambridge, MA: Harvard University Press, 1987), 258–259. Substituting "Chinese medicine" for "technoscience," animal tissue remains a significant boundary object in Chinese medicine, placed inside or outside that domain depending on who is speaking and in what historical circumstances.

4. The literature on wildlife conservation is rarely informed by mainstream academic works on Chinese medicines, while works on medicine are generally uninformed by the literature on wildlife or animal studies. One of the few works that has attempted to bridge this gap, though for a popular audience, is Richard Ellis's *Tiger Bone and Rhino Horn: The Destruction of Wildlife for Traditional Chinese Medicine* (Washington, DC: Island Press, 2005). The scholarly work on Chinese medicine that gives greatest mention to animal tissue is Nappi's *The Monkey and The Inkpot*, though her focus is the work of a premodern physician and his text, Li Shizhen's *Bencao Gangmu*, and not modern animal-based substances.

5. Kuo Wen-Hua, "Promoting Chinese Herbal Drugs through Regulatory Globalisation: The Case of the Consortium for Globalization of Chinese Medicine," *Asian Medicine* 10 (2015): 316–339; Wu Wan-Ying, "TCM-Based New Drug Discovery and Development in China," *Chinese Journal of Natural Medicine* 12, no. 4 (2014): 0241–0250; the contradictions regarding applying biomedical standards of safety to Asian medicines are well-discussed in Paul Kadetz, "Colonizing Safety: Creating Risk through the Enforcement of Biomedical Constructions of Safety," *East Asian Science, Technology, and Society* 8 (2014): 81–106.

6. On the "worlding" of Chinese medicine, see Mei Zhan, *Otherworldly*, and Volker Sheid, "The Globalization of Chinese Medicine," *The Lancet* 354 (December 1999). The World Health Organization (WHO), influential in promoting international acceptance of Chinese medicine since the Declaration of Alma Alta in 1978, has in 2018 incorporated Chinese medicine for the first time into its influential Global Medical Compendium, signaling a heightened degree of acceptance while also generating fresh controversy. See David Cyranoski, "The Big Push for Chinese Medicine," *Nature* 561 (September 2018): 444–450; on the Nobel Prize awarded in 2015 to Tu You You for the "discovery" of artemisinin, see Elizabeth Hsu, "Reflections on the 'Discovery' of the Antimalarial Qinghao," *British Journal of Clinical Pharmacology* 61 (6) (2006): 666–670; and Marta Hanson, "Is the 2015 Nobel Prize a Turning Point for Traditional Chinese Medicine?," *The Conversation*, October 5, 2015, http://theconversation.com/is-the-2015-nobel-prize-a-turning -point-for-traditional-chinese-medicine-48643.

7. Yu Jing and Wang Xiaonan, "Will TCM Finally Gain Global Acceptance amid COVID-19?," CGTN, June 16, 2020, https://news.cgtn.com/news/2020-06-14/Will-Chinese-medicine-finally-gain-global-acceptance-amid-COVID-19--RjPubXostW/index.html.

8. The 2018 *Living Planet Report* of the World Wide Fund for Nature (WWF) estimates a "60% decline in the size of populations of mammals, birds, fish, reptiles, and amphibians" has occurred in the last forty years (M. Grooten and R. E. A. Almond, eds., *Living Planet Report: Aiming Higher* [Gland, Switzerland: WWF, 2018]). Although poaching and trafficking of "medicinal animals" accounts for only a fraction of that overall decline, it has been decisive in the case of some species, such as tigers, rhinos, pangolins, saiga antelope, musk deer, moon bears, manta rays and seahorses, among others. Most of these animals are protected by the Convention on International Trade in Endangered Species (CITES), but the global trade in protected species was estimated in 2016 to generate US $19 billion, comparable to profits from the illegal trade in narcotics and small arms ("Traditional Chinese Medical Authorities are Unable to Stop the Booming Trade in Rare Animal Parts," *Time*, November 22, 2016). The price of rhino horn on the global black market as of 2016 exceeded that of gold and cocaine (Daan P. van Uhm, *The Illegal Trade in Wildlife: Inside the World of Poachers, Smugglers, and Traders* [New York: Springer, 2016]).

9. Duncan Graham-Rowe, "Biodiversity: Endangered and In Demand," *Nature* 480 (December 2011): S101–S103.

10. A prominent spokesperson for this position is Dr. Lixin Huang, president of the American College of Traditional Chinese Medicine, who also serves on the board of the WWF.

11. Volker Scheid, "The Globalization of Chinese Medicine," *The Lancet* 354 (December 1999): SIV10.

12. Ben Blanchard, "China Defends Use of Wild Animals in Traditional Medicine," Reuters, July 2, 2016, https://www.reuters.com/article/us-china-endangered/china-defends-use-of-wild-animals-in-traditional-medicine-idUSKCN0ZI0GB; Simon Denyer, "China's Push to Export Traditional Medicine May Doom the Magical Pangolin," *Washington Post*, July 21, 2018; Song Jingli, "Boosted by Belt and Road Initiative, Spread of TCM Speeds Up," China Daily.com.cn. June 4, 2018; "Xinhua Insight: Animal Rights or Human Health? Chinese Medicine at the Crossroads," December 6, 2016, http://www.xinhuanet.com//english/2016–12/06/c_135885083.htm; Didi Tang, "Chinese Doctors Hail Return of Tiger and Rhino Remedies," *The Times,* November 3, 2018, https://www.thetimes.co.uk/article/chinese-doctors-hail-return-of-rhino-and-tiger-remedies-somvglvws.

13. The Chinese announcement of October 2018 did not apply to the 1993 ban on the importation of wild animal parts, which remained in place, but to lifting the 2007 ban on the use of even domestic "farmed" tiger and rhino parts as medicine. Chinese tiger (and now rhino) farms are widely considered, however, to be laundering sites for the trade in wild animals, and to further encourage that trade by promoting the animals as medicinal; see van Uhm, *The Illegal Trade in Wildlife*, 197–253; Kristin Nowell, "Tiger Farms and Pharmacies: The Central Importance

of China's Trade Policy for Tiger Conservation," in *Tigers of the World: The Science, Politics, and Conservation of* Panthera tigris, ed. R. Tilson and P. J. Nyhus (Amsterdam: Elsevier 2009), 463–475.

14. See, for example, Wufei Yu, "Coronavirus: Revenge of the Pangolins?," *New York Times*, March 5, 2020; Jane Goodall, "COVID-19 Is a Product of Our Unhealthy Relationship with Animals and the Environment," *Mongabay*, May 4, 2020; Rachel Fobar, "China Promotes Bear Bile as Coronavirus Treatment, Alarming Wildlife Advocates," *National Geographic*, March 25, 2020; Michael Standaert, "'This Makes Chinese Medicine Look Bad': TCM Supporters Condemn Illegal Wildlife Trade," *The Guardian*, May 26, 2020; Rajat Ghai, "Chinese Medicine's Use of Animals a Threat to the Entire World," *Down to Earth*, April 7, 2020.

15. Efriam Lev, "Traditional Healing with Animals (Zootherapy): Medieval and Present-Day Levantine Practice," *Journal of Ethnopharmacology* 85 (1) (2003): 107–118; most of the recent scholarship on "zootherapy" pertains to South America and Africa. See particularly Rômulo Romeu Nóbrega Alves and Ierecê Lucena Rosa, eds., *Animals in Traditional Folk Medicine: Implications for Conservation* (Berlin: Springer, 2013).

16. Some of the established Chinese medical sayings were actually derived from works of literature. According to Wang Zhenkun, it was Tao Zongyi, a literary figure of the Ming period rather than a physician, who formulated the phrase *yi du gong du*. See Wang Zhenkun 王振坤, "Yi du gong du" 以毒攻毒 [Using poison to attack poison], *Zhongguo Weisheng Hua Bao* 2 中国卫生画报 China Hygiene Pictorial 2 (1984): 19; for discussion of the phrase *yi xing bu xing* 以形补形 [Using shape to nourish shape], see Bei Runpu 贝润浦, "Dongwu zangqi shi zhi bing de liang yao" 动物脏器是治病的良药 [Animal organs are good medicinals for treating diseases], China Hygiene Pictorial 4 (1984): 6.

17. Eugene N. Anderson, "Folk Nutritional Therapy in Modern China," in *Chinese Medicine and Healing: An Illustrated History*, ed. T. J. Hinrichs and Linda L. Barnes (Cambridge, MA: Harvard University Press, 2013), 259–260.

18. Zu Shuxian, 关于传统动物药及其疗效问题 [About traditional animal drugs and their efficacy], accessed November 1, 2019, http://shc2000.sjtu.edu.cn/article5 /guanyu.htm.

19. Michel Strickmann, *Chinese Magical Medicine* (Stanford, CA: Stanford University Press, 2002), 185.

20. Johann Frick, "Medicinal Use of Substances Derived from the Animal Organism (in Tsinghai), *Anthropo* 52 (1957): 177–198.

21. See He Shaoqi 何绍奇, "'Xuerou you qing' kaolue" "血肉有情"考略 [An examination of the saying 'Products with passion in both blood and flesh'"], *Zhongyi Zazhi* 中医杂志 Journal of Traditional Chinese Medicine 10 (1992): 58. By contrast, Qing period physician Ye Tianshi highly encouraged the use of animals as medicine and expanded the list to include marine species like mussels, sea cucumbers, and abalone.

22. Paul Unschuld, *Medical Ethics in Imperial China: A Study in Historical Anthropology* (Berkeley: University of California Press, 1979), 25.

23. Sun Simiao quoted in Unschuld, *Medical Ethics*, 30.

24. Paul Unschuld and Jinsheng Zheng, eds., *Chinese Traditional Healing: The Berlin Collections of Manuscript Volumes from the 16th through the Early 20th Century* (Leiden: Brill, 2012), 76.

25. See Nappi, *The Monkey and the Inkpot*; William C. Cooper and Nathan Sivin, "Man as a Medicine: Pharmacological and Ritual Aspects of Traditional Therapy Using Drugs Derived from the Human Body," in *Chinese Science: Explorations of an Ancient Tradition*, ed. Shigeru Nakayama and Nathan Sivin (Cambridge, MA: MIT Press, 1973), 203–272.

26. Author's observation. I regularly visited this market while in Guangzhou.

27. Nijman quoted in Robert McKie, "Jaguars Killed for Fangs to Supply Growing Chinese Medicine Trade," *The Guardian*, March 4, 2018; some sources have linked the trade in jaguar parts to the Chinese government's ban on the use of tiger parts, which follows a pattern of one species being substituted for another in the face of a legal restriction or other impediment to trade (e.g., extinction): "China's Lust for Jaguar Fangs Imperils Big Cats," *Nature*, February 23, 2018.

28. "Traditional Chinese Medical Authorities," *Time*; Joyce Wu, *Shark Fin and Mobulid Ray Gill Plate Trade in Mainland China, Hong Kong, and Taiwan* (Taipei: TRAFFIC, 2016).

29. Tom Millikan and Jo Shaw, *The South Africa-Vietnam Rhino Horn Trade Nexus* (Johannesburg: TRAFFIC, 2012).

30. Denyer, "China's Push."

31. Rachel Newer, "To Sate China's Demand, African Donkeys Are Stolen and Skinned," *New York Times*, January 2, 2018.

32. "Traditional Chinese Medical Authorities," *Time*.

33. Zhongguo yao yong dong wu zhi xie zuo zu bian zhu, ed. 中国药用动物志协作组编著, *Zhongguo yao yong dong wu zhi* 中国药用动物志 [Chinese medicinal animals], vol. 1. (Tianjin shi: Tianjin ke xue ji shu chu ban she, 1979). Volume 2 of this two-volume work was published in 1983.

34. Li Junde 李军德, Huang Luqi 黄璐琦, and Qu Xiaobo 曲晓波, eds., *Zhongguo yao yong dong wu zhi* 中国药用动物志 [Chinese medicinal animals], 2nd ed., vols. 1–3 (Fujian: Fujian Science and Technology Press, 2013).

35. Gross, *Farewell to the God of Plague*.

36. Sigrid Schmalzer, *Red Revolution, Green Revolution: Scientific Farming in Socialist China* (Chicago: University of Chicago Press, 2016).

37. For case studies highlighting innovation over the long history of Chinese medicine, see Hsu, ed., *Innovation in Chinese Medicine*. For the Republican and early Communist period, and particularly the innovation of acupuncture therapies, see Andrews, *The Making of Modern Chinese Medicine*; and Lei, *Neither Donkey nor Horse*, who provides detailed case studies of science-based innovation on Chinese herbs.

38. See Zhan, *Otherworldly*, especially chapter 3, for discussion of the role of miracle cures in contemporary clinical practice. Although this phenomenon has a long history outside animal-based medicines, faunal medicalization has been particularly subject to (and generative of) this expectation.

39. Hoai Nam Dang Vu and Martin Reinhardt Nielsen, "Understanding Utilitarian and Hedonic Values Determining the Demand for Rhino Horn in Vietnam,"

Human Dimensions of Wildlife 23, no. 5 (2018): 417–432. In email correspondence, Jill Robinson of the Animals Asia Foundation commented, "A significant amount of bear bile is simply sold in the form of expensive 'gifts,' which then sit on the shelf of a rich client or friend, literally collecting dust. Bile is also increasingly sold in hospitals by doctors who have been 'encouraged' to buy it from the trade" (comment made on January 6. 2013). This phenomenon of using certain medicinals as luxury gift items applies also to cordyceps fungus, or *yarsagumbu* in the Tibetan language. See the documentary *Himalayan Gold Rush* (Eric Valli, director, 2011).

40. Zhan, *Otherworldly*, 1.

41. Stephan Kloos, "The Pharmaceutical Assemblage: Rethinking Sowa Rigpa and the Herbal Pharmaceutical Industry in Asia," *Current Anthropology* 58, no. 6(2017): 694.

42. Notable exceptions in the English-language literature include Unschuld, *Medicine in China*; Cochran, *Chinese Medicine Men*; Saxer, *Manufacturing Tibetan Medicine*; and Lei, *Neither Donkey nor Horse*, though the focus of each of these works is on periods before or after the one covered in this book. Chinese sources include Yang Nianqun 杨念群, *Zai Zao "Bing Ren": Zhong Xi Yi Chong Tu Xia De Kongjian Zhengzhi (1832–1985)* 再造 '病人': 中西医冲突下的空间政治 (1832–1985) [Remaking "patients"] (Beijing: Zhongguo Renmin Daxue Chu Ban She, 2006); Wang Zhipu 王致谱 and Cai Jingfeng 蔡景峰, eds., *Zhongguo Zhong Yiyao 50 Nian (1949–1999)* 中国中医药 50 年 (1949–1999) [Fifty years of Chinese *yiyao* (1949–1999)] (Fujian: Fujian Kexue Jishu Chu Ban She, 1999); Deng Liqun 邓力群 et al., eds., *Dang Dai Zhongguo Cong Shu: Dang Dai Zhongguo De Yaoye Shiye* 当代中国丛书: 当代中国的药业事业 [A compendium of contemporary China: The pharmaceutical business of contemporary China] (Beijing: Zhongguo Shehui Kexue Chu Ban She, 1988); for Chinese histories of drug-making, see for instance Zhu Chao 朱潮 and Zhang Weifeng 张慰丰, eds., *Xin Zhongguo Yixue Jiao Yu Shi* 新中国医学教育史 [Chinese medicine educational history of new China] (Beijing: Beijing Yike Daxue and Zhongguo Xiehe Yike Daxue, 1990); Cheng Xinqian 陈新谦 and Zhang Tianlu 张天禄, eds., *Zhongguo Jin Dai Yaoxue Shi* 中国近代药学史 [A history of medicine in modern China] (Beijing: Renmin Weisheng Chu Ban She, 1992); Zhang Minggao 张鸣皋, *Yaoxue Fazhan Jian Shi* 药学发展简史 [A history of the development of pharmaceutics] (Beijing: Zhongguo Yiyao Keji Chu Ban She, 1993).

43. Committee on Scholarly Communication with the People's Republic of China, *Herbal Pharmacology in the People's Republic of China: A Trip Report of the American Herbal Pharmacology Delegation* (Washington, DC: National Academy of Sciences, 1975). These were the findings of a twelve-member Herbal Pharmacology Study Group, which was hosted by the Chinese Medical Association in 1974, during the period of restored relations between China and the United States. Acupuncture therapy became world famous as a result of similar high-level study trips in this period, but Chinese pharmacology became known in the West mainly in relation to the barefoot doctor program.

44. Laurent Pordie and Jean-Paul Gaudilliere, "Reformulation Regimes in Drug Discovery: Revisiting Polyherbals and Property Rights in the Ayurvedic Industry," *East Asian Science, Technology, and Society* 8, no. 1 (2014): 57–80.

45. Laurent Pordie and Anita Hardon, "'Drugs' Stories and Itineraries: On the Making of Asian Industrial Medicines," *Anthropology and Medicine* 22, no. 1 (2015): 1–6.

46. Stephan Kloos, ed., *Asian Medical Industries: Contemporary Perspectives on Traditional Pharmaceuticals* (London: Routledge, forthcoming).

47. Zhan, *Otherworldly*.

48. See, for example, Fang, *Barefoot Doctors*; see also Zheng Hong 郑洪 et al., "Ming fen you guan: jin dai zheng zhi zhong de zhong xi yi cheng wei zhi zheng" 名分攸关: 近代政制中的中西医称谓之争 [Of names and status: The battle between "Chinese medicine" and "Western medicine" in modern governance], in *Zhongguo Shehui Lishi Pinglun* 中国社会历史评论 [A commentary on the social history of China 13] (Tianjin: Tianjin Guji Chu Ban She, 2012), 338–352.

49. Lei, *Neither Donkey nor Horse*, 15.

50. Andrews, *Making of Modern Chinese Medicine*.

51. Benjamin Elman points out that Chinese scholars began adopting Japanese terms after the First Sino-Japanese War, including the word *kagaku* to mean "science." Writes Elman, "Thousands of Chinese students who studied modern science and medicine in Meiji Japan quickly assimilated the Japanese terminology for the modern sciences under the Meiji neologism for 'science' as 'organized fields of learning' (*kexue* 科学; Japanese, *kagaku*)." See "Toward a History of Modern Science in Republic China," in *Science and Technology in Modern China, 1880s–1940s*, ed. Jing Tsu and Benjamin Elman (Leiden: Brill, 2014).

52. For more discussion of "Mr. Science," see Nancy Chunjuan Wei and Darryl E. Brock, eds., *Mr Science and Chairman Mao's Cultural Revolution: Science and Technology in Modern China* (Lanham, MD: Lexington Books, 2013). Lei devotes a whole chapter, titled "Science as a Verb," in *Neither Donkey nor Horse*.

53. Kloos, "Pharmaceutical Assemblage," 699.

54. Meryl Theng, "Consumption of Endangered Antelope's Horn Remains High in Singapore," Saiga Conservation Alliance, August 13, 2018, https://saiga -conservation.org/2018/08/13/consumption-of-the-endangered-saiga-antelopes -horn-remains-high-in-singapore/.

55. Kanitha Krishnasamy and Monica Zavagli, *Southeast Asia: At the Heart of Wildlife Trade* (Petaling Jaya, Malaysia: TRAFFIC, 2020).

56. The first bear farm in Laos was established in 2000, and there were eleven by 2012, containing more than 120 bears. For an overview of bear farms in the Lao PDR, see Emily Livingston and Chris R. Shepherd, "Bear Farms in Lao PDR Expand Illegally and Fail to Conserve Wild Bears," *Oryx* 50, no. 1 (2016): 176–184; and Emily Livingston, I. Gomez, and J. Bouhuys, "A Review of Bear Farming and Bear Trade in Lao People's Democratic Republic," *Global Ecology and Conservation* 13 (January 2018): 1–9.

57. The nascent attempt by my organization to halt bear farming in Boten was ultimately unsuccessful. An investigation of the wildlife trade in Boten by a team from the NGO TRAFFIC in 2016 documented the same conditions I describe here, with bear bile farms still operating unchecked, and the product being sold openly, in violation of Lao law. Kanitha Krishnasamy, Chris R. Shepherd, and Oi Ching Or, "Observations of Illegal Wildlife Trade in Boten, a Chinese Border

Town within a Specific Economic Zone in Northern Lao PDR," *Global Ecology and Conservation* 14 (April 2018).

58. Japanese introduced *kyuushingan* to Taiwan during the occupation period, and to this day, elderly Taiwanese still travel to Japan to stock up on the drug. Lin Zhaogeng 林昭庚 et al., *Rizhi Shiqi (Xiyuan 1895–1945) No Taiwan Zhongyi* 日治时期 (西元1895–1945) の台湾中医 [Chinese medicine in Taiwan during the Japanese occupation] (Xiyuan 1895–1945) (Taipei: Guoshi Guan, 2011), 164.

59. One source places Japan's annual consumption of bear bile at 200 kilograms, which is far above the official figure. Suvendrini Kakuchi, "Japan: Demand Continues to Fuel Trade in Bear Products," accessed October 6, 2017, http://www.ipsnews.net/2002/02/japan-demand-continues-to-fuel-trade-in-bear -products/.

60. Elizabeth Hsu, "Commentary on Stephan Kloos' 'The Pharmaceutical Assemblage,'" *Current Anthropology* 58, no. 6 (2017): 708.

One. "Abandon Chinese Medicine, Retain Chinese Drugs"

1. For a history of Chinese medical education in Guangdong province, see Liu Xiaobin 刘小斌, *Guangdong Zhongyi Jiaoyu Shi: Qing Dai Zhi Jiefang Chu Qi* 广东中医教育史: 清代至解放初期 [Guangdong Chinese Medical College and its education history: From Qing Dynasty to the Early Liberation Period] (Guangzhou: Guangzhou Zhongyi Xue Yuan 广州: 广州中医学院 Guangzhou Chinese Medical College, 1983), PhD dissertation; and *Guangdong Zhongyi Yu Ying Cai* 广东中医育英才 [Nurturing talents at Guangdong Chinese Medical College] (Guangzhou: Guangdong Sheng Weisheng Ting Zhongyi Chu 广州: 广东省卫生厅中医处 Guangdong Province Health Department Chinese Medicine Section, 1988). See also Liu Xiaobin "Guangdong jin dai de zhongyi jiaoyu" 广东近代的中医教育 [Chinese medicine education in contemporary Guangdong], *Zhongguo Yishi Zazhi* 中国医史杂志 Chinese Journal of Medical History 12, no. 3 (1982): 133–138.

2. Henan Chinese Medical College established its *yao* department even earlier, in 1959. This was one of the few Chinese medical colleges that had been founded prior to the Revolution. Henan Zhongyi Xue Yuan Jiao Wu Chu 河南中医学院教务处 [Henan Chinese Medical College Administrative Office], "Henan zhongyi xue yuan zhongyao xi di yi jie xuesheng biye" 河南中医学院中药系第一届学生毕业 [First-batch students of Henan Chinese Medical College Zhongyao Department graduate], *Yaoxue Tongbao* 药学通报 Pharmaceutical Bulletin 9, no. 9 (1963): 406.

3. The new professional was also a hybrid in bridging the gap between Chinese medicine and biomedicine. Students from the *yao* departments of Chinese medical colleges were taught mainly bioscience, and even today are allowed to dispense biomedical as well as Chinese drugs. Postgraduate research in pharmacology also came to be geared toward drug discovery based on bioscientific understandings and protocols rather than the principles of Chinese medicine, even when Chinese herbs were the raw ingredients. This had to do with the emphasis on *xin yao* or

"new drug" formulation. Despite the strong emergence of *yao*, Chinese medical colleges to this day call themselves "*zhongyi* institutes" (*zhongyi xue yuan*), placing the main emphasis on medicine rather than on pharmacology.

4. Hsiang-lin Sean Lei, "From Changshan to a New Anti-Malarial Drug: Re-Networking Chinese Drugs and Excluding Chinese Doctors," *Social Studies of Science* 29, no. 3 (1999): 323-358.

5. Lei, "From Changshan."

6. Andrews, *Making of Modern Chinese Medicine*; Benjamin Elman, *On Their Own Terms: Science in China, 1550-1900* (Cambridge, MA: Harvard University Press, 2005), xxxvii.

7. Lü Jiage 吕嘉戈, *Wanjiu Zhongyi: Zao Yu De Zhidu Xianjing He Ziben Yinmou* 挽救中医: 中医遭遇的制度陷阱和资本阴谋 [Rescuing Chinese medicine: The institutional trap and capital conspiracy] (Guangxi: Guangxi Normal University Press, 2006), 53-78.

8. Yang Nianqun 杨念群, *Zai Zao "Bing Ren"* 再造'病人 [Remaking "patients"], 252-253; Gao Xi, "Between the State and the Private Sphere: Chinese State Medicine Movement, 1930-1949," in *Science, Public Health and the State in Modern Asia*, ed. Bu Liping, Darwin H. Stapleton, and Ka-che Yip (New York: Routledge, 2012), 144-160.

9. Yang Nianqun 杨念群, *Zai Zao "Bing Ren"* 再造'病人 [Remaking "patients"], 254.

10. Yang Nianqun 杨念群, *Zai Zao "Bing Ren"* 再造'病人 [Remaking "patients"], 254.

11. Lei, "From Changshan."

12. The Chinese Pharmacological Association held a meeting in Beijing on March 8, 1955, to criticize Wang Bin, details of which (including the quotations in the preceding text) are found in Xie Haizhou 谢海洲, "Pipan zhi jieshou zhongyao er bu jieshou zhongyi de cuo wu sixiang" 批判只接受中药而不接受中医的错误思想 [Criticizing the wrong thinking of accepting Zhongyi but rejecting Zhongyao], *Yaoxue Tongbao* 药学通报 Pharmaceutical Bulletin 3, no. 4 (1955): 148-149. In 1944, Mao coined the phrase *tuanjie zhongxiyi* (团结中西医) (to combine Chinese and Western medicines). See chapter 2 of Taylor, *Chinese Medicine*.

13. On November 19, 1955, He Cheng wrote a public apology that was published in the *People's Daily*. See sections 3 and 4 of Lü Jiage 吕嘉戈, *Wanjiu Zhongyi* 挽救中医, 79-181.

14. Xie Haizhou, 谢海洲, "Pipan zhi jieshou" [Criticizing the wrong thinking], 148.

15. Gong Yuzhi 龚育之 and Li Peishan 李佩珊, "Pipan wang bin zai yixue he weisheng gongzuo zhong de zichan jieji sixiang" 批判王斌在医学和卫生工作中的资产阶级思想 [Criticizing the capitalist thoughts of Wang Bin in medical and health matters], *Yaoxue Tongbao* 药学通报 Pharmaceutical Bulletin 3, no. 10 (1955): 434-438.

16. Chen Xianyu 陈先瑜, "Xuexi zhongyi de yi dian tihui" 学习中医的一点体会 [Some reflections from learning Chinese medicine], *Yaoxue Tongbao* 药学通报 Pharmaceutical Bulletin 7, no. 2 (1959): 63.

17. Xie Haizhou 谢海洲, "Pipan zhi jieshou" [Criticizing the wrong thinking], 149.

18. Linda L. Barnes, *Needles, Herbs, Gods, and Ghosts: China, Healing, and the West to 1848.* (Cambridge, MA: Harvard University Press, 2007), 285.

19. Wang Jinghui, Yan Li, Yinfeng Yang, Xuetong Chen, Jian Du, Qiusheng Zheng, Zongsuo Liang, and Yonghua Wang, "A New Strategy for Deleting Animal Drugs from Traditional Chinese Medicines Based on Modified Yimusake Formula," *Scientific Reports* 7, no. 1504 (2017).

20. Makino Isao and Tanaka Hirotoshi, "From a Choleretic to an Immuno-modulator: Historical Review of Ursodeoxycholic Acid as a Medicament," *Journal of Gastroenterology and Hepatology* (1998) 13: 659–664.

21. Sigrid Schmalzer, *Red Revolution, Green Revolution: Scientific Farming in Socialist China* (Chicago: University of Chicago Press, 2016), esp. 33–46.

22. Yan Cangshan 严苍山, "Zhongyi jinxiu zhi tujing" 中医进修之途径 [The way to advance Chinese medicine], *Xin Zhong Yiyao* 新中医药 New Chinese Medicine 2, no. 2 (1950): 5. Contemporary textbooks attribute the phrase *zhongyi kexuehua* 中医科学化 ("To scientize *zhongyi*") to Lu Yuanlei 陆渊雷. See Zhen Zhiya 甄志亚, ed., *Gao Deng Yiyao Yuan Xiao Jiao Cai: Zhongguo Yixue Shi* 高等医药院校教材: 中国医学史 [Teaching materials for higher medical colleges: Chinese medical history] (Shanghai: Shanghai Kexue Jishu Chu Ban She 上海科学技术出版社, 1997), 149–151.

23. The twelve meridians, or *jingluo* 经络, are believed to define the path where *qi* (life energy) flows. Xu Yecheng 许业诚, "Zhongyi kexue hua yi ban dou ren zuo xiyi hua" 中医科学化一般都认作西医化 [Many confuse "Scientize Chinese medicine" with "Westernize Chinese medicine"], *Xin Zhong Yiyao* 新中医药 New Chinese Medicine 2, no. 11 (1950): 14.

24. Lei, "From Changshan."

25. Yan Cangshan 严苍山, "Zhongyi jinxiu zhi tujing" 中医进修之途径 [Way to Advance], 5; Lei, "From Changshan."

26. The mission statement was printed on the front page of early issues. The journal's separation of *yi* and *yao* is noteworthy, although here they are considered to merit equal attention. Contributors to *Xin Zhong Yiyao* came from diverse backgrounds. For instance, Yan Cangshang was a Chinese medicine physician, while Yu Yunxiu (or Yu Yan) claimed to have been trained in Western science.

27. Pang Jingzhou 庞京周 et al., "Yanjiu zhongyao de fangxiang he shunxu" 研究中药的方向和顺序 [Researching Chinese medicine and the direction and order to take], *Xin Zhong Yiyao* 新中医药 New Chinese Medicine 2, no. 1 (1951): 4–6.

28. "Zhongguo yiyao gongsi que ding zengjia zuzhi guo chan huoyuan, cujin xin yao xia xiang" 中国医药公司确定增加组织国产资源, 促进新药下乡 [The Chinese Medicinal Company confirms increasing and organizing sources of supply, and also promoting new drugs in villages], *Yaoxue Tongbao* 药学通报 Pharmaceutical Bulletin 2, no. 3 (1954): 128. This article had originally appeared in the newspaper *Dagong Bao* on January 15, 1954.

29. "Zhongguo yiyao gongsi que ding," 128.

30. The list of drugs produced by Beijing Pharmaceutical Factory included vitamins, calcium lactate, and santonin (extracted from a Chinese herb called *shandaonian*). It also produced compounds like those in Lysol and DDT. See

"Beijing shi zhi yao chang jianjie" 北京市制药厂简介 [An introduction to Beijing pharmaceutical factories], *Yaoxue Tongbao* 药学通报 Pharmaceutical Bulletin 2, no. 4 (1954): 173. The article had originally appeared in the newspaper *Guangming* on January 30, 1953.

31. Xue Yu, "Zheng li he yanjiu zu guo kexue wenhua yichan—zhongyao" 整理和研究祖国科学文化遗产— 中药 [Organize and research on our country's scientific and cultural legacy—Chinese medicinals], *Yaoxue Tongbao* 药学通报 Pharmaceutical Bulletin 3, no. 1 (1955): 5–9; Zhongguo Shengli Kexue Hui Yaoli Zhuanye Mishu Zu, ed. 中国生理科学会药理专业秘书组 [Chinese Physiological Science Society Pharmacology Secretariat], *Xunzhao Xin Yao De Lilun Jichu He Linchuang Shiji: Zhongguo Shengli Kexue Hui Yaoli Zhuanye Di Yi Jie Xueshu Taolun Hui Zhuan Ji* 寻找新药的理论基础和临床实际: 中国生理科学会药理专业第一届学术讨论会专集 [The theory and practice of new drug discovery: A special issue based on the first Chinese Physiological Science Society pharmacology symposium] (Shanghai: Shanghai Kexue Jishu Chu Ban She 上海科学技术出版社, 1962); Ji Ruyun 嵇汝运 and Ren Yunfeng 任云峰, *Xunzhao Xin Yao De Tujing He Fangfa* 寻找新药的途径和方法 [The ways and methods of finding new drugs] (Beijing: Renmin Weisheng Chuban She 人民卫生出版社, 1965); Gao Xiaoshan 高晓山 et al., "Wu nian lai zhongyao yanjiu gongzuo de chengjiu" 五年来中药研究工作的成就 [Five years of research on Chinese medicinals and its achievements], *Yaoxue Tongbao* 药学通报 Pharmaceutical Bulletin 10, no. 11 (1964): 481–489.

32. According to Unschuld, only twenty of the 581 drugs were raw herbs that had appeared in classical materia medica. Even then, they were analyzed and described in the 1953 pharmacopoeia in a way that distanced them from any particular medical tradition. See Unschuld, *Medicine in China: A History of Pharmaceuticals*, 276–280.

33. "Xinan zhi yao gongye you xianzhu fazhan" 西南制药工业有显著发展 [Significant developments of the southwest pharmaceutical industry], *Yaoxue Tongbao* 药学通报 Pharmaceutical Bulletin 2, no. 2 (1954): 34–35.

34. "Si nian lai wo guo yiyao gongye you xianzhu fazhan" 四年来我国医药工业有显著发展 [Our pharmaceutical industry sees significant developments in four years], *Renmin Ribao* 人民日报 People's Daily 133 (January 1954), http://www.ziliaoku.org/rmrb/1954-01-28-2. Similar articles also appeared in health journals. For instance, "Si nian lai wo guo yiyao gongye ri yi fazhan zhuang da" 四年来我国医药工业日益发展壮大 [Our pharmaceutical industry grows steadily in four years], later published in the journal *Yaoxue Tongbao* 药学通报 Pharmaceutical Bulletin, originally appeared in *The Health Journal* (*Jian Kang Bao* 健康报), 319.

35. "[Yixue shi] 20 shiji 40 nian dai wo guo de qingmeisu yan zhi gongzuo" [医学史] 20实际 40 年代我国的青霉素研制工作 [(Medical history) Our country's research and work on penicillin during the 1940s], accessed September 14, 2013, http://bbs.club.sohu.com/read_elite.php?b=144278397&a=1875458. Like the rest of the world, China in the early 1950s was searching for the means to mass-produce penicillin, or *qingmeisu*. The first experiment was started in November 1949, and it took Chinese researchers Ma Yucheng and Liupu only a month to obtain penicillin in crystallized form. Zhang Weishen made refinements to the 1949

experiment, and on May 1, 1953, the Shanghai Number Three Pharmaceutical Factory was set up solely to manufacture the drug. See Ma Yucheng 马誉澄, "Yong cusuanjia zuo wei zhibei bian qingmeisu jiayan de jie jing fanying ji" 用醋酸钾作为制备苄青霉素钾盐的结晶反应剂 [Using potassium acetate as the reactant in the making of benzylpenicillin sodium], *Yaoxue Tongbao* 药学通报 Pharmaceutical Bulletin 2, no. 5 (1954): 191–193.

36. See also Jiang Daqu's (姜達衢) contribution, "Ru he zhengli he fayang zuguo yaoxue yichan" 如何整理和发扬祖国药学遗产 [How to organize and carry forward our country's pharmaceutical legacy], *Yaoxue Tongbao* 药学通报 Pharmaceutical Bulletin 2, no. 9 (1954): 368–369. Sean Lei's work has demonstrated that the process by which the antimalarial properties of *changshan* were recognized by the community of biomedical doctors was actually far more complex. Reference to historic texts did not play as large a part in this story as "common understanding" of the drug's effectiveness among Chinese physicians, and other social and political factors, which Lei meticulously traces (see Lei, "From Changshan to a New Anti-Malarial Drug"). *Zhouhou Fang* was written by the famous physician Ge Hong during the Jin Dynasty. *Zhou* means elbow, and *zhouhou fang* means "prescriptions at the back of the elbow" (it was common during the Jin period to carry a small sling bag on the arm, so the title relates to its portability and usefulness). It's notable that the remedies he recorded contained few if any expensive herbs or animal parts and tissues. *Waitai Miyao* was written by Wang Tao of the Tang period. It is the largest surviving record of prescriptions used by Tang-period physicians. Li Jingwei 李经纬, *Zhongguo Yixue Tong Shi* 中国医学通史 [Chinese medical history] (Beijing: Renmin Weisheng Chu Ban She 人民卫生出版社, 2000).

37. Xue Yu 薛愚, "Zheng li he yanjiu zuguo kexue wenhua yichan—zhongyao" 整理和研究祖国科学文化遗产— 中药 [Organize and research], 7–9.

38. Xie Haizhou 谢海洲, "Zhongguo yaoxue hui ge di fen hui jiji kaizhan zhongyao de yanjiu zheng li gongzuo" 中国药学会各地分会积极开展中药的研究整理工作 [All branches of the Chinese Pharmacology Association are actively carrying out research and organization work], *Yaoxue Tongbao* 药学通报 Pharmaceutical Bulletin 3, no. 2 (1955): 94–95.

39. Fang, *Barefoot Doctors*, 74.

40. Yan Cangshan 严苍山, "Zhongyi jinxiu zhi tujing" 中医进修之途径 [Way to Advance], 5.

41. Wang Jiuxiang, "Gan kuai peiyang zhongyao qing nian gongren" 赶快培养中药青年工人 [Hurry up and nurture pharmaceutical youth workers], *Zhongyao Tongbao* 2, no. 6 (1956): 260.

42. Xue Yu 薛愚, "Yong shiji xing dong yonghu renmin zi ji de xianfa" 用实际行动拥护人民自己的宪法 [Use practical actions to protect the people's constitution], *Yaoxue Tongbao* 中药通报 Pharmaceutical Bulletin 2, no. 7 (1954): 269–271.

43. Xue Yu 薛愚, "Yong shiji xing dong yonghu renmin zi ji de xianfa" [Use practical actions], 271.

44. Li Weizhen 李维祯, "Xuexi guojia zong luxian gaijin yaoxue gongzuo" 学习国家总路线改进药学工作 [Learn the country's general trajectory and improve pharmacy work], *Yaoxue Tongbao* 药学通报 Pharmaceutical Bulletin 2, no. 1 (1954): 2–3.

45. Wen Zhou 文周, "Ping 'zhongyao yaoli xue'" 评中药药理学 [Reviewing *Chinese medicine pharmacology*], *Yaoxue Tongbao* 药学通报 Pharmaceutical Bulletin 2, no. 12 (1954): 544-546; Ni Guangping 倪广平, "'Zhongyao yaoli xue' du hou gan" 中药药理学 "读后感 [My Feelings after reading *Chinese medicine pharmacology*], *Yaoxue Tongbao* 药学通报 Pharmaceutical Bulletin 2, no. 12 (1954): 546; Zhejiang Yixue Yuan Yaoxue Xi Yaoji Xue Jiaoyan Zu 浙江医学院药学系药剂学教研组 [Zhejiang Medical College Department of Pharmacy Teaching and Research Team for Pharmaceutics], "Ping li jiaren bian zhu 'shi yong tiaoji yu zhiji xue,'" 评李佳仁编著 "实用调剂与制剂学" [A criticism of *Practical pharmacy and pharmaceutics* by Li Jiaren], *Yaoxue Tongbao* 药学通报 Pharmaceutical Bulletin 3, no. 3 (1955): 123-126. Such reviews continued into the 1960s. Chen Shenquan 陈莘泉 and Wu Yundong 吴运东, "Ping yaoji shi zhuanye yong 'yaowu huaxue'" 评药剂士专业用 "药物化学" [An assessment of pharmacists and their professional application of *Medicinal chemistry*], *Yaoxue Tongbao* 药学通报 Pharmaceutical Bulletin 9, no. 9 (1963): 425-426.

46. Liao Qingjiang 廖清江, "Tantan yaoji ye xiao de kecheng wenti" 谈谈药剂夜校的课程问题 [On the problems concerning pharmacy night classes], *Yaoxue Tongbao* 药学通报 Pharmaceutical Bulletin 2, no. 2 (1954): 66-67.

47. Liao Qingjiang 廖清江, "Tantan yaoji ye xiao de kecheng wenti" [On the problems].

48. Zhang Zhongde 张忠德, "Zhi yao ken zhuanyan, jiu neng xue hui: jieshao wo zen yang xue hui feng anbu" 只要肯专研, 就能学会: 介绍我怎样学会封安瓿 [Learning through experimentation: How we learned to seal an ampoule], *Yaoxue Tongbao* 药学通报 Pharmaceutical Bulletin 2, no. 7 (1954): 309-310.

49. Cai Yumin 蔡玉珉, "Tantan tiaoji gongzuo ji yaoji zhiliang wenti" 谈谈调剂工作及药剂质量问题 [On pharmacy work and quality control issues with pharmaceutics], *Yaoxue Tongbao* 药学通报 Pharmaceutical Bulletin 3, no. 5 (1955): 216.

50. Wu Ming 吴明, "'Da cai xiao yong' yu 'yao qiu guo gao'" 大材小用" 与 "要求过高" ["Putting fine timber to petty use" and "Too high an expectation"], *Yaoxue Tongbao* 药学通报 Pharmaceutical Bulletin 3, no. 6 (1955): 274.

51. Ziwei 紫蔚, "Wo re ai zi ji de yaofang gongzuo" 我热爱自己的药房工作 [I love my pharmacy job], *Yaoxue Tongbao* 药学通报 3, no. 12 (1955): 555; Wang Fang 王芳, "Fang xia ge ren de mingli baofu, yukuai di danfu qi renmin gei yu de wei da renwu ba!" 放个人的名利包袱, 愉快地担负起人民给予的伟大任务吧! [Let's put aside fame and fortune, and happily take on the noble task given by the people!], *Yaoxue Tongbao* 药学通报 3, no. 12 (1955): 555-556.

52. Liu Guosheng 刘国声, "Xizang de yaocai he yaoxue shiye" 西藏的药材和药学事业 [Tibetan medicinals and pharmacy business], *Yaoxue Tongbao* 药学通报 Pharmaceutical Bulletin 2, no. 7 (1954): 276-279.

53. Well into the late 1950s, pharmaceutical companies and Chinese scientists, including those who had studied in the Soviet Union, continued research into lanolin. See Shanghai Putao Tang Chang 上海葡萄糖场 [Shanghai Glucose Factory], "Yang Mao Zhi" 羊毛脂 [Lanolin], *Yaoxue Tongbao* 药学通报 Pharmaceutical Bulletin 7, no. 3 (1959): 103-105.

54. Wang Shizhong 汪时中, "Cong niuxue zhong zhi qu dan yansuan zuzhi anjisuan (histidine monohydrochloride) de shiyan baogao" 从牛血中制取单盐酸

组织胺基酸的实验报告 [A report on the experiment to extract histidine monohy-drochloride from cow blood], *Yaoxue Tongbao* 药学通报 Pharmaceutical Bulletin 2, no. 1 (1954): 24–26.

55. Walter Sneader, *Drug Discovery: A History* (New York: Wiley, 2005), 6.

56. Zhang Tianmin 张天民, "Zangqi shenghua yaowu de gai kuang he zhan wang" 脏器生化药物的概况和展望 [Organo-pharmaceutics: Present and future], *Yaoxue Tongbao* 药学通报 14, no. 6 (1979): 273.

57. Zhang Yingguang 张迎光, "Cong dongwu danzhi zhong zhi qu yang dansuan yu dansuan" 从动物胆汁中制取去氧胆酸与胆酸 [Preparing deoxycholic acid and cholic acid from animal bile], *Yaoxue Tongbao* 药学通报 Pharmaceutical Bulletin 6, no. 11 (1958): 532.

58. Hebei Sheng Shangye Ting, Hebei Sheng Weisheng Ting 河北省商业厅, 河北省卫生厅 [Hebei Province Department of Commerce, Hebei Province Department of Health], "Wei jia qiang shougou niu, zhu, yang danzhi gongying niuhuang shengchan de tongzhi" 为加强收购牛, 猪, 羊胆汁供应牛黄生产的通知 [A notice to increase the purchase of cow, pig, and sheep bile for bezoar produc-tion], April 1, 1960.

59. See chapter 5, "Zhongyao xue de fazhan" 中药学的发展 [The development of pharmacology], in *Zhongguo Zhong Yiyao 50 Nian* [Fifty years of Chinese *yiyao*], ed. Wang Zhipu 王致谱 and Cai Jingfeng 蔡景峰, 326.

60. The history of Tongrentang is well-chronicled in Cochran, *Chinese Medicine Men*; Chinese accounts include Beijing Tongrentang Laonian Bao Jian Yanjiu Suo, ed. 北京同仁堂老年保健研究所编 [Beijing Tongrentang Time-Honored Healthcare Research Center], *Beijing Tongrentang Mingyao* 北京同仁堂名药 [The famous medicines of Beijing Tongrentang] (Beijing: Zhongyi Guji Chu Ban She 中医古籍出版社, 1986); Yang Guoxuan 杨国萱, *Darentang De Gushi* 达仁堂的故事 [The story of Darentang] (Tianjin: Tianjin Renmin Chu Ban She 天津人民出版社, 2004); Huang Yiwen 黄一文, "Tongxin jishi shu bainian—guangzhou chenliji yaochang" 同心济世数百年— 广州陈李济药厂 [Saving lives together for hundreds of years—Guangzhou Chenliji Pharmaceutical Factory], in *Guangzhou Wen Shi Di 61 Ji Guangzhou Lao Zihao Xia Ce* 广州文史第六十一 集: 广州老字号下册 [Guangzhou cultural history part 61: Guangzhou time-honored brands vol. 2] (Guangzhou: Guangdong Renmin Chu Ban She 广东人民出版社, 2003), 3–9.

61. Regarded as China's oldest medicine shop, Chenliji was founded by two families with the surnames Chen and Li. During the Mao period, the families went their separate ways, with the Chens taking over the Hong Kong branch, while descendants of the Li family were relegated to employee status at the new state-owned Chenliji in Guangzhou. Danny Li, a family descendant, wrote about this in his blog. See "Shen wei 'chenliji' hou ren de gankai" 身为 "陈李济" 后人的感慨 [My feelings as a descendant of Chenliji], accessed July 27, 2013, http://blog.sina .com.cn/s/blog_648e221f0100089r.html. See also *Guangzhou Wen Shi Di 61 Ji Guang-zhou Lao Zihao* [Guangzhou cultural history part 61: Guangzhou time-honored brands vol. 2], 4.

62. Prior to the merger, there were 119 individual companies in Guangzhou. Deng Liqun et al., 邓力群, 马洪, 武衡, *Dang Dai Zhongguo Cong Shu: Dangdai Zhong-*

guo De Yaoye Shiye 当代中国丛书: 当代中国的药业事业 [A compendium of contemporary China: The pharmaceutical business of contemporary China] (Beijing: Zhongguo Shehui Kexue Chu Ban She 中国社会科学出版社, 1988), 116. Accordingly, Chenliji Joint Pharmaceutical Factory was formed out of eleven Chinese medicinal and related shops. *Guangzhou Wen Shi Di 61 Ji Guangzhou Lao Zihao* [Guangzhou cultural history part 61: Guangzhou time-honored brands vol. 2], 5.

63. Zhang Zhihou 张执侯, "Wei da zuguo de yaowu ziyuan ji qi liyong—chong la yu feng la" 伟大祖国的药物资源及其利用— 虫蜡与蜂蜡 [The medicinal resources of our great motherland and tapping them—insect wax and beeswax], *Yaoxue Tongbao* 药学通报 Pharmaceutical Bulletin 3, no. 3 (1955): 130-131. Waxes produced in Sichuan province were much sought after abroad. The two types, white and yellow, were first gathered in Chongqing before making their way to Hankou and Shanghai, and then being redistributed to other parts of China and overseas. Hong Kong, Vietnam, Japan, and France were among the foreign markets.

64. Zhang Zhihou 张执侯, "Wei da zuguo de yaowu ziyuan ji qi liyong—chong la yu feng la" [Medicinal resources of our great motherland].

65. Song Xijing 宋希璟 and Zhao Baozhen 赵宝贞, "Zai tongrentang xuexi zhongyao de ji dian tihui" 在同仁堂学习中药的几点体会 [Some experiences from learning Chinese medicine at Tongrentang], *Zhongyao Tongbao* 中药通报 Bulletin of Chinese Medicinals 2, no. 6 (1954): 260.

66. By 1955, there were at least seven factories in charge of producing Chinese pharmaceuticals. "Ge di da liang zhizao zhongyao chengyao" 各地大量制造中药成药 [Manufacturing of Chinese pharmaceuticals on a massive scale], *Yaoxue Tongbao* 药学通报 Pharmaceutical Bulletin 3, no. 10 (1955): 479-480. The report was first published in the sixth issue of the magazine *Zhongguo Qing Gongye* 中国轻工业, or China's Light Industry.

67. The five key positions were production, planning, finance, general affairs, and safeguarding of the company's assets. Each of the four manufacturing workshops had a different responsibility: drug-making, packaging, wax production, and cutting. In 1955, Tongrentang reportedly produced a daily average of twelve thousand pills for each drug type, compared to nine thousand the previous year. "Gu lao de Beijing Tongrentang bian nian qing le" 古老的北京同仁堂变年轻了 [Age-old Beijing Tongrentang has turned younger], *Yaoxue Tongbao* 药学通报 Pharmaceutical Bulletin 3, no. 6 (1955): 288.

68. "Gu lao de Beijing Tongrentang bian nian qing le" [Age-old Beijing Tongrentang].

69. Pang Jingzhou 庞京周 et al., "Yanjiu zhongyao de fangxiang he shunxu" [Researching Chinese medicine], 5.

70. Xiao Ge 萧戈, "Ying gai zhong shi yaocai shengchan" 应该重视药材生产 [Giving importance to medicinal production], *Zhongyao Tongbao* 中药通报 Bulletin of Chinese Medicinals 2, no. 3 (1956): 93.

Two. "To Learn from the Soviet Union"

1. See, in particular, Elman, *On Their Own Terms*; Lei, *Neither Donkey nor Horse*, Andrews, *Making of Modern Chinese Medicine*.

2. "To Learn from the Soviet Union" was an official slogan across many domains.

3. Taylor, *Chinese Medicine*.

4. Chinese translations of Russian-language articles I have used in this section often give imprecise renderings of the names of the original authors. Some have been difficult to retranslate into Roman characters with certainty or precision, particularly if the Russian author was obscure. I have therefore accompanied most such Russian author names with [*sic*] to denote the possibility that they are misspelled.

5. Tang Guang 汤光, "Sulian shengyao yanjiu gongzuo de chengjiu" 苏联生药研究工作的成就 [The achievements of Soviet Union's research on raw medicinals], *Yaoxue Tongbao* 药学通报 Pharmaceutical Bulletin 2, no. 5 (1954): 186–188.

6. A. P. Kiriyanov [*sic*], trans. Huang Junhua 基里扬诺夫 (黄俊华), "Si shi nian lai sulian zai yao yong zhiwu fangmian de chengjiu" 四十年来苏联在药用植物方面的成就 [Forty years of Soviet achievements in utilizing plant-based medicinals], *Zhongyao Tongbao* 中药通报 Bulletin of Chinese Medicinals 3, no. 6 (1957): 223.

7. Tang Guang, "Sulian shengyao yanjiu gongzuo de chengjiu" [Achievements of Soviet Union's research], 186–188.

8. Conroy writes, "The Soviet pharmaceutical industry, despite creative scientists, fell behind American, British, Western European, Japanese, and even Eastern European pharmaceutical firms, not only in output but in research and development." Mary Schaeffer Conroy, "The Soviet Pharmaceutical Industry and Dispensing, 1945-1953," *Europe-Asia Studies* 56, no. 7 (2004): 963–991.

9. Tang Guang, "Sulian shengyao yanjiu gongzuo de chengjiu" [Achievements of Soviet Union's research], 187.

10. The article appeared a month later in the journal *Yaoxue Tongbao* 药学通报 Pharmaceutical Bulletin. A. Zhivkov [*sic*] 西瓦柯夫 (*Sulian "Yiwu Gongzuo Zhe" Bao Zhubian*) (苏联'医务工作者'报主编) (Trans. Bai Hanyu) 白汉玉, "Sulian de yaoji ye" 苏联的药剂业 [Soviet Union and its pharmacy], *Yaoxue Tongbao* 药学通报 Pharmaceutical Bulletin 3, no. 10 (1955): 443–444.

11. Xi Gao, "Foreign Models of Medicine in Twentieth-Century China," in *Medical Transitions in Twentieth-Century China*, ed. Mary Brown Bullock and Bridie Andrews (Bloomington: Indiana University Press, 2014), 203–206.

12. Nonetheless, technical programs were also created to train those "working directly in pharmacies and related organizations like medical shops and warehouses." Students took between two to three years to graduate depending on their qualifications upon enrollment. P. Senov [*sic*] 谢诺夫, "Sulian de yaoxue kexue he yaoxue shiye—wei 'yaoxue tongbao' zuo" 苏联的药学科学和药学事业— 为 "药学通报" 作 [Pharmaceutical science and pharmaceutical work in Soviet Union—For the Pharmaceutical Bulletin], *Yaoxue Tongbao* 药学通报 Pharmaceutical Bulletin 3, no. 11 (1955): 482–483.

13. A. P. Kiriyanov [*sic*], trans. Huang Junhua 基里扬诺夫 (黄俊华), "Si shi nian lai sulian zai yao yong zhiwu fangmian de chengjiu" 四十年来苏联在药用植物方面的成就 [Forty years of Soviet achievements], 223.

14. Ye Sanduo 叶三多, "Xue xi sulian xian jin jingyan wo men ying gai zi ji shengchan yaowu" 学习苏联先进经验我们应当自己生产药物 [We should learn from Soviet Union's advanced experience and produce our own drugs], *Yaoxue Tongbao* 药学通报 Pharmaceutical Bulletin 2, no. 1 (1954): 16.

15. This edition was a compilation of three previous volumes, released in 1940, 1942, and 1944, respectively.

16. Tang Guang, "Sulian yaodian zhong zhiwu xing shengyao de yan ge" 苏联药典中植物性生药的沿革 [The history of the documentation of raw herbs in Soviet pharmacopoeia], in "Sulian shengyao yanjiu gongzuo de chengjiu" 苏联生药研究工作的成就 [Achievements of Soviet Union's research], 188.

17. V. P. Kalashnikov 卡拉尼可夫, trans. Zhu Yan 朱颜 and Tu Guorui 屠国瑞, "Guan yu zhiwu yao de yanjiu" 关于植物药的研究 [Regarding plant-based medicinal research], "Liang wei sulian xue zhe guan yu yanjiu zhiwu yao de yijian" 两位苏联学者关于研究植物药的意见 [The opinions of two Russian scholars on plant-based medicinal research], *Zhongyao Tongbao* 中药通报 Bulletin of Chinese Medicinals 4, no. 3 (1958): 74.

18. Both digalen and digifolin are drugs derived from the plant genus *Digitalis*. The common name for digitalis is foxglove; a common name for *Rehmannia* in English is Chinese foxglove.

19. Ye Sanduo 叶三多, "Xue xi sulian xian jin jingyan wo men ying dang ziji shengchan yaowu" 学习苏联先进经验我们应当自己生产药物 [We should learn], 17.

20. This and other examples were solicited by the journal *Yaoxue Tongbao* to document creative approaches to the use of *zhongyao* in hospital pharmacies. "Ying jie wo kan chuang kan hou de di san nian" 迎接我刊创刊后的第三年 [Welcoming the third year of the founding of our journal], *Yaoxue Tongbao* 药学通报 Pharmaceutical Bulletin 3, no. 1 (1955): 24.

21. Ye Sanduo, "Xue xi sulian xian jin jingyan wo men ying dang ziji shengchan yaowu" [We should learn], 17.

22. V. P. Kalashnikov 卡拉希尼可夫, "Guan yu zhiwu yao de yanjiu" 关于植物药的研究 [Regarding plant-based medicinal research], in "Liang wei sulian xue zhe guan yu yanjiu zhiwu yao de yijian" 两位苏联学者关于研究植物药的意见 [Opinions of two Russian scholars], 73–74.

23. V. P. Kalashnikov 卡拉希尼可夫, "Guan yu zhiwu yao de yanjiu" [Regarding plant-based medicinal research], in "Liang wei sulian xue zhe guan yu yanjiu zhiwu yao de yijian" [Opinions of two Russian scholars], 73–74.

24. Y. P. Kefalov [*sic*] 戈伏罗夫, "Guan yu V. P. Kalashnikov de "guan yu zhiwu yao de yanjiu" yi wen 关于 B.II. 卡拉希尼可夫的 "关于植物药的研究"一文 [V. P. Kalashnikov's "Regarding plant-based medicinal research"], in "Liang wei sulian xue zhe guan yu yanjiu zhiwu yao de yijian" [Opinions of two Russian scholars], 75.

25. A. A. Tatarinov, "Catalogus medicamentorum Sinensium, quae Pekini comparanda et determinanda curavit Alexander Tatarinov, Doctor medicinae, medicus Missionis Russicae Pekinensis spatio annorum 1840–1850" (St. Petersburg:

Petropoli, 1856). Quotation from Ye Sanduo, "Xue xi sulian xian jin jingyan wo men ying dang ziji shengchan yaowu" [We should learn], 17.

26. Emil Bretschneider, *Botanicon Sinicum: Notes on Chinese Botany from Native and Western Sources Parts 1-3* (London: Trubner, 1882, 1892, 1895).

27. For the electronic version of *Botanicon Sinicum*, see https://archive.org /details/mobot31753000532124.

28. Zhu Sheng 朱晟, "E guo xue zhe bulaixilide he ta de zhu zuo 'zhongguo zhiwu': you wang jimin: 'bencao gangmu wai wen yi ben tan' yi wen tan qi" 俄国学者布来希里德和他的著作 "中国植物"— 由王吉民: "本草纲目外文译本谈"一文谈起 [Russian scholar Bretschneider and his work "Chinese botany"—A discussion starting from Wang Jimin's "Foreign translations of *Bengcao Gangmu*"], *Yaoxue Tongbao* 药学通报 Pharmaceutical Bulletin 3, no. 8 (1954): 362-363.

29. Alexander N. Shikov et al., "Medicinal Plants of the Russian Pharmacopoeia: Their History and Applications," *Journal of Ethnopharmacology* 154, no. 3 (2014): 481-536; Alexander Panossian and Georg Wikman, "Pharmacology of *Shisandra chinensis* Bial.: An Overview of Russian Research and Uses of Medicine," *Journal of Ethnopharmacology* 118 (2008): 183-212.

30. Fang Kun 方堃, "Guan yu renshen shangpin guige he jiagong wenti de shang que" 关于人参商品规格和加工问题的商榷 [Discussing the standards for ginseng as a sales product and issues with methods of processing], *Zhongyao Tongbao* 中药通报 Bulletin of Chinese Medicinals 1, no. 2 (1955): 54.

31. Liu Tiecheng 刘铁城, "Sulian de renshen zaipei fa jieshao" 苏联的人参栽培法介绍 [Introducing Soviet methods of cultivating ginseng], *Zhongyao Tongbao* 中药通报 Bulletin of Chinese Medicinals 1, no. 2 (1955): 56-58.

32. A. P. Kiriyanov [sic] 基里扬诺夫, "Si shi nian lai sulian zai yao yong zhiwu fangmian de chengjiu" 四十年来苏联在药用植物方面的成就 [Forty years of Soviet achievements], 224.

33. Xiao Peigen 萧培根and Huang Junhua 黄俊华 [Zhongyang Weisheng Yanjiu Yuan 中央卫生研究院 Central Hygiene Research Institute], "He sulian zhuanjia zai yiqi" 和苏联专家在一起 [Spending time with a Soviet expert], *Yaoxue Tongbao* 药学通报 Pharmaceutical Bulletin 3, no. 10 (1955): 470.

34. Jian Kang Bao Xun 健康报讯 [Health report], "Renshen zaipei zhong da chengjiu: rengong shi fei zi duo shu kuai gen zi zhong" 人参栽培重大成就: 人工施肥籽多熟快根子重 [Great achievements with ginseng cultivation: More seeds faster growth and heavier roots with artificial fertilizers], *Zhongyao Tongbao* 中药通报 Bulletin of Chinese Medicinals 4, no. 10 (1958): 360.

35. A. P. Kiriyanov 基里扬诺夫, "Dongbei guoying shen chang zhongzhi renshen de jingyan" 东北国营参场种植人参的经验 [Experience with ginseng cultivation in government-owned ginseng farms in the northeast region], *Zhongyao Tongbao* 中药通报 Bulletin of Chinese Medicinals 4, no. 7 (1958): 238-239.

36. Kiriyanov 基里扬诺夫, "Dongbei guoying shen chang zhongzhi renshen de jingyan" 东北国营参场种植人参的经验 [Experience with ginseng cultivation], 237.

37. Xi Gao, "Foreign Models of Medicine," 203-206.

38. Nicolai Krementsov, *Revolutionary Experiments: The Quest for Immortality in Bolshevik Science and Fiction* (Oxford: Oxford University Press, 2013), 101-105. See

also Krementsov, "Hormones and the Bolsheviks: From Organotherapy to Experimental Endocrinology, 1918–1929," *Isis* 99 (2008): 486–518; and *A Martian Stranded on Earth: Alexander Bogdanov, Blood Transfusions, and Proletarian Science* (Chicago: University of Chicago Press, 2011).

39. On the rise and fall of organotherapy, see Martin Edwards, *Control and Therapeutic Trial: Rhetoric and Experimentation in Britain* (Amsterdam: Rodopi, 2006), 41–46; and Walter Sneader, *Drug Discovery*, 152. Sneader describes experiments by George Murray in 1891 as having removed "the taint of organotherapy" from "the developing field of endocrinology," but, as Edwards points out, the two communities continued to coexist. The *Journal of Organotherapy* continued to be published in the US into the mid-1930s. See also "The Antiquity of Animal Therapy," in Henry R. Harrower, *Practical Hormone Therapy: A Manual of Organotherapy for General Practitioners*, accessed October 19, 2014, http://archive.org /stream/practicalhormoneooharr/practicalhormoneooharr_djvu.txt.

40. Krementsov, "Hormones and the Bolsheviks."

41. Rowena Meyer, "Vladimir Petrovich Filatov," *American Review of Soviet Medicine* (December 1944); V. P. Filatov, "Tissue Therapy in Cutaneous Leishmaniasis," *American Review of Soviet Medicine* (August 1945).

42. Wang Sufu 王素孚, trans., "Zuzhi liaofa he sheng yuan ciji wuzhi" 组织疗法和生原刺激物质 [Tissue therapy and (other) stimulants], *Liangshi Yiyou* 良师益友 Good Teacher Good Friend Zhongguo Yida Xuexi Hui Jishu Tongxun 中国医大学习会技术通讯 China Medical University Study Association Technology Newsletter 1 (1951): 19–21; Xi Gao, "Foreign Models of Medicine," 206–207; see also Vladimir P. Filatov, *Tissue Therapy: Teaching on Biogenic Stimulators* (Honolulu: University Press of the Pacific, 2003).

43. There were accordingly more than two hundred publications on tissue therapy by the late 1940s. See Zhongyang Renmin Zhengfu Weisheng Bu Yizheng Chu 中央人民政府卫生部医政处 [Medical Department of the Ministry of Health for the Central People's Government], "Zuzhi liaofa zai wo guo de fazhan" 组织疗法在我国的发展 [The development of tissue therapy in our country], *Liangshi Yiyou* 良师益友 Good Teacher Good Friend no. Z2 (special edition on tissue therapy) (1951): 218–220.

44. "Ren zhen zuzhi he tuixing zuzhi liaofa" 认真组织和推行组织疗法 [Seriously organize and promote tissue therapy], *Liangshi Yiyou* 良师益友 Good Teacher Good Friend 3 (1951): 75; and *Liangshi Yiyou* 良师益友 Good Teacher Good Friend Z2 (1951): 218–220.

45. Zhongyang Renmin Zhengfu Weisheng Bu 中央人民政府卫生部 [Central People's Government Ministry of Health], "Guan yu zuzhi liaofa de wu xiang zan xing gui ding" 关于组织疗法的五项暂行规定 [About tissue therapy and five interim regulations], *Liangshi Yiyou* 良师益友 Good Teacher Good Friend 3 (1951): 75–80.

46. Wang Sufu 王素孚, trans., "Zuzhi liaofa he shengyuan ciji wuzhi" 组织疗法和生原刺激物质 [Tissue therapy and (other) stimulants], and "Zuzhi liaofa suo caiyong de zhongzhi zuzhi yingfou xuanze" 组织疗法所采用的种植组织应否选择 [Whether or not to go for substances used in tissue therapy], both in *Liangshi Yiyou* 良师益友 Good Teacher Good Friend 1 (1951): pp. 19–21, and pp. 21–23, respectively.

The latter article claimed that by 1951 tissue therapy had cured more than 28,000 diseases in China.

47. Xi Gao, "Foreign Models of Medicine," 206–207.

48. Harrower, *Practical Hormone Therapy*.

49. Vyazemsky, E. S. 刘泽先 译, "Sulian dui zhongyao de zhong shi" 苏联对中药的重视 [The Soviet Union places importance on Chinese herbs], *Yaoxue Tongbao* 药学通报 Pharmaceutical Bulletin 2, no. 2 (1954): 64–65.

50. Vyazemsky 刘泽先 译, "Sulian dui zhongyao de zhong shi" 苏联对中药的重视 [Soviet Union places importance], 64–65.

51. Vyazemsky 刘泽先 译, "Sulian dui zhongyao de zhong shi" 苏联对中药的重视 [Soviet Union places importance], 64–65. The article was originally published in the fourth issue of the Russian journal *Aptechnoe Delo* [Pharmaceutical Careers] in 1953.

52. According to one source, the region had nine deer farms by 1947. See Yan Chaofu 晏朝福 and Chen Yinqing 陈寅卿, "Dongbei di fang guoying luchang shengchan qing kuang he lurong zhibei fang fa de diaocha" 东北地方国营鹿场生产情况和鹿茸制备方法的调查 [An investigation of deer antler production and preparation methods at government-owned deer farms in the northeast region], *Zhongyao Tongbao* 中药通报 Bulletin of Chinese Medicinals 1, no. 1 (1955): 15.

53. Mary Schaeffer Conroy, *Medicines of the Soviet Masses during World War II* (Lanham, MD: University Press of America, 2008), 161.

54. "Zui chang yong zhongyao jieshao (Shi'er)" 最常用中药介绍(十二) [Introducing the most commonly used Chinese medicinals (12)], *Yaoxue Tongbao* 药学通报 Pharmaceutical Bulletin 4, no. 8 (1956): 361; Sun Zulie 孙祖烈, "Lun lurong" 论鹿茸 [On deer antler], *Minsheng Yiyao* 民生医药 People's Medicine 17 (1953): 12–13. One Chinese text mentions *shen xu zheng* (literally, kidney deficiency syndrome) as the primary condition the medicinal was used to treat. This did not refer to the kidney itself but a series of symptoms related to aging or deteriorating health. Beijing Zhongyi Xue Yuan Yi Jiu Wu Qi Nian Ban北京中医学院 1957 年班 [The class of 1957 of the Beijing Chinese Medicine College], *Zhongyao Jianshi* 中药简史 [A history of Chinese medicinals] (Beijing: Kexue Jishu Chu Ban She, 1960), 198; Pavel Metveevich Kurennov, *Russian Folk Medicine* (London: W. H. Allen, 1970), 104–105.

55. Sun Zulie, "Lun lurong," 12–13.

56. Conroy, *Medicines of the Soviet Masses*, 89, 97–98, 208.

57. Igor Vilevich Zevin, *A Russian Herbal: Traditional Recipes for Health and Healing* (Rochester, VT: Healing Arts Press, 1997), 10.

Three. The Great Leap Forward and the Rise of Medicinal Animal Farming

1. See, for instance, Kimberly Ens Manning and Felix Wemheuer, eds., *Eating Bitterness: New Perspectives on China's Great Leap Forward and Famine* (Vancouver: University of British Columbia Press, 2011); Yang Jisheng, *Tombstone: The Great Chinese Famine, 1958–1962* (New York: Farrar, Straus and Giroux, 2012); Frank Dikötter, *Mao's Great Famine: The History of China's Most Devastating Catastrophe,*

1958-1962 (London: Bloomsbury, 2010); Jasper Becker, *Hungry Ghosts: Mao's Secret Famine* (New York: Free Press, 1996).

2. For a fuller explanation of the slogan, "Let a hundred flowers bloom, let a hundred schools of thought contend," see Roderick MacFarquhar et al., eds., *The Secret Speeches of Chairman Mao: From the Hundred Flowers to the Great Leap Forward* (Cambridge, MA: Harvard University Press, 1989). See also Andrew G. Walder, *China under Mao: A Revolution Derailed* (Cambridge, MA: Harvard University Press, 2015).

3. Meng Qian 孟谦, "Fazhan shengchan, ti gao zhiliang, zuzhi zhongyaocai gongzuo da yuejin" 发展生产, 提高质量, 组织中药材工作大跃进 [Increase production, improve quality, organize work on Chinese medicinals for the Great Leap Forward], *Zhongyao Tongbao* 中药通报 Bulletin of Chinese Medicinals 4, no. 5 (1958): 150. This metaphor (*pao xin po*) was coined by Meng, who was then department head for *yao* administration within the health ministry.

4. Wang Zhipu 王致谱 and Cai Jingfeng 蔡景峰, eds., *Zhongguo Zhong Yiyao 50 Nian (1949-1999)* 中国中医药 50 年 (1949-1999) (Fifty years of Chinese *yiyao*), 327.

5. Meng Qian 孟谦, "Da po mixin jishu gexin duo kuai hao sheng di zuo hao zhongyaocai de shengchan gongying gongzuo" 打破迷信技术革新多快好省地做好中药材的生产供应工作 [Dispel superstition and conduct technological innovation to efficiently increase, accelerate, and improve medicinal production], *Zhongyao Tongbao* 中药通报 Bulletin of Chinese Medicinals 4, no. 9 (1958): 298.

6. The actual Chinese expression is "Fang zhi bian di kai hua" 防止遍地开花.

7. For an in-depth study of the emergence of the Great Leap Forward, see Frederick C. Teiwes and Warren Sun, *China's Road to Disaster: Mao, Central Politicians, and Provincial Leaders in the Unfolding of the Great Leap Forward 1955-1959* (New York: M.E. Sharpe, 1999). See also Roderick MacFarquhar, *The Origins of the Cultural Revolution*, vol. 1: *Contradictions among the People 1956-57* (New York: Columbia University Press, 1974), and vol. 2: *The Great Leap Forward 1958-1960* (New York: Columbia University Press, 1983).

8. Beijing Zhongyi Xue Yuan Yi Jiu Wu Qi Nian Ban 北京中医学院 1957 年班 [The class of 1957 of the Beijing Chinese Medicine College], *Zhongyao Jianshi* 中药简史 [A history of Chinese medicinals], 171.

9. Editors of Ta Kung Pao, *Trade with China: A Practical Guide* (Hong Kong: Ta Kung Pao, 1957), 2.

10. Guan Qixue 关其学 and Zhu Huiqiang 朱慧强, eds., *Guangdong Dui Wai Maoyi Yanjiu* 广东对外贸易研究 [A research on Guangdong's foreign trade] (Guangzhou: Huanan Ligong Daxue Chu Ban She [South China University of Technology Press], 1992), 41; Xie Yongguang 谢永光, *Xiang Gang Zhong Yiyao Shi Hua* 香港中医药史话 [A history of traditional Chinese medicine in Hong Kong] (Hong Kong: Joint Publishing, 1998), 54.

11. Zhou Lushan 周路山, *Zhongyao Shijia Caizhilin: Guangzhou Caizhilin Yaoye Youxian Gongxi Fazhan shi* 中药世家采芝林: 广州采芝林药业有限公司发展史 [Caizhilin: The development history of Guangzhou Caizhilin Pharmaceutical Co. Ltd.] (Guangzhou: Guangdong Keji Chu Ban She 广东科技出版社, 2011), 28.

12. Zhonghua Renmin Gonghe Guo Dui Wai Jingji Maoyi Bu 中华人民共和国对外经济贸易部 [People's Republic of China Foreign Trade Department], *Dui Wai*

Maoyi Tongji Ziliao Huibian, 1950–1989 对外贸易统计资料汇编 1950–1989 [Compilation of foreign trade statistics 1950–1989 (October 1990)], 184.

13. This is the second of a two-volume statistics compilation by the bureau, which focuses on export figures. Hebei Sheng Dui Wai Maoyi Ju 河北省对外贸易局 [Heibei Province Foreign Trade Bureau], *1953–1963 Nian Hebei Sheng Tianjin Kou'an Dui Wai Maoyi Tongji Ziliao (Chu Kou Bufen), Di Er Ce* 河北省天津口岸对外贸易资料 (出口部分), 第二册 [Hebei province Port of Tianjin foreign trade documents (export), vol. 2] (Tianjin: Hebei Sheng Dui Wai Maoyi Ju, 1965).

14. Hebei Sheng Dui Wai Maoyi Ju [Heibei Province Foreign Trade Bureau], *1953–1963 Nian Hebei Sheng Tianjin Kou'an Dui Wai Maoyi Tongji Ziliao (Chu Kou Bufen), Di Er Ce* [Hebei province Port of Tianjin], 492.

15. The full official slogan was *Kuai Ma Jia Bian Gan Shang Yingguo, Wu Nian Gui Hua Er Nian Wan Cheng* 快马加鞭赶上英国, 五年规划二年完成 [Catch Up with Britain at Top Speed, Accomplish the Five-Year Plan by the Second Year]. See Hua Gong Bu Yanjiu Gongzuo Huiyi Yiyao Zu Tichu Kouhao He Fendou Zhi Biao 化工部研究工作会议医药组提出口号和奋斗指标 [A slogan and instruction raised by the Ministry of Chemical Industry in Research Conference on Medicine], "Kuai ma jia bian gan shang Yingguo" 快马加鞭, 赶上英国 [Whip the horse to speed it up, catch up with Britain], *Yaoxue Tongbao* 药学通报 Pharmaceutical Bulletin 6, no. 5: 247.

16. The Chinese article that made this claim cited an unknown British magazine as its source. "Yingguo yiyao gongye gai kuang" 英国医药工业概况 [An overview of the medical industry in Britain], *Yaoxue Tongbao* 药学通报 Pharmaceutical Bulletin 6, no. 6 (1958): 287.

17. "Yingguo yiyao gongye gai kuang" [An overview], 287. According to the same Chinese source, Britain's exports of pharmaceuticals in 1957 had increased by 10 percent over the previous year, and were at the highest point since World War II. Overall, according to the same Chinese source, this was "a sevenfold increase in the total production value of Britain's pharmaceutical sector in the last twenty years." All kinds of antibiotics and vitamins were among the top export items. For instance, half the supply of British-produced penicillin was for export purposes. Britain had also established the world's third-largest factory to produce vitamin A.

18. Weisheng Bu Zhi Shu Danwei 卫生部直属单位 [Ministry of Health Directed Unit], "Sixiang jiefang gongzuo yuejin zhanlan hui" 思想解放工作跃进展览会 [Thought emancipation work leap exhibition], *Zhongyao Tongbao* 中药通报 Bulletin of Chinese Medicinals 4. no. 9 (1958): 300.

19. Liu Zhijun 刘志俊, "Zhongyaocai shouce" 中药材手册 [A Handbook on Chinese medicinals], *Yaoxue Tongbao* 药学通报 Bulletin of Chinese Medicinals 8, no. 2 (1960): 107–108.

20. All service and production units in China were required to meet the four standards of *duo kuai hao sheng*, that is, "to be productive, to speed up, to be of good quality, and to save." To achieve all these, they were encouraged to engage in "friendly competitions" or *youyi jingsai* 友谊竞赛. See Gao Enming 高恩铭, "Jing jin hu deng di yiyuan yaofang fenfen ding li yuejin jihua touru shehui zhuyi jingsai"

京津滬等地医院药房纷纷订立跃进计划投入社会主义竞赛 [Beijing, Tianjin, Shanghai hospitals and pharmacies commit to the Great Leap Movement and engage in socialist competitions], *Yaoxue Tongbao* 药学通报 Pharmaceutical Bulletin 4 (1958): 154–155; and Fan Peifu 樊培福, "Tianjin yixue yuan fushu yiyuan yaofang xiang quanguo yiyuan yaofang changyi zhankai youyi jingsai" 天津医学院附属医院药房向全国医院药房倡议展开友谊竞赛 [Tianjin Medical College affiliated pharmacy proposed all hospital pharmacies to engage in friendly matches], *Yaoxue Tongbao* 药学通报 Pharmaceutical Bulletin 4 (1958): 155.

21. Zheng Qidong 郑启栋, "Beijing tongrentang yaopu zai yuejin zhong" 北京同仁堂药铺在跃进中 [Beijing Tongrentang Medicinal Shop is in the Leap Movement], *Zhongyao Tongbao* 中药通报 Bulletin of Chinese Medicinals 4, no. 4 (1958): preface.

22. Tianjin Shi Yaocai Gongsi Yanjiu Shi 天津市药材公司研究室 [Tianjin City Medicinal Company Research Laboratory], "Xijiao bei" 犀角杯 [The rhinoceros cup], *Zhongyao Tongbao* 中药通报 Bulletin of Chinese Medicinals 4, no. 5 (1958): 164.

23. Zhongguo Yaocai Gongsi Tianjin Shi Gongsi 中国药材公司天津市公司 [Chinese Medicinal Company Tianjin Office], "Shenqing Difang Waihui Zuzhi Huanglian Xijiao Jin kou Jiejue Shichang Gongying Jinzhang You" 申请地方外汇组织黄连犀角进口解决市场供应紧张由 [An appeal to import rhinoceros horn and *huanglian* to ease market supply crisis], July 4, 1957.

24. "Chong zhu guangjiao ti zhu fu bufen reng ke shiyong" 虫蛀广角剔蛀腐部分仍可使用 [Infected rhinoceros horn usable after removing the infected area], *Zhongyao Tongbao* 中药通报 Bulletin of Chinese Medicinals 2, no. 5 (1956): 219.

25. Zhongguo Yaocai Gongsi Tianjin Shi Gongsi 中国药材公司天津市公司 [Chinese Medicinal Company Tianjin Office], "Shenqing Difang Waihui Zuzhi Huanglian Xijiao Jin kou Jiejue Shichang Gongying Jinzhang You" 申请地方外汇组织黄连犀角进口解决市场供应紧张由 [An appeal to import rhinoceros horn and *huanglian* to ease market supply crisis].

26. C. W. Hobley, "The Rhinoceros," *Journal of the Society for the Preservation of the Wild Fauna of the Empire* 14 (1931): 18–23, esp. 20–21.

27. Esmond Bradley Martin, *The International Trade in Rhinoceros Products* (Gland, Switzerland: World Wildlife Fund, 1980). Martin's groundbreaking report found that the prices of traded rhino horn had increased "21-fold" between 1976 and 1979, accompanied by the killing of 90 percent of African rhinos, making the 1970s the truly critical decade in the destruction of rhino populations. The Yemenis were the major purchasers of the material (for nonmedicinal purposes), but China had by this decade risen to second place in demand despite domestic pressure to find and use alternatives. The total amount of rhino horn imported into the rest of East Asia (Taiwan, Korea, Japan, and Southeast Asia) in the same period was even larger than the amount consumed in China, however, indicating that any serious study of this trade need take a global or at least regional approach.

28. "Rare White Rhino Dies, Leaving Only Four Left on the Planet," July 29, 2015, http://news.nationalgeographic.com/2015/07/150729-rhinos-death-animals-science-endangered-species/.

29. Liz P. Y. Chee, "'Health Products' at the Boundary between Food and Pharmaceuticals: The Case of Fish Liver Oil," in *Circulation and Governance of Asian Medicine*, ed. Celine Coderey and Laurent Pordie (London: Routledge, 2019), 109–111. On the wartime use of shark liver oil in the West, see, for example, J. Herbert Duckworth. "Shark Liver Oil," *Science* (New Series) 96, no. 2485 (1942): 8; "Save the Sharks! Strange Cry Raised on West Coast," *Science News Letter* 41, no. 8 (1942): 120; on the decline of the Atlantic coast shark fishery after the war see, "Synthetic Vitamin A Halts Shark Industry in Florida," *New York Times*, July 23, 1950.

30. Chee, "Health Products." Shark liver oil also faced stigma in India, where the wartime government established factories and promoted the product into the postwar period. U. Sundar Kani, "Fish Oils," in *Fisheries of the West Coast of India*, ed. S. Jones (India, 1958), http://eprints.cmfri.org.in/5579/.

31. "Gaijin rubai yugan you zhiliang, gan shang yingguo mingpai "sigetuo" 改进乳白鱼肝油质量, 赶上英国名牌 "司各脱" [Improving the quality of creamy white fish liver oil, and catching up with Britain's famous brand Scott's], *Yaoxue Tongbao* 药学通报 Pharmaceutical Bulletin 6, no. 12 (1958): 561.

32. "Gaijin rubai yugan you zhiliang, gan shang yingguo mingpai "sigetuo" 改进乳白鱼肝油质量, 赶上英国名牌 "司各脱" [Improving the quality], 561.

33. Huabei Yaochang Zhongxin Shiyan Shi 华北药厂中心实验室 [Huabei Pharmaceutical Factory Central Laboratory], "Huabei yaochang da fang weixing" 华北药厂大放卫星 [Huabei pharmaceutical factory launches satellite in a big way], *Yaoxue Tongbao* 药学通报 Pharmaceutical Bulletin 6, no. 11 (1958): 509.

34. Hebei Sheng Zhongyi Zhongyao Zhanlan Hui Shennong Guan Che Ji Zhi Er 河北省中医中药展览会神农馆侧记之二 [Hebei Province Chinese Medicine Exhibition Shennong Pavilion Sidelight 2], "Da gao jia zhong jia yang, meng zeng yaocai shengchan" 大搞家种家养, 猛增药材生产 [Carrying out home cultivation and home rearing on a big scale to drastically increase medicinal production], *Yaoxue Tongbao* 药学通报 Pharmaceutical Bulletin 7, no. 2 (1959): 65.

35. Zhou Enlai 周恩来, "Ba yesheng zhiwu chong fen li yong qi lai guowu yuan zhishi ge di quan mian guihua tongyi an'pai ding qi jiancha" 把野生植物充分利用起来国务院指示各地全面规划统一安排定期检查 [The State Council for Full Utilization of Wild Fauna and Flora instructs all parts of China to plan, standardize, and conduct regular checks], *Zhonyao Tongbao* 中药通报 Bulletin of Chinese Medicinals 4, no. 6 (1958): 181.

36. Liu Jiaqi 刘家琪 and Sun Shujin 孙书缙, *Ye Sheng Dongwu Yangzhi Xue Xunlian Ban Jiang Yi* 野生动物养殖学训练班讲义 [Lectures on wildlife farming] (Beijing: Quan Guo Shoulie Shiye Jingying Guanli Gan Bu Xunlian Ban Bian Wei Hui 全国狩猎事业经营管理干部训练班编委会 [Editorial Committee for National Training of Cadres in Business Hunting Management], 1960), 1.

37. Beijing Zhongyi Xue Yuan Yi Jiu Wu Qi Nian Ban 北京中医学院 1957 年班 [The class of 1957 of the Beijing Chinese Medicine College], *Zhongyao Jianshi* 中药简史 [A history of Chinese medicinals], 176. See also Ao Zhixiong's 敖志雄, "Ren gong yangzhi baihua she" 人工养殖百花蛇 [Artificial farming of the Chinese sharp-nosed viper], *Zhongyao Tongbao* 中药通报 Bulletin of Chinese Medicinals 4, no. 12 (1958): 415–416.

38. See subsection "Bian ye sheng dong zhiwu yaocai wei jia yang jia zhong" 变野生东植物药材为家养家种 [Converting wild fauna and flora into home rearing home cultivation], in "Wei chuang li zuguo de xin yixue er fendou: quan guo zhongyi zhongyao gongzuo huiyi zai baoding juxing" 为创立祖国的新医学而奋斗: 全国中医中药工作会议在保定举行 [Strive to establish a new medicine in our motherland: National Chinese medicine conference held in Baoding], *Yaoxue Tongbao* 药学通报 Pharmaceutical Bulletin 6, no. 12 (1958): 557. On knowledge of the danger of extinction, see Liu Jiaqi 刘家琪 and Sun Shujin 孙书缙, *Ye Sheng Dongwu Yangzhi Xue Xunlian Ban Jiang Yi* [Lectures on wildlife farming], 2.

39. Yan Chaofu 晏朝福 and Chen Yinqing 陈寅卿, "Dongbei di fang guoying luchang shengchan qing kuang he lurong zhibei fang fa de diaocha" 东北地方营 鹿场生产情况和鹿茸制备方法的调查 [An investigation of deer antler production], 15.

40. Zhong Yuan 仲远, "Ji Chuan Xi Lurong Shenghui" 记川西鹿茸盛会 [On Chuanxi deer antler event], *Xian Dai Yiyao Zazhi* 现代医药杂志 Journal of Contemporary Medicine 3, nos. 35/36 (1949): 11-12.

41. Chen Chunyuan 陈春源, "Lurong wei yao zhong zhenpin jia ji ang'gui, wu guo bei di suo chan zhe zui zhuming" 鹿茸为药中珍品价极昂贵, 吾国北地所产者最 著名 [Deer antler as the most expensive of luxury medicinals, products from the northern region the most famous], *Xinjiapo Hua Bao* 新加坡画报 Singapore Pictorial 106 (1930): 26.

42. "Lurong qu fa yu yingye gai kuang" 鹿茸取法与营业概况 [Method to remove deer antler and business overview], *Dong Sheng Jingji Gai Kuang* 东省经济月刊 Eastern Province Economic Monthly 4, no. 8 (1928): 19-20.

43. "Lurong qu fa yu yingye gai kuang" 鹿茸取法与营业概况 [Method to remove deer antler], 19-20. The common method of processing raw deer antler in China was to boil it in hot water and then hang it to dry. The same procedure was to be repeated nine times, which is why this method was called Nine Boil, Nine Dry (*Jiu Zheng, Jiu Liang* 九蒸九晾). The entire process was said to last about twenty days. The end product was soft and delicate and ready to be sliced into thin strips like the ones sold in contemporary medicinal markets.

44. Pei Weng 培翁, "Lurong de gushi" 鹿茸的故事 [The story of deer antler], *Da Di Zhouba* 大地周报 Earth Weekly 126 (1948): 11.

45. For instance, it was reported that the total number of deer owned by three or four households in Dongfeng county ranged between four to five hundred. "Lurong qu fa yu yingye gai kuang" 鹿茸取法与营业概况 [Method to remove deer antler].

46. "Lurong qu fa yu yingye gai kuang" 鹿茸取法与营业概况 [Method to remove deer antler].

47. In 1963, Zhang Zidong had written to the journal *Yaoxue Tongbao* in response to a reader's query on the expiration date for injectable substances made from deer antlers. He cited the eighth edition (1946) of the *Soviet Pharmacopoeia* as having provided an answer. See Zhang Zidong 张紫洞, "Lurong jing zhushe ye de zhiliang yaoqiu ru he? guo qi wu ge yue hou shang ke yingyong fou? shifou hui fasheng buliang fanying?" 鹿茸精注射液的质量要求如何? 过期五个月后尚可应用否? 是否会发生不良反应? [What is the quality requirement for deer essence injec-

tion substance? Still possible to use five months past expiry date? Will there be negative side effects?], *Yaoxue Tongbao* 药学通报 Pharmaceutical Bulletin 9, no. 5 (1963): 200.

48. Staff at Harbin Pharmaceutical Factory wrote an article explaining the different types and forms of antler essence it was producing. See Ha'erbin Zhi Yao Chang 哈尔滨制药厂 [Harbin Pharmaceutical Factory], "Lurong jing, mirong jing de zhi fa ji liaoxiao" 鹿茸精, 麋茸精的制法及疗效 [The making of deer antler and elk antler essence and their efficacies], *Yaoxue Tongbao* 药学通报 Pharmaceutical Bulletin 8, no. 9 (1958): 426–427. See also Yan Chaofu 晏朝福 and Dong Yinqing 陈寅卿, "Dongbei di fang guoying luchang shengchan qing kuang he lurong zhibei fang fa de diaocha" [An investigation of deer antler production].

49. Lu Wei 陆伟, "Jieshao dongfeng yang lu chang de jingyan" 介绍东丰养鹿场的经验 [Introducing the experience of Dongfeng Deer Farm], *Zhongyao Tongbao* 中药通报 Bulletin of Chinese Medicinals 3, no. 5 (1957): 187–189. Wang Lingyun 王凌云, "Jilin sheng zheng zai choujian yi ge da xing luchang" 吉林省正在筹建一个大型鹿场 [Jilin province making preparations to construct large-scale deer farm], *Zhongyao Tongbao* 中药通报 Bulletin of Chinese Medicinals 2, no. 4 (1956): 176.

50. See "Wei chuang li zuguo de xin yixue er fendou" 为创立祖国的新医学而奋 [Strive to establish], 557.

51. Zhong Yuan 仲远, "Ji Chuan Xi Lurong Shenghui" 记川西鹿茸盛会 [On Chuanxi deer antler event], 11–12.

52. Liu Jiaqi 刘家琪 and Sun Shujin 孙书缙, *Ye Sheng Dongwu Yangzhi Xue Xunlian Ban Jiang Yi* [Lectures on wildlife farming].

53. Guangdong Sheng Shantou Zhuan Shu Shuili Ju 广东省汕头专属水利局 [Water Resources Department of Shantou Guangdong Province], "Guangdong shantou de haima yangzhi fa" 广东汕头的海马养殖法 [Seahorse farming at Guangdong Shantou], *Yaoxue Tongbao* 药学通报 Pharmaceutical Bulletin 7, no. 4: 166.

54. Guangdong Sheng Shantou Zhuan Shu Shuili Ju 广东省汕头专属水利局 [Water Resources Department of Shantou Guangdong Province], "Guangdong shantou de haima yangzhi fa" 广东汕头的海马养殖法 [Seahorse farming], 170.

55. Zhonghua Renmin Gonghe Guo Weisheng Bu Yaozheng GuanLi Ju 中华人民共和国卫生部药政管理局 [People's Republic of China Health Ministry Drug Administration Bureau], *Zhongyaocai Yesheng Bian Jia Zhong Jia Yang Chenggong De Jingyan Di Yi Ji* 中药材野生变家种家养成功的经验介绍 第一集 [Introducing the successful experiences of converting wild Chinese medicinals into home cultivation, home rearing, part 1] (Beijing: Renmin Weisheng Chu Ban She 人民卫生出版社, 1959), 47–59.

56. Xi Tongsheng 喜桐生, "Siyang dibi chong de chu bu jingyan" 饲养地必虫的初步经验 [Preliminary experiences of rearing ground beetle], *Zhongyao Tongbao* 中药通报 Bulletin of Chinese Medicinals 4, no. 12 (1958): 421.

57. Xi Tongsheng 喜桐生, "Siyang dibi chong de chu bu jingyan" 饲养地必虫的初步经验 [Preliminary experiences of rearing ground beetle].

58. Zhonghua Renmin Gonghe Guo Weisheng Bu Yaozheng Guanli Ju 中华人民共和国卫生部药政管理局 [People's Republic of China Health Ministry Drug Administration Bureau], *Zhongyaocai Yesheng Bian Jia Zhong Jia Yang Chenggong De*

Jingyan Jieshao Di Yi Ji 中药材野生变家种家养成功的经验介绍 第一集 [Introducing the successful experiences, part 1], 37–39; see also Zhonghua Renmin Gonghe Guo Weisheng Bu Yaozheng Guanli Ju 中华人民共和国卫生部药政管理局, ed., *Zhongyaocai Feng Chan Zaipei Jingyan Jieshao Di Yi Ji* [Introducing the cultivation experiences of Chinese medicinals with high yield part 1: Production technology]. Beijing: Renmin Weisheng Chu Ban She 人民卫生出版社, 1959; Nongye Bu Gongye Yuanliao Ju, Weisheng Bu Yaozheng Guanli Ju 农业部工业原料局, 卫生部药政管理局, *Zhongyaocai Shengchan Jishu* 中药材丰产栽培经验介绍 第一集: 中药材生产技术 [Introducing the cultivation experiences of Chinese medicinals with high yield, part 1: Production technology] (Beijing: Renmin Weisheng Chu Ban She 人民卫生出版社, 1960).

59. Yang Guoxuan 杨国萱, *Darentang De Gushi* 达仁堂的故事 [The story of Darentang], 77–80.

60. Guangxi Tong Zu Zi Zhi Qu Shangye Ting Yaocai Zhongzhi Shiyan Chang 广西僮族自治区商业厅药材种植实验场 [Guangxi Zhuang Autonomous Region Commerce Department for Experimental Farms in Medicinal Cultivation], "Rengong siyang gejie shiyan chenggong 人工饲养蛤蚧实验成功 [Successful experimentation with tokay gecko farming], *Zhongyao Tongbao* 中药通报 Bulletin of Chinese Medicinals 4, no. 11 (1958): 388.

61. Guangxi Tong Zu Zi Zhi Qu Shangye Ting Yaocai Zhongzhi Shiyan Chang 广西僮族自治区商业厅药材种植实验场 [Guangxi Zhuang Autonomous Region Commerce Department for Experimental Farms in Medicinal Cultivation], "Rengong siyang gejie shiyan chenggong 人工饲养蛤蚧实验成功 [Successful experimentation], 388.

62. Guangxi Tong Zu Zi Zhi Qu Shangye Ting Yaocai Zhongzhi Shiyan Chang 广西僮族自治区商业厅药材种植实验场 [Guangxi Zhuang Autonomous Region Commerce Department for Experimental Farms in Medicinal Cultivation], "Rengong siyang gejie shiyan chenggong 人工饲养蛤蚧实验成功 [Successful experimentation], 388.

63. Scorpions and centipedes are actually arachnids, but Chinese pharmaceutical journals of this period did not make distinctions between insects and other land-based arthropods.

64. Meng Qian 孟谦, "Da po mixin jishu gexin duo kuai hao sheng di zuo hao zhongyaocai de shengchan gongying gongzuo" 打破迷信技术革新多快好省地做好中药材的生产供应工作 [Dispel superstition], 299.

65. I thank one of the anonymous reviewers of my manuscript for this reference.

66. Ye Niandao 叶年道, "Ying zhong shi jineijin de shougou gongzuo" 应重视鸡内金的收购工作 [Placing importance on chicken gizzard procurement], *Zhongyao Tongbao* 中药通报 Bulletin of Chinese Medicinals 4, no. 6 (1958).

67. Li Rongsheng 李荣升, "Jineijin" 鸡内金 [Chicken gizzard], *Zhongyao Tongbao* 中药通报 Bulletin of Chinese Medicinals 4, no. 5 (1958): 164.

68. Gao Minggong 高铭功, "Wei da zuguo de yaowu ziyuan ji qi liyong: guochan shexiang" 伟大祖国的药物资源及其利用: 国产麝香 [The medical resources of our Great Motherland and their utilization: State-produced musk], *Yaoxue Tong-*

bao 药学通报 Pharmaceutical Bulletin 3, no. 5 (1955): 229; another source included Qinghai, Gansu, Shanxi, and Guangxi as provinces with substantial musk deer populations. Di Er Junyi Daxue Yaoxue Xi Zhong Caoyao Jiaoyan Shi 第二军医大学药学系中草药教研室 [The Second Army Medical University School of Pharmacy Research Laboratory for Chinese Medicinals], "Wuchan jieji wenhua da geming yi lai wo guo zhongyaocai shengchan ji qi keyan de xin chengjiu (xu)" 无产阶级文化大革命以来我国中药材生产及其科研的新成就 (续) [New achievements in the research and production of Chinese medicinals since the Great Proletarian Cultural Revolution (continued)], *Zhong Caoyao Tongxun* 中草药通讯 Chinese Traditional and Herbal Drugs 9 (1976): 41.

69. Di Er Junyi Daxue Yaoxue Xi Zhong Caoyao Jiaoyan Shi 第二军医大学药学系中草药教研室 [The Second Army Medical University School of Pharmacy Research Laboratory for Chinese Medicinals], "Wuchan jieji wenhua da geming yi lai wo guo zhongyaocai shengchan ji qi keyan de xin chengjiu (xu)" 无产阶级文化大革命以来我国中药材生产及其科研的新成就 (续) [New achievements], 41.

70. Even in 1950, Xikang province produced eight hundred *jin* of musk compared to the rest of the musk-producing regions and provinces, which produced from three to 162 *jin*. Gao Minggong 高铭功, "Wei da zuguo de yaowu ziyuan ji qi liyong" 伟大祖国的药物资源及其利用 [Medical resources], 229.

71. It was claimed that about twenty deer were required to produce one *jin* of musk. See Cai Shoubai 蔡受白, "Zhongguo shexiang ye zhuang kuang: shexiang wei wo guo zhi techan" 中国麝香业状况: 麝香为我国之特产 [The situation of China's musk industry: Musk as our country's specialty], *Shanghai Zong Shanghui Yuebao* 上海总商会月报 Shanghai General Chamber of Commerce Monthly 5, no. 3 (1925): 13–17.

72. Gao Minggong 高铭功, "Wei da zuguo de yaowu ziyuan ji qi liyong" 伟大祖国的药物资源及其利用 [Medical resources].

73. A 1925 article reported that China also exported musk for perfume making to Japan, where demand was increasing. Cai Shoubai 蔡受白, "Zhongguo shexiang ye zhuang kuang" 中国麝香业状况 [Situation of China's musk industry].

74. China's musk exports to France dropped from a total of 746,000 grams, for the three years between 1936 and 1938, to 127,500 grams for the same duration a decade later. Cai Shoubai 蔡受白, "Zhongguo shexiang ye zhuang kuang" 中国麝香业状况 [Situation of China's musk industry], 230. For musk export figures during the Republican period, see "Qu nian changyi shexiang chu kou e, changyi san shi yi yuan shexiang shi yi yuan" 去年肠衣麝香出口额, 肠衣三十亿元麝香十亿元 [Last year's export value for (sausage) casing and musk, casing 30 billion yuan musk 10 billion yuan], *Zhengxin Suo Bao* 征信所报 Zhengxin Report 263 (1947): 4.

75. Beijing Shi Yaocai Gongsi Di Yi Pifa Bu 北京市药材公司第一批发部 [Beijing Medicinal Company No. 1 Wholesale Department], "Shexiang nei yi shiyong jingyan jieshao" 麝香内衣使用经验介绍 [Introducing experiences in using "musk inner wear"], *Zhongyao Tongbao* 中药通报 Bulletin of Chinese Medicinals 2, no. 4 (1956): 150–151.

76. Beijing Shi Yaocai Gongsi Di Yi Pifa Bu 北京市药材公司第一批发部 [Beijing Medicinal Company No. 1 Wholesale Department], "Shexiang nei yi shiyong jingyan jieshao" 麝香内衣使用经验介绍 [Introducing experiences], 150–151.

77. Beijing Shi Yaocai Gongsi Di Yi Pifa Bu 北京市药材公司第一批发部 [Beijing Medicinal Company No. 1 Wholesale Department], "Shexiang nei yi shiyong jingyan jieshao" 麝香内衣使用经验介绍 [Introducing experiences], 150–151.

78. Guangdong Sheng Shantou Zhuan Shu Shuili Ju 广东省汕头专属水利局 [Water Resources Department of Shantou Guangdong Province], "Guangdong shantou de haima yangzhi fa" 广东汕头的海马养殖法 [Seahorse farming], 170.

79. Guangzhou Zhongyi Xue Yuan 广州中医学院 [Guangzhou Medical College], *Shengwu Xue Jiang Yi* 生物学讲义 [Biology lectures] (1959), 35.

80. Guangzhou Zhongyi Xue Yuan 广州中医学院 [Guangzhou Medical College], *Shengwu Xue Jiang Yi* 生物学讲义 [Biology lectures].

81. Tianjin Shi Jingji Jihua Weiyuan Hui 天津市经济计划委员会 [Tianjin Economic Planning Committee], "Wei jianyi zhiding shengchu zonghe liyong de tongyi guihua ji qingshi jiejue niuhuang deng yaopin yong liao you" 为建议制定牲畜综合利用的统一规划及请示解决牛黄等药品用料由 [Proposal to plan for all-around use of livestock and a request to resolve medical resources like bezoar], May 15, 1959.

82. "Niuhuang shizhi chenggong touru shengchan" 牛黄试制成功投入生产 [Trial manufacturing of bezoar a success leading to actual production], *Zhongyao Tongbao* 中药通报 Bulletin of Chinese Medicinals 2, no. 4 (1956) (originally published in *Yiyao Gongye Tongxun* 医药工业通讯 Medical Industry Newsletter 5 [1956]: 161).

83. Fu Yunsheng 付云升, "Guan yu tianjin shi rengong hecheng niuhuang shengchan wenti de diaocha baogao" 关于天津市人工合成牛黄生产问题的调查报告 [An investigative report on the problems concerning artificial bezoar production in Tianjin City], July 20, 1965; see also Beijing Zhongyi Xue Yuan Yi Jiu Wu Qi Nian Ban 北京中医学院 1957 年班 [The class of 1957 of the Beijing Chinese Medicine College], *Zhongyi Jianshi* 中药简史 [A history of Chinese medicinals]; Su Huaide 苏怀德, ed., "Cong tianran niuhuang dao rengong niuhuang" 从天然牛黄到人工牛黄 [From natural bezoar to artificial bezoar], in *Yaowu Yanjiu Shi Xuan Jiang* 药物研究史选讲 [Lectures on the history of drug research] (Beijing: Beijing Yike Daxue 北京医科大学, 1992); Tianjin Zhi Yao Chang 天津制药厂 [Tianjin Pharmaceutical Factory], "Guoying tianjin zhi yao chang guan yu jin yi bu gaijin niuhuang chejian sanfa qiwei de cuoshi" 国营天津制药厂关于进一步改进牛黄车间散发气味的措施 [Measures to improve the condition of odor emission from state-owned Tianjin pharmaceutical factory bezoar workshop], February 23, 1957.

84. Hebei Sheng Shangye Ting, Hebei Sheng Weisheng Ting 河北省商业厅, 河北省卫生厅 [Hebei Province Department of Commerce, Hebei Province Department of Health], "Wei jia qiang shougou niu, zhu, yang danzhi gongying niuhuang shengchan de tongzhi" 为加强收购牛, 猪, 羊胆汁供应牛黄生产的通知 [A notice to increase the purchase].

85. Tianjin Shi Jingji Jihua Weiyuan Hui 天津市经济计划委员会 [Tianjin Economic Planning Committee], "Wei jianyi zhiding shengchu zonghe liyong de tongyi guihua ji qingshi jiejue niuhuang deng yaopin yong liao you" 为建议制定牲畜综合利用的统一规划及请示解决牛黄等药品用料由 [Proposal to plan]. See also "Guan yu jin chan rengong niuhuang deng yaopin yuanliao gongying jinzhang qing qiu tongyi anpai de baogao" 关于津产人工牛黄等药品原料供应紧张请求统一安排的报告 [A report to request that standardized arrangements be made to solve a short-

age of medical ingredients like Tianjin artificial bezoar], April 14, 1959 (written on behalf of Tianjin Shi Huaxue Gongye Ju 天津市化学工业局 [Tianjin Chemical Industry Department]). By 1963, Shanghai, Beijing, Tianjin, and Guangzhou had become the four main production centers for artificial bezoar. Beijing and Guangzhou needed only to ensure sufficient supply in their own cities, while Tianjin and Shanghai had to produce for the rest of China. Fu Yunsheng 付云升, "Guan yu tianjin shi rengong hecheng niuhuang shengchan wenti de diaocha baogao" 关于天津市人工合成牛黄生产问题的调查报告 [An investigation report].

86. China's first method for producing artificial bezoar was invented by a pharmacist, not a scientist or physician, whose name was Guogong. See Su Huaide 苏怀德, ed., "Chong tianran niuhuang dao rengong niuhuang" 从天然牛黄到人工牛黄 [From natural bezoar to artificial bezoar], in *Yaowu Yanjiu Shi Xuan Jiang* 药物研究史选讲 [Lectures on the history of drug research].

87. Beijing Zhongyi Xue Yuan Yi Jiu Wu Qi Nian Ban 北京中医学院 1957 年班 [The class of 1957 of the Beijing Chinese Medicine College], *Zhongyi Jianshi* 中药简史 [History of Chinese medicinals], 177–178. Despite that innovation, the hunting of tigers in China increased in this period in response to the official directive to gather medicinals from the wild. Tiger bones were largely destined for export markets like Hong Kong, Singapore, and Malaysia, where they were made into products like tiger-bone wine. The extensive deforestation that took place in this period throughout China, described by Judith Shapiro, likely contributed to the large numbers of tigers caught during the Great Leap Forward period. See Shapiro, *Mao's War against China: Politics and the Environment in Revolutionary China* (Cambridge: Cambridge University Press, 2009).

88. It was believed that the earliest study on bezoar was conducted in 1931 by the Japanese researcher Tsubura Shirō. See Liu Shoushan 刘寿山, "Guan yu niuhuang cheng fen, liao xiao ji yaoli de yi xie bu chong" 关于牛黄成分, 疗效及药理的一些补充 [Supplementary notes on the components, efficacies and pharmacology of bezoar], *Zhongyao Tongbao* 中药通报 Bulletin of Chinese Medicinals 2, no. 1 (1956): 23.

89. Japanese scientist Sugimoto Shigetoshi conducted experiments to ascertain the drug action of bezoar, the results of which were published in 1940 in a Manchuria-based medical journal (*Manzhou Yixue Zazhi*). Liu Shoushan 刘寿山, "Guan yu niuhuang cheng fen, liao xiao ji yaoli de yi xie bu chong" 关于牛黄成分, 疗效及药理的一些补充 [Supplementary notes], 23. For Japanese scientific activity in Manchuria, see Timothy Yang, "Selling an Imperial Dream: Japanese Pharmaceuticals, National Power, and the Science of Quinine Self-Sufficiency," *EASTS* 6 (2012): 101–125.

90. Zhang Yingcai 张颖才, "Yaocai shengchan fangmian cun zai de ji ge wenti" 药材生产方面存在的几个问题 [Some problems regarding medicinal production], *Zhongyao Tongbao* 中药通报 Bulletin of Chinese Medicinals 4, no. 5 (1958): 153.

91. Section 5, "Pochu mixin gui zhong yaopin de sixiang" 破除迷信贵重药品的思想 [Break the superstitious mindset of luxury medicinals], in "1958 nian guangdong sheng liuxing xing yixing naoyan zhongyi zhiliao gongzuo zong jie" 1958年广东省流行性乙型脑炎中医治疗工作总结 1958 [Summary of using Chinese medicine to treat epidemic encephalitis B in Guangdong province], *Guangdong Zhongyi* 广东

中医 Guangdong Chinese Medicine 10 (1958): 3; Huang Zizhan 黄子瞻 et al., "Yong shuiniu jiao daiti lingyang jiao xijiao zhiliao 35 li liuxing xing yixing naoyan linchuang chubu baogao" 用水牛角代替羚羊角犀角35例流行性乙型脑炎临床初步报告 [A preliminary report of using water buffalo horns as a replacement for antelope and rhinoceros horns to treat 35 cases of epidemic encephalitis B], *Guangdong Zhongyi* 广东中医 Guangdong Chinese Medicine 10 (1958): 14.

Four. The Quest for Innovation

1. Zhan, *Otherworldly*, chapter 3.

2. Schmalzer, *Red Revolution, Green Revolution*.

3. Gross, *Farewell to the God of Plague*.

4. Fa-ti Fan, "Collective Monitoring, Collective Defense: Science, Earthquakes, and Politics in Communist China," *Science in Context* 25, no. 1 (2012): 127–154. See also Schmalzer, "On the Appropriate Use of Rose-Colored Glasses: Reflections on Science in Socialist China," *Isis* 98, no. 3 (2007): 571–583.

5. "Jiefang sixiang, da dan chuangzao—Beijing shi gong gong weisheng ju yan yi fu juzhang zai 4 yue 27 ri zhongguo yaoxue hui beijing fen hui he beijing shi wei xie yaoshi hui lianhe zhaokai de yaofang jishu gexin baogao hui shang de baogao" 解放思想, 大胆创造— 北京市公共卫生局阎毅副局长在 4 月 27 日中国药学会北京分会 和北京市卫协药师会联合召开的药房技术革新报告会上的报告 [Liberal thoughts, bold inventions—A report on 27 April by deputy director of Beijing Public Health Bureau Yan Yifu at the Pharmaceutical Technology Innovation Symposium jointly organized with the Chinese Pharmaceutical Association Beijing office], *Yaoxue Tongbao* 药学通报 Pharmaceutical Bulletin 6, no. 6 (1958): 254–255.

6. See also Schmalzer, "Youth and the 'Great Revolutionary Movement' of Scientific Experiment in 1960s–1970s Rural China," in *Maoism at the Grassroots: Everyday Life in China's Era of High Socialism*, ed. Jeremy Brown and Matthew D. Johnson (Cambridge, MA: Harvard University Press, 2015).

7. Cui Luchun 崔禄春, "Keji 'da yuejin' yundong pingxi" 科技 "大跃进" 运动评析 [A comment on the technological "Great Leap Forward" movement], *Beijing Dangshi* 北京党史 Beijing Party History 2 (2013): 12–14.

8. Fu Lianzhang 傅连璋, "Wei gao sudu di fazhan shehui zhuyi de weisheng shiye er fendou" 为高速度地发展社会主义的卫生事业而奋斗 [Strive for the healthcare of a society gearing for fast-paced development], *Yaoxue Tongbao* 药学通报 Pharmaceutical Bulletin 6, no. 9 (1958): 401.

9. One example was the Chinese pharmaceutical journal *Yaoxue Tongbao* 药学通报 Pharmaceutical Bulletin.

10. Shanghai Shi Chuban Geming Zu 上海市出版革命组 [Shanghai Publishing Revolutionary Team], *Mao Zedong Sixiang Zhao Liang Le Woguo Yixue Fazhan De Daolu* 毛泽东思想照亮了我国医学发展的道路 [Shining the thoughts of Mao Zedong on our path toward medical development] (Shanghai: Shanghaishi Chuban Geming Zu, 上海市出版革命组 [Shanghai Publishing Revolutionary Team] 1970), 3.

11. Qinqiu Guxun, Bocai Zhongfang 勤求古训, 博采众方. *Guxun* means "the teachings and experiences of past generations." Zhang Zhongjing's advice was to

"collect broadly the medical formulations of the wider population." See Zhongyi Yanjiu Yuan Zhongyao Yanjiu Suo 中医研究院中药研究 [Chinese Medicine Research Institute Department for Research on Chinese Drugs], "Jian guo shi nian lai zhongyao yanjiu gongzuo de chengjiu" 建国十年来中药研究工作的成就 [Research on Chinese medicinals and its achievements during the ten years of nation-building], *Yaoxue Tongbao* 药学通报 Pharmaceutical Bulletin 7, no. 9 (1959): 441.

12. "Zhongyi Yanfang Huibian Di Yi Ji" 中医验方汇编第一集 [Experience-based Chinese medical prescriptions, part 1], *Yaoxue Tongbao* 药学通报 Pharmaceutical Bulletin 7, no. 9 (1959): 441.

13. "Zhongyi Yanfang Huibian Di Yi Ji" 中医验方汇编第 [Experience-based Chinese medical prescriptions], 441.

14. "Jiaoyu yu shengchan laodong xiang jiehe" 教育于生产劳动相结合 basically means that education should serve a practical purpose; Huanan refers to the provinces of Guangdong, Guangxi, and Hainan. See Guangzhou Zhongyi Xue Yuan Bianxie 广州中医学院编写 [Guangzhou Chinese Medical College], *Linchuang Shiyong Zhongyao* 临床使用中药 [Bedside application of Chinese medicinals] (Guangdong Renmin Chu Ban She 广东人民出版社, 1960), 1–2.

15. Zhongyi Yanjiu Yuan Zhongyao Yanjiu Suo 中医研究院中药研究所 [Chinese Medicine Research Institute Department for Research on Chinese Drugs], "Jian guo shi nian lai zhongyao yanjiu gongzuo de chengjiu" 建国十年来中药研究工作的成就 [Research on Chinese medicinals].

16. "Tufang tufa wenzhai" 土方土法文摘 [Folk ways and methods: An abstract], *Yaoxue Tongbao* 药学通报 Pharmaceutical Bulletin 12, no. 4 (1966): 178–183.

17. Fang Xiaoping, *Barefoot Doctors*, 77.

18. See Yuan Shicheng 袁士诚 and Kang Tai 康泰, "Zhonghua renmin gonghe guo yaodian 1963 nian ban jianjie" 中华人民共和国药典 1963 年版简介 [An Introduction to the People's Republic of China pharmacopoeia 1963 edition], *Yaoxue Tongbao* 药学通报 Pharmaceutical Bulletin 10, no. 7 (1964): 289.

19. Gao Xiaoshan 高晓山 et al., "Wu nian lai zhongyao yanjiu gongzuo de chengjiu" 五年来中药研究工作的成就 [Five years of research], 482–483.

20. Yuan Shicheng 袁士诚 and Kang Tai 康泰, "Zhonghua renmin gonghe guo yaodian 1963 nian ban jianjie" [An Introduction], 290.

21. Gao Xiaoshan 高晓山 et al., "Wu nian lai zhongyao yanjiu gongzuo de chengjiu" [Five years of research].

22. The only detailed English-language account of this phenomenon is a web-based translation by Joel Martinson, of Du Xing, "Why Was the Preposterous 'Chicken Blood Injection' Therapy So Popular during the CR Era?" [Wenge shi 'da jixue' de huangmiu liaofa wei he neng gou shengxing? 文革时 "打鸡血" 的荒谬疗法为何能够盛行?], *Wanxia* 晚霞 Sunset (July 20, 2012), in Martinson, "Chicken Blood Injections and Other Health Crazes," January 13, 2015, http://www.danwei.org/health_care_diseases_and_pharmaceuticals/chicken_blood_injections.php.

23. Qinghai Sheng Ba Yi Ba Youdian Zaofan Tuan Bianyin 青海省八一八邮电造反团编印, *Jixue Liaofa* 鸡血疗法 [Chicken blood therapy] (Qinghai Province Eight-One-Eight Post and Telecommunications Revolutionary Team, 1967). This booklet was compiled in 1967 by the so-called Qinghai Province Eight-One-Eight Post

and Telecommunications Revolutionary Team to promote the therapy during the Cultural Revolution. It includes the sole published narrative by the inventor, Yu Changshi 俞昌时, titled "Jixue liaofa de kaishi" 鸡血疗法的开始 [The beginning of chicken blood therapy]. Yu's testament had previously been circulated in the form of handwritten copies after the government had officially banned his therapy the previous year (1966).

24. Chicken blood injection was still included in a 1971 instruction manual for barefoot doctors, long after it had gone out of fashion in cities. Hai Bazi 海巴子, "Fengmi yi shi de 'jixue liaofa'" 风靡一时的鸡血疗法 [Fashionable chicken blood therapy in 1960s], *Dang'an Chunqiu* 档案春秋 Spring and Autumn Archives (December 10, 2009), 24.

25. Wu Zhijing 伍稚荆, "Lao cheng jishi: huang tang de jixue liaofa" 老城纪事: 荒唐的鸡血疗法 [Old town chronicle: The absurd chicken blood therapy], in *Zha Wen Xuan Kan* 杂文选刊 Journal of Selected Essays (March 21, 2008): 42.

26. Xi'an Shi Di Si Yiyuan Yaofang 西安市第四医院药房 [Xi'an Number Four Hospital Pharmacy], "Xiongdan, xiong she jiemo xia zhuseye zhibei jieshao" 熊胆、熊麝结膜下注射液制备介绍 [Introducing the preparation of injectable substance targeting the conjunctiva using bear bile and bear bile-musk], *Yaoxue Tongbao* 药学通报 Pharmaceutical Bulletin 7, no. 3 (1959): 122–123; see also Zhang Zidong 张紫洞 and Huang Wenda 黄文达, "Qiuyin zhushe ye zhiliao zhiqiguan xiaochuan de liaoxiao guancha" 蚯蚓注射液治疗支气管哮喘的疗效观察 [An observation of the efficacy of earthworm-based injectable substance in curing bronchial asthma], *Yaoxue Tongbao* 药学通报 Pharmaceutical Bulletin 11, no. 10 (1965): 479; Gu Kelin 顾克霖, "Yugan you suan'na zhushe ye yu weisheng su A, D zhushe ye shi bu shi yi zhong yao?" 鱼肝油酸钠注射液与维生素 A, D 注射液是不是一种药? [Are sodium morrhuate and vitamins A and D considered medicine?], *Yaoxue Tongbao* 药学通报 Pharmaceutical Bulletin 11 no. 5 (1965): 237–238; Liu Mohui 刘谟慧, "'Kang chuansi shuan' he 'zhu danzhi zhushe ye'" 抗喘息栓" 和 "猪胆汁注射液 [Battling agonal breathing and pig bile injectable substance], *Yaoxue Tongbao* 药学通报 Pharmaceutical Bulletin 12, no. 3 (1966): 129.

27. Yu Changshi 俞昌时, "Jixue liaofa de kaishi" 鸡血疗法的开始 [Beginning of chicken blood therapy], in Qinghai Sheng Ba Yi Ba Youdian Zaofan Tuan Bianyin, *Jixue Liaofa* 鸡血疗法 [Chicken blood therapy]. It is not clear from his account which classical texts Yu was referring to. But according to Hai Bazi 海巴子, there was mention of chicken blood in the Ming materia medica compilation *Jiying Gangmu* 济阴纲目, written by the famous Shanxi physician Wu Zhiwang 武之望. According to that text, chicken blood was used mainly to cure gynecological problems and was suitable for *both* internal and external use. See Hai Bazi 海巴子, "Fengmi yi shi de 'jixue liaofa'" 风靡一时的鸡血疗法 [Fashionable chicken blood therapy], 25. Also, "black chicken and white chicken pills" were among the medicinals in the prewar product lines of the drug companies Tongrentang and Darentang and were intended to "prevent irregular menstruation." See Cochran, *Chinese Medicine Men*, 33.

28. Yu Changshi 俞昌时, "Jixue liaofa de kaishi" 鸡血疗法的开始 [Beginning of chicken blood therapy], 25.

29. Yu Changshi 俞昌时, "Jixue liaofa de kaishi" 鸡血疗法的开始 [Beginning of chicken blood therapy], 25.

30. Krementsov, *Martian Stranded on Earth*, 2011.

31. Hebei Xin Yi Daxue "Chijiao Yisheng Cankao Cong Shu" Bianxie Zu 河北新医大学 '赤脚医生参考丛书' 编写组 [Hebei New Medical College Barefoot Doctors Reference Series Editorial Team], *Jichu Yixue Wenda: Xueye Xitong* 基础医学问答: 血液系统 [Fundamental questions of medicine: The blood system] (Beijing: Renming Weisheng Chu Ban She 人民卫生出版社, 1976), 14–15.

32. For a history of blood transfusion and blood banking in China, and its relation to wartime needs, see Wayne Soon, "Blood, Soy Milk, and Vitality: The Wartime Origins of Blood Banking in China, 1943–45," *Bulletin of the History of Medicine* 90, no. 3 (2016).

33. Yu Changshi 俞昌时, "Jixue liaofa de kaishi" 鸡血疗法的开始 [Beginning of chicken blood therapy], 25–26.

34. Du Xing 杜兴, "Da jixue wang shi" 打鸡血往事 [The historical "injecting chicken blood" event], *Dushu Wenzhai* 读书文摘 Reader Digest (August 1, 2009): 12; see also "Guoren ceng fengkuang da jixue" 国人曾疯狂打鸡血 [The once-crazed chicken blood therapy], *Gongchan Dang Yuan* 共产党员 Communist Party Member (August 15, 2010): 48; and Hai Bazi 海巴子, "Fengmi yi shi de 'jixue liaofa'" 风靡一时的鸡血疗法 [Fashionable chicken blood therapy], 25.

35. Yu Changshi 俞昌时, "Jixue liaofa de kaishi" 鸡血疗法的开始 [Beginning of chicken blood therapy]. Du Xing believes that Yu was inspired to come forward and make his invention known because of a speech made by Premier Zhou Enlai in 1958 at the launch of the Great Leap Forward (later published as a New Year's speech in the national newspaper *Renmin Ribao* on January 1, 1959, under the headline "Usher the New Year with a Glorious Victory"). Zhou had encouraged the limitless display of technological innovation (*jishu gexin*). Du Xing 杜兴, "Wenge shi 'da jixue' de huangmiu liaofa wei he neng gou shengxing?" 文革时 "打鸡血" 的荒谬疗法为何能够盛行? [Why was the preposterous "chicken blood injection" therapy so popular during the CR era?], *Wanxia* 晚霞 Sunset (July 20, 2012): 54; Du Xing 杜兴, *Dushu Wenzhai* 读书文摘 Reader Digest, 12.

36. Hai Bazi 海巴子, "Fengmi yi shi de 'jixue liaofa'" 风靡一时的鸡血疗法 [Fashionable chicken blood therapy], 25.

37. Du Xing 杜兴, *Dushu Wenzhai* 读书文摘 Reader Digest, 12.

38. Yu Changshi 俞昌时, "Jixue liaofa de kaishi" 鸡血疗法的开始 [Beginning of chicken blood therapy], 30.

39. Yu Changshi 俞昌时, "Jixue liaofa de kaishi" 鸡血疗法的开始 [Beginning of chicken blood therapy], 31–32.

40. Yu quoted the health ministry as advising, "This therapy has surpassed international standards, and so we should keep it a secret." Yu Changshi 俞昌时, "Jixue liaofa de kaishi" 鸡血疗法的开始 [Beginning of chicken blood therapy], 26.

41. "Guoren ceng fengkuang da jixue" 国人曾疯狂打鸡血 [Once-crazed chicken blood therapy], 48; Du Xing 杜兴, *Dushu Wenzhai* 读书文摘 Reader Digest, 13.

42. Yu Changshi 俞昌时, "Jixue liaofa de kaishi" 鸡血疗法的开始 [Beginning of chicken blood therapy], 43.

43. Du Xing 杜兴, *Dushu Wenzhai* 读书文摘 Reader Digest, 13.

44. Hai Bazi 海巴子, "Fengmi yi shi de 'jixue liaofa'" 风靡一时的鸡血疗法 [Fashionable chicken blood therapy], 26.

45. Du Xing 杜兴, *Dushu Wenzhai* 读书文摘 Reader Digest, 13-14; "Guoren ceng fengkuang da jixue" 国人曾疯狂打鸡血 [Once-crazed chicken blood therapy], 48.

46. Qinghai Sheng Ba Yi Ba Youdian Zaofan Tuan Bianyin 青海省八一八邮电造反团编印, *Jixue Liaofa* 鸡血疗法. This section of the book was entitled "Chicken blood therapy—Basic victory of the bourgeois reactionary line."

47. Qinghai Sheng Ba Yi Ba Youdian Zaofan Tuan Bianyin 青海省八一八邮电造反团编印, *Jixue Liaofa* 鸡血疗法.

48. Qinghai Sheng Ba Yi Ba Youdian Zaofan Tuan Bianyin 青海省八一八邮电造反团编印, Jixue Liaofa 鸡血疗法. One handbook cost *yijiao wufen* 五角一分 (fifteen cents). See Su Zhiwu 苏志武, "Wenge zhong 'da jixue' zhi guai zhuang" 文革中 "打鸡血" 之怪状 [The strange occurrence of chicken blood therapy during the Cultural Revolution], in *Wen Shi Jing Hua* 文史精华 Essence of Literature and History (May 6, 2012): 45.

49. Hai Bazi 海巴子, "Fengmi yi shi de 'jixue liaofa'" 风靡一时的鸡血疗法 [Fashionable chicken blood therapy], 28.

50. Yi Qie Niu Gui She Shen 一切牛鬼蛇神 [All the cows, ghosts, snakes, and gods]; see "Pipan zichan jieji fandong luxian: zaofan yundong de xianqi" 批判资产阶级反动路线: 造反运动的掀起 [Criticizing the bourgeois reactionary line: The start of the rebel movement], http://www.cuhk.edu.hk/ics/21c/issue/articles/031_95206.pdf.

51. Sections titled "Geming de xin shengwu" 革命的新生物 [Revolutionary New Matter], and "Zai yiyao keyan shang wei mao zedong sixiang fan'an (geming zaofan xuanyan)" 在医药科研上为毛泽东思想翻案 (革命造反宣言) [In defense of medical research on behalf of Mao Zedong's thoughts], in Qinghai Sheng Ba Yi Ba Youdian Zaofan Tuan Bianyin 青海省八一八邮电造反团编印, *Jixue Liaofa* 鸡血疗法, 3-9.

52. Section titled "Che di wei yiyao keyan zhong de xin sheng shiwu—jixue liaofa fan'an (gao quanguo geming renmin de gongkai xin)" 彻底为医药科研中的新生物— 鸡血疗法翻案 (搞全国革命人民的公开信) [All for the new matters in medical research—In defense of chicken blood therapy (Public letter for the people involved in the nation-wide revolution)], in Qinghai Sheng Ba Yi Ba Youdian Zaofan Tuan Bianyin 青海省八一八邮电造反团编印, *Jixue Liaofa* 鸡血疗法, 15.

53. Section titled "Gao ju mao zedong sixiang wei da hong qi che di pipan zichan jieji fandong luxian zai qinghai sheng de liu du" 高举毛泽东思想伟大红旗彻底批判资产阶级反动路线在青海省的流毒 [Raise the Great Red Flag of Mao Zedong's thoughts and criticize the pernicious influence of the bourgeois reactionary line in Qinghai], in Qinghai Sheng Ba Yi Ba Youdian Zaofan Tuan Bianyin 青海省八一八邮电造反团编印, *Jixue Liaofa* 鸡血疗, 55-63.

54. Deng Liqun 邓力群 et al., eds., *Dang Dai Zhongguo De Yiyao Shiye* 当代中国丛书 [A compendium of contemporary China], 66.

55. Jing Fang 荆方, *Wo Shi Liu Ling Hou* 1969-1978 我是 60 后 1969-1978 [I belong to the post-60s generation 1969-1978] (Beijing: Xinxing Chu Ban She 新星出版社, 2010), 69-71.

56. Wu Zhijing 伍稚荆, "Lao cheng jishi" 老城纪事 [Old town chronicle], 42.

57. Sang Ye 桑晔, "Guoren meng yi xing?" 国人梦已醒? [Have the people awakened from their dreams?], *Dushu* 读书 Reading 1 (March 1992): 144.

58. Sang Ye 桑晔, "Guoren meng yi xing?" 国人梦已醒? [Have the people awakened], 144.

59. Chen Shuyu 陈淑玉, "'Wenge' qi jian da jixue" "文革" 期间打鸡血 [Chicken blood therapy of the Cultural Revolution], *Shoudu Yiyao* 首都医药 City Medicine 9 (May 1, 2008): 43.

60. Hai Bazi 海巴子, "Fengmi yi shi de 'jixue liaofa'" 风靡一时的鸡血疗法 [Fashionable chicken blood therapy], 28.

61. Du Xing 杜兴, *Dushu Wenzhai* 读书文摘 Reader Digest.

62. Su Zhiwu 苏志武, "Wenge zhong 'da jixue' zhi guai zhuang" 文革中 "打鸡血" 之怪状 [Strange occurrence], 45.

63. Su also recalled that the best foreign breeds could cost between six to seven *jiao* 角 (sixty to seventy cents) per *jin* 斤, 45.

64. Wu Zhijing 伍稚荆, "Lao cheng jishi" 老城纪事 [Old town chronicle], 42.

65. Chen Shuyu 陈淑玉, "'Wenge' qi jian da jixue" "文革" 期间打鸡血 [Chicken blood therapy], 43.

66. Chen Shuyu 陈淑玉, "'Wenge' qi jian da jixue" "文革" 期间打鸡血 [Chicken blood therapy], 43; Wu Zhijing 伍稚荆, "Lao cheng jishi" 老城纪事 [Old town chronicle], 42.

67. Section titled "Fazhan qian tu" 发展前途 [Prospects for development], in Qinghai Sheng Ba Yi Ba Youdian Zaofan Tuan Bianyin 青海省八一八邮电造反团编印, *Jixue Liaofa* 鸡血疗法, 35.

68. Section titled "Ji de xuan ze" 鸡的选择, in Qinghai Sheng Ba Yi Ba Youdian Zaofan Tuan Bianyin 青海省八一八邮电造反团编印, *Jixue Liaofa* 鸡血疗法, 23.

69. Liang Jielian 梁洁莲, *Wu Tong Zhushe Fa Jiang Hua* 无痛注射法讲话 [A conversation on no pain injection] (Beijing: Renmin Weisheng Chu Ban She 人民卫生出版社, 1957).

70. Liang Jielian 梁洁莲, *Wu Tong Zhushe Fa Jiang Hua* 无痛注射法讲话 [A conversation on no pain injection].

71. Ma Qinlin 马钦林, "Bu yao lan yong zhenji" 不要滥用针剂 [Do not misuse injection], *Yaoxue Tongbao* 药学通报 Pharmaceutical Bulletin 11, no. 11 (1965): 517–518.

72. See Zhu Longyu 朱龙玉, *Shenjing Zhushe Liao Fa* 神经注射疗法 [Nerve injection therapy] (Xi'an: Shanxi Renmin Chu Ban She 陕西人民出版社, 1959).

73. Section titled "Fazhan qian tu" 发展前途 [Prospects for development], in Qinghai Sheng Ba Yi Ba Youdian Zaofan Tuan Bianyin 青海省八一八邮电造反团编印, *Jixue Liaofa* 鸡血疗法, 34–35.

74. Du Xing 杜兴, *Dushu Wenzhai* 读书文摘 Reader Digest, 14.

75. Du Xing 杜兴, *Dushu Wenzhai* 读书文摘 Reader Digest, 16.

76. According to historian Zheng Hong, who is also a trained physician, toads were believed to help relieve constant coughing, which is one sign of aging. Interview with Zheng, conducted on January 8, 2013.

77. Ge Hanshu 葛汉枢, "Laihama zai linchuang shang de yingyong" 癞蛤蟆在临床上的应用 [Bedside application of toad], *Xin Zhongyi* 新中医 New Chinese Medicine 5 (1976): 46-47.

78. Ge Hanshu 葛汉枢, "Laihama zai linchuang shang de yingyong" 癞蛤蟆在临床上的应用 [Bedside application of toad], 47.

79. Ge Hanshu 葛汉枢, "Laihama zai linchuang shang de yingyong" 癞蛤蟆在临床上的应用 [Bedside application of toad], 47-48.

80. Zhang Mengnong 张梦侬, "Guan yu e ya xue zhi yege yu wei'ai de ji dian kan fa" 关于鹅鸭血治噎膈与胃癌的几点看法 [Some thoughts on using the blood of goose and duck to cure dysphagia and stomach cancer], *Xin Zhongyi* 新中医 New Chinese Medicine 6 (1976): 39.

81. Zhang Mengnong 张梦侬, "Guan yu e ya xue zhi yege yu wei'ai de ji dian kan fa" 关于鹅鸭血治噎膈与胃癌的几点看法 [Some thoughts], 40.

82. Zhang used the word *xiao shuo* 小说, or novel, to describe the two books, but in fact they were collections of stories and events.

83. Zhang Mengnong 张梦侬, "Guan yu e ya xue zhi yege yu wei'ai de ji dian kan fa" 关于鹅鸭血治噎膈与胃癌的几点看法 [Some thoughts], 40-41.

84. Zhang Mengnong 张梦侬, "Guan yu e ya xue zhi yege yu wei'ai de ji dian kan fa" 关于鹅鸭血治噎膈与胃癌的几点看法 [Some thoughts], 41.

85. Zhang Mengnong 张梦侬, "Guan yu e ya xue zhi yege yu wei'ai de ji dian kan fa" 关于鹅鸭血治噎膈与胃癌的几点看法 [Some thoughts], 41-42.

86. Shanghai Renmin Chu Ban She Bian 上海人民出版社编 [Shanghai People's Publishing House], *Qunzhong Yixue Cong Kan* 群众医学丛刊 2 [Medicine for the masses, series no. 2] (Shanghai People's Publishing House, 1974).

87. Shanghai Renmin Chu Ban She Bian 上海人民出版社编 [Shanghai People's Publishing House], *Qunzhong Yixue Cong Kan* 群众医学丛刊 2 [Medicine for the masses].

88. The first two stanzas went like this:

> Mao issued an instruction
> To carry out the "Criticize Lin, Criticize Kong" Movement
> To insist on the revolution and oppose all attempts to *fupi*
> Promote the use of new matters
>
> Barefoot doctors are good
> They have a high understanding of the struggle between two lines
> Relying on the masses to pluck herbs
> Independently execute medical care

See Wang Zhongliang 王忠良, "Caoyao ge" 草药歌, in *Qunzhong Yixue Cong Kan*, no. 2 群众医学丛刊 2 [Medicine for the masses, series 2] (Shanghai People's Publishing House, 1974), 41.

89. Clinical trials for various cancer types using duck and goose blood were recorded in section 12 of chapter 6, Zhang Mengnong 张梦侬, "Guan yu e ya xue zhi yege yu wei'ai de ji dian kan fa" 关于鹅鸭血治噎膈与胃癌的几点看法 [Some thoughts].

90. According to Zhang, the use of duck blood was unrecorded as a folk healing method while Qing-period *Zhang's Medical Annals* 张氏医通 gave it only scant mention: "If goose blood can cure dysphagia and stimulate digestion, why not consider raw duck blood?" "Guan yu e ya xue zhi yege yu wei'ai de ji dian kan fa" 关于鹅鸭血治噎膈与胃癌的几点看法 [Some thoughts], 40.

91. Zhang wrote that only patients experiencing blood stasis and a feeling of an overly full stomach would throw up clots of goose blood.

92. Ke's article had appeared in a special column titled "Barefoot Doctor's Garden" (Chijiao Yisheng Yuandi 赤脚医生园地). Most articles in this column were the personal accounts of barefoot doctors in their treatment of patients. Ke Zexun 柯泽训, "Ji guan xue zhiliao qian du huo tang shang" 鸡冠血治疗浅度火烫伤 [Blood from chicken combs to treat light burns], *Xin Zhongyi* 新中医 New Chinese Medicine 3 (1976): 46.

93. Ke Zexun 柯泽训, "Ji guan xue zhiliao qian du huo tang shang" 鸡冠血治疗浅度火烫伤 [Blood from chicken combs], 46.

94. Ke Zexun 柯泽训, "Ji guan xue zhiliao qian du huo tang shang" 鸡冠血治疗浅度火烫伤 [Blood from chicken combs], 46.

95. Guangdong Sheng Jieyang Xian Yunlu Gongshe Weisheng Yuan 广东省揭阳县云路公社卫生院 [Guangdong Province Jieyang County Yunlu Commune Health Center], "Yong chong lei yao zhiliao sheng jie chang ai yi li baogao" 用虫类药治疗升结肠癌一例报告 [A report on using insect-based medicinals to cure ascending colon cancer], *Xin Zhongyi* 新中医 New Chinese Medicine 3 (1976): 24.

96. Ye claimed that in ancient times, lizards were also called "salted snakes" since they were regarded as "salty" and "cold" under the *siqi wuwei* 四气五味 (or *sixing wuwei* 四性五味, which means, literally, four characteristics, five tastes) classification system. One ancient prescription he found was called "salted snake powder," which consisted of lizards, amber, vermilion, *bingpian* or borneol, musk, pearl, and cow bezoar. See Ye Haichang 叶海昌, "Bihu zai linchuang shang de yingyong" 壁虎在临床上的应用 [Bedside application of lizards], *Xin Zhongyi* 新中医 New Chinese Medicine 1 (1976): 50.

97. Scrofula, for instance, was better known in Chinese medicine as *luoli* 瘰疬 and resulted from the accumulation of two kinds of poison in the liver and lung channels. One poison was manifested in form of phlegm (*tandu*) 痰毒, while the other was supposedly caused by heat (*redu*) 热毒.

98. Ye Haichang 叶海昌, "Bihu zai linchuang shang de yingyong" 壁虎在临床上的应用 [Bedside application of lizards], 50.

99. Ye Haichang 叶海昌, "Bihu zai linchuang shang de yingyong" 壁虎在临床上的应用 [Bedside application of lizards], 50.

100. Zheng Yihua 郑亦化, "Bihu zuzhi ye de zhibei he yingyong" 壁虎组织液的制备和应用 [The preparation and application of lizard extract], *Yaoxue Tongbao* 药学通报 Pharmaceutical Bulletin 2, no. 2 (1954): 81.

101. Gold and silver refer to a specification found in an old textbook, requiring needles to be made of such materials to remove cataracts. Wu Ruimin 伍锐敏 and Zang Fuke 臧福科, "Yi luxian wei gang, che di gai ge jiu jiaocai" 以路线为纲, 彻底改

革旧教材 [The trajectory as main, thoroughly revise old textbooks], *Xin Zhongyi* 新中医 New Chinese Medicine 5 (1974): 3.

102. Wu Ruimin 伍锐敏 and Zang Fuke 臧福科, "Yi luxian wei gang, che di gai ge jiu jiaocai" 以路线为纲, 彻底改革旧教材 [The trajectory as main], 3.

103. This phrase was popularized during the Mao period.

104. "Shuiniu jiao ju you xiniu jiao xiang tong de liao xiao" 水牛角具有犀牛角相同的疗效 [Water buffalo horns possess the same efficacy as rhinoceros horns], *Shangchang Xiandai Hua* 商场现代化 Market Modernization Magazine 6 (1977): 24.

105. "Shuiniu jiao ju you xiniu jiao xiang tong de liao xiao" 水牛角具有犀牛角相同的疗效 [Water buffalo horns], 24.

106. Mention of rhino horn as a medicinal was first made in the Han period, in the *Shennong Bencao Jing* 神农本草经 [Shennong materia medica]. It was believed to remove all kinds of poison, cure miasma (*zhang qi*) 瘴气, and expel evil spirits.

107. Zhejiang Huzhou Zhi Yao Chang 浙江湖州制药厂 [Zhejiang Huzhou Pharmaceutical Factory], "Shuiniu jiao bang pian he jiao jian fensui de gongyi gaijin" 水牛角镑片和角尖粉碎的工艺改进 [Technique improvement on converting water buffalo horn slices and apex into powder form], *Zhong Chengyao Yanjiu* 中成药研究 Chinese Medicine Research 2 (1979): 22.

108. Another article claimed that, according to classical materia medica compilations such as *Benjing* 本经 and Li Shizhen's *Bencao Gangmu* 本草纲目, the term "cow" also referred to oxen and water buffalo, meaning that all three horns had the same properties. It also gave examples of folk preparation methods using the horns of oxen. Another preparation mentioned in the August issue of the journal *Harbin Zhongyi* 哈尔滨中医 (1965) required that the buffalo horn be placed under a fire until burnt, then scraped with a knife into powder form, and finally mixed in *huangjiu* 黄酒 (a wine commonly used for cooking, now more popularly known as *shaoxingjiu* 绍兴酒). The recommended dosage was one *qian* 钱 per application. Jilin Medical College agreed with the use of ox horn in its journal *Dongbei Dongwuyao* 东北动物药 (Northeast Animal Yao) but recommended 2–4 *qian* 钱. It also claimed that ox horn could stop all kinds of bleeding, such as excessive menstruation or following a miscarriage. There was also mention of barefoot doctors from Zhaodong county, Heilongjiang province, treating external wounds with the horns of oxen, which were able to "enliven blood and reduce swelling" (*huo xue xiao zhong* 活血消肿). In the south, such compounds were applied on the chests of children suffering from fever and a swollen pharynx. See Chang Minyi 常敏毅, "Guan yu huang niujiao de yiliao zuo yong" 关于黄牛角的医疗作用 [On ox horn and its medical use], *Zhong Yiyao Xuebao* 中医药学报 Acta Chinese Medicine and Pharmacology 1 (1976): 44–46.

109. Zhang Haoliang 张浩良, "Jie shao xijiao dai yong pin" 介绍犀角代用品 [Introducing replacements for rhinoceros horns], *Jiangsu Yiyao* 江苏医药 Jiangsu Medical Journal 3 (1977): 34.

110. "xie ganhuo, qingluo, xifeng" 泻肝火, 清洛, 熄风. Feng in this instance refers to spasm.

111. "xiehuo jiedu, liangxue, qingxin" 泻火解毒, 凉血, 清心. Simply put, it was believed that rhino horns could prevent the occurrence of high fever.

112. Dongguan Xian Zhongyi Yuan Liu Yi Bu 东莞县中医院留医部 [Dongguan Country Chinese Medicine Hospital Intensive Care Unit], "Zhongyi zhiliao yinao de ji dian tihui" 中医治疗乙脑的几点体会 [Few thoughts on using Chinese medicine to treat encephalitis], *Xin Zhongyi* 新中医 New Chinese Medicine 2 (1973): 21.

113. Shandong Sheng Gougu Jiao Yaojiu Xiezuo Zu 山东省狗骨胶药酒协作组 [Shandong Province Dog Bone Glue Wine Collaboration Team], "Gougu jiao yaojiu de yanjiu" 狗骨胶药酒的研究 [Research on dog bone glue wine], *Zhong Caoyao Tongxun* 中草药通讯 Chinese Traditional and Herbal Drugs Newsletter 12 (1976): 12–15.

114. "Shuiniu jiao ju you xiniu jiao xiang tong de liao xiao" 水牛角具有犀牛角相同的疗效 [Water buffalo horns]. Research on substitutions for rhino horn would continue at least into the 1980s. See, for example, Yu Zhongfan 于仲范, "Guangjiao ban yu shuiniu jiao ban de jianbie" 广角瓣与水牛角瓣的鉴别 [Identifying rhinoceros horn parts from water buffalo horn parts], *Zhongyao Tongbao* 中药通报 Bulletin of Chinese Medicinals 11, no. 7 (1986): 16.

115. "Jiji kai zhan quan chong bushou gongzuo" 积极开展全虫捕收工作 [Giving the work of gathering whole insects an active kickstart], *Zhong Caoyao Tongxun* 中草药通讯 Chinese Traditional and Herbal Drugs Newsletter 5, no. 5 (1973): 29.

116. "Jiji kai zhan quan chong bushou gongzuo" 积极开展全虫捕收工作 [Giving the work], 29.

117. Jiangsu Sheng Yizheng Xian Maji Gongshe Jinqiao Dadui Weisheng Shi 江苏省仪征县马集公社金桥大队卫生室 [Jiangsu Province Yizheng County Maji Commune Jinqiao Brigade Health Corner], "Tubie chong de si yang he guanli" 土鳖虫的饲养和管理 [The rearing and management of ground beetles], *Zhong Caoyao Tongxun* 中草药通讯 Chinese Traditional and Herbal Drugs Newsletter 2 (1974): 63.

118. Duan Weihe 段维和, "Shenrong de jiagong fang fa ying gai gai ge" 参茸的加工方法应该改革 [Ginseng and deer antler processing methods should be reformed], *Zhong Caoyao Tongxun* 中草药通讯 Chinese Traditional and Herbal Drugs Newsletter 5 (1976): 19.

119. "Xia shou zhi yin'gan" 夏收之阴干; "Po zhi huo gan" 破之火干; despite the word *huo* or fire, the article interpreted it to mean drying the deer antler under natural heat.

120. The Chinese phrase was "Bu qi yi jingxue" 补气益精血. Duan Weihe 段维和, "Shenrong de jiagong fang fa ying gai gai ge" 参茸的加工方法应该改革 [Ginseng and deer antler processing methods should be reformed].

121. Duan Weihe 段维和, "Shenrong de jiagong fang fa ying gai gai ge" 参茸的加工方法应该改革 [Ginseng and deer antler processing methods should be reformed].

122. Shaanxi Sheng Shengwu Ziyuan Kaocha Dui 陕西省生物资源考察队 [Shaanxi Province Biological Resources Expedition Team], Shaanxi Sheng Zhenping Xian Yang She Shiyan Chang 陕西省镇坪县养麝实验场 [Shaanxi Province Zhenping Country Musk Dear Experimental Farm], "Xun She Qu Xiang" 驯麝取香 [Training musk deer and collecting musk], *Zhong Caoyao Tongxun* 中草药通讯 Chinese Traditional and Herbal Drugs Newsletter 4 (1973): 32–42.

123. Shandong Haiyang Yanjiu Suo Yaoyong Zu 山东海洋研究所药用组 [Shandong Marine Research Institute Medicinal Team], "Haiyang shengwu yao yong

yanjiu jian kuang" 海洋生物药用研究简况 [An update on research on marine-based medicinals], *Zhong Caoyao Tongxun* 中草药通讯 Chinese Traditional and Herbal Drugs Newsletter 6 (1972): 11.

124. "Qing re yi yin, zhen xin an shen, ming mu jie du" 清热益阴, 镇心安神, 明目解毒.

125. By the late 1970s, China had replaced Japan as the world's largest exporter of pearl. See Paul Southgate and John Lucas, eds., *The Pearl Oyster* (Oxford: Elsevier, 2008), 306.

126. "Wu.Qi" Gan Xiao 五七干校. The school was named after the official "Five-Seven" instruction (Wu.Qi Zhishi 五七指示), whereby urbanites were sent to schools in the countryside to be "reeducated." There is evidence, however, that many used their skills and knowledge to conduct experiments there.

127. Seahorse and starfish are two examples of medicinals whose mass harvesting and national use likely became common only in this period. Although seahorse is mentioned in classical texts, its sale as medicine is likely a twentieth-century innovation. There is no record of scientific medicinal studies on seahorse until the late 1990s. The first reference I can find on starfish is from the 1950s.

128. Zhang Feng Ying 张凤瀛 and Wu Baoling 吴宝铃, "Woguo de haixing" 我国的还行 [The starfish of our country], 生物学通报 [Bulletin of biology] 6 (1956): 5–9.

129. "Xin de yi dai yisheng zai chengzhang—ji guangdong zhongyi xue yuan ji ge gongnongbing biye sheng" 新的一代医生在成长— 记广东中医学院几个工农兵毕业生 [The rise of a new generation doctors—Remembering the few worker-peasant-soldier student graduates of Guangdong Chinese Medical College], *Xin Zhongyi* 新中医 New Chinese Medicine 5 (1974): 10.

130. Jiangsu Xinyi Xue Yuan 江苏新医院 [Jiangsu New Medical College], *Zhongyao Da Cidian* 中药大辞典 [Chinese medicine dictionary] (Shanghai: Shanghai Renmin Chu Ban She 上海人民出版社, 1977).

131. Then again, Western (and Japanese) researchers were experimenting with the use of cow bile in the early twentieth century, well before barefoot doctors. Jin Yilang 金贻郎, "Dongwu yao yanjiu de jin kuang" 动物药研究的近况 [An update on animal-based medicinal research], *Zhejiang Zhongyi Xue Yuan Tongxun* 浙江中医学院通讯 Zhejiang Chinese Medical College Newsletter 1 (1977): 47–50. Animal bile was considered a common folk ingredient and believed to "clear heat and counteract the effects of poison," although there were cases of poisoning from ingesting the bile of fish. Hunan Xinhua Xian Renmin Yiyuan Neike 湖南新化县人民医院内科 [Hunan Xinhua County People's Hospital Internal Medicine], "Caoyu dan zhong du yi li baogao" 草鱼胆中毒—例报告 [A case of poisoning from the bile of grass carp], *Zhong Caoyao Tongxun* 中草药通讯 Chinese Traditional and Herbal Drugs Newsletter 1 (1974): 56. A "hygiene team" learned that soaking green bean powder in pig's bile could cure dysentery and enteritis. Yi San Jiu Liu Budui Weisheng Dui 1396 部队卫生队 [Platoon 1936 Hygiene Team], "Yong zhu danzhi jinpao lüdou fen zhiliao liji, changyan" 用猪胆汁浸泡禄豆粉治疗痢疾, 肠炎 [Treating dysentery and enteritis with green bean powder soaked in pig bile], *Zhong Caoyao Tongxun* 中草药通讯 Chinese Traditional and Herbal Drugs Newsletter 1 (1971): 45.

Five. "Economic Animals"

1. Zhang Tianmin 张天民, Shandong Yixue Yuan Yaoxue Xi 山东医学院药学系 [Shandong Medical College School of Pharmacy], "Zangqi shenghua yaowu de gai kuang he zhan wang" 脏器生化药物的概况和展望 [Organo-pharmaceutics: Present and future], *Yaoxue Tongbao* 药学通报 Pharmaceutical Bulletin 14, no. 6 (1979): 272.

2. Zhang Tianmin 张天民, "Zangqi shenghua yaowu de gai kuang he zhan wang" 脏器生化药物的概况和展望 [Organo-pharmaceutics], 273.

3. "X quan shen dou shi bao" X 全身都是宝 (the entire body of X is a treasure).

4. Chi Cheng 迟程, "Dongwu yao qian zai ziyuan de kaifa he liyong" 动物药潜在资源的开发和利用 [The potential to develop and use animal-based medicines], *Chengdu Zhongyi Xue Yuan Xuebao* 成都中医学院学报 Journal of Chengdu University of Traditional Chinese Medicine 12, no. 4 (1989): 39-41.

5. See Liu Wengang 刘永纲, "Ren zhen guan che hu yaobang tongzhi zhongyao pi shi nu li jie jue zhongyaocai gongying jin que wen ti" 认真贯彻胡耀邦同志重要批示努力解决中药材供应紧张问题 [Seriously consider comrade Hu Yaobang's instruction to work hard at solving the crisis of herb shortage], in *Zhongyi Nianjian (1983)* 中医年鉴 [Yearbook of traditional Chinese medicine of China 1983], ed. Shanghai Zhongyi Xue Yuan 上海中医学院 (now Shanghai University of Traditional Chinese Medicine) (Beijing: Renmin Weisheng Chu Ban She, 1984), 18-19.

6. See "Nongfu chanpin yi gou yi xiao jiage zan xing guanli ban fa (cao'an) 农副产品议购议销价格暂行管理办法 (草案) [Preliminary guidelines for the purchase and sale of agricultural products through the price negotiation scheme (draft)], in *Zhonghua Renmin Gonghe Guo Xian Xing Zhong Yiyao Fa Gui Huibian (1949-1991)* 中华人民共和国现行中医药法规汇编 1949-1991 [A compilation of laws governing traditional Chinese medicine in the People's Republic of China 1949-1991], ed. Guojia Zhong Yiyao Guanli Ju Zheng Ce Fa Gui Si 国家中医药管理局政策法规司 [State Administration of Traditional Chinese Medicine Policy and Regulation Division] (Beijing: Zhongguo Zhongyiyao Chu Ban She, 1991), 361.

7. This was the Guojia Yiyao Guanli Ju 国家医药管理局 [State Department for the Administration of Pharmaceuticals].

8. The terms "modern drugs" (*xiandai yao*) and "traditional drugs" (*chuantong yao*) were also used in this document to distinguish between Western and non-Western medicinals. Zhonghua Renmin Gonghe Guo Yaopin Guanli Fa 中华人民共和国药品管理法 [Drug Control Law of the People's Republic of China] was released on September 20, 1984, by the Standing Committee of the National People's Congress, 264-269.

9. Zhonghua Renmin Gonghe Guo Yaopin Guanli Fa 中华人民共和国药品管理法 [Drug Control Law of the People's Republic of China], 362.

10. Qi Fang 齐放, "Chong fen fahui you shi fazhan chuanghui nongye—guan yu jilin sheng fazhan chuanghui nongye de tantao" 充分发挥优势发展创汇农业—关于吉林省发展创汇农业的探讨 [Fully unleash potential and develop export-oriented agriculture—Exploring Jilin province's development of export-oriented agriculture], *Yanbian Nongye Xue Yuan Xuebao* 延边农业学院学报 Journal of Yanbian Agricultural College 2 (1987): 80.

11. Liu Dezu 刘德祖, "Ban hao shiyan chang zhan shixing jiao xue, keyan he tui guang san jiehe qian yi" 办好实验场站实行教学，科研和推广三结合浅议 [Effectively run experimental farm stations to teach, research and promote the "three combines": A discussion], *Jilin Nongye Daxue Xuebao* 吉林农业大学学报 Journal of Jilin Agricultural University 7, no. 2 (1985): 103–107.

12. Liu used the word *xiaqian* 下迁 (literally, to move down). Liu Dezu 刘德祖, "Ban hao shiyan chang zhan shixing jiao xue" 办好实验场站实行教学 [Effectively run experimental farm], 105.

13. Liu Dezu 刘德祖, "Ban hao shiyan chang zhan shixing jiao xue" 办好实验场站实行教学 [Effectively run experimental farm], 105.

14. It was reported that farms affiliated with Jilin Agricultural University made a loss totaling almost 40 million yuan between 1971 and 1978. The turning point was in 1984 when, in that year alone, the farms made a profit of more than 30 million yuan. Liu Dezu 刘德祖, "Ban hao shiyan chang zhan shixing jiao xue" 办好实验场站实行教学 [Effectively run experimental farm], 106.

15. Liu Dezu 刘德祖, "Ban hao shiyan chang zhan shixing jiao xue" 办好实验场站实行教学 [Effectively run experimental farm], 107.

16. Liu Dezu 刘德祖, "Ban hao shiyan chang zhan shixing jiao xue" 办好实验场站实行教学 [Effectively run experimental farm], 106.

17. Qin Rongqian 秦荣前 et al., "Kong guang cujin lurong shengzhang fayu de yanjiu" 控光促进鹿茸生长发育的研究 [Research on light and its role in promoting growth in deer antlers], *Jilin Nongye Daxue Xuebao* 吉林农业大学学报 Journal of Jilin Agricultural University 7, no. 2 (1985): 31.

18. See "Richard J. Goss, 1925–1996," accessed April 19, 2014, http://www .sdbonline.org/sites/archive/SDBMembership/Goss.html.

19. "Zhongguo linye keji chengguo guanli xinxi xitong" 中国林业科技成果管理信息系统 [Chinese forestry science and technology results and information management system], accessed April 20, 2014, http://smbk.forestry.gov.cn:8099 /lyj/main/ShowDetail.jsp?id=13790.

20. Liang Fengxi 梁凤锡, "Dongbei yuan she de shengtai diaocha" 东北原麝的生态调查 [An investigation into the ecology of northeastern musk deer], *Jilin Nongye Daxue Xuebao* 吉林农业大学学报 Journal of Jilin Agricultural University 7, no. 2 (1985): 41.

21. Gao Xufen 高绪芬 and Jie Jue 解觉, "He (Nyctereutes procyonoides) zhen liangxing ti (tsue hermaphrodite) zuzhi jiegou de yanjiu" 貉 (Nyctereutes procyonoides) 真两性体 (true hermaphrodite) 组织结构的研究 [Anatomical study on true hermaphroditism in raccoon dog], *Jilin Nongye Daxue Xuebao* 吉林农业大学学报 Journal of Jilin Agricultural University 7, no. 2 (1985): 37–40.

22. Bi Pengfei wrote, "After that (the 1984 research), scholars and research units from all parts of China began to extract and conduct qualitative analysis of bear bile. Research was also done to develop chemical restraint drugs for the bears. For instance, Qin Hesheng (1985) and Chen Jiapu (1984) conducted studies on anesthesia for bears. The research of Lin Shizhen (1986) and Jin Guangzhu (1987) concentrated on bile extraction. New techniques are kept a secret, however, and it is impossible to provide detailed information." Bi Pengfei 毕鹏飞,

"Xiong lei de shengtai xue yanjiu jinzhan ji zhanwang" 熊类的生态学研究进展及展望 [Conducting ecological studies of bears: Current development and future], *Yanbian Nongxue Yuan Xuebao* 延边农学院学报 Journal of Yanbian Agricultural College 2 (1988): 71.

23. Jin Yuquan, Jin Jichun, Jin Renshu, and Jin Xiangquan, 金禹权, 金吉春, 金仁淑, 金享权 *Xiong Lei Yu Xiong Dan* 熊类与熊胆 [Types of bear species and bear bile] (Heilongjiang: Heilongjiang Chaoxian Minzu Chu Ban She, 1993).

24. Jin Yuquan et al., *Xiong Lei Yu Xiong Dan* 熊类与熊胆 [Types of bear species], 210.

25. The two companies that merged were Jilin Sheng Baitoushan Xiong Da Zhi Yao Youxian Gongsi 吉林省白头山熊大制药有限公司 [Jilin Province Baitoushan Bear Pharmaceutical Co., Ltd.] and Yanbian Baitoushan Renshen Huishe 延边白头山人参会社 [Yanbian Baitoushan Ginseng Co.].

26. To quote the book, "The company's main goal is to tap the rich natural resources of Changbaishan, and build an integrated and outward-looking enterprise with bear farming as its foundation." Jin Yuquan et al., *Xiong Lei Yu Xiong Dan* 熊类与熊胆 [Types of bear species], 211.

27. Jin Yuquan et al., *Xiong Lei Yu Xiong Dan* 熊类与熊胆 [Types of bear species], 212.

28. See "Spark Programme," http://ie.china-embassy.org/eng/ScienceTech/ScienceandTechnologyDevelopmentProgrammes/t112842.htm; and "National Programs for Science and Technology," http://www.china.org.cn/english/features/Brief/193304.htm.

29. "Xingxing zhi huo keyi liao yuan" 星星之火可以燎原 [A single spark can start a prairie fire].

30. "Spark Programme," http://ie.china-embassy.org/eng/ScienceTech/ScienceandTechnologyDevelopmentProgrammes/t112842.htm.

31. Jin Yuquan et al., *Xiong Lei Yu Xiong Dan* 熊类与熊胆 [Types of bear species], 213–214.

32. Jin Yuquan et al., *Xiong Lei Yu Xiong Dan* 熊类与熊胆 [Types of bear species], 214–216.

33. Yanji Shi Renmin Gongyuan 延吉市人民公园. The other two bureaucracies were the city science committee (Yanji Shi Kewei 延吉市科委) and the city hospital (Yanji Shi Yiyuan 延吉市医院). Jin Guangzhu, Jin Guangling, and Jin Changhao, 金光株, 金光凌, 金昌浩 "Xiongdan huo ti qu zhi shiyan baogao" 熊胆活体取汁实验报告 [A report on the experiment to extract bile from live bears], *Yanbian Nongxue Yuan Xuebao* 延边农学院学报 Journal of Yanbian Agricultural College 2 (1987): 61–65.

34. Jin Guangzhu et al., "Xiongdan huo ti qu zhi shiyan baogao" 熊胆活体取汁实验报告 [A report], 61.

35. In the table provided by the researchers, however, only ursodeoxycholic acid and chenodeoxycholic acid were specifically mentioned. A third category was simply named "bile acid." Jin Guangzhu et al., "Xiongdan huo ti qu zhi shiyan baogao" 熊胆活体取汁实验报告 [A report], 63.

36. Researchers also wrote that hunting "has caused destruction to animal resources," suggesting that they understood farming as a conservation method. Jin Guangzhu et al., "Xiongdan huo ti qu zhi shiyan baogao" 熊胆活体取汁实验报告 [A report], 62.

37. Zhongguo Yaoxue Nianjian Bian Ji Weiyuan Hui 中国药学年鉴编辑委员会 [China Pharmaceutical Yearbook Editorial Committee], *Zhongguo Yaoxue Nianjian 1991* 中国药学年鉴 1991 [China pharmaceutical yearbook 1991], 5.

38. Li Shouwan 李寿万 et al., "Xiao hei xiong she ci (issa, lyssa) de weixi jiegou" 小黑熊舌刺 (いっさ, lyssa) 的微细结构 [Microstructure of the tongue of bear cub], *Yanbian Nong Xue Yuan Xuebao 1988* 延边农学院学报 Journal of the Yanbian Agricultural College 2:76–78.

39. Bi Pengfei 毕鹏飞, "Xiong lei de shengtai xue yanjiu jinzhan ji zhanwang" 熊类的生态学研究进展及展望 [Conducting ecological studies], 72.

40. Other animals that became subjects for zoological research because of medicinal farming included the big-eyed ratsnake, dwarf musk deer, sika deer, seahorse, and ground beetle. Zhongguo Yaoxue Nianjian Bianji Weiyuan Hui 中国药学年鉴编辑委员会 [China Pharmaceutical Yearbook Editorial Committee], *Zhongguo Yaoxue Nianjian 1991* 中国药学年鉴 1991 [China Pharmaceutical Yearbook 1991], 5.

41. According to an official Chinese travel website, "The [Yanbian Korean Autonomous Prefecture] is home to China's largest concentration of people of the Korean ethnic group, whose ancestors migrated from the Korean peninsula into northeast China in the late 17th century. Yanbian has a population of some two million, 40 percent of whom are Koreans." See "The Yanbian Korean Autonomous Prefecture," accessed December 25, 2014, http://www.china.org.cn/english/travel/53647.htm.

42. Cited in Lin Lianjie 林廉结, "Chaoxian minzu yiyao de xingcheng ji tedian" 朝鲜民族医药的形成及特点 [The making of ethnomedicine in North Korea and its characteristics], in *Zhongyi Nianjian 1986* 中医年鉴 1986 [1986 yearbook of traditional Chinese medicine of China], ed. Shanghai Zhongyi Xue Yuan 上海中医学院 (now Shanghai University of Traditional Chinese Medicine) (Beijing: Renmin Weisheng Chu Ban She, 1987), 423–424.

43. Jin Zhuzhe 金洙哲 and Wu Yonghuan 吴永焕, "Jilin sheng yanbian chaoxian zu yong yao" 吉林省延边朝鲜族用药 [The North Korean community in Yanbian Jilin province and their use of medicines], *Yanbian Nong Xue Yuan Xuebao* 延边农学院学报 Journal of Yanbian Agricultural College 2 (1988): 17–20.

44. The Chinese name for ursodeoxycholic acid is *xiongquyangdansuan*. *Xiongdan* was first mentioned in the Tang period pharmacopoeia *Xin Xiu Bencao* 新修本草 (Pan Shasha 潘莎莎 and Li Ruzhen 李儒珍, "Fufang xiongdan yanyao shui dui shiyan xing tu jiaomo baiban de liaoxiao guancha" 复方熊胆眼药水对实验性兔角膜白斑的疗效观察 [Laboratory observations of the efficacy of compound drug bear bile eye drops on rabbits with corneal infections], *Guangzhou Zhonyi Xueyuan Xuebao* 广州中医药学院学报 Journal of Guangzhou Chinese Medical College 6, no. 3 [1989]: 143–145); a similar history is given in Yamazaki Mitsuyoshi 山崎三省,

"Kumanoi no kagaku to yakuri sayō" 熊胆の化学と 药理作用, *Wakan Yaku* 和漢藥 Rinjin zō kango 臨時増刊号 10 (1973): 295-299.

45. Pan Shasha 潘莎莎 and Li Ruzhen 李儒珍, "Fufang xiongdan yanyao shui dui shiyan xing tu jiaomo baiban de liaoxiao guancha" 复方熊胆眼药水对实验性兔角膜白斑的疗效观察 [Laboratory observations of the efficacy of compound drug bear bile eye drops on rabbits with corneal infections].

46. Bear bile was first documented in Japan in the Heian period, but only in the seventeenth century did the physician Gotō Konzon popularize its use. Gotō argued that all diseases were a result of blockage (*ryuutai*) of the *qi* and recommended three therapeutic methods, among which was the use of bear gallbladder (Yamazaki Mitsuyoshi 山崎三省, "Kumanoi no kagaku to yakuri sayō" 熊胆の化学と药理作用, *Wakan Yaku*). Gotō had even created a drug called "black pill," using bear bile as the main ingredient, that became popular during the Edo period (Shanqi Guangfu 山崎光夫 [Yamasaki Mitsuo], *Riben Mingyao Daoyou* 日本名藥導遊 [A guide to famous Japanese drugs] (Taipei: Wangwen She, 2005), 47-52. Originally translated from Nihon No Meiyaku 日本の名薬 [Tokyo: Toyo Keizai Inc., 2000]). Later the physician Ono Ranzan 小野蘭山, in *Honzō Hōmoku Keimō* 本草綱目啓蒙, described the changing quality and characteristics of bear bile according to seasonality and species. See Makino Isao 牧野勲 and Takebe Kazuo 武部和夫, "Yuutan to Ursodeoxycholic acid" 熊胆と Ursodeoxycholic acid, *Sogo Rinshō* 綜合臨 Comprehensive Clinical 31, no. 9 (1982): 2385-2387.

47. Makino Isao and Tanaka Hirotoshi, "From a Cholerectic to an Immunomodulator," 659-664.

48. "'Kuma no yi' yu nyū ha da me" くまのい"原料輸入はダメ [Import of bear bile comes to a halt], *Asahi Shimbun* (June 30, 1988): 3; "Kuma no tannō fusei yunyū" クマの胆のう不正輸入 [Illegal import of bear bile], *Asahi Shimbun* (April 16, 1988): 3; Kawahara Kazuhito et al., "Report on Quality and Manufacturing of Bear Bile from Living Bear," *Natural Medicines* 49, no. 2 (1995): 158-163.

49. Takahashi Shintaro 高橋真太郎 and Nishikawa Misako 西川ミサ子, "Shihan, Yuutan no Hinshitsu Kenkyu" 市販. 熊胆の品質研究 [A study of the quality of bear bile sold in the market], *Yakugaku Kenykyū* 30:16-19; Melissa Lewis and Takahashi Mitsuhiko, "A Prescription for Conservation: Strengthening Japan's Role in Curbing the Illegal International Trade of Bear Bile for Medicinal Use," *Asia-Pacific Journal of Environmental Law* 15 (2013): 95-124.

50. Andrew Jacobs, "A Movement to Rescue Bears in China: Growing Movement Stands Up for Bears," *International Herald Tribune* (May 23, 2013): 4. See also, "The Bear Facts: The East Asian Market for Bear Gall Bladder," A TRAFFIC Network report, July 1995. http://www.google.com.sg/url?url=http://www.traffic .org/species-reports/traffic_species_mammals10.pdf&rct=j&q=&esrc=s&sa=U&ei =yh62VKXXD5eVuATF4IDIBw&ved=0CBMQFjAA&usg=AFQjCNGBvba4Vw9 -kYqihTzWwRMV2qeVmA.

51. The Chinese name for bilirubin is *danhongsu* 胆红素.

52. See *Zhonghua Renmin Gonghe Guo Yaodian 1953 Nian Ban* 中华人民共和国药典1953年版 [The pharmacopoeia of the People's Republic of China 1953 edition] (Shanghai: Shangwu Yinshu Guan Chuban 商务印书馆出版, 1953).

53. One example of the growing sophistication of pharmacological laboratory processes was the rise of drug authentication (*jian ding* 鉴定 in Chinese), which was established as a legitimate field only in the 1980s through the efforts of Xu Luoshan and Xu Guojun (interview with Mr. Hu Zhinan of Guangzhou Huahai Pharmaceuticals Co. Ltd., February 21, 2017).

54. The term *shiyi* (literally, food-medicine) can be cited as early as the Zhou Dynasty. A list of foods that also performed as medicine was compiled during this time under the title *Shiwu Bencao* 食物本草. During the Tang dynasty, the term *shizhi* or "food cures" also became common. It was believed that famous Chinese physician Sun Simiao had popularized the use of food as medicine, and the term *shiliao* has been attributed to him (interview with Professor Zheng Hong on June 1, 2014).

55. See Mark Grant, *Galen on Food and Diet* (London: Routledge, 2000).

56. Ute Engelhardt, "Dietetics in Tang China and the First Extant Works on Materia Dietetica," in *Innovation in Chinese Medicine*, ed. Elisabeth Hsu (Cambridge: Cambridge University Press, 2001).

57. The article educating readers on displaying kitchenware in a "scientific" way came under the section "Lifestyle Hygiene" (*Shenghuo Weisheng* 生活卫生). See Yuan Qingcheng 袁庆成 and Liu Hong 刘宏, "Chufang li wupin de kexue bu zhi" 厨房里物品的科学布置 [Displaying kitchenware the scientific way], *Zhongguo Weisheng Huakan* 中国卫生画刊 China Hygiene Pictorial 2 (1984): 23. On eating fish bile, see Yu Xiao 欲晓, "Yudan zhi bing ye zhi ming" 鱼蛋治病也致命 [Fish roe can cure and also kill], *Zhongguo Weisheng Huakan* 中国卫生画刊 China Hygiene Pictorial 1 (1984): 47. Zu Guodong 祖国栋, who wrote the article on eating rejected eggs, was reportedly a researcher from the nutrition department of China Medical University (Zhongguo Yike Daxue 中国医科大学). See his "Jing fu hua de jidan neng chi ma?" 经孵化的鸡蛋能吃吗？ [Are incubated eggs edible?], *Zhongguo Weisheng Huakan* 中国卫生画刊 China Hygiene Pictorial 2 (1984): 39.

58. It was believed that Ming physician Li Shizhen had coined the name Xuan Ju 玄蚼 for ants. Xin Dingkang, 忻定康, "Qite de mayi shiliao" 奇特的蚂蚁食料 [The strange food cure that is ants], *Zhongguo Weisheng Huakan* 中国卫生画刊 China Hygiene Pictorial 4 (1987): 23.

59. Ant farming, which took off around this time, was driven largely by multiple claims about the insects' curative powers. The publication by Chinese physician Zhu Liangchun 朱良春 of the book *Chong Lei Yao De Yingyong* 虫类药的应用 (Using insects as medicine) (Nanjing: Jiangsu Keji Chu Ban She, 1981) helped give new impetus to such theories, which had earlier energized Mao-period beetle farming. A 1995 Chinese article even claimed that scientists had found a cure for AIDS using ants: "In recent years, a number of entomologists experimented with ant farming. So far, only the edible black ant (*Polyrhachis vicina* Roger) has been successfully farmed. This type of ants has both medicinal and nutritional benefits. . . . This is a highly feasible farming project." Han Guoyan 韩国彦, "Mayi rengong yangzhi chu tan" 蚂蚁人工养殖初探 [A preliminary investigation into ant farming], *Shengwu Xue Zazhi* 生物学杂志 Journal of Biology 1 (1995): 34. For a detailed report on the scientific studies of ants, see Zhou Jun 周军 et al., "Mayi de

yao yong yanjiu jinzhan" 蚂蚁的药用研究进展 [Current research on ants for medicinal purpose], *Guangxi Zhong Yiyao* 广西中医药 Guangxi Journal of Traditional Chinese Medicine 14, no. 2 (1991): 90–92.

60. In 1987, however, the health ministry released a list of food ingredients that could also be considered as "drugs." The information is found in no. 8 of the 1987 Food Hygiene Law of the People's Republic of China (Zhonghua Renmin Gonghe Guo Shipin Weisheng Fa 中华人民共和国食品卫生法). Some examples were Chinese ratsnake, chrysanthemum, and gingko. See "Weisheng bu ban bu ji shi shipin you shi yaopin mingdan" 卫生部颁布既是食品又是药品名单 [Ministry of Health releases a list of products to be both food and drug], *Zhong Yiyao Xinxi* 中医药信息 Chinese Journal of Information on Traditional Chinese Medicine 2 (1988): np.

61. "Weisheng bu qiang diao: zhongyao baojian yao yilü buzhun baoxiao" 卫生部强调: 中药保健药一律不准报销 [Ministry of Health stresses all TCM health products to be non-reimbursable], *Zhong Yiyao Xinxi* 中医药信息 Chinese Journal of Information on Traditional Chinese Medicine 2 (1988): np.

62. Zhong Jianguang 钟建光, "'Shi zihao' yu 'yao jian zihao' de qubie" "食字号"与"药健字号"的区别 [The difference between "a number in the food category" and "a number in the drug category"], *Hunan Laonian* 湖南老年 Hunan Old Age 12 (1995): 36.

63. See "'Jianzihao' yaopin san nian hou jiang xiaoshi" '健字号'药品三年后将消失 [Drugs registered as "health products" to be phased out in three years], *Zhongguo Jingji Xinxi* 中国经济信息 China Economic Information Journal 7 (2000): 28.

64. "Guizhentang she xian lan yong xiongdan fen xiongdan cha yi qiaoran xia jia" 归真堂涉嫌滥用熊胆粉熊胆茶已悄然下架 [Guizhentang's bear bile tea products quietly removed from shelves], accessed August 30, 2015, http://finance.china.com.cn/stock/special/gzt/20120216/536711.shtml.

65. See "Zhonggyao Baojian Yaopin De Guanli Guiding" 中药保健药品的管理规定 [Regulations on the management of health supplement-drug products in TCM], Zhongguo Baojian Xiehui 中药保健协会 [China Health Care Association], June 30, 2011, http://www.chc.org.cn/; Tan Min 谭敏 and Ma Shuming 马书明, "Zhongguo baojian yaopin shichang bingdu yingxiao chuanbo yiyuan yanjiu" 中国保健药品市场病毒营销传播意愿研究 [A study of the toxic spread of China's "health-drug product" market], *Jingying Guanli Zhe* 经营管理者 Manager's Journal 16 (2016): 263–265.

66. The China Food and Drug Administration website presently organizes substances under the categories "food product," "health-food product," and "drug." At the time of writing, two of Guizhentang's products were registered under the "drug" category: bear bile capsule (Xiongdan Jiaonang) and bear bile powder (Xiongdan Fen). Some manufacturers have also reproduced bear bile in the form of eye drops (registered as drug), which among all uses for that product is closest to Chinese tradition. China Food and Drug Administration, http://www.sfda.gov.cn/WS01/CL0001/.

67. See the 1987 report, "Ye sheng yaocai ziyuan baohu guanli tiaoli" 野生药材资源保护管理条例 [Regulations on managing and protecting wildlife medicinal resources], in *Zhonghua Renmin Gonghe Guo Xian Xing Zhong Yiyao Fa Gui Huibian (1949–1991)* 中华人民共和国现行中医药法规汇编 (1949–1991), 363–368. For English

translations of both laws, see the State Administration of Traditional Chinese Medicine of People's Republic of China, *Anthology of Policies, Regulations and Laws of The People's Republic of China on Traditional Chinese Medicine* (Beijing, 1997), 55–57, 61–62. For Hong Kong law, see chapter "Guanzhi ye sheng dong zhiwu yao tiaoli" 管制野生动植物药条例 [Regulations on the management of wildlife and plant-based medicinals], in Xie Yongguang 谢永光, *Xiang gang Zhong Yiyao Shi Hua* 香港中医药史话 [A history], 241–244.

Conclusion

1. Pordie and Hardon, "Drugs' Stories and Itineraries," 1–6.

2. Kim Taylor has argued that the popularization of traditional Chinese medicine (TCM) in the West since the 1970s has had a kickback effect on Chinese medicine in China, specifically in helping create a "unified theory" of TCM from the 1980s onward. Such theory-building made less allowance for innovation in drug development, however. Taylor, "Divergent Interests and Cultivated Misunderstandings: The Influence of the West on Modern Chinese Medicine," *Social History of Medicine* 17, no. 1 (2004): 93–111.

3. Beijing Tongrentang Laonian Bao Jian Yanjiu Suo, ed. 北京同仁堂老年保健研究所编 [Beijing Tongrentang Time-Honored Healthcare Research Center], *Beijing Tongrentang Mingyao* 北京同仁堂名药 [Famous medicines], 9–10.

4. According to both Chinese government and unofficial sources, the consumption of shark fin soup in China has decreased by as much as 80 percent since 2011, partly in response to China's declared policy of banning it from official banquets. This represents one area of conservation policy in which Chinese efforts have succeeded ahead of those in Hong Kong, Singapore, Vietnam, and other regional states. Simon Denyer, "Even as China Turns Away from Shark Fin Soup, the Prestige Dish Is Gaining Popularity Elsewhere in Asia," *Washington Post*, February 15, 2018. For the modern history and politics of shark fin soup, see Liz P. Y. Chee, "'Down with Shark Fin!': The Politics of Eating Shark Fin and Its Shifting Nationality in Republican China," in *Consuming. Eating. Well-being: Proceedings of the 2016 Food and Society Conference*, ed. Eric Olmedo et al., 21–27 (Bangi, Malaysia: KITA-UKM Press, 2018).

5. Animals Asia Foundation, accessed November 11, 2019, https://www .animalsasia.org/intl/end-bear-bile-farming-2017.html. The industry has since consolidated around several large firms. The *Washington Post* estimated that about ten thousand bears lived on seventy Chinese bear farms in 2018. Simon Denyer, "China's Bear Bile Industry Persists Despite Growing Awareness of the Cruelty Involved," *Washington Post*, June 3, 2018; "Duoshao yang xiongchang bu zhongguo, duoshao xiongdan yao xing renjian" 多少养熊场布中国, 多少熊胆药行人间 [How many bear farms distributed throughout China? How many bear bile products are there?], accessed April 24, 2014, http://www.infzm.com/content/55575.

6. Adam Minter, "Bull Market for Bear Bile Leads to China IPO," Bloomberg, February 23, 2012, http://www.bloomberg.com/news/2012-02-23/bull-market-for -bear-bile-leads-to-china-ipo-adam-minter.html.

7. "Cruelty Free Alternatives to Bear Bile: Affordable and Effective Herbal and Synthetic Options Available," accessed September 7, 2013, http://www.animalsasia .org/index.php?UID=PBJUOGNYTNG1; see also "[enviro-vlc] New PSA Released: Bear Bile Is Not a Magic Medicine," accessed September 4, 2013, http://mailman .anu.edu.au/pipermail/enviro-vlc/2011-January/003442.html.

8. Jin Yuquan et al., *Xiong Lei Yu Xiong Dan* 熊类与熊胆 [Types of bear species], 86.

9. Jin Yuquan et al., *Xiong Lei Yu Xiong Dan* 熊类与熊胆 [Types of bear species], 46–47.

10. Professor Li also argued that authentic bear bile would have been a much more effective antidote during the SARS epidemic than Tamiflu. See interview conducted by Chinese news portal Siyuewang, or m4, [Siyue mian dui mian] yuanshi li lianda: xiongdan fen yu yazhou"四月网 (M4.CN) [四月面对面] 院士李连达: 熊 胆粉与亚洲 [(April face to face) scholar Li Lian Da: Bear bile powder and Asia], accessed October 27, 2017, http://v.youku.com/v_show/id_XNDAxMTIxMDIo .html. The Golden Bear Company, which I discussed in the introduction, also features this interview within a DVD they include in their advertising kit.

11. Three of these are reproduced in Jill Robinson's blog, "China Rises against Bear Farming," Animals Asia, February 24, 2012, https://www.animalsasia.org/intl/social /jills-blog/2012/02/24/china-rises-against-bear-farming. The most compelling series of cartoons was produced by the Weibo user @zeeko, who used the controversy to draw comparisons between the exploitation of bears and regular Chinese in what he called "Guizhenland." These are reproduced and translated at "Cartoon: Guizhenland, on Bear Bile Controversy," *China Digital Times*, February 25, 2012, https:// chinadigitaltimes.net/2012/02/cartoon-guizhenland-on-bear-bile-controversy.

12. Accordingly, Ningbo Pharmaceutical Co., Ltd., and the *zhongyao* department of Zhejiang Pharmaceutical College coauthored a paper claiming that farmed bears were as healthy as non-farmed ones based on testing blood and urine samples. See "Huo xiong qu dan bei zhi bing wu kexue yiju jishu cong chaoxian yinjin" 活熊取胆被指并无科学依据技术从朝鲜引进 [Bear farming technique]. Mental health was not considered as a factor.

13. "Traditional Chinese Medicine: China's Bear Farms Prompt Public Outcry," *Nature* 484 (April 26, 2012), https://doi.org/10.1038/484455c.

14. *South China Morning Post* (online edition), October 21, 2006; *China Daily*, Hong Kong Edition (online edition), November 22, 2006, and March 22, 2007; *Xinhua* (online edition), March 1, 2007; *Xinhua*, March 23, 2007.

15. "Ji zhe fu guizhentang jidi shi wen 'huo xiong qu dan' tan jiu wu tong lun" 记者赴归真堂基地十问"活熊取胆"探究无痛论 [Reporter made site visit to Guizhentang to explore the "no pain" argument], accessed April 22, 2014, http://news.sohu .com/20120220/n335301850.shtml.

16. "Bio-pharmaceutical in 2010," accessed April 22, 2014, http://www .investguangzhou.gov.cn/web/eng/jsp/content/content_detail.jsp?catEncode =001006003002004&contentId=28395.

17. "Fan dui wo men deng yu fan dui guojia" 反对我们等于反对国家 [To go against us is to go against the country], in "Fan huo qu xiongdan shi fan guojia, Guizhentang kou maozi hu shui" 反活取熊胆是反国家, 归真堂扣帽子唬谁？["To go

against bear farming is to go against the country," Who is Guizhentang trying to fool with such label?], accessed April 24, 2014, http://bbs.chinanews.com/web/65/2012/0220/33900.shtml.

18. See Ellis, *Tiger Bone and Rhino Horn*; see also Animals Asia Foundation, accessed December 25, 2014, https://www.animalsasia.org/.

19. Personal observations of author. Students at Tembusu College at NUS have also formed the Tembusu Wildlife Association in order to activate awareness about endangered Asian animal species. They annually nominate an "animal of the year" and raise funds to visit a site where that species lives, or is being protected/conserved.

20. Animal Concerns Research and Education Society, "Keep Endangered Species Out of TCM," accessed November 11, 2019, https://acres.org.sg/campaigns/current-campaigns/keep-endangered-species-out-of-tcm-cuurent-campaign/.

21. These include the Animals Asia Foundation and ADM Capital Foundation in Hong Kong, the Taiwan Environmental Information Association, and the Environment and Animal Society of Taiwan, among others.

22. Laura Tensen, "Under What Circumstances Can Wildlife Farming Benefit Species Conservation?" *Global Ecology and Conservation* 6 (April 2016): 286–298; Laurine Croes, "Tiger and Rhino Farms Set to Rise to Meet Chinese Demand," *Nikkei Asian Review*, November 12, 2018, https://asia.nikkei.com/Politics/International-relations/Tiger-and-rhino-farms-set-to-rise-to-meet-Chinese-demand; Javier C. Hernández, "China, after Outcry, Reinstates Ban on Rhino and Tiger Parts in Medicine," *New York Times*, November 12, 2018.

23. Michael Standaert, "China Raises Protection for Pangolins by Removing Scales from Medicine List," *The Guardian*, June 9, 2020. The article quotes Zhou Jinfeng, secretary-general of the CBCGDF, as saying in relation to the pangolin's removal from the 2020 pharmacopeia that "our continuous efforts for several years have not been in vain."

24. Aron White, "Chinese Government Policy on Wildlife Trade: What Has Changed, What Has Not, and Why It Matters," RUSI.org, July 13, 2020; Elizabeth Claire Alberto, "China Offers Buyouts to Wildlife Farmers in Response to Pandemic," *Mongabay*, May 20, 2020.

25. Mike Gaworecki, "Chinese Government Reportedly Recommending Bear Bile Injections to Treat Coronavirus," *Mongabay*, March 23, 2020.

26. Alberto, "China Offers Buyouts to Wildlife Farmers"; White, "Chinese Government Policy on Wildlife Trade." White provides a link to (and translation of) NFGA Notification No. 42 (2020), which suggests that some now-banned farmed wild animals might relocate to non-banned categories, including medicine.

GLOSSARY

Terms

Baojian	protector of health
Baojianpin	health supplements
Bingli	medical records
Busheng or *Yangsheng*	nourishment or preservation of health
Chengshi laoye	old city masters (referring to city dwellers in general)
Chuangxin	to innovate
Chuantong zhongyao	traditional Chinese drugs
Daifu	archaic expression for doctors
Dajixue	injecting chicken blood
Danfang	single-herb prescriptions
Didao yaocai	Regional medicinals
Dongyi	Eastern medicine (i.e., North Korean medicine)
Gewei weisheng ju	Revolutionary Committee Public Health Bureau
Gongren yisheng	worker doctors
Gufang	old prescriptions
Guizhong yaocai	high-end or luxury medicinals
Guizhong yaopin	valuable drugs
Hongyi	red medicine
Jiben luxian	basic trajectory
Jineijin	inner membrane of chicken gizzards
Jingji dongwu	economic animals
Jishu renyuan	technician
Jixue liaofa	chicken blood therapy

Kexuehua	to scientize
Lujiao	antler of older deer
Lujiaojiao	antler of older deer in paste form
Lurong	antler of young deer
Mifang	secret recipes
Minzuyao	folk medicinals
Nongcun yisheng	village doctors
Nongfu chanpin	agricultural products
Qiangzhuang liaofa	health-boosting therapy
Quanchong	whole insects
Rengong hugujiao	artificial tiger-bone paste
Sanlao	three olds (old physicians, old yaogong, old folk healers)
Sexiangzi or Sexiang neiyi	inner lining of a musk pouch
Shan (or Zhong) caoyao	Chinese herbs
Shangpinhua	to commercialize
Shehui zhuyi nongye jihua	socialist-based farming enterprise
Shenjing fanshe xue	neural reflex theory
Shenjing xuewei zhushe liaofa	nerve-acupuncture point-injection theory (a term of the 1950s)
Shenjing zhushe liaofa	nerve injection therapy
Shenrong	literally, deer antler and ginseng, but more generally high-end medicinals
Shiliao	food cures
Shiyan or Shijian	to experiment based on trial and error
Shiyanchang zhan	experimental farm stations
Shizihao	a registered product in the food category
Tianjian shiyanshi	laboratory in the field
Tiaojishi	druggists, but used interchangeably with yaogongshi during the Mao period
Tufa	indigenous methods
Tuyao	folk medicinals
Tu zhuanjia	indigenous experts
Weisheng	hygiene
Weisheng fangyi zhan	sanitary (or hygiene) and epidemic prevention stations
Weisheng yuan	hygiene institute
Xiandaihua	to modernize
Xiangzhen qiye	township enterprise
Xinghuo jihua	China Spark Program
Xin sheng shiwu	new matters
Xin yao	new drugs
Xin yi	new medicine
Xiyihua	to westernize
Xuerong	blood antlers

Xuewei zhushe liaofa	acupuncture point-injection therapy (used in present-day China)
Yanfang	prescriptions based on experience rather than science
Yaocai shougou zhan	herb collection stations
Yaogongshi	medicine shop workers, but referred to Western-trained pharmacologists and pharmacists during the Mao period
Yaojian zihao	a registered product in the drug category
Yaojiu	medicinal wine
Yiliao zhan	medical stations
Yishi	physicians
Yiyao gongsi	state-owned Chinese drug companies
Yizhu	medical assistants
Yuanliao yaocai	crude drugs
Yufang	to prevent (or defend)
Yumin yisheng	fishermen doctors
Zangqi shenghua yaowu	organo-biochemical drugs
Zangqi zhiji	organo-pharmaceutics
Zaofan tuan	Revolutionary Team
Zhi baibing	to cure a hundred diseases
Zhi fu	to bring wealth
Zhiliao or Zhiyu	to cure
Zhong chengyao	Chinese patent drugs
Zhonghe jingluo liaofa	integrated meridian therapy
(Zhong) yao (cai)	(Chinese) drugs or medicinals
(Zhong) yi	(Chinese) medical theory and practice
Zhuanyan	to research
Zhuanyehua	to professionalize
Zuzhi liaofa	tissue therapy

Slogans

Bei Zhan Bei Huang Wei Renmin	Prepare for War, Prepare for Famine, Serve the People
Dadan Chuangzao	Dare to Create
Dapo Mixin	Down with Superstitions
Fang Weixin	Launching of Satellites (new initiatives)
Fei Yi, Cun Yao	Abandon Chinese Medicine, Retain Chinese Drugs
Ganshuo, Ganxiang, Ganzuo	Dare to Speak, Dare to Think, Dare to Do
Gu Wei Jin Yong Yang Wei Zhong Yong	find new ways in old methods, and sinicize all ways Western
Jia Yang Jia Zhong	Home Rearing, Home Cultivation
Jiefang Sixiang	Liberate one's thoughts

Jishu Geming or Jishu Gexin	technological innovation
Kuai Ma Jia Bian	whip the horse to speed it up
Pilin Pikong	Criticize Lin Biao, Criticize Confucius
Qunzhong Luxian	mass line (i.e., collective efforts)
Qunzhong Yundong	The People's Movement
San Jiehe	Three Combines
San Kao	three dependables
San Zhua	three catches
Tuyang Jiehe	combining indigenous and foreign methods
Wu Fan Yundong	Five-Anti Movement
You Hong You Zhuan	Red and Expert
Zhongxiyi Jiehe	combine Chinese and Western medicines
Zhongyi Kexuehua Xiyi Zhongguohua	Scientize Chinese Medicine, Sinicize Western Medicine

BIBLIOGRAPHY

Alberto, Elizabeth Claire. "China Offers Buyouts to Wildlife Farmers in Response to Pandemic." *Mongabay*, May 20, 2020.

Alves, Rômulo Romeu Nóbrega, and Ierecê Lucena Rosa, eds. *Animals in Traditional Folk Medicine: Implications for Conservation*. Berlin: Springer, 2013.

Anderson, Eugene N. "Folk Nutritional Therapy in Modern China." In *Chinese Medicine and Healing: An Illustrated History*, edited by T. J. Hinrichs and Linda L. Barnes, 259–260. Cambridge, MA: Belknap Press of Harvard University Press, 2013.

Andrews, Bridie. "China: Medicine." In *Reader's Guide to the History of Science*, edited by Arne Hessenbruch, 135–137. New York: Routledge, 2000.

Andrews, Bridie. *The Making of Modern Chinese Medicine, 1850–1960*. Honolulu: University of Hawai'i Press, 2015.

Andrews, Bridie. "The Republic of China." In *Chinese Medicine and Healing: An Illustrated History*, edited by T. J. Hinrichs and Linda L. Barnes, 234–238. Cambridge, MA: Belknap Press of Harvard University Press, 2013.

Animal Concerns Research and Education Society (ACRES). "Keep Endangered Species Out of TCM." Accessed November 11, 2019. https://acres.org.sg /campaigns/current-campaigns/keep-endangered-species-out-of-tcm -cuurent-campaign/.

Animals Asia Foundation. Accessed December 25, 2014. https://www.animalsasia .org/.

Ao Zhixiong 敖志雄. "Ren gong yangzhi baihua she" 人工养殖百花蛇 [Artificial farming of the Chinese sharp-nosed viper]. *Zhongyao Tongbao* 中药通报 Bulletin of Chinese Medicinals 4, no. 12 (1958): 415–416.

"Awardee of Chemistry Prize Yuan Chengye." Accessed December 18, 2013. http:// www.hlhl.org.cn/english/showsub.asp?id=392.

Barnes, Linda L. *Needles, Herbs, Gods, and Ghosts: China, Healing, and the West to 1848.* Cambridge, MA: Harvard University Press, 2007.

"Bear Facts: The East Asian Market for Bear Gall Bladder." A TRAFFIC Network report. July 1995. http://www.google.com.sg/url?url=http://www.traffic .org/species-reports/traffic_species_mammals10.pdf&rct=j&q=&esrc =s&sa=U&ei=yh62VKXXD5eVuATF4IDIBw&ved=0CBMQFjAA&usg =AFQjCNGBvba4Vw9-kYqihTzWwRMV2qeVmA.

Becker, Jasper. *Hungry Ghosts: Mao's Secret Famine.* New York: Free Press, 1996.

Bei Runpu 贝润浦. "Dongwu zangqi shi zhi bing de liang yao" 动物脏器是治病的良药 [Animal organs are good medicinals for treating diseases]. *Zhongguo Weisheng Hua Bao* 中国卫生画报 China Hygiene Pictorial 4 (1984): 6–7.

Beijing Shi Yaocai Gongsi Di Yi Pifa Bu 北京市药材公司第一批发部 [Beijing Medicinal Company Number One Wholesale Department]. "She xiang nei yi shiyong jingyan jieshao" 麝香内衣使用经验介绍 [Introducing experiences in using "musk inner wear"]. *Zhongyao Tongbao* 中药通报 Bulletin of Chinese Medicinals 2, no. 4 (1956): 150–151.

"Beijing shi zhi yao chang jianjie" 北京市制药厂简介 [An introduction to Beijing pharmaceutical factories]. *Yaoxue Tongbao* 药学通报 Pharmaceutical Bulletin 2, no. 4 (1954): 173.

Beijing Tongrentang Laonian Bao Jian Yanjiu Suo, ed. 北京同仁堂老年保健研究所编 [Beijing Tongrentang Time-Honored Healthcare Research Center]. *Beijing Tongrentang Mingyao* 北京同仁堂名药 [The famous medicines of Beijing Tongrentang]. Beijing: Zhongyi Guji Chu Ban She 中医古籍出版社, 1986.

Beijing Zhongyi Xue Yuan Yi Jiu Wu Qi Nian Ban 北京中医学院1957年班 [The class of 1957 of the Beijing Chinese Medicine College]. *Zhongyao Jianshi* 中药简史 [A history of Chinese medicinals]. Beijing: Kexue Jishu Chu Ban She 科学技术出版社, 1960.

Bi Pengfei 毕鹏飞. "Xiong lei de shengtai xue yanjiu jinzhan ji zhanwang" 熊类的生态学研究进展及展望 [Conducting ecological studies of bears: Current development and future]. *Yanbian Nong Xue Yuan Xuebao* 延边农学院学报 Journal of Yanbian Agricultural College 2 (1988): 69–75.

Bianchi, L., et al., eds. *Trends in Hepatology: A Symposium in Honour of Dr. Dr. Herbert Falk on the Occasion of his 60th Birthday.* Oxford: Michael Terence Publishing, 1985.

"Bio-pharmaceutical in 2010." Accessed April 22, 2014. http://www .investguangzhou.gov.cn/web/eng/jsp/content/content_detail.jsp ?catEncode=001006003002004&contentId=28395.

Blanchard, Ben. "China Defends Use of Wild Animals in Traditional Medicine." July 2, 2016. https://www.reuters.com/article/us-china -endangered/china-defends-use-of-wild-animals-in-traditional-medicine -idUSKCN0ZI0GB.

Bretschneider, Emil. *Botanicon Sinicum: Notes on Chinese Botany from Native and Western Sources.* London: Trubner, 1882, 1892, 1885. Accessed March 10, 2014. https://archive.org/details/mobot31753000532124.

Brown, Jeremy, and Matthew D. Johnson, eds. *Maoism at the Grassroots: Everyday Life in China's Era of High Socialism*. Cambridge, MA: Harvard University Press, 2015.

Bu Liping, Darwin H. Stapleton, and Ka-che Yip, eds. *Science, Public Health and the State in Modern Asia*. New York: Routledge, 2012.

Cai Shoubai 蔡受白. "Zhongguo shexiang ye zhuang kuang: shexiang wei wo guo zhi techan" 中国麝香业状况：麝香为我国之特产 [The situation of China's musk industry: Musk as our country's specialty]. *Shanghai Zong Shanghui Yuebao* 上海总商会月报 Shanghai General Chamber of Commerce Monthly 5, no. 3 (1925): 13–17.

Cai Yumin 蔡玉珉. "Tantan tiaoji gongzuo ji yaoji zhiliang wenti" 谈谈调剂工作及药剂质量问题 [On pharmacy work and quality control issues with pharmaceutics]. *Yaoxue Tongbao* 药学通报 Pharmaceutical Bulletin 3, no. 5 (1955): 216–218.

"Cartoon: Guizhenland, on Bear Bile Controversy." *China Digital Times*, February 25, 2012. https://chinadigitaltimes.net/2012/02/cartoon-guizhenland-on-bear-bile-controversy.

Chang Minyi 常敏毅. "Guan yu huang niujiao de yiliao zuo yong" 关于黄牛角的医疗作用 [On ox horn and its medical use]. *Zhong Yiyao Xuebao* 中医药学报 Acta Chinese Medicine and Pharmacology 1 (1976): 44–46.

Chee, Liz P. Y. "'Down with Shark Fin!': The Politics of Eating Shark Fin and Its Shifting Nationality in Republican China." In *Consuming. Eating. Well-being: Proceedings of the 2016 Food and Society Conference*, edited by Eric Olmedo et al., 21–27. Bangi, Malaysia: KITA-UKM Press, 2018.

Chee, Liz P. Y. "'Health Products' at the Boundary between Food and Pharmaceuticals: The Case of Fish Liver Oil." In *Circulation and Governance of Asian Medicine*, edited by Celine Coderey and Laurent Pordie, 103–117. London: Routledge, 2019.

Chee, Liz P. Y. "Reformulating New Drugs within Traditional Chinese Medicine: Inside Guangzhou Huahai Pharmaceuticals Co., Ltd." In *Asian Medical Industries: Contemporary Perspectives on Traditional Pharmaceuticals*, edited by Stephan Kloos. London: Routledge, forthcoming.

Chee, Liz P. Y., and Gregory Clancey. "The Human Proteome and the Chinese Liver." *Science, Technology, and Society* 18, no. 3 (2013): 307–319.

Chen Chunyuan 陈春源. "Lurong wei yao zhong zhenpin jia ji ang'gui, wu guo bei di suo chan zhe zui zhuming" 鹿茸为药中珍品价极昂贵，吾国北地所产者最著名 [Deer antler as the most expensive of luxury medicinals, products from the northern region the most famous]. *Xinjiapo Hua Bao* 新加坡画报 Singapore Pictorial 106 (1930): 26.

Chen Haoran 陈浩然. "Wo men xue xi sulian xian jin jingyan fangmian de shouhuo" 我们学习苏联先进经验方面的收获 [What we've learned from Soviet Union's advanced experience]. *Yaoxue Tongbao* 药学通报 Pharmaceutical Bulletin 2, no. 4 (1954):161–162.

Chen Lanying 陈兰英. "Dui yaoxue jiaoyu de yi dian yi jian" 对药学教育的一点意见 [Some opinions on pharmacy education]. *Yaoxue Tongbao* 药学通报 Pharmaceutical Bulletin 2 no. 7 (1954): 309.

Chen Shenquan and Wu Yundong 陈莘泉, 吴运东. "Ping yaoji shi zhuanye yong 'yaowu huaxue'" 评药剂士专业用 "药物化学" [An assessment of pharmacists and their professional application of *Medicinal chemistry*]. *Yaoxue Tongbao* 药学通报 Pharmaceutical Bulletin 9, no. 9 (1963): 425–426.

Chen Shuyu 陈淑玉. "'Wenge' qi jian da jixue" "文革"期间打鸡血 [Chicken blood therapy of the Cultural Revolution]. *Shoudu Yiyao* 首都医药 City Medicine 9 (2008): 43.

Chen Xianyu 陈先瑜. "Xue xi zhongyi de yi dian tihui" 学习中医的一点体会 [Some reflections from learning Chinese medicine]. *Yaoxue Tongbao* 药学通报 Pharmaceutical Bulletin 7, no. 2 (1959): 63–64.

Chen Yixin. "Cold War Competition and Food Production in China, 1957–1952." *Agricultural History* 83, no. 1 (2009): 51–78.

Cheng Xinqian and Zhang Tianlu 陈新谦, 张天禄, eds. *Zhongguo Jin Dai Yaoxue Shi* 中国近代药学史 [A history of medicine in modern China]. Beijing: Renmin Weisheng Chu Ban She, 1992.

Chengshi Yi Liao Weisheng Gongzuo Geming Hua: Xuexi Ziliao Di Yi Ji 城市医疗卫生工作革命化: 学习资料第一集. Beijing: Renmin Weisheng Chu Ban She, 1966.

Chi Cheng 迟程. "Dongwu yao qian zai ziyuan de kaifa he liyong" 动物药潜在资源的开发和利用 [The potential to develop and use animal-based medicines]. *Chengdu Zhongyi Xue Yuan Xuebao* 成都中医学院学报 Journal of Chengdu University of Traditional Chinese Medicine 12, no. 4 (1989): 39–41.

China Food and Drug Administration. http://www.sfda.gov.cn/WS01/CL0001/.

"China's Lust for Jaguar Fangs Imperils Big Cats." *Nature*, February 23, 2018.

"Chong zhu guangjiao ti zhu fu bufen reng ke shiyong" 虫蛀广角剃蛀腐部分仍可使用 [Infected rhinoceros horn usable after removing the infected area]. *Zhongyao Tongbao* 中药通报 Bulletin of Chinese Medicinals 2, no. 5 (1956).

Cochran, Sherman. *Chinese Medicine Men: Consumer Culture in China and Southeast Asia*. Cambridge, MA: Harvard University Press, 2006.

Committee on Scholarly Communication with the People's Republic of China. *Herbal Pharmacology in the People's Republic of China: A Trip Report of the American Herbal Pharmacology Delegation*. Washington, DC: National Academy of Sciences, 1975.

Conroy, Mary Schaeffer. *Medicines of the Soviet Masses during World War II*. Lanham, MD: University Press of America, 2008.

Conroy, Mary Schaeffer. "The Soviet Pharmaceutical Industry and Dispensing, 1945–1953." *Europe-Asia Studies* 56, no. 7 (2004): 963–991.

Cooper, William C., and Nathan Sivin. "Man as a Medicine: Pharmacological and Ritual Aspects of Traditional Therapy Using Drugs Derived from the Human Body." In *Chinese Science: Explorations of an Ancient Tradition*, ed. Shigeru Nakayama and Nathan Sivin, 203–272. Cambridge, MA: MIT Press, 1973.

Croes, Laurine. "Tiger and Rhino Farms Set to Rise to Meet Chinese Demand." *Nikkei Asian Review*, November 12, 2018. https://asia.nikkei.com/Politics/International-relations/Tiger-and-rhino-farms-set-to-rise-to-meet-Chinese-demand.

"Cruelty Free Alternatives to Bear Bile: Affordable and Effective Herbal and Synthetic Options Available." Accessed September 7, 2013. http://www.animalsasia.org/index.php?UID=PBJUOGNYTNG1.

Cui Luchun 崔禄春. "Keji 'da yuejin' yundong pingxi" 科技 "大跃进"运动评析 [A comment on the technological "Great Leap Forward" movement], *Beijing Dangshi* 北京党史Beijing Party History 2 (2013): 12-14.

Cyranoski, David. "The Big Push for Chinese Medicine." *Nature* 561 (2018): 444-450.

"Daonian wo men jing'ai de dao shi he pengyou—jiliyangnuofu tong zhi" 悼念我们敬爱的导师和朋友-基里扬诺夫同志. *Zhongyao Tongbao* 中药通报 4, no. 9 (1958).

Davis, Arthur T. "The History of Organotherapy." *Lancet* 168, no. 4339 (1906): 1169.

Deng Liqun, Ma Hong, and Wu Heng, eds. 邓力群, 马洪, 武衡. *Dang Dai Zhongguo Cong Shu: Dangdai Zhongguo De Yaoye Shiye* 当代中国丛书: 当代中国的药业事业 [A compendium of contemporary China: The pharmaceutical business of contemporary China]. Beijing: Zhongguo Shehui Kexue Chu Ban She 中国社会科学出版社, 1988.

Deng Tietao and Cheng Zhifan 邓铁涛, 程之范. *Zhongguo Yixue Tong Shi (Jin Dai Juan)* 中国医学通史 (近代卷). Beijing: Renmin Weisheng Chu Ban She, 1999.

Denyer, Simon. "China's Bear Bile Industry Persists Despite Growing Awareness of the Cruelty Involved." *Washington Post*, June 3, 2018.

Denyer, Simon. "China's Push to Export Traditional Medicine May Doom the Magical Pangolin." *Washington Post*, July 21, 2018.

Denyer, Simon. "Even as China Turns Away from Shark Fin Soup, the Prestige Dish Is Gaining Popularity Elsewhere in Asia." *Washington Post*, February 15, 2018.

"Development, Prosperity, Decline of Chinese Tea Trading." Accessed October 23, 2013. http://www.lcsd.gov.hk/ce/Museum/Arts/7thingsabouttea/en/ch4_2_0.htm.

Di Er Junyi Daxue Yaoxue Xi Zhong Caoyao Jiaoyan Shi 第二军医大学药学系中草药教研室 [The Second Army Medical University School of Pharmacy Research Laboratory for Chinese Medicinals]. "Wu chan jieji wenhua da geming yi lai wo guo zhongyaocai shengchan ji qi keyan de xin chengjiu (xu)" 无产阶级文化大革命以来我国中药材生产及其科研的新成就 (续) [New achievements in the research and production of Chinese medicinals since the Great Proletarian Cultural Revolution (continued)]. *Zhong Caoyao Tongxun* 中草药通讯 Chinese Traditional and Herbal Drugs 9 (1976): 40-41.

Dikkötter, Frank. *The Cultural Revolution: A People's History 1962-1976*. London: Bloomsbury, 2016.

Dikkötter, Frank. *Mao's Great Famine: The History of China's Most Devastating Catastrophe, 1958-1962*. London: Bloomsbury, 2010.

Dongguan Xian Zhongyi Yuan Liu Yi Bu 东莞县中医院留医部 [Dongguan Country Chinese Medicine Hospital Intensive Care Unit]. "Zhongyi zhiliao yinao de ji dian ti hui" 中医治疗乙脑的几点体会 [Few thoughts on using Chinese medicine to treat encephalitis]. *Xin Zhongyi* 新中医 New Chinese Medicine 2 (1973): 20-21.

"Donkey Gelatin Shortage in China Sparks Tonic Fears." *Straits Times*, January 30, 2016.

Du Xing 杜兴. "Da jixue wang shi" 打鸡血往事 [The historical "injecting chicken blood" event]. *Dushu Wenzhai* 读书文摘 Reader Digest (August 1, 2009): 12–16.

Du Xing 杜兴. "Wenge shi 'da jixue' de huangmiu liaofa wei he neng gou shengxing?" 文革时"打鸡血"的荒谬疗法为何能够盛行？[Why was the preposterous 'chicken blood injection' therapy so popular during the CR era?]. *Wanxia* 晚霞 Sunset (July 20, 2012): 54–55.

Duan Weihe 段维和. "Shenrong de jiagong fang fa ying gai gai ge" 参茸的加工方法应该改革 [Ginseng and deer antler processing methods should be reformed]. *Zhong Caoyao Tongxun* 中草药通讯 Chinese Traditional and Herbal Drugs 5 (1976): 18–19.

Duckworth, J. Herbert. "Shark Liver Oil." *Science* (New Series) 96, no. 2485 (1942): 8.

"Duoshao yang xiongchang bu zhongguo, duoshao xiongdan yao xing renjian" 多少养熊场布中国, 多少熊胆药行人间 [How many bear farms distributed throughout China? How many bear bile products are there?]. Accessed April 24, 2014. http://www.infzm.com/content/55575.

Editors of Ta Kung Pao. *Trade with China: A Practical Guide*. Hong Kong: Ta Kung Pao, 1957.

Edwards, Martin. *Control and Therapeutic Trial: Rhetoric and Experimentation in Britain*. Amsterdam: Rodopi, 2006.

Ellis, Richard. *Tiger Bone and Rhino Horn: The Destruction of Wildlife for Traditional Chinese Medicine*. Washington, DC: Island Press, 2005.

Elman, Benjamin. *On Their Own Terms: Science in China, 1550–1900*. Cambridge, MA: Harvard University Press, 2005.

Engelhardt, Ute. "Dietetics in Tang China and the First Extant Works on Materia Dietetica." In *Innovation in Chinese Medicine*, edited by Elisabeth Hsu, 173–191. Cambridge: Cambridge University Press, 2001.

"[enviro-vlc] New PSA Released: Bear Bile Is Not a Magic Medicine." January 19, 2011. http://mailman.anu.edu.au/pipermail/enviro-vlc/2011-January/003442.html.

Fan, Fa-ti. "Collective Monitoring, Collective Defense: Science, Earthquakes, and Politics in Communist China." *Science in Context* 25, no. 1 (2012): 127–154.

Fan Peifu 樊培福. "Tianjin yixue yuan fushu yiyuan yaofang xiang quanguo yiyuan yaofang changyi zhankai youyi jingsai" 天津医学院附属医院药房向全国医院药房倡议展开友谊竞赛 [Tianjin Medical College affiliated pharmacy proposed all hospital pharmacies to engage in friendly matches]. *Yaoxue Tongbao* 药学通报 Pharmaceutical Bulletin 4 (1958): 155.

Fang Kun 方堃. "Guan yu renshen shangpin guige he jiagong wenti de shang que" 关于人参商品规格和加工问题的商榷 [Discussing the standards for ginseng as a sales product and issues with methods of processing]. *Zhongyao Tongbao* 中药通报 Bulletin of Chinese Medicinals 1, no. 2 (1955): 54–56.

Fang, Xiaoping. *Barefoot Doctors and Western Medicine in China*. Rochester, NY: University of Rochester Press, 2012.

"Fan huo qu xiongdan shi fan guojia, guizhentang kou maozi hu shui?" 反活取熊胆是反国家, 归真堂扣帽子唬谁？["To go against bear farming is to go against the country," Who is Guizhentang trying to fool with such label?]. Accessed April 24, 2014. http://bbs.chinanews.com/web/65/2012/0220/33900.shtml.

Farquhar, Judith. *Knowing Practice: The Clinical Encounter of Chinese Medicine*. Boulder, CO: Westview Press, 1996.

Filatov, Vladimir P. "Tissue Therapy in Cutaneous Leishmaniasis." *American Review of Soviet Medicine* (August 1945).

Filatov, Vladimir P. *Tissue Therapy: Teaching on Biogenic Stimulators*. Honolulu: University Press of the Pacific, 2003.

Fobar, Rachel. "China Promotes Bear Bile as Coronavirus Treatment, Alarming Wildlife Advocates." *National Geographic*, March 25, 2020.

"For Generations—Fitness for a King." Accessed April 10, 2014. http://www.brandsessence.co.uk/about.asp.

Frick, Johann. "Medicinal Use of Substances Derived from the Animal Organism (in Tsinghai). *Anthropo* 52 (1957): 177–198.

"From Beijing to New York: The Dark Side of Traditional Chinese Medicine—Age-Old Remedies Drive Trade in Endangered Species and Promote Animal Suffering, Despite Alternatives." *Science Online*. NYU Science, Health, and Environment Reporting System. June 29, 2011. http://scienceline.org/2011/06/from-beijing-to-new-york-the-dark-side-of-traditional-chinese-medicine/.

Fu Lianzhang 傅连璋. "Wei gao sudu di fazhan shehui zhuyi de weisheng shiye er fendou" 为高速度地发展社会主义的卫生事业而奋斗 [Strive for the healthcare of a society gearing for fast-paced development]. *Yaoxue Tongbao* 药学通报 Pharmaceutical Bulletin 6, no. 9 (1958): 401–405.

Fu Yunsheng 付云升. "Guan yu tianjin shi rengong hecheng niuhuang shengchan wenti de diaocha baogao" 关于天津市人工合成牛黄生产问题的调查报告 [An investigative report on the problems concerning artificial bezoar production in Tianjin City]. July 20, 1965. Unpublished report.

"Gaijin rubai yugan you zhiliang, gan shang yingguo mingpai "sigetuo" 改进乳白鱼肝油质量, 赶上英国名牌 "司各脱" [Improving the quality of creamy white fish liver oil, and catching up with Britain's famous brand Scott's]. *Yaoxue Tongbao* 药学通报 Pharmaceutical Bulletin 6, no. 12 (1958): 561.

Gao Enming 高恩铭. "Jing jin hu deng di yiyuan yaofang fenfen ding li yuejin jihua touru shehui zhuyi jingsai" 京津滬等地医院药房纷纷订立跃进计划投入社会主义竞赛 [Beijing, Tianjin, Shanghai hospitals and pharmacies commit to the Great Leap Movement and engage in socialist competitions]. *Yaoxue Tongbao* 药学通报 Pharmaceutical Bulletin 4 (1958): 154–155.

Gao Minggong 高铭功. "Wei da zuguo de yaowu ziyuan ji qi liyong: guo chan shexiang" 伟大祖国的药物资源及其利用: 国产麝香 [The medical resources of our Great Motherland and their utilization: State-produced musk]. *Yaoxue Tongbao* 药学通报 3, no. 5 (1955): 228–230.

Gao Xi. "Between the State and the Private Sphere: Chinese State Medicine Movement, 1930–1949." In *Science, Public Health and the State in Modern Asia*, edited by Bu Liping, Darwin H. Stapleton, and Ka-che Yip, 144–160. New York: Routledge, 2012.

Gao Xiaoshan, Xie Zongwan, Wang Xiaotao, Liu Jingming, Yu Guoyuan, and Jiang Fengwu 高晓山, 谢宗万, 王孝涛, 刘静明, 余国瑗, 姜凤梧. "Wu nian lai zhongyao yanjiu gongzuo de chengjiu" 五年来中药研究工作的成就 [Five years of research on Chinese medicinals and its achievements]. *Yaoxue Tongbao* 药学通报 Pharmaceutical Bulletin 10, no. 11 (1964): 481-489.

Gao Xufen and Jie Jue 高绪芬, 解觉. "He (Nyctereutes procynoides) zhen liangxing ti (tsue hermaphrodite) zuzhi jiegou de yanjiu" 貉 (Nyctereutes procynoides) 真两性体 (tsue hermaphrodite) 组织结构的研究 [Anatomical study on true hermaphroditism in raccoon dog]. *Jilin Nongye Daxue Xuebao* 吉林农业大学学报 Journal of Jilin Agricultural University 7, no. 2 (1985): 37-40.

Gao Zheng 高正. "Canguan tongrentang zhongyao dian yi hou de ganxiang" 参观同仁堂中药店以后的感想 [My feelings after visiting Tongrentang Medicinal Shop]. *Yaoxue Tongbao* 药学通报 Pharmaceutical Bulletin 3, no. 3 (1955): 132.

Gaworecki, Mike. "Chinese Government Reportedly Recommending Bear Bile Injections to Treat Coronavirus." *Mongabay*, March 23, 2020.

Ge Hanshu 葛汉枢. "Laihama zai linchuang shang de yingyong" 癞蛤蟆在临床上的应用 [Bedside application of toad]. *Xin Zhongyi* 新中医 New Chinese Medicine 5 (1976): 46-48.

"Ge di da liang zhizao zhongyao chengyao" 各地大量制造中药成药 [Manufacturing of Chinese pharmaceuticals on a massive scale]. *Yaoxue Tongbao* 药学通报 Pharmaceutical Bulletin 3, no. 10 (1955): 479-480.

Ghai, Rajat. "Chinese Medicine's Use of Animals a Threat to the Entire World." *Down to Earth*, April 7, 2020.

Gong Yuzhi and Li Peishan 龚育之, 李佩珊. "Pipan wang bin zai yixue he weisheng gongzuo zhong de zichan jieji sixiang" 批判王斌在医学和卫生工作中的资产阶级思想 [Criticizing the capitalist thoughts of Wang Bin in medical and health matters]. *Yaoxue Tongbao* 药学通报 Pharmaceutical Bulletin 3, no. 10 (1955): 434-438.

Goodall, Jane. "COVID-19 Is a Product of Our Unhealthy Relationship with Animals and the Environment." *Mongabay*, May 4, 2020.

Graham-Rowe, Duncan. "Biodiversity: Endangered and in Demand." *Nature* 480 (December 2011): S101-S103.

Grant, Mark. *Galen on Food and Diet*. London: Routledge, 2000.

Grooten, M., and R. E. A. Almond, eds. *Living Planet Report: Aiming Higher*. Gland, Switzerland: WWF, 2018.

Gross, Miriam. *Farewell to the God of Plague: Chairman Mao's Campaign to Deworm China*. Berkeley: University of California Press, 2014.

Gu Kelin 顾克霖. "Yugan you suan'na zhushe ye yu weisheng su A, D zhushe ye shi bu shi yi zhong yao?" 鱼肝油酸钠注射液与维生素 A, D 注射液是不是一种药？[Are sodium morrhuate and vitamins A and D considered medicine?]. *Yaoxue Tongbao* 药学通报 Pharmaceutical Bulletin 11, no. 5 (1965): 237-238.

Guan Qixue and Zhu Huiqiang 关其学, 朱慧强. *Guangdong Dui Wai Maoyi Yanjiu* 广东对外贸易研究 [A research on Guangdong's foreign trade]. Guangzhou:

Huanan Ligong Daxue Chu Ban She [South China University of Technology Press], 1992.

Guangdong Sheng Huiyang Diqu Weisheng Ju Zhong Xi Yi Jiehe Diaocha Zu 广东省惠阳地区卫生局中西医结合调查组. "Diaocha zong jie 'sanlao' jingyan, fajue minjian tufang tufa—jieshao ji ge diaocha cailiao" 调查总结 "三老 "经验, 发掘民间土方土法— 介绍几个调查材料. *Xin Zhongyi* 新中医 2 (1976): 11–18.

Guangdong Sheng Jieyang Xian Yunlu Gongshe Weisheng Yuan 广东省揭阳县云路公社卫生院 [Guangdong Province Jieyang County Yunlu Commune Health Center]. "Yong chong lei yao zhiliao sheng jie chang ai yi li baogao" 用虫类药治疗升结肠癌一例报告 [A report on using insect-based medicinals to cure ascending colon cancer]. *Xin Zhongyi* 新中医 New Chinese Medicine 3 (1976): 24–25.

Guangdong Sheng Shantou Zhuan Shu Shuili Ju 广东省汕头专属水利局 [Water Resources Department of Shantou Guangdong Province]. "Guangdong shantou de haima yangzhi fa" 广东汕头的海马养殖法 [Seahorse farming at Guangdong Shantou]. *Yaoxue Tongbao* 药学通报 Pharmaceutical Bulletin 7, no. 4 (1960): 166–170.

"Guangdong xinhui xian siqian gongshe liyong shan caoyao zhi bing, shou dao qunzhong huan ying" 广东新会县司前公社利用山草药治病, 受到群众欢迎. *Yaoxue Tongbao* 药学通报 7, no. 8 (1959): 429–430.

Guangxi Tong Zu Zi Zhi Qu Shangye Ting Yaocai Zhongzhi Shiyan Chang 广西僮族自治区商业厅药材种植实验场 [Guangxi Zhuang Autonomous Region Commerce Department for Experimental Farms in Medicinal Cultivation]. "Rengong siyang gejie shiyan chenggong" 人工饲养蛤蚧实验成功 [Successful experimentation with tokay gecko farming]. *Zhongyao Tongbao* 中药通报 Bulletin of Chinese Medicinals 4, no. 11 (1958): 388.

Guangzhou Junqu Houqinbu Weishengbu, ed. 广州军区后勤部卫生部编. *Chang Yong Xin Yiliao Fa Shouce* 常用新医疗法手册. Beijing: Remin Weisheng Chu Ban She, 1970.

Guangzhou Shi Zheng Xie Xuexi He Wen Shi Ziliao Weiyuan Hui, Guangzhou Shi Difang Zhi Bianzuan Weiyuan Hui Bangong Shi, eds. 广州市政协学习和文史资料委员会, 广州市地方志编纂委员会办公室合编. *Guangzhou Wen Shi Di 61 Ji Guangzhou Lao Zihao Xia Ce* 广州文史第六十一 集 广州老字号下册 [Guangzhou cultural history part 61: Guangzhou time-honored brands vol. 2]. Guangzhou: Guangdong Renmin Chu Ban She 广东人民出版社, 2003.

Guangzhou Zhongyi Xue Yuan 广州中医学院 [Guangzhou Medical College]. *Shengwu Xue Jiang Yi* 生物学讲义 [Biology lectures]. 1959. Unpublished.

Guangzhou Zhongyi Xue Yuan Bianxie 广州中医学院编写 [Guangzhou Chinese Medical College]. *Linchuang Shi Yong Zhongyao* 临床使用中药 [Bedside application of Chinese medicinals]. Guangzhou: Guangdong Renmin Chu Ban She 广东人民出版社, 1960.

"Guizhentang she xian lan yong xiongdan fen xiongdan cha yi qiaoran xia jia" 归真堂涉嫌滥用熊胆粉熊胆茶已悄然下架 [Guizhentang's bear bile tea products quietly removed from shelves]. Accessed August 30, 2015. http://finance.china.com.cn/stock/special/gzt/20120216/536711.shtml.

"Gu lao de Beijing Tongrentang bian nian qing le" 古老的北京同仁堂变年轻了 [Age-old Beijing Tongrentang has turned younger]. *Yaoxue Tongbao* 药学通报 Pharmaceutical Bulletin 3, no. 6 (1955): 288.

Guojia Zhong Yiyao Guanli Ju Zheng Ce Fa Gui Si, ed. 国家中医药管理局政策法规司 [State Administration of Traditional Chinese Medicine Policy and Regulation Division]. *Zhonghua Renmin Gonghe Guo Xian Xing Zhong Yiyao Fa Gui Huibian (1949–1991)* 中华人民共和国现行中医药法规汇编 1949–1991 [A compilation of laws governing traditional Chinese medicine in the People's Republic of China 1949–1991]. Beijing: Zhongguo Zhongyiyao Chu Ban She, 1991.

"Guoren ceng fengkuang da jixue" 国人曾疯狂打鸡血 [The once-crazed chicken blood therapy]. *Gongchan Dang Yuan* 共产党员 Communist Party Member, August 15, 2010.

Ha'erbin Zhi Yao Chang 哈尔滨制药厂 [Harbin Pharmaceutical Factory]. "Lurong jing, mirong jing de zhi fa ji liao xiao" 鹿茸精, 麋茸精的制法及疗效 [The making of deer antler and elk antler essence and their efficacies]. *Yaoxue Tongbao* 药学通报 Pharmaceutical Bulletin 8, no. 9 (1958): 426–427.

Hai Bazi 海巴子. "Feng mi yi shi de 'jixue liaofa'" 风靡一时的鸡血疗法 [Fashionable chicken blood therapy in 1960s]. *Dang'an Chunqiu* 档案春秋 Spring and Autumn Archives (December 10, 2009): 24–28.

Han Guoyan 韩国彦. "Mayi rengong yangzhi chu tan" 蚂蚁人工养殖初探. *Shengwu Xue Zazhi* 生物学杂志 1 (1995): 34–35.

Han Yi 韩毅. *Song Dai Wenyi De Liuxing Yu Fangzhi* 宋代瘟疫的流行与防止. Beijing: Shangwu Yin Shu Guan, 2015.

Hangzhou Ribao 杭州日报. "Liyong yulin tilian kafei yin chu bu chenggong" 利用鱼鳞提炼咖啡因初步成功 [Extracting caffeine from fish scales a preliminary success]. *Yaoxue Tongbao* 药学通报 Pharmaceutical Bulletin 4, no. 8 (1956): 384.

Hanson, Marta. "Is the 2015 Nobel Prize a Turning Point for Traditional Chinese Medicine?" *The Conversation*. October 5, 2015. http://theconversation.com /is-the-2015-nobel-prize-a-turning-point-for-traditional-chinese-medicine -48643.

Harrower, Henry R. *Practical Hormone Therapy: A Manual of Organotherapy for General Practitioners*. Accessed October 19, 2014. http://archive.org/stream /practicalhormoneooharr/practicalhormoneooharr_djvu.tx.

He Shaoqi 何绍奇. "'Xuerou you qing' kaolue" "血肉有情"考略 [An examination of the saying "Products with passion in both blood and flesh"]. *Zhongyi Zazhi* 中医杂志 Journal of Traditional Chinese Medicine 10 (1992): 58.

Hebei Sheng Dui Wai Maoyi Ju 河北省对外贸易局 [Heibei Province Foreign Trade Bureau]. *1953–1963 Nian Hebei Sheng Tianjin Kou'an Dui Wai Maoyi Tongji Ziliao (Chu Kou Bufen), Di Er Ce* 1953–1963 河北省天津口岸对外贸易资料 (出口部分), 第二册 [Hebei province Port of Tianjin foreign trade documents (export), vol. 2]. Tianjin: Hebei Sheng Dui Wai Maoyi Ju, 1965.

Hebei Sheng Shangye Ting, Hebei Sheng Weisheng Ting 河北省商业厅, 河北省卫生厅 [Hebei Province Department of Commerce, Hebei Province Department of Health]. "Wei jia qiang shougou niu, zhu, yang danzhi gongying

niuhuang shengchan de tongzhi" 为加强收购牛, 猪, 羊胆汁供应牛黄生产的通
知 [A notice to increase the purchase of cow, pig, and sheep bile for bezoar
production], April 1, 1960.

Hebei Sheng Zhongyi Zhongyao Zhanlan Hui Shennong Guan Che Ji Zhi Er
河北省中医中药展览会神农馆侧记之二 [Hebei Province Chinese Medicine
Exhibition Shennong Pavilion Sidelight 2]. "Da gao jia zhong jia yang, meng
zeng yaocai shengchan" 大搞家种家养, 猛增药材生产 [Carrying out home
cultivation and home rearing on a big scale to drastically increase medicinal production]. *Yaoxue Tongbao* 药学通报 Pharmaceutical Bulletin 7, no. 2
(1959): 65–66.

Hebei Xin Yi Daxue "Chijiao Yisheng Cankao Congshu" Bianxie Zu 河北新医大
学 '赤脚医生参考丛书'编写组 [Hebei New Medical College Barefoot Doctors
Reference Series Editorial Team]. *Jichu Yixue Wenda: Xueye Xitong* 基础医学
问答: 血液系统 [Fundamental questions of medicine: The blood system].
Beijing: Renming Weisheng Chu Ban She 人民卫生出版社, 1976.

Henan Zhongyi Xue Yuan Jiao Wu Chu 河南中医学院教务处 [Henan Chinese
Medical College Administrative Office]. "Henan zhongyi xue yuan zhongyao xi di yi jie xuesheng biye" 河南中医学院中药系第一届学生毕业 [First-
batch students of Henan Chinese Medical College Zhongyao Department
graduate]. *Yaoxue Tongbao* 药学通报 Pharmaceutical Bulletin 9, no. 9 (1963):
406.

Hernández, Javier C. "China, after Outcry, Reinstates Ban on Rhino and Tiger
Parts in Medicine." *New York Times*, November 12, 2018.

Hinrichs, T. J., and Linda L. Barnes, eds. *Chinese Medicine and Healing*. Cambridge,
MA: Belknap Press of Harvard University Press, 2013.

Hobley, C. W. "The Rhinoceros." *Journal of the Society for the Preservation of the Wild
Fauna of the Empire* 14 (1931): 18–23.

Hsu, Elizabeth. "Commentary on Stephan Kloos' 'The Pharmaceutical Assemblage.'" *Current Anthropology* 58, no. 6 (2017): 708–709.

Hsu, Elizabeth. "Reflections on the 'Discovery' of the Antimalarial Qinghao." *British Journal of Clinical Pharmacology* 61, no. 6 (2006): 666–670.

Hsu, Elizabeth, ed. *Innovation in Chinese Medicine*. Needham Research Institute
Studies 3. Cambridge: Cambridge University Press, 2001.

Huabei Yaochang Zhongxin Shiyan Shi 华北药厂中心实验室 [Huabei Pharmaceutical Factory Central Laboratory]. "Huabei yaochang da fang weixing" 华
北药厂大放卫星 [Huabei Pharmaceutical Factory launches satellite in a big
way]. *Yaoxue Tongbao* 药学通报 Pharmaceutical Bulletin 6, no. 11 (1958): 509.

Hua Gong Bu Yanjiu Gongzuo Huiyi Yiyao Zu Tichu Kouhao He Fendou Zhi
Biao 化工部研究工作会议医药组提出口号和奋斗指标 [A slogan and instruc-
tion raised by the Ministry of Chemical Industry in research conference on
medicine]. "Kuai ma jia bian, gan shang Yingguo" 快马加鞭, 赶上英国 [Whip
the horse to speed it up, catch up with Britain]. *Yaoxue Tongbao* 药学通报
Pharmaceutical Bulletin 6, no. 5:247.

Huang Wenda 黄文达. "Qiuyin zhushe ye zhiliao zhiqiguan xiaochuan de liaoxiao
guancha" 蚯蚓注射液治疗支气管哮喘的疗效观察 [An observation of the

efficacy of earthworm-based injectable substance in curing bronchial asthma].
Yaoxue Tongbao 药学通报 Pharmaceutical Bulletin 11, no. 10 (1965): 479.

Huang Zizhan, Zhao Dieru, and Li Zhiguan 黄子瞻, 赵眎如, 黎志贯. "Yong shuiniu jiao daiti lingyang jiao xijiao zhiliao 35 li liuxing xing yixing naoyan linchuang chubu baogao" 用水牛角代替羚羊角犀角 35 例流行性乙型脑炎临床初步报告 [A preliminary report of using water buffalo horns as a replacement for antelope and rhinoceros horns to treat 35 cases of epidemic encephalitis B]. *Guangdong Zhongyi* 广东中医 Guangdong Chinese Medicine 10 (1958): 14–18.

Hunan Xinhua Xian Renmin Yiyuan Neike 湖南新化县人民医院内科 [Hunan Xinhua County People's Hospital Internal Medicine]. "Caoyu dan zhong du yi li baogao" 草鱼胆中毒一例报告 [A case of poisoning from the bile of grass carp]. *Zhong Caoyao Tongxun* 中草药通讯 Chinese Traditional and Herbal Drugs 1 (1974): 56.

"Huo xiong qu dan bei zhi bing wu kexue yiju jishu cong chaoxian yinjin" 活熊取胆被指并无科学依据技术从朝鲜引进 [Bear farming technique introduced from North Korea faced backlash for lacking scientific basis]. Accessed April 21, 2014. http://finance.qq.com/a/20120217/007542.htm.

Jacobs, Andrew. "A Movement to Rescue Bears in China: Growing Movement Stands Up for Bears." *International Herald Tribune* (May 23, 2013): 4.

Ji Ruyun and Ren Yunfeng 稔汝运, 任云峰, eds. *Xunzhao Xin Yao De Tujing He Fangfa* 寻找新药的途径和方法 [The ways and methods to finding new drugs]. Beijing: Renmin Weisheng Chuban She 人民卫生出版社, 1965.

Jiang Daqu 姜達衢. "Ru he zhengli he fayang zuguo yaoxue yichan" 如何整理和发扬祖国药学遗产 [How to organize and carry forward our country's pharmaceutical legacy]. Yaoxue Tongbao 药学通报 Pharmaceutical Bulletin 2, no. 9 (1954): 368–369.

Jiangsu Sheng Yizheng Xian Maji Gongshe Jinqiao Dadui Weisheng Shi 江苏省仪征县马集公社金桥大队卫生室 [Jiangsu Province Yizheng County Maji Commune Jinqiao Brigade Health Corner]. "Tubie chong de si yang he guanli" 土鳖虫的饲养和管理 [The rearing and management of ground beetles]. *Zhong Caoyao Tongxun* 中草药通讯 Chinese Traditional and Herbal Drugs 2 (1974): 63.

Jiangsu Xinyi Xue Yuan 江苏新医院 [Jiangsu New Medical College]. *Zhongyao Da Cidian* 中药大辞典 [Chinese medicine dictionary]. Shanghai: Shanghai Renmin Chu Ban She 上海人民出版社, 1977.

Jian Kang Bao Xun 健康报讯 [Health report]. "Renshen zaipei zhong da chengjiu: rengong shi fei zi duo shu kuai gen zi zhong" 人参栽重大成就: 人工施肥籽多熟快根子重 [Great achievements with ginseng cultivation: More seeds faster growth and heavier roots with artificial fertilizers]. *Zhongyao Tongbao* 中药通报 Bulletin of Chinese Medicinals 4, no. 10 (1958): 360.

"'Jianzihao' yaopin san nian hou jiang xiaoshi" 健字号﹡药品三年后将消失 [Drugs registered as "health products" to be phased out in three years]. *Zhongguo Jingji Xinxi* 中国经济信息 China Economic Information Journal 7 (2000): 28.

"Jiefang sixiang, da dan chuangzao—Beijing shi gong gong weisheng ju yan yi fu juzhang zai 4 yue 27 ri zhongguo yaoxue hui beijing fen hui he beijing shi

wei xie yaoshi hui lianhe zhaokai de yaofang jishu gexin baogao hui shang
de baogao" 解放思想, 大胆创造— 北京市公共卫生局阎毅副局长在4月27日中国
药学会北京分会和北京市卫协药师会联合召开的药房技术革新报告会上的报告
[Liberal thoughts, bold inventions—A report on 27 April by deputy director
of Beijing Public Health Bureau Yan Yifu at the Pharmaceutical Technology
Innovation Symposium jointly organized with the Chinese Pharmaceutical
Association Beijing office]. *Yaoxue Tongbao* 药学通报 Pharmaceutical Bulletin
6, no. 6 (1958): 254–255.

"Jiji kai zhan quan chong bushou gongzuo" 积极开展全虫捕收工作 [Giving the
work of gathering whole insects an active kickstart]. *Zhong Caoyao Tongxun*
中草药通讯 Chinese Traditional and Herbal Drugs 5 (October 1973): 29.

Jin Guangzhu, Jin Guangling, and Jin Changhao 金光株, 金光凌, 金昌浩. "Xiong-
gdan huo ti qu zhi shiyan baogao" 熊胆活体取汁实验报告 [A report on the
experiment to extract bile from live bears]. *Yanbian Nong Xue Yuan Xuebao*
延边农学院学报 Journal of Yanbian Agricultural College 2 (1987): 61–65.

Jin Yilang 金贻郎. "Dongwu yao yanjiu de jin kuang" 动物药研究的近况 [An update
on animal-based medicinal research]. *Zhejiang Zhongyi Xue Yuan Tongxun* 浙江
中医学院通讯 Zhejiang Chinese Medical College Newsletter 1 (1977): 47–50.

Jin Yuquan, Jin Jichun, Jin Renshu, and Jin Xiangquan 金禹权, 金吉春, 金仁淑,
金享权. *Xiong Lei Yu Xiong Dan* 熊类与熊胆 [Types of bear species and bear
bile]. Heilongjiang: Heilongjiang Chaoxian Minzu Chu Ban She, 1993.

Jin Zhuzhe and Wu Yonghuan 金洙哲, 吴永焕. "Jilin sheng yanbian chaoxian zu
yong yao" 吉林省延边朝鲜族用药 [The North Korean community in Yanbian
Jilin Province and their use of medicines]. *Yanbian Nong Xue Yuan Xuebao* 延
边农学院学报 Journal of Yanbian Agricultural College 2 (1988): 17–20.

Jing Fang 荆方. *Wo Shi Liu Ling Hou 1969–1978* 我是 60 后 1969–1978 [I belong to the
post-60s generation 1969–1978]. Beijing: Xinxing Chu Ban She 新星出版社,
2010.

"Ji zhe fu guizhentang jidi shi wen 'huo xiong qu dan' tan jiu wu tong lun" 记者赴
归真堂基地十问"活熊取胆" 探究无痛论 [Reporter made site visit to Guizhen-
tang to explore the "no pain" argument]. Accessed April 22, 2014. http://
news.sohu.com/20120220/n335301850.shtml.

Kadetz, Paul. "Colonizing Safety: Creating Risk through the Enforcement of
Biomedical Constructions of Safety." *East Asian Science, Technology, and Society*
8 (2014): 81–106.

Kalashnikov, V. P. 卡拉希尼可夫. "Guan yu zhiwu yao de yanjiu" 关于植物药的研
究 [Regarding plant-based medicinal research]. In "Liang wei sulian xue zhe
guan yu yanjiu zhiwu yao de yijian" 两位苏联学者关于研究植物药的意见 [The
opinions of two Russian scholars on plant-based medicinal research]. *Zhongyao Tongbao* 中药通报 Bulletin of Chinese Medicinals 4, no. 3 (1958): 73–74.

Kani, U. Sundar. "Fish Oils." In *Fisheries of the West Coast of India*, edited by S.
Jones, 101–105. India, 1958. http://eprints.cmfri.org.in/5579/.

Kawahara Kazuhito, Kitani Chiho, Yoshimura Chiaki, and Tanaka Toshihiro. "Report on Quality and Manufacturing of Bear Bile from Living Bear." *Natural
Medicines* 49, no. 2 (1995): 158–163.

Ke Zexun 柯泽训. "Ji guan xue zhiliao qian du huo tang shang" 鸡冠血治疗浅度 火烫伤 [Blood from chicken combs to treat light burns]. *Xin Zhongyi* 新中医 New Chinese Medicine 3 (1976): 46.

Kefalov [*sic*], Y. P. 戈伏罗夫. "Guan yu V. P. Kalashnikov de 'guan yu zhiwu yao de yanjiu' yi wen 关于 B.II. 卡拉希尼可夫的 "关于植物药的研究"—文 [V. P. Kalashnikov's "Regarding plant-based medicinal research"]. In "Liang wei sulian xue zhe guan yu yanjiu zhiwu yao de yijian" 两位苏联学者关于研究植物药的意见 [The opinions of two Russian scholars on plant-based medicinal research]. *Zhongyao Tongbao* 中药通报 Bulletin of Chinese Medicinals 4, no. 3 (1958): 75.

Kiriyanov [*sic*], A. P. Trans. Huang Junhua 基里扬诺夫 (黄俊华 译). "Dongbei guoying shen chang zhongzhi renshen de jingyan" 东北国营参场种植人参的经验 [Experience with ginseng cultivation in government-owned ginseng farms in the northeast region]. *Zhongyao Tongbao* 中药通报 Bulletin of Chinese Medicinals 4, no. 7 (1958): 237–239.

Kiriyanov [*sic*], A. P. Trans. Huang Junhua. "Si shi nian lai sulian zai yao yong zhiwu fangmian de chengjiu" 四十年来苏联在药用植物方面的成就 [Forty years of Soviet achievements in utilizing plant-based medicinals]. *Zhongyao Tongbao* 中药通报 Bulletin of Chinese Medicinals 3, no. 6 (1957): 222–224.

Kloos, Stephan, ed. *Asian Medical Industries: Contemporary Perspectives on Traditional Pharmaceuticals*. London: Routledge, forthcoming.

Kloos, Stephan. "The Pharmaceutical Assemblage: Rethinking Sowa Rigpa and the Herbal Pharmaceutical Industry in Asia." *Current Anthropology* 58, no. 6 (2017): 693–705.

Krementsov, Nikolai. "Hormones and the Bolsheviks: From Organotherapy to Experimental Endocrinology, 1918–1929." *Isis* 99 (2008): 486–518.

Krementsov, Nikolai. *A Martian Stranded on Earth: Alexander Bogdanov, Blood Transfusions, and Proletarian Science*. Chicago: University of Chicago Press, 2011.

Krementsov, Nikolai. *Revolutionary Experiments: The Quest for Immortality in Bolshevik Science and Fiction*. Oxford: Oxford University Press, 2013.

Krishnasamy, Kanitha, Chris R. Shepherd, and Oi Ching Or. "Observations of Illegal Wildlife Trade in Boten, a Chinese Border Town within a Specific Economic Zone in Northern Lao PDR." *Global Ecology and Conservation* 14 (April 2018).

Krishnasamy, Kanitha, and Monica Zavagli. *Southeast Asia: At the Heart of Wildlife Trade*. Petaling Jaya, Malaysia: TRAFFIC, 2020.

"Kuma no tannō fusei yunyū" クマの胆のう不正輸入 [Illegal import of bear bile]. *Asahi Shimbun* 朝日新闻 (April 16, 1988): 3.

"'Kuma no yi' yu nyū wa da me" "くまのい"原料輸入はダメ [Import of bear bile comes to a halt]. *Asahi Shimbun* 朝日新闻 (June 30, 1988): 3.

Kuo Wen-Hua. "Promoting Chinese Herbal Drugs through Regulatory Globalisation: The Case of the Consortium for Globalization of Chinese Medicine." *Asian Medicine* 10 (2015): 316–339.

Kurennov, Pavel Metveevich. *Russian Folk Medicine*. London: W.H. Allen, 1970.

Latour, Bruno. *Science in Action: How to Follow Scientists and Engineers through Society*. Cambridge, MA: Harvard University Press, 1987.

Lei, Hsiang-lin Sean. "From Changshan to a New Anti-Malarial Drug: Re-Networking Chinese Drugs and Excluding Chinese Doctors." *Social Studies of Science* 29, no. 3 (1999): 323–358.

Lei, Hsiang-lin Sean. *Neither Donkey nor Horse: Medicine in the Struggle over China's Modernity*. Chicago: University of Chicago Press, 2014.

"*Leuzea carthamoides*." Accessed December 6, 2013. http://www.keyherbs.org/leuzea_carthamoides_rhaponticum—01.htm.

Lev, Efriam. "Traditional Healing with Animals (Zootherapy): Medieval and Present-Day Levantine Practice." *Journal of Ethnopharmacology* 85, no. 1 (2003): 107–118.

Li Jingwei 李经纬. Zhongguo Yixue Tong Shi 中国医学通史 [Chinese medical history]. Beijing: Renmin Weisheng Chu Ban She 人民卫生出版社, 2000.

Li Junde, Huang Luqi, and Qu Xiaobo 李军德, 黄璐琦, 曲晓波, eds. *Zhongguo yao yong dong wu zhi* 中国药用动物志 [Chinese medicinal animals]. 2nd ed. Vols. 1–3. Fujian: Fujian Science and Technology Press, 2013.

Li Rongsheng 李荣升. "Jineijin" 鸡内金 [Chicken gizzard]. *Zhongyao Tongbao* 中药通报 Bulletin of Chinese Medicinals 4, no. 5 (1958): 164.

Li Shouwan, Jin Hui, Wang Fujin, and Yu Shulin 李寿万, 金辉, 王富金, 俞曙林. "Xiao hei xiong she ci (issa, lyssa) de weixi jiegou" 小黑熊舌刺 (いっさ, lyssa) 的微细结构 [Microstructure of the tongue of bear cub]. *Yanbian Nong Xue Yuan Xuebao* 延边农学院学报 Journal of the Yanbian Agricultural College 2 (1988): 76–78.

Li Weizhen 李维禛. "Xuexi guojia zong luxian gaijin yaoxue gongzuo" 学习国家总路线改进药学工作 [Learn the country's general trajectory and improve pharmacy work]. *Yaoxue Tongbao* 药学通报 Pharmaceutical Bulletin 2, no. 1 (1954): 2–3.

Liang Fengxi 梁凤锡. "Dongbei yuan she de shengtai diaocha" 东北原麝的生态调查 [An investigation into the ecology of northeastern musk deer]. *Jilin Nongye Daxue Xuebao* 吉林农业大学学报 Journal of Jilin Agricultural University 7, no. 2 (1985): 41–46.

Liang Jielian 梁洁莲. *Wu Tong Zhushe Fa Jiang Hua* 无痛注射法讲话 [A conversation on no pain injection]. Beijing: Renmin Weisheng Chu Ban She 人民卫生出版社, 1957.

Liao Qingjiang 廖清江. "Tantan yaoji ye xiao de kecheng wenti" 谈谈药剂夜校的课程问题 [On the problems concerning pharmacy night classes]. *Yaoxue Tongbao* 药学通报 Pharmaceutical Bulletin 2, no. 2 (1954): 66–68.

Lin Zhaogeng, Chen Guangwei, and Zhou Peiqi 林昭庚, 陳光瑋, 周珮琪. *Rizhi Shiqi (Xiyuan 1895–1945) No Taiwan Zhongyi* 日治時期 (西元1895–1945) の台湾中医 [Chinese medicine in Taiwan during the Japanese occupation (Xiyuan 1895–1945)]. Taipei: Guoshi Guan, 2011.

Liu Dezu 刘德祖. "Ban hao shiyan chang zhan shixing jiao xue, keyan he tui guang san jiehe qian yi" 办好实验场站实行教学, 科研和推广三结合浅议 [Effectively run experimental farm stations to teach, research and promote the "three combines": A discussion]. *Jilin Nongye Daxue Xuebao* 吉林农业大学学报 Journal of Jilin Agricultural University 7, no. 2 (1985): 103–107.

Liu Guosheng 刘国声. "Xizang de yaocai he yaoxue shiye" 西藏的药材和药学事业 [Tibetan medicinals and pharmacy business]. *Yaoxue Tongbao* 药学通报 Pharmaceutical Bulletin 2, no. 7 (1954): 276–279.

Liu Jiaqi and Sun Shujin 刘家琪, 孙书缙. *Ye Sheng Dongwu Yangzhi Xue Xunlian Ban Jiang Yi* 野生动物养殖学训练班讲义 [Lectures on wildlife farming]. Beijing: Quan Guo Shoulie Shiye Jingying Guanli Gan Bu Xunlian Ban Bian Wei Hui 全国狩猎事业经营管理干部训练班编委会 [Editorial Committee for National Training of Cadres in Business Hunting Management], 1960.

Liu Mohui 刘谟慧. "'Kang chuansi shuan' he 'zhu danzhi zhushe ye'" "抗喘息栓" 和 "猪胆汁注射液" [Battling agonal breathing and pig bile injectable substance]. *Yaoxue Tongbao* 药学通报 Pharmaceutical Bulletin 12, no. 3 (1966): 129.

Liu Shoushan 刘寿山. "Guan yu niuhuang cheng fen, liao xiao ji yaoli de yi xie bu chong" 关于牛黄成分, 疗效及药理的一些补充 [Supplementary notes on the components, efficacies and pharmacology of bezoar]. *Zhongyao Tongbao* 中药通报 Bulletin of Chinese Medicinals 2, no. 1 (1956): 23.

Liu Shoushan 刘寿山, ed. *Zhongyao Yanjiu Wenxian Zhaiyao: 1820-1961* 中药研究文献摘要. Beijing: Kexue Chu Ban She, 1963.

Liu Shoushan 刘寿山. *Zhongyao Yanjiu Wenxian Zhaiyao: 1962-1974* 中药研究文献摘要. Beijing: Kexue Chu Ban She, 1979.

Liu Shoushan 刘寿山. *Zhongyao Yanjiu Wenxian Zhaiyao: 1975-1979* 中药研究文献摘要. Beijing: Kexue Chu Ban She, 1986.

Liu Tiecheng 刘铁城. "Sulian de renshen zaipei fa jieshao" 苏联的人参栽培法介绍 [Introducing Soviet methods of cultivating ginseng]. *Zhongyao Tongbao* 中药通报 Bulletin of Chinese Medicinals 1, no. 2 (1955): 56–58.

Liu Xiaobin 刘小斌. "Guangdong jin dai de zhongyi jiao yu" 广东近代的中医教育 [Chinese medicine education in contemporary Guangdong]. *Zhongguo Yishi Zazhi* 中国医史杂志 Chinese Journal of Medical History 12, no. 3 (1982): 133–138.

Liu Xiaobin 刘小斌. *Guangdong Zhongyi Jiaoyu Shi: Qing Dai Zhi Jiefang Chu Qi* 广东中医教育史: 清代至解放初期. PhD dissertation. Guangzhou: Guangzhou Zhongyi Xue Yuan 广州: 广州中医学院 [Guangzhou Medical College], 1983.

Liu Xiaobin 刘小斌. *Guangdong Zhongyi Yu Ying Cai* 广东中医育英才 [Nurturing talents at Guangdong Medical College]. Guangzhou: Guangdong Sheng Weisheng Ting Zhongyi Chu 广州: 广东省卫生厅中医处 [Guangdong Province Health Department Chinese Medicine Section], 1988.

Liu Zhijun 刘志俊. "Zhongyaocai shouce" 中药材手册 [A handbook on Chinese medicinals]. *Yaoxue Tongbao* 药学通报 Bulletin of Chinese Medicinals 8, no. 2 (1960): 107–108.

Livingston, Emily, and Chris R. Shepherd. "Bear Farms in Lao PDR Expand Illegally and Fail to Conserve Wild Bears." *Oryx* 50, no. 1 (2016): 176–184.

Livingston, Emily, I. Gomez, and J. Bouhuys. "A Review of Bear Farming and Bear Trade in Lao People's Democratic Republic." *Global Ecology and Conservation* 13 (January 2018): 1–9.

Lü Jiage 吕嘉戈. *Wanjiu Zhongyi: Zhongyi Zao Yu De Zhidu Xianjing He Ziben Yinmou* 挽救中医: 中医遭遇的制度陷阱和资本阴谋 [Rescuing Chinese medicine: The institutional trap and capital conspiracy]. Guangxi: Guangxi Normal University Press, 2006.

Lu Wei 陆伟. "Jieshao dongfeng yang lu chang de jingyan" 介绍东丰养鹿场的经验 [Introducing the experience of Dongfeng Deer Farm]. *Zhongyao Tongbao* 中药通报 Bulletin of Chinese Medicinals 3, no. 5 (1957): 187-189.

"Lurong qu fa yu yingye gai kuang" 鹿茸取法与营业概况 [Method to remove deer antler and business overview]. *Dong Sheng Jingji Gai Kuang* 东省经济月刊 Eastern Province Economic Monthly 4, no. 8 (1928): 19-20.

Ma Qinlin 马钦林. "Bu yao lan yong zhenji" 不要滥用针剂 [Do not misuse injection]. *Yaoxue Tongbao* 药学通报 Pharmaceutical Bulletin 11, no. 11 (1965): 517-518.

Ma Yucheng 马誉澄. "Yong cusuanjia zuo wei zhibei bian qingmeisu jiayan de jie jing fanying ji" 用醋酸钾作为制备苄青霉素钾盐的结晶反应剂 [Using potassium acetate as the reactant in the making of benzylpenicillin sodium]. *Yaoxue Tongbao* 药学通报 Pharmaceutical Bulletin 2, no. 5 (1954): 191-193.

MacFarquhar, Roderick. *The Origins of the Cultural Revolution*, vol. 1: *Contradictions among the People 1956-57*. New York: Columbia University Press, 1974.

MacFarquhar, Roderick. *The Origins of the Cultural Revolution*, vol. 2: *The Great Leap Forward 1958-1960*. New York: Columbia University Press, 1983.

MacFarquhar, Roderick, ed. *The Politics of China: Sixty Years of the People's Republic of China*. 3rd ed. Cambridge: Cambridge University Press, 2011.

MacFarquhar, Roderick, Timothy Cheek, and Eugene Wu, eds. *The Secret Speeches of Chairman Mao: From the Hundred Flowers to the Great Leap Forward*. Cambridge, MA: Harvard University Press, 1989.

Makino Isao and Tanaka Hirotoshi. "From a Choleretic to an Immunomodulator: Historical Review of Ursodeoxycholic Acid as a Medicament." *Journal of Gastroenterology and Hepatology* 13(1998): 659-664.

Makino Isao and Takebe Kazuo 牧野勳, 武部和夫. "Yuutan to ursodeoxycholic acid" 熊胆と Ursodeoxycholic acid. *Sogo Rinshō* 綜合臨 Comprehensive Clinical 31, no. 9 (1982): 2385-2387.

Manning, Kimberly Ens, and Felix Wemheuer, eds. *Eating Bitterness: New Perspectives on China's Great Leap Forward and Famine*. Vancouver: University of British Columbia Press, 2011.

Martin, Esmond Bradley. *The International Trade in Rhinoceros Products*. Gland, Switzerland: World Wildlife Fund, 1980.

Martinsen, Joel. "Chicken Blood Injections and Other Health Crazes." January 13, 2015. http://www.danwei.org/health_care_diseases_and_pharmaceuticals/chicken_blood_injections.php.

McKie, Robert. "Jaguars Killed for Fangs to Supply Growing Chinese Medicine Trade." *The Guardian*, March 4, 2018.

Meng Qian 孟谦. "Da po mixin jishu gexin duo kuai hao sheng di zuo hao zhongyaocai de shengchan gongying gongzuo" 打破迷信技术革新多快好省地做好中药材的生产供应工作 [Dispel superstition and conduct technological innovation to efficiently increase, accelerate and improve medicinal production]. *Zhongyao Tongbao* 中药通报 Bulletin of Chinese Medicinals 4, no. 9 (1958): 298-300.

Meng Qian 孟谦. "Fazhan shengchan, ti gao zhiliang, zuzhi zhongyaocai gongzuo da yuejin" 发展生产, 提高质量, 组织中药材工作大跃进. *Zhongyao Tongbao* 中药通报 4, no. 5 (1958): 150–151.

Meyer, Rowena. "Vladimir Petrovich Filatov." *American Review of Soviet Medicine* (December 1944).

Millikan, Tom, and Jo Shaw. *The South Africa-Vietnam Rhino Horn Trade Nexus*. Johannesburg: TRAFFIC, 2012.

Minter, Adam. "Bull Market for Bear Bile Leads to China IPO." Bloomberg. February 23, 2012. http://www.bloomberg.com/news/2012-02-23/bull-market-for-bear-bile-leads-to-china-ipo-adam-minter.html.

Mitcham, Chad J. *China's Economic Relations with the West and Japan, 1949-79: Grain, Trade and Diplomacy*. Oxford: Routledge, 2005.

Mommen, Andre. *The Belgian Economy in the Twentieth Century*. London: Routledge, 1994.

Nakayama Shigeru and Nathan Sivin, eds. *Chinese Science: Explorations of an Ancient Tradition*. Cambridge, MA: MIT Press, 1973.

Nappi, Carla. *The Monkey and the Inkpot*. Cambridge, MA: Harvard University Press, 2009.

"National Programs for Science and Technology." Accessed 14 January 2015. http://www.china.org.cn/english/features/Brief/,93304.htm.

Newer, Rachel. "To Sate China's Demand, African Donkeys Are Stolen and Skinned." *New York Times*, January 2, 2018.

Ni Guangping 倪广平. "'Zhongyao yaoli xue' du hou gan" "中药药理学" 读后感 [My feelings after reading *Chinese medicine pharmacology*]. *Yaoxue Tongbao* 药学通报 Pharmaceutical Bulletin 2, no. 12 (1954): 546.

"1958 nian guangdong sheng liuxing xing yixing naoyan zhongyi zhiliao gongzuo zong jie" 1958 年广东省流行性乙型脑炎中医治疗工作总结 1958 [Summary of using Chinese medicine to treat epidemic encephalitis B in Guangdong province]. *Guangdong Zhongyi* 广东中医 Guangdong Chinese Medicine 10 (1958): 2–4.

"Niuhuang shizhi chenggong touru shengchan" 牛黄试制成功投入生产 [Trial manufacturing of bezoar a success leading to actual production]. *Zhongyao Tongbao* 中药通报 Bulletin of Chinese Medicinals 2, no. 4 (1956) (originally published in *Yiyao Gongye Tongxun* 医药工业通讯 Medical Industry Newsletter 5 [1956]).

Nongye Bu Gongye Yuanliao Ju, Weisheng Bu Yaozheng Guanli Ju 农业部工业原料局, 卫生部药政管理局. *Zhongyaocai Shengchan Jishu* 中药材丰产栽培经验介绍第一集: 中药材生产技术 [Introducing the cultivation experiences of Chinese medicinals with high yield, part 1: Production technology]. Beijing: Renmin Weisheng Chu Ban She 人民卫生出版社, 1960.

Nowell, Kristin. "Tiger Farms and Pharmacies: The Central Importance of China's Trade Policy for Tiger Conservation." In *Tigers of the World: The Science, Politics, and Conservation of Panthera tigris*, edited by R. Tilson and P. J. Nyhus, 463-475. Amsterdam: Elsevier 2009.

Pan Shasha 潘莎莎 and Li Ruzhen 李儒珍. "Fufang xiongdan yan yaoshui dui shiyan xing tu jiaomo baiban de liaoxiao guancha" 复方熊胆眼药水对实验性兔角膜白斑的疗效观察 [Laboratory observations of the efficacy of compound drug bear bile eye drops on rabbits with corneal infections]. *Guangzhou Zhonyi Xueyuan Xuebao* 广州中医药学院学报 Journal of Guangzhou Chinese Medical College 6, no. 3 (1989): 143-145.

Pang Jingzhou, Yu Yunxiu, and He Yunhe 庞京周, 余云岫, 何云鹤. "Yanjiu zhong-yao de fangxiang he shunxu" 研究中药的方向和顺序 [Researching Chinese medicine and the direction and order to take]. *Xin Zhong Yiyao* 新中医药 New Chinese Medicine 2, no. 1 (1950): 4-6.

Panossian, Alexander, and Georg Wikman. "Pharmacology of *Shisandra chinensis* Bial.: An Overview of Russian Research and Uses of Medicine." *Journal of Ethnopharmacology* 118 (2008): 183-212.

Pei Weng 培翁. "Lurong de gushi" 鹿茸的故事 [The story of deer antler]. *Da Di Zhoubao* 大地周报 Earth Weekly 126 (1948): 11.

"Pipan zichan jieji fandong luxian: zaofan yundong de xianqi" 批判资产阶级反动路线: 造反运动的掀起 [Criticizing the bourgeois reactionary line: The start of the rebel movement]. Accessed March 30, 2014. http://www.cuhk.edu.hk/ics/21c/issue/articles/031_95206.pdf.

Pordie, Laurent, and Anita Hardon. "Drugs' Stories and Itineraries: On the Making of Asian Industrial Medicines." *Anthropology and Medicine* 22, no. 1 (2015): 1-6.

Pordie, Laurent, and Jean-Paul Gaudilliere. "Reformulation Regimes in Drug Discovery: Revisiting Polyherbals and Property Rights in the Ayurvedic Industry." *East Asian Science, Technology, and Society* 8, no. 1 (2014): 57-80.

Qi Fang 齐放. "Chong fen fahui you shi fazhan chuanghui nongye—guan yu jilin sheng fazhan chuanghui nongye de tantao" 充分发挥优势发展创汇农业— 关于吉林省发展创汇农业的探讨 [Fully unleash potential and develop export-oriented agriculture—Exploring Jilin province's development of export-oriented agriculture]. *Yanbian Nong Xue Yuan Xuebao* 延边农学院学报 Journal of Yanbian Agricultural College 2 (1987): 77-83.

Qianqian Qu. "A Study on the 'Going Out' Paths of Tourism Industry of TCM Health Preservation Culture Driven by One Belt, One Road." *Advances in Social Science, Education, and Humanities Research* 250 (2018): 253-258.

Qin Rongqian, Liang Fengxi, Bai Qingyu, Wang Shuzhi, and Chen Jinguo. 秦荣前, 梁凤锡, 白庆余, 王树志, 陈进国. "Kong guang cujin lurong shengzhang fayu de yanjiu" 控光促进鹿茸生长发育的研究 [Research on light and its role in promoting growth in deer antlers]. *Jilin Nongye Daxue Xuebao* 吉林农业大学学报 Journal of Jilin Agricultural University 7, no. 2 (1985): 31-36.

Qinghai Sheng Ba Yi Ba Youdian Zaofan Tuan Bianyin 青海省八一八邮电造反团编印. *Jixue Liaofa* 鸡血疗法 [Chicken blood therapy]. Qinghai Province Eight-One-Eight Post and Telecommunications Revolutionary Team, 1967.

"Qu nian changyi shexiang chu kou e, changyi san shi yi yuan shexiang shi yi yuan" 去年肠衣麝香出口额, 肠衣三十亿元麝香十亿元 [Last year's export value

for (sausage) casing and musk, casing 30 billion yuan musk 10 billion yuan].
Zhengxin Suo Bao 征信所报 Zhengxin Report 263 (1947).

"Rare White Rhino Dies, Leaving Only Four Left on the Planet." *National Geographic.* July 29, 2015. http://news.nationalgeographic.com/2015/07/150729 -rhinos-death-animals-science-endangered-species/.

"Ren zhen zuzhi he tui xing zuzhi liaofa" 认真组织和推行组织疗法 [Seriously organize and promote tissue therapy]. *Liangshi Yiyou* 良师益友 Good Teacher Good Friend 3 (1951): 75.

"Richard J. Goss, 1925–1996." Accessed April 19, 2014. http://www.sdbonline.org /sites/archive/SDBMembership/Goss.html.

Robinson. Jill. "China Rises against Bear Farming." Animals Asia. February 24, 2012. https://www.animalsasia.org/intl/social/jills-blog/2012/02/24/china -rises-against-bear-farming.

Sang Ye 桑晔. "Guoren meng yi xing?" 国人梦已醒？[Have the people awakened from their dreams?]. *Dushu* 读书 Reading 1 (March 1992): 141–145.

"Save the Sharks! Strange Cry Raised on West Coast." *Science News Letter* 41, no. 8 (1942): 120.

Saxer, Martin. *Manufacturing Tibetan Medicine: The Creation of an Industry and the Moral Economy of Tibetanness.* New York: Berghahn Books, 2013.

Scheid, Volker. *Chinese Medicine in Contemporary China: Plurality and Synthesis.* Durham, NC: Duke University Press, 2002.

Scheid, Volker. "Convergent Lines of Descent: Symptoms, Patterns, Constellations, and the Emergent Interface of Systems Biology and Chinese Medicine." *East Asian Science, Technology, and Society* 8, no. 1 (2014): 107–139.

Scheid, Volker. "The Globalization of Chinese Medicine." *The Lancet* 354 (December 1999): S1V10.

Scheid, Volker. "The People's Republic of China." In *Chinese Medicine and Healing,* edited by T. J. Hinrichs and Linda L. Barnes. Cambridge, MA: Belknap Press of Harvard University Press, 2013.

Schmalzer, Sigrid. "Youth and the 'Great Revolutionary Movement' of Scientific Experiment in 1960s–1970s Rural China." In *Maoism at the Grassroots: Everyday Life in China's Era of High Socialism,* edited by Jeremy Brown and Matthew D. Johnson. Cambridge, MA: Harvard University Press, 2015.

Schmalzer, Sigrid. "On the Appropriate Use of Rose-Colored Glasses: Reflections on Science in Socialist China." *Isis* 98, no. 3 (2007): 571–583.

Schmalzer, Sigrid. *Red Revolution, Green Revolution: Scientific Farming in Socialist China.* Chicago: University of Chicago Press, 2016.

Senov [*sic*], Y. P. 谢诺夫. "Sulian de yaoxue kexue he yaoxue shiye—wei "yaoxue tongbao" zuo" 苏联的药学科学和药学事业— 为"药学通报"作 [Pharmaceutical science and pharmaceutical work in Soviet Union—for the pharmaceutical bulletin]. *Yaoxue Tongbao* 药学通报 Pharmaceutical Bulletin 3, no. 11 (1955): 482–485.

Shaanxi Sheng Shengwu Ziyuan Kaocha Dui 陕西省生物资源考察队 [Shaanxi Province Biological Resources Expedition Team]. Shaanxi Sheng Zhenping Xian Yang She Shiyan Chang 陕西省镇坪县养麝实验场 [Shaanxi Province

Zhenping Country Musk Deer Experimental Farm]. "Xun she qu xiang" 驯
麝取香 [Training musk deer and collecting musk]. *Zhong Caoyao Tongxun* 中
草药通讯 Chinese Traditional and Herbal Drugs 4 (1973): 32–42.

Shandong Haiyang Yanjiu Suo Yao Yong Zu 山东海洋研究所药用组 [Shandong
Marine Research Institute Medicinal Team]. "Haiyang shengwu yao yong
yanjiu jian kuang" 海洋生物药用研究简况 [An update on research on marine-
based medicinals]. *Zhong Caoyao Tongxun* 中草药通讯 Chinese Traditional
and Herbal Drugs 6 (1972): 11–14.

Shandong Sheng Gougu Jiao Yaojiu Xiezuo Zu 山东省狗骨胶药酒协作组 [Shandong
Province Dog Bone Glue Wine Collaboration Team]. "Gougu jiao yaojiu de
yanjiu" 狗骨胶药酒的研究 [Research on dog bone glue wine]. *Zhong Caoyao
Tongxun* 中草药通讯 Chinese Traditional and Herbal Drugs 12 (1976): 12–15.

Shanghai Putao Tang Chang 上海葡萄糖场 [Shanghai Glucose Factory]. "Yang
Mao Zhi" 羊毛脂 [Lanolin]. *Yaoxue Tongbao* 药学通报 Pharmaceutical Bulletin 7, no. 3 (1959): 103–105.

Shanghai Renmin Chu Ban She Bian 上海人民出版社编 [Shanghai People's Publishing House]. *Qunzhong Yixue Cong Kan* 群众医学丛刊 2 [Medicine for the
masses, series no. 2]. Shanghai: Shanghai People's Publishing House, 1974.

Shanghai Shi Chuban Geming Zu 上海市出版革命组 [Shanghai Publishing Revolutionary Team]. *Mao Zedong Sixiang Zhao Liang Le Woguo Yixue Fazhan De Daolu* 毛
泽东思想照亮了我国医学发展的道路 [Shining the thoughts of Mao Zedong on
our path toward medical development]. Shanghai: Shanghaishi Chuban Geming Zu 上海市出版革命组 [Shanghai Publishing Revolutionary Team], 1970.

Shanghai Zhongyi Xue Yuan, ed. 上海中医学院 (now Shanghai University of Traditional Chinese Medicine). *Zhongyi Nianjian 1983* 中医年鉴 [1983 yearbook of
traditional Chinese medicine of China]. Beijing: Renmin Weisheng Chu Ban
She, 1984.

Shanghai Zhongyi Xue Yuan, ed. 上海中医学院 (now Shanghai University of
Traditional Chinese Medicine). *Zhongyi Nianjian 1986* 中医年鉴 1986 [1986
yearbook of traditional Chinese medicine of China]. Beijing: Renmin Weisheng Chu Ban She, 1987.

Shanghai Zhongyi Xue Yuan Hong Yi Ban Bianxie Zu 上海中医学院红医班编写组.
Hong Yi Ban Jiang Yi: Shiyong Jiaocai 红医班讲义: 试用教材 (1969).

Shangye Bu Yiyao Ju 商业部医药局. "Yiyao shangye shinian" 医药商业十年. *Yaoxue
Tongbao* 药学通报 7, no. 9 (1959): 433–437.

Shanqi Guangfu 山崎光夫 [Yamasaki Mitsuo]. *Riben Mingyao Daoyou* 日本名藥導遊
[A guide to famous Japanese drugs]. Taipei: Wangwen She, 2005.

Shanxi Sheng Shizhi Yanjiu Yuan Bian 山西省史志研究院编. *Shanxi Tongzhi Di 41
Juan Weisheng Yiyao Zhi Yiyao Bian* 山西通志第41卷卫生医药志: 医药编. Beijing:
Zhonghua Shuju, 1997.

Shapiro, Judith. *Mao's War against China: Politics and the Environment in Revolutionary
China*. Cambridge: Cambridge University Press, 2009.

"Shen wei 'chenliji' hou ren de gankai" 身为"陈李济"后人的感慨 [My feelings as
a descendant of Chenliji]. Accessed July 27, 2013. http://blog.sina.com.cn/s
/blog_648e221f0100089r.html.

Shikov, Alexander N., et al. "Medicinal Plants of the Russian Pharmacopoeia: Their History and Applications." *Journal of Ethnopharmacology* 154, no. 3 (2014): 481–536.

"Shuiniu jiao ju you xiniu jiao xiang tong de liao xiao" 水牛角具有犀牛角相同的疗效 [Water buffalo horns possess the same efficacy as rhinoceros horns]. *Shangchang Xiandai Hua* 商场现代化 Market Modernization Magazine 6 (1977): 24–25.

"Si nian lai wo guo yiyao gongye ri yi fazhan zhuang da" 四年来我国医药工业日益发展壮大 [Our pharmaceutical industry grows steadily in four years]. *Yaoxue Tongbao* 药学通报 Pharmaceutical Bulletin 2, no. 4 (1954): 172.

"Si nian lai wo guo yiyao gongye you xianzhu fazhan" 四年来我国医药工业有显著发展 [Pharmaceutical industry sees significant developments in four years]. *Renmin Ribao* 人民日报 People's Daily 133 (1954). http://www.ziliaoku.org/rmrb/1954-01-28-2.

"[Siyue mian dui mian] yuanshi li lianda: xiongdan fen yu yazhou" 四月网 (M4. CN) [四月面对面] 院士李连达: 熊胆粉与亚洲 [(April face to face) scholar Li Lian Da: Bear bile powder and Asia]. Accessed October 27, 2017. http://v.youku.com/v_show/id_XNDAxMTIxMDIo.html.

Sneader, Walter. *Drug Discovery: A History*. New York: Wiley, 2005.

Song Jingli. "Boosted by Belt and Road Initiative, Spread of TCM Speeds Up." China Daily.com.cn. June 4, 2018.

Song Xijing and Zhao Baozhen 宋希璟, 赵宝贞. "Zai tongrentang xuexi zhongyao de ji dian tihui" 在同仁堂学习中药的几点体会 [Some experiences from learning Chinese medicine at Tongrentang]. *Zhongyao Tongbao* 中药通报 Bulletin of Chinese Medicinals 2, no. 6 (1954): 260.

Soon, Wayne. "Blood, Soy Milk, and Vitality: The Wartime Origins of Blood Banking in China, 1943–45." *Bulletin of the History of Medicine* 90, no. 3 (2016): 424–454.

"South East MEP Pledges Support to End Animal Cruelty." Accessed April 21, 2014. http://sharonbowles.org.uk/en/article/2005/095752/south-east-mep-pledges-support-to-end-animal-cruelty.

Southgate, Paul, and John Lucas, eds. *The Pearl Oyster*. Oxford: Elsevier, 2008.

"Spark Programme." Accessed January 14, 2015. http://ie.china-embassy.org/eng/ScienceTech/ScienceandTechnologyDevelopmentProgrammes/t112842.htm.

Standaert, Michael, "China Raises Protection for Pangolins by Removing Scales from Medicine List." *The Guardian*, June 9, 2020.

Standaert, Michael. "'This Makes Chinese Medicine Look Bad': TCM Supporters Condemn Illegal Wildlife Trade." *The Guardian*, May 26, 2020.

State Administration of Traditional Chinese Medicine of People's Republic of China. *Anthology of Policies, Regulations and Laws of the People's Republic of China on Traditional Chinese Medicine*. Beijing, 1997.

Strickmann, Michael. *Chinese Magical Medicine*. Stanford, CA: Stanford University Press, 2002.

Su Huaide 苏怀德, ed. *Yaowu Yanjiu Shi Xuan Jiang* 药物研究史选讲 [Lectures on the history of drug research]. Beijing: Beijing Yike Daxue 北京医科大学, 1992.

Su Zhiwu 苏志武. "Wenge zhong 'da jixue' zhi guai zhuang" 文革中"打鸡血"之怪状 [The strange occurrence of chicken blood therapy during the Cultural Revolution], in *Wen Shi Jing Hua* 文史精华 (May 6, 2012): 41–46.

Sun Zulie 孙祖烈. "Lun lurong" 论鹿茸 [On deer antler]. *Minsheng Yiyao* 民生医药 People's Medicine 17 (1953): 12–13.

Suvendrini Kakuchi. "Japan: Demand Continues to Fuel Trade in Bear Products." Accessed October 6, 2017. http://www.ipsnews.net/2002/02/japan-demand -continues-to-fuel-trade-in-bear-products/.

"Synthetic Vitamin A Halts Shark Industry in Florida." *New York Times*, July 23, 1950.

Takahashi Shintaro and Nishikawa Misako 高橋真太郎, 西川ミサ子. "Shihan, Yuu-tan no Hinshitsu Kenkyu" 市販. 熊胆の品質研究 [A study of the quality of bear bile sold in the market]. *Yakugaku Kenykyū* 藥学研究 30:16–19.

Tan Min and Ma Shuming 谭敏, 马书明. "Zhongguo baojian yaopin shichang bingdu yingxiao chuanbo yiyuan yanjiu" 中国保健药品市场病毒营销传播意愿研究 [A study of the toxic spread of China's "health-drug product" market]. *Jingying Guanli Zhe* 经营管理者 Manager's Journal 16 (2016): 263–265.

Tan Zaiyang 谭在洋. "Jieshao chongqing shi zhongyao ren yuan ye wu xuexi de jingyan" 介绍重庆市中药人员业务学习的经验 [Introducing the business learning experiences of Chinese medicinal personnel in Chongqing City]. *Zhongyao Tongbao* 中药通报 Bulletin of Chinese Medicinals 3, no. 6 (1957): 230–235.

Tang, Didi. "Chinese Doctors Hail Return of Tiger and Rhino Remedies." *The Times*, November 3, 2018. https://www.thetimes.co.uk/article/chinese -doctors-hail-return-of-rhino-and-tiger-remedies-somvglvws.

Tang Guang 汤光. "Sulian shengyao yanjiu gongzuo de chengjiu" 苏联生药研究工作的成就 [The achievements of Soviet Union's research on raw medicinals]. *Yaoxue Tongbao* 药学通报 Pharmaceutical Bulletin 2, no. 5 (1954): 186–188.

Tatarinov, A. A. "Catalogus medicamentorum Sinensium, quae Pekini comparanda et determinanda curavit Alexander Tatarinov, Doctor medicinae, medicus Missionis Russicae Pekinensis spatio annorum 1840–1850." St. Petersburg: Petropoli, 1856.

Taylor, Kim. *Chinese Medicine in Early Communist China, 1945–63: A Medicine of Revolution*. London: Routledge, 2005.

Taylor, Kim. "Divergent Interests and Cultivated Misunderstandings: The Influence of the West on Modern Chinese Medicine." *Social History of Medicine* 17, no. 1 (2004): 93–111.

"Teaching and Research of China Pharmaceutical University." Accessed December 11, 2013. http://www.csc.edu.cn/cbu/Group2/China%20Pharmaceutical%20University.pdf.

Teiwes, Frederick C., and Warren Sun. *China's Road to Disaster: Mao, Central Politicians, and Provincial Leaders in the Unfolding of the Great Leap Forward 1955–1959*. New York: M.E. Sharpe, 1999.

Tensen, Laura. "Under What Circumstances Can Wildlife Farming Benefit Species Conservation?" *Global Ecology and Conservation* 6 (April 2016): 286–298.

Theng, Meryl. "Consumption of Endangered Antelope's Horn Remains High in Singapore." Saiga Conservation Alliance. August 13, 2018. https://saiga

-conservation.org/2018/08/13/consumption-of-the-endangered-saiga
-antelopes-horn-remains-high-in-singapore/.

Tianjin Shi Di Er Shangye Ju 天津市第二商业局. "Guan yu tongyi suoshu si ge
gongchang huagui gongye lingdao bing jianyi jiang tianjin zhi yao chang
rengong niuhuang chejian huagui wo ju lingdao de baogao" 关于同意所属
四个工厂划归工业领导并建议将天津制药厂人工牛黄车间划归我局领导的报告.
September 25, 1963. Unpublished report.

Tianjin Shi Di Er Shangye Ju 天津市第二商业局. "Guan yu zhongyaocai gongsi
muqian dui niuhuang shougou wenti de zhuanti baogao" 关于中药材公司目
前对牛黄收购问题的专题报告, June 12, 1958. Unpublished report.

Tianjin Shi Gonggong Weisheng Ju 天津市公共卫生局. "Tongyi nichang jiu
hedong qu ruwei lu 105 hao xiujian niuhuang chejian bing tichu weisheng
yaoqiu you" 同意你厂就河东区入伟路 105 号修建牛黄车间并提出卫生要求由,
June 7, 1957. Unpublished report.

Tianjin Shi Huaxue Gongye Ju 天津市化学工业局 [Tianjin Chemical Industry
Department]. "Guan yu jin chan rengong niuhuang deng yaopin yuanliao
gongying jinzhang qing qiu tongyi anpai de baogao" 关于津产人工牛黄等药
品原料供应紧张请求统一安排的报告 [A report to request for standardized arrangements to be made to solve a supply shortage of medical ingredients like
tianjin artificial bezoar]. April 14, 1959. Unpublished report.

Tianjin Shi Jingji Jihua Weiyuan Hui 天津市经济计划委员会 [Tianjin Economic
Planning Committee]. "Wei jianyi zhiding shengchu zonghe liyong de
tongyi guihua ji qingshi jiejue niuhuang deng yaopin yong liao you" 为建议
制定牲畜综合利用的统一规划及请示解决牛黄等药品用料由 [Proposal to plan
for all-around use of livestock and a request to resolve medical resources like
bezoar]. May 15, 1959. Unpublished report.

Tianjin Shi Wenhua Ju 天津市文化局. "Qing jianding hugu you wu wenhua jiazhi
you" 请鉴定虎骨有无文化价值由. December 1, 1960. Unpublished report.

Tianjin Shi Yaocai Gongsi Yanjiu Shi 天津市药材公司研究室 [Tianjin City Medicinal Company Research Laboratory]. "Xijiao bei" 犀角杯 [The rhinoceros
cup]. *Zhongyao Tongbao* 中药通报 Bulletin of Chinese Medicinals 4, no. 5
(1958): 164.

Tianjin Zhi Yao Chang 天津制药厂 [Tianjin Pharmaceutical Factory]. "Guoying
tianjin zhi yao chang guan yu jin yi bu gai jin niuhuang chejian sanfa qiwei
de cuoshi" 国营天津制药厂关于进一步改进牛黄车间散发气味的措施 [Measures
to improve the condition of odor emission from state-owned Tianjin pharmaceutical factory bezoar workshop]. February 23, 1957. Unpublished report.

"Traditional Chinese Medicine: China's Bear Farms Prompt Public Outcry." *Nature* 484 (April 26, 2012). http://www.researchgate.net/publication/224854954
_Traditional_Chinese_medicine_China's_bear_farms_prompt_public
_outcry .

Tsu Jing and Benjamin Elman, eds. *Science and Technology in Modern China, 1880s–
1940s.* Leiden: Brill, 2014.

"Tufang tufa wenzhai" 土方土法文摘 [Folk ways and methods: An abstract]. *Yaoxue
Tongbao* 药学通报 Pharmaceutical Bulletin 12, no. 4 (1966): 178–183.

Unschuld, Paul. *Medical Ethics in Imperial China: A Study in Historical Anthropology*. Berkeley: University of California Press, 1979.

Unschuld, Paul. *Medicine in China: A History of Ideas*. Berkeley: University of California Press, 2010.

Unschuld, Paul. *Medicine in China: A History of Pharmaceutics*. Comparative Studies of Health Systems and Medical Care. Berkeley: University of California Press, 1986.

Unschuld, Paul, and Jinsheng Zheng, eds. *Chinese Traditional Healing: The Berlin Collections of Manuscript Volumes from the 16th through the Early 20th Century*. Leiden: Brill, 2012.

Van Uhm, Daan P. *The Illegal Trade in Wildlife: Inside the World of Poachers, Smugglers, and Traders*. New York: Springer, 2016.

Vogel, Ezra. *One Step Ahead in China: Guangdong under Reform*. Cambridge, MA: Harvard University Press, 1989.

Vu, Hoai Nam Dang, and Martin Reinhardt Nielsen. "Understanding Utilitarian and Hedonic Values Determining the Demand for Rhino Horn in Vietnam." *Human Dimensions of Wildlife* 23, no. 5 (2018): 417–432.

Vyazemsky, E. S. Trans. Liu Zexian 刘泽先 译. "Sulian dui zhongyao de zhong shi" 苏联对中药的重视 [The Soviet Union places importance on Chinese herbs]. *Yaoxue Tongbao* 药学通报 Pharmaceutical Bulletin 2, no. 2 (1954): 64–65.

Walder, Andrew G. *China under Mao: A Revolution Derailed*. Cambridge, MA: Harvard University Press, 2015.

Walder, Andrew G. *Fractured Rebellion: The Beijing Red Guard Movement*. Cambridge, MA: Harvard University Press, 2009.

Wan Wenji 万文继. *Weitamin B1 Shenjing Xuewei Zhushe Liao Fa* 维他命 B1 神经穴位注射疗法. Wuhan: Hubei Renmin Chu Ban She, 1959.

Wang Fang 王芳. "Fang xia ge ren de mingli baofu, yukuai di danfu qi renmin gei yu de wei da renwu ba!" 放下个人的名利包袱，愉快地担负起人民给予的伟大任务吧! [Let's put aside fame and fortune, and happily take on the noble task given by the people!]. *Yaoxue Tongbao* 药学通报 Pharmaceutical Bulletin 3, no. 12 (1955): 555–556.

Wang Jinghui, Yan Li, Yinfeng Yang, Xuetong Chen, Jian Du, Qiusheng Zheng, Zongsuo Liang, and Yonghua Wang. "A New Strategy for Deleting Animal Drugs from Traditional Chinese Medicines Based on Modified Yimusake Formula." *Scientific Reports* 7, no. 1504 (2017).

Wang Jiuxiang 王九香. "Gan kuai peiyang zhongyao qing nian gongren" 赶快培养中药青年工人 [Hurry up and nurture pharmaceutical youth workers]. *Zhongyao Tongbao* 中药通报 Pharmaceutical Bulletin 2, no. 6 (1956): 260.

Wang Lingyun 王凌云. "Jilin sheng zheng zai choujian yi ge da xing luchang" 吉林省正在筹建一个大型鹿场 [Jilin province making preparations to construct large-scale deer farm]. *Zhongyao Tongbao* 中药通报 Bulletin of Chinese Medicinals 2, no. 4 (1956): 176.

Wang Ruoguang 王若光. "Dan bai zhi zu xue yanjiu yu zhong yiyao xue de yuan chuang xing fazhan" 蛋白质组学研究与中医药学的原创性发展. *Zhongguo Yiyao Xuebao* 中国医药学报 18, no. 10 (2003): 619–622.

Wang Shizhong 汪时中. "Cong niuxue zhong zhi qu dan yansuan zuzhi anjisuan (histidine monohydrochloride) de shiyan baogao" 从牛血中制取单盐酸组织胺基酸 (histidine monohydrochloride) 的实验报告 [A report on the experiment to extract histidine monohydrochloride from cow blood]. *Yaoxue Tongbao* 药学通报 Pharmaceutical Bulletin 2, no. 1 (1954): 24–26.

Wang Sufu 王素孚, trans. "Zuzhi liaofa he sheng yuan ciji wuzhi" 组织疗法和生原刺激物质 [Tissue therapy and (other) stimulants]. *Liangshi Yiyou* 良师益友 Good Teacher Good Friend, Zhongguo Yida Xuexi Hui Jishu Tongxun 中国医大学习会技术通讯 China Medical University Study Association Technology Newsletter 1 (1951): 19–21.

Wang Sufu 王素孚. "Zuzhi liaofa suo caiyong de zhongzhi zuzhi yingfou xuanze" 组织疗法所采用的种植组织应否选择 [Whether or not to go for substances used in tissue therapy]. *Liangshi Yiyou* 良师益友 Good Teacher Good Friend, Zhongguo Yida Xuexi Hui Jishu Tongxun 中国医大学习会技术通讯 China Medical University Study Association Technology Newsletter 1 (1951): 21–23.

Wang Wannan, Yongsong Liu, and Yunlong Duan. "Analysis on the Barriers and Countermeasures of Chinese Medicine Enterprises for Countries along the Belt and Road." *Advances in Economics, Business, and Management Research* 58 (2018): 316–322.

Wang Zhenkun 王振坤. "Yi du gong du" 以毒攻毒 [Using poison to attack poison]. *Zhongguo Weisheng Hua Bao* 中国卫生画报 China Hygiene Pictorial 2 (1984): 19.

Wang Zhipu and Cai Jingfeng, eds. 王致谱, 蔡景峰. *Zhongguo Zhong Yiyao 50 Nian (1949–1999)* 中国中医药 50 年 (1949–1999) [Fifty years of Chinese *yiyao*]. Fujian: Fujian Kexue Jishu Chu Ban She 福建科学出版社, 1999.

"Wei chuang li zuguo de xin yixue er fendou: quan guo zhongyi zhongyao gongzuo huiyi zai baoding juxing" 为创立祖国的新医学而奋斗: 全国中医中药工作会议在保定举行 [Strive to establish a new medicine in our motherland: National Chinese medicine conference held in Baoding]. *Yaoxue Tongbao* 药学通报 Pharmaceutical Bulletin 6, no. 12 (1958): 553–557.

Wei Chunjuan, Nancy, and Darryl E. Brock, eds. *Mr Science and Chairman Mao's Cultural Revolution: Science and Technology in Modern China*. Lanham, MD: Lexington Books, 2013.

"Weisheng bu ban bu ji shi shipin you shi yaopin mingdan" 卫生部颁布既是食品又是药品名单 [Ministry of Health releases a list of products to be both food and drug]. *Zhong Yiyao Xinxi* 中医药信息 Chinese Journal of Information on Traditional Chinese Medicine 2 (1988).

"Weisheng bu qiang diao: zhongyao bao jian yao yi lü bu zhun bao xiao" 卫生部强调: 中药保健药一律不准报销 [Ministry of health stresses all TCM health products to be non-reimbursable]. *Zhong Yiyao Xinxi* 中医药信息 Chinese Journal of Information on Traditional Chinese Medicine 2 (1988).

Weisheng Bu Zhi Shu Danwei 卫生部直属单位 [Ministry of Health Directed Unit]. "Sixiang jiefang gongzuo yuejin zhanlan hui" 思想解放工作跃进展览会 [Thought emancipation work leap exhibition]. *Zhongyao Tongbao* 中药通报 Bulletin of Chinese Medicinals 4, no. 9 (1958): 300.

Wen Musheng 温木生. *Xuewei Zhushe Liao Fa zhi Baibing* 穴位注射疗法治百病. Beijing: Renming Junyi Chu Ban She, 2003.

Wen Zhou 文周. "Ping 'zhongyao yaoli xue'" 评中药药理学 [Reviewing *Chinese medicine pharmacology*]. *Yaoxue Tongbao* 药学通报 Pharmaceutical Bulletin 2, no. 12 (1954): 544-546.

White, Aron. "Chinese Government Policy on Wildlife Trade: What Has Changed, What Has Not, and Why It Matters." RUSI.org, July 13, 2020.

Wu, Joyce. *Shark Fin and Mobulid Ray Gill Plate Trade in Mainland China, Hong Kong, and Taiwan*. Taipei: TRAFFIC, 2016.

Wu Ming 吴明. "'Da cai xiao yong' yu 'yao qiu guo gao'" "大材小用"与"要求过高" ["Putting fine timber to petty use" and "Too high an expectation"]. *Yaoxue Tongbao* 药学通报 Pharmaceutical Bulletin 3, no. 6 (1955): 274.

Wu Ruimin and Zang Fuke 伍锐敏, 臧福科. "Yi luxian wei gang, che di gai ge jiu jiaocai" 以路线为纲, 彻底改革旧教材 [The trajectory as main, thoroughly revise old textbooks thoroughly revise old textbooks]. *Xin Zhongyi* 新中医 New Chinese Medicine 5, no. 5 (1974): 2-4.

Wu Wan-Ying. "TCM-Based New Drug Discovery and Development in China." *Chinese Journal of Natural Medicine* 12, no. 4 (2014): 0241–0250.

Wu Weiyao 邬威尧. *Gu Jin Yin Zheng, Fo Yao Feng Liaoxing: Foshan Feng Liaoxing Yaoye Youxian Gongsi Fazhan Shi* 古今印证, 佛药冯了性: 佛山冯了性药业有限公司发展史. Guangzhou: Guangdong Keji Chu Ban She, 2012.

Wu Zhijing 伍稚荆. "Lao cheng jishi: huang tang de jixue liaofa" 老城纪事: 荒唐的鸡血疗法 [Old town chronicle: The absurd chicken blood therapy]. *Za Wen Xuan Kan* 杂文选刊 Journal of Selected Essays (March 21, 2008): 42.

Xi Gao. "Foreign Models of Medicine in Twentieth-Century China." In *Medical Transitions in Twentieth-Century China*, edited by Mary Brown Bullock and Bridie Andrews. Bloomington: Indiana University Press, 2014.

Xi Tongsheng 喜桐生. "Siyang dibi chong de chu bu jingyan" 饲养地必虫的初步经验 [Preliminary experiences of rearing ground beetle]. *Zhongyao Tongbao* 中药通报 4, no. 12 (1958): 421.

Xi'an Shi Di Si Yiyuan Yaofang 西安市第四医院药房 [Xi'an Number Four Hospital Pharmacy]. "Xiongdan, xiong she jiemo xia zhushe ye zhibei jieshao" 熊胆, 熊麝结膜下注射液制备介绍 [Introducing the preparation of injectable substance targeting the conjunctiva using bear bile and bear bile-musk]. *Yaoxue Tongbao* 药学通报 Pharmaceutical Bulletin 7, no. 3 (1959): 122–123.

Xiao Ge 萧戈. "Ying gai zhong shi yaocai shengchan" 应该重视药材生产 [Giving importance to medicinal production]. *Zhongyao Tongbao* 中药通报 Bulletin of Chinese Medicinals 2, no. 3 (1956): 93–94.

Xiao Peigen and Huang Junhua 萧培根, 黄俊华 [Zhongyang Weisheng Yanjiu Yuan 中央卫生研究院 Central Hygiene Research Institute]. "He sulian zhuanjia zai yi qi" 和苏联专家在一起 [Spending time with a Soviet expert]. *Yaoxue Tongbao* 药学通报 Pharmaceutical Bulletin 3, no. 10 (1955): 470.

Xie Haizhou. "Pipan zhi jieshou zhongyao er bu jieshou zhongyi de cuo wu sixiang" 批判只接受中药而不接受中医的错误思想 [Criticizing the wrong thinking of accepting Zhongyi but rejecting Zhongyao]. *Yaoxue Tongbao* 药学通报 Pharmaceutical Bulletin 3, no. 4 (1955): 148–149.

Xie Haizhou. "Zhongguo yaoxue hui ge di fen hui jiji kaizhan zhongyao de yanjiu zheng li gongzuo" 中国药学会各地分会积极开展中药的研究整理工作 [All branches of the Chinese pharmacology association are actively carrying out research and organization work]. *Yaoxue Tongbao* 药学通报 Pharmaceutical Bulletin 3, no. 2 (1955): 94–95.

Xie Yongguang 谢永光. *Xiang Gang Zhong Yiyao Shi Hua* 香港中医药史话 [A history of traditional Chinese medicine in Hong Kong]. Hong Kong: Joint Publishing, 1998.

Ximen Lusha. "Herbal Medicines a Boon to Co-op Medical Care." *Medicine in China* (1979; China Reconstructs issue): 35–40.

"Xin de yi dai yisheng zai cheng zhang—ji guangdong zhongyi xue yuan ji ge gong-nongbing biye sheng" 新的一代医生在成长— 记广东中医学院几个工农兵毕业生 [The rise of a new generation doctors—Remembering the few worker-peasant-soldier student graduates of Guangdong Chinese Medical College]. *Xin Zhongyi* 新中医 New Chinese Medicine 5 (1974): 9–11.

Xin Dingkang 忻定康. "Qite de mayi shiliao" 奇特的蚂蚁食料 [The strange food cure that is ants]. *Zhongguo Weisheng Huakan* 中国卫生画刊 China Hygiene Pictorial 4 (1987): 23.

"Xinan zhi yao gongye you xianzhu fazhan" 西南制药工业有显著发展 [Significant developments of the southwest pharmaceutical industry]. *Yaoxue Tongbao* 药学通报 Pharmaceutical Bulletin 2, no. 2 (1954): 34–35.

"Xinghuo jihua" 星火计划. Accessed April 16, 2014. https://zh.wikipedia.org/wiki/星火计划.

"Xinhua Insight: Animal Rights or Human Health? Chinese Medicine at the Crossroads." December 6, 2016. http://www.xinhuanet.com//english/2016-12/06/c_135885083.htm.

Xu Chang Di Gewei Kewei 许昌地革委科委. *Zhong Caoyao Zhushe Ji Ziliao Ke Xuan Bian* 中草药注射剂资料科选编. Xu Chang Di Kewei Weisheng Ju, 1979.

Xu Yecheng 许业诚. "Zhongyi kexue hua yi ban dou ren zuo xiyi hua" 中医科学化一般都认作西医化 [Many confuse "Scientize Chinese medicine" with "Westernize Chinese medicine"]. *Xin Zhong Yiyao* 新中医药 New Chinese Medicine 2, no. 11 (1950): 14.

Xue Yu 薛愚. "Jieke siluo fa'ke de yaoxue jiaoyu" 捷克斯洛伐克的药学教育 [The pharmaceutical education of Czechoslovakia]. *Yaoxue Tongbao* 药学通报 Pharmaceutical Bulletin 2, no. 1 (1954): 35–37.

Xue Yu 薛愚. "Yong shiji xing dong yonghu renmin zi ji de xianfa" 用实际行动拥护人民自己的宪法 [Use practical actions to protect the people's constitution]. *Yaoxue Tongbao* 药学通报 Pharmaceutical Bulletin 2, no. 7 (1954): 269–271.

Xue Yu 薛愚. "Zheng li he yanjiu zu guo kexue wenhua yichan—zhongyao" 整理和研究祖国科学文化遗产— 中药 [Organize and research on our country's scientific and cultural legacy—Chinese medicinals]. *Yaoxue Tongbao* 药学·通报 Pharmaceutical Bulletin 3, no. 1 (1955): 5–9.

Yamazaki Mitsuyoshi 山崎三省. "Kumanoi no kagaku to yakuri sayō" 熊胆の化学と薬理作用. *Wakan Yaku* 和漢藥 Rinjin zō kango 臨時増刊号 10 (1973): 295–299.

Yan Cangshan 严苍山. "Zhongyi jinxiu zhi tujing" 中医进修之途径 [The way to advance Chinese medicine]. *Xin Zhong Yiyao* 新中医药 New Chinese Medicine 2, no. 2 (1950): 5–6.

Yan Chaofu and Chen Yinqing 晏朝福, 陈寅卿. "Dongbei di fang guoying luchang shengchan qing kuang he lurong zhibei fang fa de diaocha" 东北地方国营鹿场生产情况和鹿茸制备方法的调查 [An investigation of deer antler production and preparation methods at government-owned deer farms in the northeast region]. *Zhongyao Tongbao* 中药通报 Bulletin of Chinese Medicinals 1, no. 1 (1955): 15–17.

"Yanbian Korean Autonomous Prefecture, The." Accessed December 25, 2014. http://www.china.org.cn/english/travel/53647.htm.

Yang Bin. Review of *Birds and Beast in Chinese Texts and Trade: Lectures Related to South China and the Overseas World*, Roderick Ptak. *East Asian Science, Technology, and Medicine* 37 (2013): 107–110.

Yang Guoxuan 杨国萱. *Darentang De Gushi* 达仁堂的故事 [The story of Darentang]. Tianjin: Tianjin Renmin Chu Ban She 天津人民出版社, 2004.

Yang Jisheng. *Tombstone: The Great Chinese Famine, 1958-1962*. New York: Farrar, Straus and Giroux, 2012.

Yang Nianqun 杨念群. *Zai Zao "Bing Ren": Zhong Xi Yi Chong Tu Xia De Kongjian Zhengzhi (1832-1985)* 再造 '病人': 中西医冲突下的空间政治 (1832-1985) [Remaking "patients": The spatial politics of Chinese-Western medicines]. Beijing: Zhongguo Renmin Daxue Chu Ban She, 2006.

Yang, Timothy. "Selling an Imperial Dream: Japanese Pharmaceuticals, National Power, and the Science of Quinine Self-Sufficiency." *EASTS* 6 (2012): 101–125.

Yang Xionghui 杨雄辉, ed. *De Zai Yao Zhong, Yao Wei Dazhong: Foshan Dezhong Yaoye Youxian Gongsi Fazhan Shi* 德在药中 药为大众: 佛山德众药业有限公司发展史. Guangzhou: Guangdong Keji Chu Ban She, 2011.

Yaoxue Tongbao 药学通报. "Ying jie wo kan chuang kan hou de di san nian" 迎接我刊创刊后的第三年. *Yaoxue Tongbao* 药学通报 3, no. 1 (1955): 24.

Ye Haichang 叶海昌. "Bihu zai linchuang shang de yingyong" 壁虎在临床上的应用. *Xin Zhongyi* 新中医 1 (1976): 50.

Ye Niandao 叶年道. "Ying zhong shi jineijin de shougou gongzuo" 应重视鸡内金的收购工作 [Placing importance on chicken gizzard procurement]. *Zhongyao Tongbao* 中药通报 Bulletin of Chinese Medicinals 4, no. 6 (1958): 217.

Ye Sanduo 叶三多. "Xue xi sulian xian jin jingyan wo men ying dang ziji shengchan yaowu" 学习苏联先进经验我们应当自己生产药物 [We should learn from Soviet Union's advanced experience and produce our own drugs]. *Yaoxue Tongbao* 药学通报 Pharmaceutical Bulletin 2, no. 1 (1954): 16–17.

Ye Sanduo 叶三多. "Zheng li zhongyao yao xishou sulian xian jin jingyan" 整理中药要吸收苏联先进经验 [Absorb the advanced experience of Soviet Union when organizing Chinese medicinals]. *Yaoxue Tongbao* 药学通报 Pharmaceutical Bulletin 2, no. 5 (1954): 188–190.

Yerka, Bob. "Chinese Scientists Call for Ban on Bear Farming." Accessed April 23, 2014. http://phys.org/news/2012-04-chinese-scientists-farming.html.

Yi San Jiu Liu Budui Weisheng Dui 1396 部队卫生队 [Platoon 1936 Hygiene Team]. "Yong zhu danzhi jinpao lüdou fen zhiliao liji, changyan" 用猪胆汁浸泡禄豆粉治疗痢疾, 肠炎 [Treating dysentery and enteritis with green bean powder soaked in pig bile]. *Zhong Caoyao Tongxun* 中草药通讯 Chinese Traditional and Herbal Drugs 1 (1971): 45.

"[Yixue shi] 20 shiji 40 nian dai wo guo de qingmeisu yan zhi gongzuo" [医学史] 20 实际40年代我国的青霉素研制工作 [(Medical history) Our country's research and work on penicillin during the 1940s]. Accessed September 14, 2013. http://bbs.club.sohu.com/read_elite.php?b=144278397&a=1875458.

Yu Changshi 俞昌时, "Jixue liaofa de kaishi" 鸡血疗法的开始 [The Beginning of chicken blood therapy]. In Qinghai Sheng Ba Yi Ba Youdian Zaofan Tuan Bianyin, *Jixue Liaofa* 鸡血疗法 [Chicken blood therapy]. Qinghai Province Eight-One-Eight Post and Telecommunications Revolutionary Team, 1967.

Yu Jing and Wang Xiaonan. "Will TCM Finally Gain Global Acceptance amid COVID-19?" CGTN. June 16, 2020. https://news.cgtn.com/news/2020-06-14/Will-Chinese-medicine-finally-gain-global-acceptance-amid-COVID-19--RjPubXostW/index.html.

Yu, Wufei. "Coronavirus: Revenge of the Pangolins?" *New York Times*, March 5, 2020.

Yu Xiao 欲晓. "Yudan zhi bing ye zhi ming" 鱼蛋治病也致命 [Fish roe can cure and also kill]. *Zhongguo Weisheng Huakan* 中国卫生画刊 China Hygiene Pictorial 1 (1984): 47.

Yu Zhongfan 于仲范. "Guangjiao ban yu shuiniu jiao ban de jianbie" 广角瓣与水牛角瓣的鉴别 [Identifying rhinoceros horn parts from water buffalo horn parts]. *Zhongyao Tongbao* 中药通报 Bulletin of Chinese Medicinals 11, no. 7 (1986): 16.

Yuan Chengye 袁承业. "Sulian de zhi yao huaxue yanjiu gongzuo ji huaxue zhi yao gong ye—zai zhongguo yaoxue hui beijing fen hui ji shanghai fen hui de jiang gao" 苏联的制药化学研究工作及化学制药工业— 在中国药学会北京分会及上海分会的讲稿 [Pharmaceutical chemistry research and the synthetic drug industry of Soviet Union—Lectures made by the Beijing and Shanghai branches of the Chinese Pharmaceutical Association]. *Yaoxue Tongbao* 药学通报 Pharmaceutical Bulletin 4, no. 4 (1956): 148–151.

Yuan Qingcheng and Liu Hong 袁庆成, 刘宏. "Chufang li wupin de kexue bu zhi" 厨房里物品的科学布置 [Displaying kitchenware the scientific way]. *Zhongguo Weisheng Huakan* 中国卫生画刊 China Hygiene Pictorial 2 (1984): 23.

Yuan Shicheng 袁士诚. "Wei da zuguo de yaowu ziyuan ji qi liyong kafei yin de yuanliao—cha ye" 伟大祖国的药物资源及其利用咖啡因的原料— 茶叶 [The drug resources of our great motherland and their utilization: The source of caffeine—tea leaves]. *Yaoxue Tongbao* 药学通报 Pharmaceutical Bulletin 2, no. 1 (1954): 38–40.

Yuan Shicheng and Kang Tai 袁士诚, 康泰. "Zhonghua renmin gonghe guo yao-dian 1963 nian ban jianjie" 中华人民共和国药典 1963 年版简介 [An introduction to the People's Republic of China pharmacopoeia 1963 edition]. *Yaoxue Tongbao* 药学通报 Pharmaceutical Bulletin 10, no. 7 (1964): 289–292.

Zeng Shaoqi 曾绍奇. "Beijing shi zhongyao dian men shi gongzuo zhong de que dian" 北京市中药门市工作中的缺点. *Zhongyao Tongbao* 中药通报 4, no. 3 (1958): 107.

Zevin, Igor Vilevich. *A Russian Herbal: Traditional Recipes for Health and Healing.* Rochester, VT: Healing Arts Press, 1997.

Zhan, Mei. *Otherworldly: Making Chinese Medicine through Transnational Frames.* Durham, NC: Duke University Press, 2009.

Zhang Feng Ying 张凤瀛 and Wu Baoling 吴宝铃. "Woguo de haixing" 我国的还行 [The starfish of our country]. 生物学通报 [Bulletin of biology] 6 (1956): 5–9.

Zhang Haoliang 张浩良. "Jie shao xijiao dai yong pin" 介绍犀角代用品 [Introducing replacements for rhinoceros horns]. *Jiangsu Yiyao* 江苏医药 Jiangsu Medical Journal 3 (1977): 34.

Zhang Mengnong 张梦侬. "Guan yu e ya xue zhi yege yu wei'ai de ji dian kan fa" 关于鹅鸭血治噎膈与胃癌的几点看法 [Some thoughts on using the blood of goose and duck to cure dysphagia and stomach cancer]. *Xin Zhongyi* 新中医 New Chinese Medicine 6 (1976): 9–42.

Zhang Minggao 张鸣皋. *Yaoxue Fazhan Jian Shi* 药学发展简史 [A history of the development of pharmaceutics]. Beijing: Zhongguo Yiyao Keji Chu Ban She, 1993.

Zhang Tianmin 张天民, Shandong Yixue Yuan Yaoxue Xi 山东医学院药学系 [Shandong Medical College School of Pharmacy]. "Zangqi shenghua yaowu de gai kuang he zhan wang" 脏器生化药物的概况和展望 [Organo-pharmaceutics: Present and future]. *Yaoxue Tongbao* 药学通报 14, no. 6 (1979): 272–276.

Zhang Yingcai 张颖才. "Yaocai shengchan fangmian cun zai de ji ge wen ti" 药材生产方面存在的几个问题 [Some problems regarding medicinal production]. *Zhongyao Tongbao* 中药通报 Bulletin of Chinese Medicinals 4, no. 5 (1958): 153–154.

Zhang Yingguang 张迎光. "Cong dongwu danzhi zhong zhi qu qu yang dansuan yu dansuan" 从动物胆汁中制取去氧胆酸与胆酸 [Preparing deoxycholic acid and cholic acid from animal bile]. *Yaoxue Tongbao* 药学通报 Pharmaceutical Bulletin 6, no. 11 (1958): 532–537.

Zhang Zhihou 张执侯. "Wei da zuguo de yaowu ziyuan ji qi liyong—chong la yu feng la" 伟大祖国的药物资源及其利用— 虫蜡与蜂蜡 [The medicinal resources of our great motherland and tapping them—insect wax and beeswax]. *Yaoxue Tongbao* 药学通报 Pharmaceutical Bulletin 3, no. 3 (1955): 130–131.

Zhang Zhongde 张忠德. "Zhi yao ken zhuanyan, jiu neng xue hui: jieshao wo zen yang xue hui feng anbu" 只要肯专研, 就能学会: 介绍我怎样学会封安瓿 [Learning through experimentation: How we learned to seal an ampoule]. *Yaoxue Tongbao* 药学通报 Pharmaceutical Bulletin 2, no. 7 (1954): 309–310.

Zhang Zidong 张紫洞. "Lurong jing zhushe ye de zhiliang yaoqiu ru he? Guo qi wu ge yue hou shang ke yingyong fou? shifou hui fasheng buliang fanying?" 鹿茸精注射液的质量要求如何? 过期五个月后尚可应用否? 是否会发生不良反应? [What is the quality requirement for deer essence injection substance? Still possible to use five months past expiry date? Will there be negative side effects?]. *Yaoxue Tongbao* 药学通报 Pharmaceutical Bulletin 9, no. 5 (1963): 200.

Zhejiang Huzhou Zhi Yao Chang 浙江湖州制药厂 [Zhejiang Huzhou Pharmaceutical Factory]. "Shuiniu jiao bang pian he jiao jian fensui de gongyi gaijin" 水牛角镑片和角尖粉碎的工艺改进 [Technique improvement on converting water buffalo horn slices and apex into powder form]. *Zhong Chengyao Yanjiu* 中成药研究 Chinese Medicine Research 2 (1979): 22.

Zhejiang Yixue Yuan Yaoxue Xi Yaoji Xue Jiao Yan Zu 浙江医学院药学系药剂学
教研组 [Zhejiang Medical College Department of Pharmacy Teaching and
Research Team for Pharmaceutics]. "Ping li jiaren bian zhu 'shi yong tiaoji
yu zhiji xue'" 评李佳仁编著 "实用调剂与制剂学" [A criticism of *Practical pharmacy and pharmaceutics* by Li Jiaren]. *Yaoxue Tongbao* 药学通报 Pharmaceutical
Bulletin 3, no. 3 (1955): 123–126.

Zhen Zhiya 甄志亚, ed. *Gao Deng Yiyao Yuan Xiao Jiao Cai Zhongguo Yixue Shi* 高等
医药院校教材中国医学史 [Teaching materials for higher medical colleges:
Chinese medical history]. Shanghai: Shanghai Kexue Jishu Chu Ban She 上
海科学技术出版社, 1997.

Zheng Hong 郑洪. "Ming fen you guan: jin dai zheng zhi zhong de zhong xiyi
cheng wei zhi zheng" 名分攸关: 近代政制中的中西医称谓之争 [Of names
and status: The battle between "Chinese medicine" and "Western modern
governance medicine"]. In *Zhongguo Shehui Lishi Pinglun* 中国社会历史评论 [A
commentary on the social history of China], 338–352. Vol. 13. Tianjin: Tianjin
Guji Chu Ban she, 2012.

Zheng Qidong 郑启栋. "Beijing tongrentang yaopu zai yuejin zhong" 北京同仁堂药
铺在跃进中 [Beijing Tongrentang Medicinal Shop is in the leap movement].
Zhongyao Tongbao 中药通报 Bulletin of Chinese Medicinals 4, no. 4 (1958): 2.

Zheng Yihua 郑亦化. "Bihu zuzhi ye de zhibei he yingyong" 壁虎组织液的制备和应
用 [The preparation and application of lizard extract]. *Yaoxue Tongbao* 药学通
报 Pharmaceutical Bulletin 2, no. 2 (1954): 81.

Zhivkov [*sic*], A. (*Sulian "Yiwu Gongzuo Zhe" Bao* Zhubian). Trans. Bai Hanyu 西瓦
柯夫 (苏联'医务工作者'报主编)白汉玉译 "Sulian de yaoji ye" (苏联的药剂业)
[Soviet Union and its pharmacy]. *Yaoxue Tongbao* 药学通报 Pharmaceutical
Bulletin 3, no. 10 (1955): 443–444.

Zhong Jianguang 钟建光. "'Shi zi hao' yu 'yao jian zi hao' de qubie" 食字号"与"药
健字号"的区别 [The difference between "a number in the food category" and
"a number in the drug category"]. *Hunan Laonian* 湖南老年 Hunan Old Age
12 (1995): 36.

Zhong Yuan 仲远. "Ji Chuan Xi Lurong Shenghui" 记川西鹿茸盛会 [On Chuanxi
deer antler event]. Xian Dai Yiyao Zazhi 现代医药杂志 Journal of Contemporary Medicine 3, nos. 35/36 (1949): 11–12.

Zhongguo Baojian Xiehui 中药保健协会 [China Health Care Association]. http://
www.chc.org.cn/.

"Zhongguo linye keji chengguo guanli xinxi xitong" 中国林业科技成果管理信息系
统 [Chinese forestry science and technology results and information management system]. Accessed April 20, 2014. http://smbkforestry.gov.cn:8099
/lyj/main/ShowDetail.jsp?id=13790.

Zhongguo Renmin Jiefang Jun 157 Yiyuan 中国人民解放军157医院. "Xuexi weiwu
bianzheng fa nu li zhua hao zhong xiyi jiehe de keyan miaotou" 学习唯物辩
证法努力抓好中西医结合的科研苗头. *Xin Zhongyi* 新中医 2 (1973): 48–51.

Zhongguo Shengli Kexue Hui Yaoli Zhuanye Mishu Zu 中国生理科学会药理专业秘
书组 [Chinese Physiological Science Society Pharmacology Secretariat], ed.
Xunzhao Xin Yao De Lilun Jichu He Linchuang Shiji: Zhongguo Shengli Kexue Hui

Yaoli Zhuanye Di Yi Jie Xueshu Taolun Hui Zhuan Ji 寻找新药的理论基础和临床实际: 中国生理科学会药理专业第一届学术讨论会专集 [The theory and practice of new drug discovery: A special issue based on the First Chinese Physiological Science Society Pharmacology Symposium]. Shanghai: Shanghai Kexue Jishu Chu Ban She 上海科学技术出版社, 1962.

Zhongguo Yaocai Gongsi Tianjin Shi Gongsi 中国药材公司天津市公司 [Chinese Medicinal Company Tianjin Office]. "Shenqing Difang Waihui Zuzhi Huanglian Xijiao Jin kou Jiejue Shichang Gongying Jinzhang You" 申请地方外汇组织黄连犀角进口解决市场供应紧张由 [An appeal to import rhinoceros horn and *huanglian* to ease market supply crisis], July 4, 1957. Unpublished report.

Zhongguo Yaoxue Hui 中国药学会译 [Chinese Pharmaceutical Association], trans. *Suweiai Shehui Zhuyi Gonghe Guo Lianmeng Guojia Yaodian Di Ba Ban* 苏维埃社会主义共和国联盟国家药典第 8 版 [The pharmacopoeia of the Union of Soviet Socialist Republics, 8th ed.]. Beijing: Renmin Weisheng Chu Ban She, 1959.

Zhongguo Yaoxue Nianjian Bian Ji Weiyuan Hui 中国药学年鉴编辑委员会 [China Pharmaceutical Yearbook Editorial Committee]. *Zhongguo Yaoxue Nianjian 1991* 中国药学年鉴 1991 [China pharmaceutical yearbook 1991]. Beijing: Renmin Weisheng Chu Ban She, 1991.

Zhongguo yao yong dong wu zhi xie zuo zu bian zhu, ed. 中国药用动物志协作组编著. Zhongguo yao yong dong wu zhi 中国药用动物志 [Chinese medicinal animals], vol. 1. Tianjin shi: Tianjin ke xue ji shu chu ban she, 1979. (Volume 2 of this two-volume work published in 1983).

Zhongguo Yiyao Gongsi Jilin Sheng Gongsi 中国医药公司吉林省公司, ed. *Nongcun Changyong Chengyao Shouce* 农村常用成药手册. Changchun: Jilin Renmin Chu Ban She, 1966.

"Zhongguo yiyao gongsi que ding zengjia zuzhi guo chan huoyuan, cujin xin yao xia xiang" 中国医药公司确定增加组织国产货源, 促进新药下乡 [The Chinese Medicinal Company confirms increasing and organizing sources of supply, and also promoting new drugs in villages]. *Yaoxue Tongbao* 药学通报 Pharmaceutical Bulletin 2, no. 3 (1954): 128.

Zhongguo Zhongyi Kexue Yuan 中国中医科学院. Accessed February 6, 2014. http://www.catcm.ac.cn/.

Zhonghua Renmin Gonghe Guo Dui Wai Jingji Maoyi Bu 中华人民共和国对外经济贸易部 [People's Republic of China Foreign Trade Department]. *Dui wai maoyi tongji ziliao huibian, 1950–1989* 对外贸易统计资料汇编 1950–1989 [Compilation of foreign trade statistics 1950–1989]. October 1990. Unpublished report.

Zhonghua Renmin Gonghe Guo Weisheng Bu Yaozheng Guanli Ju 中华人民共和国卫生部药政管理局, ed. *Zhongyaocai Feng Chan Zaipei Jingyan Jieshao Di Yi Ji* 中药材丰产栽培经验介绍 第一集 [Introducing the cultivation experiences of Chinese medicinals with high yield part 1: Production technology]. Beijing: Renmin Weisheng Chu Ban She 人民卫生出版社, 1959.

Zhonghua Renmin Gonghe Guo Weisheng Bu Yaozheng Guanli Ju 中华人民共和国卫生部药政管理局 [People's Republic of China Health Ministry Drug Administration Bureau], ed. *Zhongyaocai Yesheng Bian Jia Zhong Jia Yang*

Chenggong De Jingyan Jieshao Di Yi Ji 中药材野生变家种家养成功的经验介绍 第
一集 [Introducing the successful experiences of converting wild Chinese
medicinals into home cultivation, home rearing part 1]. Beijing: Renmin
Weisheng Chu Ban She 人民卫生出版社, 1959.

Zhonghua Renmin Gonghe Guo Yaodian 1953 Nian Ban 中华人民共和国药典 1953 年版
[The pharmacopoeia of the People's Republic of China 1953 edition]. Shanghai: Shangwu Yinshu Guan Chuban 商务印书馆出版, 1953.

Zhongyang Renmin Zhengfu Weisheng Bu 中央人民政府卫生部 [Central People's
Government Ministry of Health]. "Guan yu zuzhi liaofa de wu xiang zan xing
gui ding" 关于组织疗法的五项暂行规定 [About tissue therapy and five interim
regulations]. *Liangshi Yiyou* 良师益友 Good Teacher Good Friend, Zhongguo
Yida Xuexi Hui Jishu Tongxun 中国医大学习会技术通讯 China Medical University Study Association Technology Newsletter Z2 (1951): 75–80.

Zhongyang Renmin Zhengfu Weisheng Bu Yizheng Chu 中央人民政府卫生部医政
处 [Medical Department of the Ministry of Health for the Central People's
Government]. "Zuzhi liaofa zai wo guo de fazhan" 组织疗法在我国的发展
[The development of tissue therapy in our country]. *Liangshi Yiyou* 良师益友
Good Teacher Good Friend, Zhongguo Yida Xuexi Hui Jishu Tongxun 中国
医大学习会技术通讯 China Medical University Study Association Technology Newsletter Z2 (1951): 218–220.

"Zhongyang yanjiu yuan huaxue yanjiu suo yaopin zhizao bu sheli ji zhangcheng
cao'an" 中央研究院化学研究所药品制造部设立及章程草案, September 1936.
Unpublished report.

Zhongyi Yanjiu Yuan Zhongyao Yanjiu Suo 中医研究院中药研究所 [Chinese Medicine Research Institute Department for Research on Chinese Drugs]. "Jian
guo shi nian lai zhongyao yanjiu gongzuo de chengjiu" 建国十年来中药研究
工作的成就 [Research on Chinese medicinals and its achievements during
the ten years of nation-building]. *Yaoxue Tongbao* 药学通报 Pharmaceutical
Bulletin 7, no. 9 (1959): 438–442.

Zhou, Kate. *China's Long March to Freedom: Grassroots Modernization*. New Bruns-
wick, NJ: Transaction Publishers, 2009.

Zhou Enlai 周恩来. "Ba yesheng zhiwu chong fen li yong qi lai guowu yuan zhishi
ge di quan mian guihua tongyi an'pai ding qi jiancha" 把野生植物充分利用
起来国务院指示各地全面规划统一安排定期检查 [The State Council for Full
Utilization of Wild Fauna and Flora instructs all parts of China to plan,
standardize, and conduct regular checks]. *Zhongyao Tongbao* 中药通报 Bulletin of Chinese Medicinals 4, no. 6 (1958): 181–182.

Zhou Jun 周军 et al. "Mayi de yao yong yanjiu jinzhan" 蚂蚁的药用研究进展 [Cur-
rent research on ants for medicinal purpose]. *Guangxi Zhong Yiyao* 广西中医
药 Guangxi Journal of Traditional Chinese Medicine 14, no. 2 (1991): 90–92.

Zhou Liling 周莉玲. "Zhong caoyao zhushe ji yu rong xue" 中草药注射剂与溶血.
Xin Zhongyi 2 (1980): 53–55.

Zhou Lushan 周路山. *Zhongyao Shijia Caizhilin: Guangzhou Caizhilin Yaoye Youxian
Gongxi Fazhan Shi* 中药世家采芝林: 广州采芝林药业有限公司发展史 [Caizhilin:

The development history of Guangzhou Caizhilin Pharmaceutical Co. Ltd.].
Guangzhou: Guangdong Keji Chu Ban She 广东科技出版社, 2011.

Zhu Chao and Zhang Weifeng 朱潮, 张慰丰, eds. *Xin Zhongguo Yixue Jiao Yu Shi*
新中国医学教育史 [Chinese medicine educational history of new China].
Beijing: Beijing Yike Daxue and Zhongguo Xiehe Yike Daxue, 1990.

Zhu Liangchun 朱良春. *Chong Lei Yao De Yingyong* 虫类药的应用 [Using insects as
medicine]. Nanjing: Jiangsu Keji Chu Ban She, 1981.

Zhu Longyu 朱龙玉. *Shenjing Zhushe Liao Fa* 神经注射疗法 [Nerve injection
therapy]. Xi'an: Shanxi Renmin Chu Ban She 陕西人民出版社, 1959.

Zhu Sheng 朱晟. "E guo xue zhe bulaixilide he ta de zhu zuo 'zhongguo zhiwu'—
you wang jimin: 'bencao gangmu wai wen yi ben tan' yi wen tan qi" 俄国学者
布来希里德和他的著作 "中国植物"— 由王吉民: "本草纲目外文译本谈"一文谈起
[Russian scholar Bretschneider and his work "Chinese botany"—A discussion starting from Wang Jimin's "Foreign translations of *Bengcao Gangmu*"].
Yaoxue Tongbao 药学通报 Pharmaceutical Bulletin 3, no. 8 (1954): 362–363.

Ziwei 紫蔚. "Wo re ai zi ji de yaofang gongzuo" 我热爱自己的药房工作 [I love my
pharmacy job]. *Yaoxue Tongbao* 药学通报 3, no. 12 (1955): 555.

Zu Guodong 祖国栋. "Jing fu hua de jidan neng chi ma?" 经孵化的鸡蛋能吃吗?
[Are incubated eggs edible?]. *Zhongguo Weisheng Huakan* 中国卫生画刊 China
Hygiene Pictorial 2 (1984): 39.

Zu Shuxian 关于传统动物药及其疗效问题 [About traditional animal drugs and
their efficacy]. Accessed November 1, 2019. http://shc2000.sjtu.edu.cn
/article5/guanyu.htm.

"Zui chang yong zhongyao jieshao (shi'er)" 最常用中药介绍(十二) [Introducing the
most commonly used Chinese medicinals 12]. *Yaoxue Tongbao* 药学通报 Pharmaceutical Bulletin 4, no. 8 (1956): 361–362.

INDEX

Note: The letter *f* following a page number denotes a figure; the letter *t* denotes a table.

chicken blood therapy, 10, 12, 16, 66, 105–11, 204n22; alternate accounts of the origins of, 116, 118; in comparison to later blood therapies, 125–26; and the Cultural Revolution, 112–21, 113f, 117f, 138; embarrassment about, 17; and the expression *dajixue* (injecting chicken blood), 106; as the fusion of diverse influences, 106–8, 126, 138; in the *Jiying Gangmu* of Wu Zhiwang, 205n27; and the mass line (*qunzhong luxian*), 114; resurfacing as burn treatment, 126–27; as technological innovation (*jishu gexin*), 206n35; and tissue therapy (*zuzhi liaofa*), 66, 107, 126, 138. *See also* blood therapy; duck and goose blood therapy; Yu Changshi

chicken gizzards (*jineijin*), 29, 90, 92, 125, 140

China Association of Traditional Chinese Medicine (*Zhongguo Zhongyao Xiehui*), 165–66; and Golden Bear, 25; statements ridiculed in cartoons, 167n11, 222n11

China Biodiversity Conservation and Green Development Foundation (CBCGDF), 170

Chinese Export Commodities Fair (*Zhongguo Chukou Shangpin Zhanlanhui*), 74, 75f

Chinese magnolia (*Schisandra chinensis*, limonnik), 62–63

Chinese Medicinal Animals, 137

Chinese medicine: animal bile in, 142, 152, 154–55, 213n131; "animal issue" in, 2, 164–71; and bezoar, 5, 47, 78, 91f, 96, 140, 143; boundary between "folk" and "classical" in, 8; COVID-19 and, 2–3; efficacy of, 2–6, 9, 15, 19–20, 32–33, 37, 52, 61–62, 67, 81, 89, 94, 97, 103, 109–10, 123–28, 135, 140–42, 152–55, 158, 165, 167; ethical considerations in, 1–3, 6, 15, 17, 25, 165, 167, 170–71; goal of combining with Western medicine, 14, 32–35, 123; goal of eliminating animal products in, 170; and herbology, 5–6, 8–9, 15, 18, 27–30, 33–41, 46–55, 62–68; innovation

in, 8–11, 13, 18–19, 177n37; as intangible cultural heritage, 168; Mao's support of, 18, 31, 102, 135, 181n12; and North Korean medicine, 153–54; and politics, 4, 7, 9–15, 25–35, 66–67, 69, 86–87, 107, 112–14, 130, 138, 141, 162, 171; polyherbal recipes in, 6, 10, 36–37, 84, 100; popularization in the West of, 221n2; raw herbs in, 183n32; Russian interest in, 61–62; safety of, 2, 103, 109–11, 128, 156–57, 174n5; skepticism about synthetic substitutes in, 166–67; speciation of, 14; state-supported institutionalization of, 2; Western perceptions of, 1, 33, 66, 174n2; and wildlife conservation, 2–3; worlding of, 2–3, 153, 174n6. *See also* faunal medicalization; folk medicine; herbs and herbology; medical sayings; pharmaceuticalization; pharmacology

Chinese Pharmacology Association: and "new drugs," 40; in the early 1950s, 44–45

Chinese State Council: ban on tiger and rhino parts lifted by (2018), 3, 6, 170; and wild medicinals (1987), 159

Chou, Jay, 169

cicadas, 90

civet cats, 132

classical sayings. *See* medical sayings; Sun Simiao

cod liver oil. *See* fish liver oil; sharks: shark liver oil

Convention on International Trade in Endangered Species (CITES): ban on rhino horns and tiger-bone products, 159; and bear products, 155; list of critically endangered species in, 7, 175n8

cordyceps, 6, 177–78n39

COVID-19, 2–3, 7, 170

cows: bezoar of, 5, 75, 96, 123, 140, 210n96, 213n131; bile of, 47, 96, 137; breeding of, 95; in Chinese pharmacopoeia, 46; and expansion of Five-Anti Movement, 114; hooves of, 131; insulin from, 46; oxen and water buffalo as categories of, 211n108

Cultural Revolution (1966–1976): animals and insects harvested during, 90, 91f, 92, 130, 133, 135, 137; and attack on elite knowledge, 130, 209n88; and beetle farming, 133–34; and chicken blood therapy, 106–7, 112–21, 125–27, 138–39, 160; and drug exports, 75; and "luxury" medicinals, 129–30, 133; medicinal properties of plants as a focus in, 40–41, 91f; and the People's Movement (*Qunzhong Yundong*), 101; processing deer during, 134–35; view of science during, 9. *See also* barefoot doctors; Red Guards

Darentang: honey products of, 49; deer farms of, 83; proprietary medicines of, 48
Daxin Pharmaceutical Factory, 39
Declaration of Alma Alta, 174n6
deer: antlers of, 49–52, 54, 105, 143; export demand for products of, 73, 75–76, 144; farming of, 10, 13, 19, 23, 67, 81–86; as influence on bear farming, 139, 148; as influence on tiger and rhino farming, 170; injectable substances from antlers of, 106, 197–98n47; reform in processing of (during Cultural Revolution), 134; Soviet influence on Chinese farming of, 10, 18–19, 25, 67–68, 153, 160; wine made from, 24. *See also* musk deer; red deer; sika deer
Deng Xiaoping's reforms: and bear-bile farming, 19–20, 139–40, 160; and "economic animals," 139–42, 147, 153, 160, 163; and the pricing of agricultural products (*nongfu chanpin*), 143–44; and rare animal parts as "good investments," 11
Ding Fubao, 30
dis-assembly line, 85
dog-bone, 132
Dongfeng Deer Farm, 85
donkeys, 7, 132, 144, 177n31
drugs. *See* pharmacology

duck and goose blood therapy, 12, 123–26, 142, 162; cancer trials using, 125, 209n89; not recorded as a folk healing method, 210n90; Qing-period novels used as evidence for, 124–25. *See also* blood therapy; chicken blood therapy
dung beetles. *See* beetles
dwarf musk deer. *See* musk deer
dysentery, 56, 154, 213n131
dysphagia, 122–23

earthquake prediction, 100
earthworms, 106
endocrinology, 65
environmental conservation. *See* wildlife conservation
Environment and Animal Society of Taiwan, 223n21
ephedrine, 35
experimental farms, 144–45
extinction, 3, 11, 83, 92, 165, 177n27

faunal medicalization: and awareness-raising at NUS, 169; and the black market, 38, 159, 175n8; and China's medical marketplaces, 6–8, 155–56, 159; concept of, 5–8; and COVID-19, 2–3, 7, 170; and the Cultural Revolution, 130, 133–35, 137–38; and the decline of species, 7, 155, 175n8, 195n27; and Deng-period targeting of "economic animals," 142, 160; and ignoring of differences in sub-species, 40; and "new drugs," 8–10, 28, 49; and organo-pharmaceuticals, 140–41; and the pharmaceuticalization of Chinese medicine, 8–13, 49, 161–63, 167; and premodern practice in China, 5–8; response of the Chinese state to, 2–3, 170–71; and "wild" medicinals, 13, 144, 166, 170–71, 223n26; and zoo-therapy, 176n15. *See also* blood therapy; chicken blood therapy; duck and goose blood therapy; medicinal animal farming; organotherapy
Filatov, Vladimir P., 65, 107. *See also* tissue therapy

fisherman doctors, 136

fish liver oil, 46, 79–81, 106. *See also* sharks: shark liver oil

Five-Anti Movement, 107, 114

Five-Year Plans: first (1953–1957), 27–28, 37–38, 76t; second (1958–1962), 73–76, 76t; seventh (1986–1990), 144

flatworms, 68

folk medicine: chicken blood therapy and, 105–7; compilations of, 103–4, 125; ideological turn to, 10, 18, 100, 104–5, 129–30, 139, 162; as initially outside state pharmacology, 45; in relation to Chinese medicine, 7, 13; Soviet interest in, 54, 59–60, 63, 68–69

food cures (*shiliao*): as an ancient category, 156; and ants, 157, 219n58; and Sun Simiao, 219n54

forestry authorities, 141, 150, 171

Four Modernizations, 139

Four Pests Campaign, 87

France, as export market for musk, 93; drugs supplied to the Russian Empire by, 55

Frick, Johann, 5–6

frogs, 15, 22

geckos. *See* tokay geckos

geese. *See* duck and goose blood therapy

Ge Hanshu, 121–22

Germany: and Bretschneider (Emil), 62; and drug exports, 77; drugs supplied to the Russian Empire by, 55–56; Ursofalk (synthetic bear bile) produced in, 24

gifting economy. *See* medicinals as luxury gifts (*guizhong yaocai*)

Gilman, Henry, 46

ginseng, 5, 18, 50–51, 54, 67–68, 70, 105, 133, 141, 149, 164; Soviet study and farming of, 63–64. See also *shenrong*

goats, 65, 132

Golden Bear Private, Ltd., 23–25, 169, 222n10

Golden Boten City, 20–25, 179n57

golden money leopards. *See* leopards

goose blood therapy. *See* duck and goose blood therapy

grassroots innovation, 54, 93, 99–101, 112. *See also* mass line

Great Leap Forward, 18–19, 27–28, 34, 45, 47; Britain as target of, 76–77; and chicken blood therapy, 66, 109; deforestation during, 202n86; difficulty of discussing, 17; and farms as labs, 144–45; and faunal medicalization, 138, 163; and folk medicine, 102–5, 137; and medical exports, 74–75; and medicinal animal farming, 71–72, 81–82, 85–86, 89–92, 97, 129, 133, 147; and rhino horn imports, 74

Great Leap Forward, slogans of: "Dare to Create" (*Dadan Chuangzao*), 100–101; "Down with Superstitions" (*Dapo Mixin*), 74; "Home Rearing, Home Cultivation" (*Jia Yang Jia Zhong*), 82, 88, 97, 141, 144; "Let a hundred flowers bloom," 71; "Overtake Britain in 15 Years," 71; "Red and Expert" (*You Hong You Zhuan*), 100–101; satellite launching (*fang weixing*), 81; technological innovation (*jishu gexin*), 101, 206n35

ground beetles. *See* beetles

Guangdong Health Bureau, 95

Guangzhou: as center for drug trade, 72, 74–75, 78; chicken blood therapy in, 116; as production center for bezoar, 201–2n85; Qingping Market in, 8, 135

Guangzhou Chenliji Joint Pharmaceutical Factory, 48. *See also* Chenliji

Guangzhou University of Chinese Medicine (GUCM), 16, 23, 28

guinea pigs, 64

Guizhenland cartoons, 222n11

Guizhentang Pharmaceutical: controversy over, 165–69; and product registration, 159, 220n66. *See also* bear bile; bears: farming of

Harbin Chemical and Pharmaceutical Factory, 68, 84

Harper, Donald, 174n2

hawksbill turtles, 132. *See also* turtles

health and hygiene: educational programs related to, 42; and the medical efficacy of health supplements, 158; Sanitary and Epidemic Prevention Stations (*weisheng fangyi zhan*), 110–11; *Zhongguo Weisheng Huakan* (China health pictorial), 157. *See also* food cures (*shiliao*)

Health Ministry: and campaign against Britain, 77; and chicken blood therapy, 110–12; criticism of during the Cultural Revolution, 102, 112–15; and medicinal exports, 72; in the Republican period, 29; and tissue therapy, 66

health supplements (*baojianpin*), 155–60

Hebei province: *dihuang* cultivation in, 81; folk prescriptions collected in, 104; foreign trade of, 74–76; insect collection stations (*shougou zhan*) in, 133; medicinal animal farming encouraged in, 82; medicinal animal products from, 76t; medicinal animals and lab-based research in, 95–96

heparin, 47, 52, 166

hepatitis, 155

Herbal Pharmacology Study Group, 178n43

herb collection stations, 38, 73

herbs and herbology, 5–6, 8–9, 15, 18, 27–30, 33–41, 46–55, 62–68; and botany, 33, 40; and phytotherapy, 60–61

histotherapy. *See* tissue therapy

"Home Rearing, Home Cultivation" (*Jia Yang Jia Zhong*), 82, 88, 97, 141, 144

honey, 49, 78, 89, 127

Hong Kong: advertisement of medicinal company in, 50f; animal welfare groups in, 169–70, 223n21; bear bile customers in, 24; and British pharmaceuticals, 72, 77; and Chinese medicinal exports, 13, 74, 187n63; endangered species traded in, 159; musk imported to, 93; rhino horn shipments through, 79; shark fin soup consumption in, 221n4; and tiger bone products,

202n87. *See also* ADM Capital Foundation; Animals Asia Foundation

hormone therapy. *See* organotherapy

horses, 66, 91f, 111, 123; Mongolian wild horses, 82

Huang Lixin, 175n10

hunting: banned for "protected" animals (1987), 159; of bear, 152, 217n36; of deer, 83, 86, 147; of tigers, 202n87

India: bear parts and, 155; bezoar and, 96; musk production in, 93, 96; shark liver oil in, 196n30

industrialization: bear farming as, 139, 148–53, 166; and grassroots innovation, 100–105, 112, 133, 137; and health supplements, 158–59; pharmaceuticals as contributing to, 42, 51, 71–73. *See also* Beijing Pharmaceutical Factory; British medicinal industry; faunal medicalization; medicinal animal farming; pharmacology; Tongrentang Pharmaceutical Factory

injection, popularization and abuse of, 119–120

innovation, 4, 8–13, 18–21, 97, 137, 161, 168, 177n37; with animal tissue, 67, 80; chicken blood therapy as, 107–9, 112–14, 126; in drug discovery, 45, 52–57, 77, 221n2; grassroots innovation, 99–102; injection as, 120; in medicinal animal farming, 85, 89, 93–95, 149; versus tradition, 160, 164; Zhou Enlai's encouragement of, 206n35

insects: farming of, 82, 87–90, 133–34; collection of, 29, 71, 90, 133; curing cancer with, 127; in prescriptions, 104, 127–28. *See also* ants; beetles; cicadas

insulin, 46–47, 52

Japan: bear bile alternative developed in, 166; consumption of bear bile in, 180n59; chemical research on Chinese herbs in, 30, 36–37; and Chinese medicinal exports, 13; and cow-bile research, 213n131; drug exports of,

77; and *kyuushingan,* 24, 180n58; and patent drug Rokushingan (*liushen wan*), 155; and North Korean medicine, 153, 160; research on bezoar in, 96, 202n89; scholarly interest in Chinese herbology in, 62; ursodeoxycholic acid (UDCA) isolated by researchers in, 20, 34, 52, 142, 154–55

jaundice, 154

Jiang Daqu, 39–40

Jiang Qi, 166–67

Jilin Agricultural University: bear farming and, 150; experimental farm stations (*shiyan zhan*) in, 145–46; experiments on raccoon dogs in, 147–48; profitability of, 145, 215n14

Jilin province: and bear farming, 85, 148; bile factories in, 152; deer owned by households in, 197n45; Dongfeng Deer Farm in, 85

Jin Jichun, 149–51, 169

Kalashnikov, V. P., 60

Kang Sheng, 112

Kefalov, Y. P., 60–61

Ke Zexun, 126–27, 210n92

Kiriyanov, A. P., 63

Korea: bear farming in North Korea, 4, 20, 142, 148–49, 151, 153–54; and Chinese medicinal exports, 13, 76; and *Dongyi* (Eastern medicine), 153–54; rhino horn consumption by, 79. *See also* Yanbian Korean Autonomous Prefecture

Korean War, 108

Kuomintang, 119; and chicken blood therapy, 116; and Chinese pharmacology, 42; and "political tutelage" (*xunzheng*), 114

laboratories in the field (*tianjian shiyan shi*). *See* experimental farms

Lang Lang, 169

lanolin, 46

Laos, 20–22, 179n56, 179–80n57. *See also* Golden Boten City

leopards, 7, 142, 144, 159, 175n8

Liang Fengxi, 147

Liang Jielian, 119–20

Li Bingbing, 169

Li Lianda, 167, 222n10

Li Shizhen: on antler processing, 134; and ants, 219n58; on bear gallbladder, 154; and duck and goose blood, 123; and lizards, 123. *See also Bencao Gangmu*

Liu Dezu, 144–46, 215n12

Liu Yanhua, 168

lizards: and cancer treatments, 127–28; and the medicinal marketplace, 6, 163; eggs of, 138; Li Shizhen's research on, 123; Ye Haichang on, 128–29, 210n96; Zheng Yihua's research on *zuzhiye* (tissue fluid) from, 129

Lu Yuanlei, 182n22

mahuang, 35, 37

Manchuria, 61, 96, 202n89

manta-rays, 7, 175n8

Mao Zedong: and advocacy of Chinese medicine, 29–31; and Caifeng movement, 101; on combining Chinese and Western medicines, 17, 32–33, 35, 181n12; and criticism of Health Ministry, 102; declining health of, 121; and Five-Anti Movement, 107; and mass line, 57, 100–101, 114; and textbooks, 130

marine-based medicinal animals. *See* fish liver oil; manta-rays; pearl and oyster shells; seahorses; sharks; starfish

Martin, Esmond Bradley, 195n27

mass line (*qunzhong luxian*), 100, 114. *See also* grassroots innovation

medical sayings: *bu yi jingxue* (enriching and benefiting essence and blood), 5, 6; and works of literature, 5, 176n16; *xuerou you qing zhi pin* (products with passion in both blood and flesh), 5; *yi du gong du* (using poison to attack poison), 5, 176n16; *yi xing bu xing* (using shape to nourish shape), 5 medicinal animal farming: and bear, 85, 148–54, 166; beekeeping as, 49, 78, 88–89; and deer, 67–68, 81, 83–86, 146–47; and the early Communist period, 9–10; and experimental-farm stations, 144–48; and the Great Leap Forward, 18–19, 71–98; and grassroots innovation, 100, 114; and *fang weixing* (satellite launching), 81; and "Home Rearing, Home Cultivation," 82, 97, 144; in Jilin province, 85, 148–54; and the state pharmaceutical sector, 27; and *tianjian shiyan shi* (laboratory in the field), 144–45. *See also* ants: farming of; bears: farming of; beetles: farming of; deer: farming of; insects: farming of; musk deer: farming of; rhinoceros: farming of; seahorses: farming of; snakes: farming of; tigers: farming of

medicinal animals. *See* abalone; ants; bears; beeswax; beetles; bezoar; blood therapy; cat placenta; chickens; cicadas; civet cats; cows; deer; dog-bone; donkeys; ducks; earthworms; faunal medicalization; flatworms; frogs; geese; goats; guinea pigs; hawksbill turtles; horses; insects; leopards; lizards; manta rays; medicinal animal farming; monkeys; mussels; organotherapy; oxen and water buffalo; pangolins; pearls and oyster shells; pigs; rhinoceros; saiga antelope; scorpions; sea cucumbers; seahorses; sharks; sheep; silkworms; snakes; spiders; starfish; tigers; toads; tokay geckos; turtles; white foxes; wolves

medicinals as luxury gifts (*guizhong yaocai*): bear bile and, 21, 168, 177–78n39; cordyceps fungus (*yarsagumbu*) and, 6, 177–78n39; the pouch of musk deer and, 147; and species extinction, 11

medicine shops: in China, 17, 20, 38, 41–42, 48–49, 57, 62, 79, 104; in the Soviet Union, 57

medicine shop workers (*yaogongshi*), 28, 40–41, 105, 134. *See also* pharmacists

Meng Qian, 72–74

meningitis, 130–31

minerals as drugs, 6, 15, 39, 105, 129

Ministry of Health. *See* Health Ministry

Mitsui Pharmaceutical Company, 24

monkeys, 65

Moscow Organo-Therapeutic Drug Factory, 67

moxibustion, 14

Mr. Science, 15

musk deer: farming of, 92–93; domestication of, 92, 147; endangerment of, 85–86, 175n8; experiments with, 135; and northeast China, 92, 146–47, 200n70; and *sexiang neiyi* (inner lining of a musk pouch), 93–94; zoological research on, 147, 217n40. *See also* deer; red deer; sika deer

mussels, 176n21

National Academy of Sciences (American), 11

National Medicine Movement, 30

National Pharmaceutical Research Institute, 42

National University of Singapore (NUS): faunal medicalization awareness-raising projects at, 169; Tembusu Wildlife Association at, 223n19

Needham, Joseph, 174n2

nervism, 64

Ni Minggao, 93–94

Northeast Forestry University, 147

North Korea. *See* Korea

organopharmaceuticals (*zangqi zhiji*), 140–41, 155

organotherapy: and Brown-Séquard, 64–65, 108; and male vitality enhancement, 67; and pantocrin, 67–68, 69, 83; the rise and fall of, 191n39; Soviet interest in, 4, 18, 65–69, 164; and tissue therapy (*zuzhi liaofa*), 65–66, 107, 191n43

oxen and water buffalo: folk preparations using the horns of, 211n108;

heparin manufactured from lungs of, 166; horns of substituted for rhino and antelope, 96–97, 130–32

Sinicize Western Medicine" (*zhongyi kexuehua, xiyi zhongguohua*), 34–35

snail fever, 100

snakes: farming of, 82, 171; zoological research on, 217n40; venom of, 68

South Africa, 170

Soviet Union: blood science in, 107–8; influence on Chinese policies and practices, 10, 18, 38, 53–61, 160; and *limonnik* (*Schisandra chinensis*, Chinese magnolia), 62–63; medicine and pharmacology of, 14, 18, 55–57; and "new drugs," 56–57, 59, 64; and organotherapy, 4, 18, 65–69, 164; pharmaceutical education in, 57; pharmacopoeia of, 46, 58–61; phytotherapy movement in, 60–61; self-sufficiency in medicinals as policy in, 54; surveys of medicinal resources in, 55. *See also* nervism; Pavlovian science; Russian Far-East

spiders, 6, 129

starfish: in the Qingping Market, Guangzhou, 136f; zoological research on, 213n127

Sun Li, 169

Sun Simiao: ethical concerns of, 6; and the term *bu yi jingxue* (enriching and benefiting essence and blood), 6; and the term *shiliao* (food cure), 219n54

Su Zhiwu, 119

Taiwan: animal welfare groups in, 170, 223n21; and Chinese medicinal exports to, 13; and *kyuushingan*, 24, 180n58; rhino horn imported into, 195n27

Taiwan Environmental Information Association, 223n21

Tatarinov, Alexander A., 61–62

Tembusu College (National University of Singapore), 169, 223n19

Tianjin: as center for drug trade, 72, 74–75, 78; and bezoar production, 96, 201–2n85; as headquarters of Darentang, 48; beekeeping around, 49; water buffalo horns analyzed in, 131

Tianjin Drug Testing Center, 105

Tianjin Medicinal Company, 78

Tibet, 92, 177–78n39

tigers: bones of, 6, 13, 76, 88, 96, 105, 132, 143, 155; and the Chinese medicinal marketplace, 3, 6, 13, 17–18, 49, 170; and the medicinal marketplace in Singapore, 20; confounding of subspecies, 40; endangerment of, 7, 82, 159, 163, 165, 175n8, 202n87; farming of, 3, 170, 175n13; jaguar parts substituted for, 7, 177n27; parts as export items, 43–44, 76, 202n87; stomach of, 123; Sun Simiao and, 6; wildness as medicinal attribute of, 7, 52; wine made from bones of, 18, 49–50, 132, 164, 202n87

tissue therapy (*zuzhi liaofa*), 10, 18, 53, 65–66, 69, 164; and chicken blood therapy, 106–7, 126–27; and lizard therapy, 129; numbers of Chinese publications on, 191n43

toads, 121–22, 126, 138, 141, 162–63, 208n76; venom of, 144

tokay geckos, 15, 19, 82, 89–90, 129

Tongrentang Pharmaceutical Factory: deer farms of, 83–84; drug production of, 187n67; history of, 48, 186n60; international reputation of, 73; medicinals produced from chicken blood by, 205n27; performance and productivity efforts by, 78; *sexiangzi* (musk-based) pills of, 94; *shenrong* production of, 49–51, 52; tiger-bone wine sales of, 50, 164

traditional Chinese medicine (TCM). *See* Chinese medicine

TRAFFIC, 20

tuberculosis, 89–90, 128

tufa, 101

turtles, 91f. *See also* hawksbill turtles

typhoid fever, 56

United States: drug exports of, 77; food trends of, 157; research on deer antler growth in, 146; scholarly interest in Chinese herbology in, 62